ROMANTICISM AND THE ANGLICAN NEWMAN

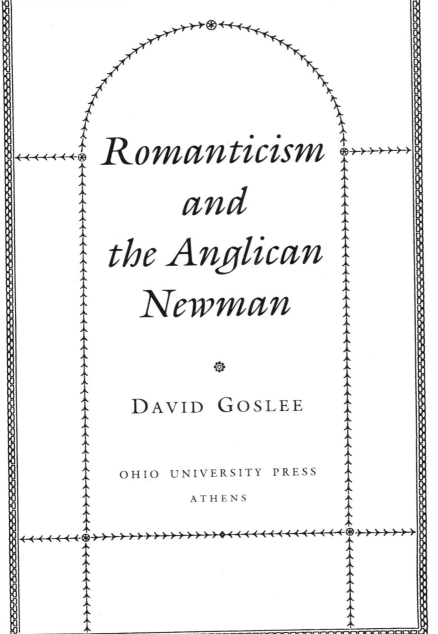

Romanticism
and
the Anglican
Newman

DAVID GOSLEE

OHIO UNIVERSITY PRESS

ATHENS

Ohio University Press, Athens, Ohio 45701
© 1996 by David Goslee
Printed in the United States of America
All rights reserved

Ohio University Press books are printed on acid-free paper ∞

01 00 99 98 97 96   5 4 3 2 1

Library of Congress Cataloging-in-Publication Data

Goslee, David.
Romanticism and the Anglican Newman / David Goslee.
      p.   cm.
Includes bibliographical references and index.
ISBN 0-8214-1126-8
1. Newman, John Henry, 1801–1890. 2. Romanticism—Religious
aspects—Christianity—History of doctrines—19th century.
3. Church of England—Doctrines—History—19th century. 4. Anglican
Communion—England—doctrines—History—19th century. I. Title.
BX4705.N5G67   1995   95-31944
282'.092—dc20   CIP

DESIGNED BY LAURY A. EGAN

For Brenda

CONTENTS

ACKNOWLEDGMENTS

I WOULD LIKE TO THANK the Trustees of the Hodges Fund of the University of Tennessee Department of English for awarding me a sabbatical during the spring semester of 1992. The uninterrupted time allowed me to complete a draft of this book. The whole department has been unfailingly generous with support, time, and materials. I need to thank the editors of *Modern Language Quarterly* for permission to incorporate into chapters 6 and 11 paragraphs from my "Rhetoric as Confession in Newman's Parochial Sermons," *MLQ* 48 (1987), 339–63; also Ed Block and the editors of the series *English Literary Studies* for allowing me to insert into chapters 2, 3, 7, and 11 portions of my "Newman, Gibbon, and New-Testament Christianity," *Critical Essays on John Henry Newman,* ed. Ed Block Jr. (Victoria: U of Victoria P, 1992), 75–87.

Like all students of Newman, I owe a great debt to Charles Stephen Dessain and the other fathers of the Birmingham Oratory, whose *Letters and Diaries* sets high standards for insight and scholarship. Trying to compensate for the four volumes of letters still in progress made me appreciate our good fortune in having all the others available to us. I have also made extensive use of the editorial apparatus of Martin Svaglic and I. T. Ker in their editions of the *Apologia* and the *Idea of a University* respectively.

Several friends and colleagues have read earlier portions of the manuscript and have made very helpful suggestions (which I probably should have used even more than I did). In particular I need to thank David DeLaura at Pennsylvania, David Dungan in Religious Studies at Tennessee, and Thomas Hummel at Episcopal High School in Alexandria. Problems still remaining in the book remain my responsibility.

I am much indebted to Andrew Bongiorno, who first introduced me to Newman at Oberlin, and to Dwight Culler (also one of his students), who taught me Newman at Yale. His *Imperial Intellect* remains my favorite Newman study. In countless phone conversations, my daughter Susan repeated like a mantra her assurances that the book would be finished, would be placed, would be published—and she was right. Finally I thank my wife, Brenda, to whom this book is dedicated. Even though her heart is with Charles Kingsley, she graciously helped me write on Newman anyway.

ABBREVIATIONS

THE FOLLOWING ABBREVIATIONS for Newman's works, used parenthetically throughout the book, have been adapted from those in Ian Ker's *John Henry Newman: A Biography*. With the exception of Harrold's edition of the *Development*, the volumes published by Longmans, Green are all part of the uniform edition, begun in 1868 and concluded in 1881. These volumes have been reissued virtually unchanged, but they are gradually being replaced by newer critical editions, which usually give marginal indications of the original pagination. I have referred to the Oxford edition of the *Prophetical Office* as "*PO*" because the new volume's title, *The Via Media*, duplicates that of the uniform two-volume edition. While I have checked my quotations against editions published while Newman was still an Anglican, it seemed more convenient to cite the readily available later editions, especially since the differences between them are usually slight.

Apo.   *Apologia Pro Vita Sua*. Ed. Martin J. Svaglic. Oxford: Clarendon, 1967.

Ari.   *The Arians of the Fourth Century*. London: Longmans, Green, 1908.

AW   *Autobiographical Writings*. Ed. Henry Tristram. New York: Sheed and Ward, 1957.

DA   *Discussions and Arguments on Various Subjects*. London: Longmans, Green, 1899.

Dev.   *An Essay on the Development of Christian Doctrine*. Ed. C. F. Harrold. New York: Longmans, Green, 1949.

Diff.   *Certain Difficulties Felt by Anglicans in Catholic Teaching*. London: Longmans, Green, 1908.

Ess.   *Essays Critical and Historical*. 2 vols. London: Longmans, Green, 1903.

GA   *An Essay in Aid of a Grammar of Assent*. Ed. I. T. Ker. Oxford: Clarendon, 1985.

HS   *Historical Sketches*. 3 vols. London: Longmans, Green, 1901.

Idea   *The Idea of a University Defined and Illustrated*. Ed. I. T. Ker. Oxford: Clarendon, 1976.

Jfc.   *Lectures on the Doctrine of Justification*. London: Longmans Green, 1900.

KC   *Correspondence of John Henry Newman with John Keble and Others*. London: Longmans, Green, 1917.

LD   *The Letters and Diaries of John Henry Newman*. Ed. Charles Stephen Dessain, et al. Vols. 1-6 (Oxford: Oxford UP, 1978–84), 11–22 (London: Thoms Nelson, 1961–72), 23–31 (Oxford: Oxford UP, 1973–77).

LG   *Loss and Gain: The Story of a Convert*. London: Longmans, Green, 1910.

Mir.   *Two Essays on Biblical and on Ecclesiastical Miracles*. London: Longmans, Green, 1907.

Moz.   *Letters and Correspondence of John Henry Newman*. 2 vols. Ed. Anne Mozley. London: Longmans Green, 1903.

PL   *A Packet of Letters: A Selection from the Correspondence of John Henry Newman*. Ed. Joyce Sugg. Oxford: Clarendon, 1983.

PO   *Lectures on the Prophetical Office of the Church. The* Via Media *of the Anglican Church*. Ed. H. D. Weidner, 58–358. Oxford: Clarendon, 1990.

PS   *Parochial and Plain Sermons*. 8 vols. London: Longmans, Green, 1901.

SD   *Sermons Bearing on Subjects of the Day*. London: Longmans, Green, 1902.

US   *Fifteen Sermons Preached before the University of Oxford*. London: Longmans, Green, 1901.

VM   *The Via Media*. 2 vols. London: Longmans, Green, 1908.

VV   *Verses on Various Occasions*. London: Longmans, Green, 1903.

It must surely be profitable for our thoughts to be sent backward and forward to the beginning and the end of the Gospel times. . . . What we want, is to *understand* that we are in the place in which the early Christians were, with the same covenant, ministry, sacraments, and duties;—to realize a state of things long past away . . .—to have our hearts awake, as if we had seen CHRIST and His Apostles, and seen their miracles.

—Tract 83: *Advent Sermons on Antichrist* (1838)

The Reformation produced such immediate and great benefits, that Protestantism was considered under the immediate eye of heaven, and its own remaining Dogmas and superstitions . . . constituted those resting places and seeming sure points of Reasoning. . . . Milton . . . appears to have been content with these by his writings—He did not think into the human heart, as Wordsworth has done—Yet Milton as a Philosop[h]er, had sure as great powers as Wordsworth—What is then to be inferr'd? O many things—It proves there is really a grand march of intellect—, It proves a mighty providence subdues the mightiest Minds to the service of the time being, whether it be in human Knowledge or Religion.

—Keats to Reynolds (1818)

The remark has been made that the history of an author is the history of his works; it is far more exact to say that, at least in the case of great writers, the history of their works is the history of their fortunes or their times. Each is, in his turn, the man of his age, the type of a generation, or the interpreter of a crisis. He is made for his day, and his day for him.

—"English Catholic Literature," *The Idea of a University* (1854)

INTRODUCTION

IN "MR. KINGSLEY'S METHOD OF DISPUTATION," included in the first edition of his *Apologia Pro Vita Sua,* Newman complains bitterly of his opponent's effort

> to cut the ground from under my feet;—to poison by anticipation the public mind against me, John Henry Newman, and to infuse into the imaginations of my readers, suspicion and mistrust of everything that I may say in reply to him. . . . If I am natural, he will tell them, 'Ars est celare artem'; if I am convincing, he will suggest that I am an able logician; if I show warmth, I am acting the indignant innocent; if I am calm, I am thereby detected as a smooth hypocrite; if I clear up difficulties, I am too plausible and perfect to be true. The more triumphant are my statements, the more certain will be my defeat. (*Apo.* 395–96)

Although his Anglican period comprised half his life and more than half of his published writings, the Anglican Newman remains mired today in an analogous double bind.[1] Both his religious and his secular critics, from his day to our own, have carefully placed him at the margins of their particular projects. To be fair, however, we must acknowledge that Newman made himself complicit in this marginalization. As a Catholic, he reinterpreted his Anglican thought as partial and incomplete; as an Anglican, he constructed a history and a theology that divorced him from the entire post-Enlightenment world. His writings of the 1830s and 1840s place him outside the emerging constellation of issues, attitudes, and practices which we identify as Victorian. If we look closely at these writings, however, we find them complicit with a deeper intellectual and emotional current flowing from English and German Romanticism. In fact the most visionary, most overtly religious passages within them reinterpret Romantic transcendence within a uniquely dialogic paradigm. It is this paradigm which modern (and postmodern) critics need to test as a possible bridge over the widening gap between sacred and secular domains within Victorian culture.

[3]

Newman among the Critics

Among those who acknowledge Newman, it is probably Catholic scholars who claim him most wholeheartedly. With them, however, the Catholic works and the Catholic Newman understandably hold pride of place. For those who revere him as a spiritual guide, including those actively working for his canonization, his Anglican writings offer much of value, but his political machinations within the Oxford Movement remain almost as embarrassing as his later difficulties with the Catholic hierarchy in England and Rome.[2] Others celebrate these later difficulties and celebrate the Catholic Newman as harbinger of Vatican II; for them the reactionary stance of his Anglican writing makes it convenient to see his Catholic hardships as winning him over to a belated (albeit covert) liberalism. Still others prize his work on the intersection of theology, psychology, and philosophy; these critics focus on his study of religious belief, particularly in the late *Grammar of Assent*.[3] While Newman hoped this work would render belief accessible to all, his earlier Anglican writings exalt a visionary Christianity so modelled on his own experience that to follow Newman's thought and to follow Newman became virtually synonymous.

Newman's secular critics, from his Oxford days to the present, have respected him when he followed the norms of a cultured academic and attacked him when he did not. Newman's educational ideal has remained his most accessible legacy to the academy, and his portrait of the gentleman, however problematic he may have intended it, was not challenged outside the Catholic hierarchy until Marxists and feminists began probing its cultural base. Newman himself pleaded with Kingsley to respect him as a gentleman (*Apo.* 352) and his return to popular favor with the *Apologia* grew from the public's perception that the work epitomized the traditional English virtues of honesty, tact, loyalty, and general good breeding. Thirty years earlier, however, Rene Hampden had pleaded in vain to the Anglican Newman for a similar respect: "Have you (to take the lowest ground) acted towards me in the manner due from one gentleman to another?" (*LD* 5: 83). And Newman's own account of this time admits that "In one of my first Sermons I said, '. . . it would be a gain to the country were it vastly more superstitious, more bigoted, more gloomy, more fierce in its religion than at present'" (*Apo.* 52). Another contemporary sermon even describes "civilized" Christianity as Satanic: "What is Satan's device in this day? . . . What is the world's religion now? . . . Our manners are courteous; we avoid giving pain or offence. . . . Benevolence is the chief virtue; intolerance, bigotry, excess of zeal, are the first of sins" (*PS* 1 [24]: 311–12). Newman's younger brother Frank waited until John was safely dead before venting eighty years of sibling hostility in an attack which surpasses even Kingsley's in uncivilized spite. Yet his *Early History of Cardinal Newman* accuses John of this same lack of civilized tolerance: "It did not occur to him that he might have something himself *to learn,* as well as to *teach*" (91–92).

William Robbins's *The Newman Brothers,* focusing on their earlier controversies, finds Frank's position the more appealing, but David DeLaura dismisses the book as "a skillfully staged attempt to discredit Newman's entire career and his apologetic as a mixture of sophistry and self-deception" ("Prophecy" 493). DeLaura argues that in any attack on Newman, the attacker confesses him- or herself to be threatened by Newman's power. For DeLaura, he is still perceived as dangerous because he stands "as a permanent standard of judgment against the complacent secularism of the modern world" (498). Newman's "implicit object," according to DeLaura, is a "uniquely personal way of looking at things which in his view is the uniquely personal context for the 'habit' of supernatural faith. Newman . . . does not seek our admiration but our joint commitment transacted through a joint experience" (494). The *Apologia,* with its stated purpose of clearing his name by vindicating his life (12), may sanction such a strategy, but this "joint commitment transacted through a joint experience" has always been part of Newman's strategy; he has always insisted that his experience remains both uniquely personal and universally normative. When we study his early controversial works in the context of his Anglican sermons and his Tractarian correspondence, we find his most abstract ideas paralleled by visionary moments and embodied in a life which wins its identity through these moments. Byron, shaping his own life in the image of his fictional characters, may be more flamboyant than the Anglican Newman, but he is no more rigorous in living his ideal and idealizing a role that only he could live.

The commentators most sensitive to this early religious radicalism have been mostly Protestant and mostly hostile. All have had their own theological and sectarian biases, and all have at some point imputed themselves. Edwin Abbott's pre-Freudian psychologizing espouses an impossible fusion of liberal Christianity and naturalism. Owen Chadwick, following Bremond, claims that Abbott "treats Newman like an old title-deed, and by the time he has finished[,] the life of Newman resembles a very old printed volume gnawed by generations of insects" ("Bremond" 175).[4] Bremond himself, however, evaluates Newman and his achievement from the perspective of his own Modernist agenda. Newman's brother-in-law, Thomas Mozley, on the other hand, wrote his gossipy, tabloid-quality *Reminiscences* when his "eyesight was bad. He could not check anything. He had a mass of old letters but he could hardly read them" (Chadwick, "Reminiscences," 141).[5]

[5]

The various appreciations of D. G. James, Alexander Whyte, and Yngve Brilioth all strive to give Newman his due, but they box him into a delimited "Catholic" perspective which can set off their broader vision of early twentieth-century Protestantism. For Harold Weatherby, by contrast, the Newman of the *Apologia* shows himself a closet Romantic by privileging his individual conscience and scripting his religious history as a self-determined quest; yet Weatherby laments that he has abandoned the capacious social and ontological hierarchies of the Scholastics and the Caroline Divines. Stephen Prickett allies him with Keble in a belated effort to imitate Coleridge's project of baptizing the Romantic imagination.[6] For Owen Chadwick, Newman rendered doctrinal development orthodox enough that conservative theologians, at least those outside the Roman hierarchy, could again acknowledge historical change.

Several recent apologists, recognizing the value of reading Newman against the grain, have discovered sanction for such a project within Newman himself. An unpublished passage quoted by John Coulson suggests that we "put ourselves on the guard as to our proceeding, and protest against it, while we do it. We can only set right one error of expression by another. By this method of antagonism we steady our minds . . . by saying and unsaying to a positive result" (64). By celebrating the gaps and absences within his own text, by acknowledging the inevitability of figurative slippage, Newman looks backward to Coleridge's reconciliation of opposites and forward to a conception of language as both symbolic and social construct.[7] As these apologists interpret him, Newman's characteristic appeal to his individual conscience is grounded within the interactive relationships and intersubjective language of a religious community. Yet within all these recent studies, both Catholic and Protestant, lurks a certain theological decorum which renders their sincere appreciation slightly patronizing. In particular, I think, they assume that because the Anglican Newman invokes his God through traditional, Scriptural, orthodox language, his image of God remains equally so. In context, I will argue, his God shares more traits with the "god terms" of his secular contemporaries than he or his critics would admit.

Curiously enough, secular postmodern critics may have more invested in Newman's orthodoxy than their religious counterparts. Michael Ryan, writing more as a deconstructionist than a Marxist, sees the *Apologia* as Newman's effort to support a theocentric universe within a logocentric tissue of metaphors; this structure finally collapses when Newman cannot find his own face within his figurative mirror.[8] In "The Meaning of the Ancient Mariner," Jerome McGann carefully distances the orthodox Newman from what he sees as self-mystified Romantic escapism: "When Newman watched Coleridge replace the Truth with the Imagination of the

Truth, he concluded that Coleridge had 'indulged a liberty of speculation which no Christian can tolerate, and advanced conclusions which were often heathen rather than Christian.' Newman's analysis, like his orthodox fears, were both correct and farsighted, for Coleridge's own method would necessarily place his interpretive scheme beneath the critical razor he first employed" (236). For such critics, Newman's rejection of liberalism makes him a convenient ally in their effort to expose Victorian platitudes as a series of ideological constructs. For them, of course, Newman's own orthodoxy has itself been so thoroughly reduced to ideology by Strauss, Feuerbach, Marx, and Nietzsche that no time need be wasted in marginalizing him further. A similar condescension undermines Geoffrey Faber's Freudian approach in *Oxford Apostles*. Arguing that the internalized voice of a domineering mother drove Newman to a deeply repressed homosexuality, Faber confines him to the margins of gender and dismisses his Anglican period as the neurotic reenactment of this trauma.[9] Two recent studies exploit Newman's own efforts to escape his age. Robert Pattison's *The Great Dissent* shapes Newman's religious conflicts into an impressive case against modern relativism, a case which remains a bit too Scholastic and too coherent. Stephen Thomas's *Newman and Heresy*, by contrast, focuses on his Anglican encounters with Patristic theology, but this painstaking historical study shows him strangely uncomfortable and ineffectual.[10]

Newman himself, of course, would have accepted all such charges of irrelevance rather than accept the self-absorbed subjectivity of "modern" religious experience. He came to believe that by heeding the commands, reprimands, and commendations from a source beyond his own conscious desires, he could grow transparent to this presence. Through lifelong obedience, he hoped to see into the presence itself and, as if in a mirror, to see himself objectively reflected. On purely psychological grounds, we need not be orthodox Freudians or Lacanians to question his supposition that this inner voice of prohibition must have a divine source. Naturalistic explanations for Newman's voice abound in the unconscious mind, or in later reflections of childhood experience, or in children's larger-than-life image of their parents.[11] This exclusive identification of God with prohibition now seems only one of the less savory manifestations of a distinctively Victorian idolatry.

The Romantic in Spite of Himself

It is from these overlapping agendas of historical, theological, and intellectual marginalization that I hope to rescue the Anglican Newman. In this quest to restore him to cultural centrality, my study divides neatly into three main sections: chapters 1-3 will first explain, then describe, and then critique Newman's early renunciation of modern thought; chapters 4-9 will analyze the dialogic Romanticism within his Anglican works and its power to expand his notions of personal identity, spiritual election, militant purpose, self-criticism, and cultural critique; finally, chapters 10-11 will chart the progressive collapse of this Romantic synthesis under the burden of its own success as first natural and preternatural presences break into Newman's dialogue with his God and then this God becomes transformed into a threatening presence that must be constrained within an institutional church.

The analysis of Newman's childhood in chapter 1 describes his adolescent conversion as a search for some substitute for his ineffectual father. In this search, he first reverses the moral hierarchies within his family, becoming husband to his mother and father to his siblings. Next, he adopts and then discards a series of human mentors and father substitutes, always on the grounds that they have somehow distorted the divine voice within him. When his siblings tire of being patronized and assert their own convictions, he fears that they may contextualize him and breaks with the older three. As his sister Harriett described him, "John *can* be most amiable, most generous . . . but to become his friend, the essential condition is, that you see everything along his lines, and accept him as your leader" (quoted in F. Newman, *Early History,* 72).[12] He even selects his closest friends for their ability to further his quest; if they fail or are otherwise taken from him, he learns to appropriate their spirits so thoroughly that their loss cannot compromise his autonomy. In all these wrenching dislocations, just as painful to him as to the other parties, Newman comes to define the power of his God as the power to reject all substitutes, a rejection that includes both people and the cultural forms they inhabit. In his quest for what Harold Weatherby describes as "a 'portable' Christianity" (76), one independent of any culture or polity, Newman uses his proximity to God as the *pou sto* from which, if not to move his world, at least to critique it.

As chapter 2 will explore, Newman's religious contemporaries professed a solid faith in the Bible, in the figure of Jesus, *and* in their own powers of subjective self-definition. The Anglican Newman insisted that both their faith and their subjectivity were coopted by a blind participation in specifically Victorian patterns of economic and psychological self-interest. Because Newman's Jesus remained so transcendent and the Bible so historically suspect, neither allowed him to escape this same cultural complicity. Hence he came to invoke an authority not only outside himself but outside the intellectual horizons of the Enlightenment; he came to see his materialistic age as paralleled and overshadowed by a spiritual realm first envisioned by the fourth-century Alexandrian Church. Since these visions matched his own, they allowed him to move, first into the Patristic past and then into the divine source of their common faith. Enfolded, comforted, and empowered by the Alexandrian community, he could claim that Romanticism, the Enlightenment, the Renaissance, and even the Reformation were all modern aberrations. Chapter 3 examines this visionary domain itself, the witness it offers of its own origins, and the path by which Newman hopes to reach it. From this perspective, his quest appears even more complicit with Enlightenment subjectivity than those of his religious contemporaries.[13] He may present himself as what Schiller called a naive and Keble a primary poet of the spirit; in practice, however, he constantly reshapes the historical and spiritual realities which he claims to have discovered.

When he suspends his defensive attacks on contemporary secularism to explore what appears an exclusively religious universe, chapter 4 sees him shaping this subjectivity into an original and vital variant on the projects of his Romantic predecessors. He may participate implicitly in the Idealism of a Fichte or in the imaginative recreation of the English Romantics, but he neither endows his own unaided subjectivity with transcendent power nor relinquishes it to God in a gesture of orthodox self-transcendence. Instead, through the dialogue within Newman's conscience, self and God are conceived (and conceived of), grow, and fulfill themselves within an ongoing process of mutual redefinition. Where Fichte's apparently God-centered rhetoric overlay a foundation of self, where a Derridean critique reveals Rousseau's rhetoric of self as overlying a God-secured metaphysics of presence, Newman's dialogue continually renegotiates its theology and its metaphysics as it proceeds.

So described, this reading may seem only to recapitulate the critique which underlies those of Marx and Freud, that of Feuerbach; it may seem to reduce Newman's God to a complex of human fears, desires, and ideals projected onto some spiritual fantasy world. In his practice, however, if not always in his theory, Newman's response to this world and its author grows increasingly active. Hence, even if these remain projections of the self, this self grows more complex and dynamic.[14] Newman thus reengages the riddling questions surrounding the Romantic imagination: are its visions illusions or truths, and if truths, are they discovered or invented? In the process, however, he superimposes on these questions the classic religious paradoxes of finding and being found, creating and being created. Throughout his Anglican career, his changing formulations and answers mark out a special locus for the religious imagination, one which is neither within the outer world, as in Coleridge's early pantheism, nor within the subject as a means of perception, as proleptically in Kant or more stridently in Fichte, nor within the cozier confines of a sacramental universe, as in Keble and some contemporary apologists. From a place in which to stand, his God grows into a participant in Newman's ongoing quest to redefine himself and his world.

Having analyzed the development and the shape of Newman's quasi-Romantic synthesis, the book goes on to analyze its relation to the Romantic project itself, whether as practiced by earlier poets and philosophers or as critiqued by their successors. Chapter 5 opens with Newman's religious variant on Wordsworth's effort to reconstruct his adult identity through a series of childhood epiphanies; it concludes with the challenges which this newly formed identity encountered during his 1832–33 Mediterranean tour—the pagan grandeur of classical Sicily and the subsequent trauma of his near-fatal fever. Such challenges forced Newman to redescribe the grandeur of his mystical visions in the more secular terms of the Romantic sublime, as exemplified in Wordsworth and analyzed by Kant. When he reinterprets the hallucinations of his Sicilian fever as divine epiphanies, these rival sublimities transform his spiritual dialogue into an agon of self and God.

This same tension, as we will see in chapter 6, prompts Newman to borrow from Calvinistic election and Catholic sainthood in order to synthesize his own ideal of spiritual privilege. Within such an ideal, he can reconcile his sense of spiritual exaltation, his ecclesiastical ambition, his need for physical self-discipline, his dependance upon visionary moments to escape the prosaic, his reverence for Patristic models and his concomitant need to adapt them for his own age and his own self-conscious psyche. So strenuous that few could even attempt it, this ideal offers Newman both a criterion for friendship and a means of celebrating the select circle of friends whose personalities helped to form the ideal itself. Secular critics may see him as selling his Romantic birthright for religious comfort, religious critics may see him as perverting Christian humility into Romantic willfulness, yet Newman's spiritual dialogue gives rise to an exaltation at once Romantic and Christian.

The stay which prevents this exaltation from degenerating into self-worship is Newman's conscience, his obedience to a voice he can never completely appropriate. As he works to identify that voice with the God he has encountered in the Bible and the Patristic Church, however, chapter 7 finds him threatened by philosophical and psychological relativism. His own response thus replicates the response to a chaotic universe proposed by Goethe and preached in England by Carlyle, an insistence on action as somehow self-authenticating. As Newman implements it, this militancy wins him individual autonomy, sweeping rhetorical freedom, and power to instantiate his subjective vision within his followers. Much as the Romantics invoked imagination to reshape their own worlds, he can invoke the gift of intercession, the spiritual counterpart of action, to reshape the course of Providence.

Because such claims, like those of the Romantics, rest on a subjective base, they remain equally vulnerable to self-doubt and self-criticism. As chapter 8 will show, the relapses Newman experienced throughout his Anglican career threatened to cripple his own spiritual aspirations by allying him with the empiricism of Hume and Gibbon and the more free-floating skepticism of Byron. So described, Newman's Romantic self-consciousness implicates him within the current debate over whether such moves anticipate those of postmodern critique or merely disguise an aesthetic escapism. By retaining dialogue as the medium for criticism itself, Newman's variant holds open the potentially reductive, potentially circular redefinition of poetry as criticism. In practice, he predicates engagement with some outside entity as a precondition for empathy with even the most skeptical of his covert mentors.

As chapter 9 moves from self-criticism to social criticism, Newman would seem far more vulnerable than the more radical of his Romantic predecessors. Although less bound to a pre-Enlightenment theology than he claimed to be, he stands condemned by this very complicity with his age, a complicity only exacerbated by his reactionary Tory politics. Taken on his own terms, however, Newman can expose the self-serving rationalizations of his religious contemporaries. In addition, his dialogic paradigm incorporates both a critique from outside the ideological horizons of Victorian society and a simultaneous stance at its core. From the first position, he exposes the inevitable contingency and human suffering which must compromise any secular utopia; from the second, he posits a spiritual center within individuals, institutions, and nations, a center that reinscribes their apparently random motions as errant and centrifugal. This relational, value-laden center keeps Newman's critique from privileging negativity as its own culturally contingent norm.

The last two chapters of this study will trace Newman's discovery, as if in response to some implicit critique, that the God of his cozy spiritual dialogue has grown too pliable to his own needs and too vulnerable in his ever-more-frequent encounters with natural and preternatural forces. These marginally Romantic intruders seem to have originated on his Mediterranean tour, lain latent throughout the glory days of the Tractarian movement, and then resurfaced during his religious setbacks in the early 1840s. They include ironic visions of an anarchic nature, preternatural specters, Patristic miracle stories, Old Testament savagery, and intimations of an immanent, pantheistic Deity. In trying to baptize phenomena usually associated with gothic, satanic, sublime, or ironic Romanticism, Newman sought to encompass them within a more capacious image of God. In so doing, as chapter 11 will detail, he discovered that a God who can encompass such irrationality demands a response much like the fear and trembling demanded of Kierkegaard. First Newman brooded over the destruction of Old Testament figures who had also claimed too close a visionary partnership in providence. Then he brooded over the spiritual impotence of contemporary Anglicanism. Finally, he turned to Catholicism, not just because it offered a bulwark against the predations of secular power, but because it subsumed within itself the same imperious, untrammeled spiritual power which he had come to find in nature, in preternatural visitants, and in God himself.

Text as Catena

In tracing this progression, I have employed a hermeneutic strategy suggested by Thomas's more chronological study and supported by Newman's own descriptions of his character and compositional practice. Thomas follows Newman through a sequence of discoveries: first, that concepts—ancient and modern—followed an inevitable progression; [15] second, that they could carry even the most astute thinkers to unforeseen conclusions;[16] third, that this progression informed the development of doctrine, and finally that a similar progression had been unconsciously subverting and redirecting his own thought.[17] Analyzing Newman's prejudice against Rome in the *Apologia* (20), for example, Leonard Deen claims that the passage itself "endows ideas as they exist in a living mind with potentialities for development or decay; it insists on a rigorous consistency of ideas, and forecasts the struggle between inconsistent ideas and the attendant 'unrest of mind'" (230).

Mulling over the spiritual meaning of his fever in Sicily, Newman himself admitted that his "professed [he first wrote "apparent"] principles [seemed] mere intellectual deductions from one or two admitted truths. . . . I have a vivid perception of the[ir] consequences . . . , have a considerable intellectual capacity of drawing them out, have the refinement to admire them, & a rhetorical or histrionic power to represent them" (*AW* 125). Three years later he confessed: "My constant feeling when I write is, that I . . . am merely drawing out intellectual conclusions— which, I need not say, is very uncomfortable" (*LD* 6: 353–54). The consequences of such concatenation he explores within the autonomous development of religious consciousness in others: "They hold the notions they have been taught for a long while, not perceiving that the character forming within them is at variance with these, till at length the inward growth forces itself forward, . . . and the dead outward surface of error, which has no root in their minds, . . . suddenly falls off; suddenly,—just as a building might suddenly fall, which had been going many years" (*PS* 8 (15): 226-27). His conflicting figures for this development—both organic growth and architectural collapse—lend credence to his admission that he is far more certain of the process itself than of its results.

I have chosen, therefore, to follow this process as my own vulnerable via media between a traditional chronology on the one hand and a discontinuous deconstruction on the other. I will not focus exclusively on the anomalies between passages or the gaps and absences within them; nor will I track Newman in his incessant "saying and unsaying." Yet I will also be warned by Thomas's admission that "The complicated chronology of Newman's encounter with Sabellianism and Apollinarianism stretches the narrator's art to its limits. . . . [P]roblems of simultaneity will not be artificially smoothed out, and constant cross-referencing will be necessary" (66-67). To render my own study somewhat more "reader-friendly"—and more appreciative of its subject—I have strung together thematically related passages from different times and contexts in order to see just how far Newman's ideas may take him.[18] Through this procedure I have created and/or discovered subtexts, elegantly defined by Tilottama Rajan as "subversive and repressed text[s] not consistent with the explicit text, in relation to which [they stand] as the subconscious to the conscious" (21n). I would suggest that such subtexts can assume a cogency and direction independent of either context or authorial intention; once reassembled, they can sanction a reading of the Anglican Newman not unlike the one I have just summarized.

Methodology

In working out this reading, I have adopted a flexible—I hope not a cavalier—approach to (1) temporal progression, (2) historical context, (3) textual context, and (4) disciplinary boundaries.

1. Because each of Newman's stages first challenges and then subsumes those before it, their dialectical progression forms a narrative of spiritual growth, a narrative that parallels yet subverts those which Newman told and retold within his contemporary letters, within the *Apologia,* and within the still later *Memoir.* Examined individually, however, each of these conceptual threads weaves itself back into his childhood and forward into his later life as a Catholic. And because these threads are both logical and causal, as Newman works with them, he sometimes picks up

one end and sometimes the other. To do justice both to his practice and to the stubbornly autonomous development of these subtexts, I have had to adopt an approach simultaneously diachronic and synchronic. Most of the passages quoted early in the study come from early in his life and most of those quoted late come from his last days as an Anglican; yet Newman's brooding, implicitly Romantic consciousness is continually throwing out early prefigurations of later ideas or later reformulations of early ones.

2. This focus on internal continuities among passages also slights the historical circumstances which occasioned them. Attention to such contemporary issues can admittedly prove crucial. Robert Pattison has shown, for example, that Newman's vendetta against Rene Hampden's liberal theology owed much to Hampden's beating him out for the professorship of moral theology (*Dissent* 64–65). Donald Capps has also found correlations between the biblical subjects in two sets of sermons and Newman's disagreements with two former mentors, Hawkins and Whately ("Sunden" 62–69). And, for Thomas, the pervasive analogies Newman discovers between contemporary and ancient controversies deny him and us the luxury of focusing on either in isolation from the other.[19] Newman himself acknowledged his need for controversy as a stimulus to composition (*LD* 5: 133), but the apparent occasions of his work often seem like excuses to work out deeper and more ongoing problems. Every student of Newman will acknowledge that his most evocative ideas crop up within the most unlikely contexts. The particular subtexts I consider, in fact, rather than being called up by context, seem to appropriate almost any context as a vehicle for their expression.

Nor do I see my methodology as short-changing the role of Newman's audience. Skilled as he was in sizing them up, he usually works to reduce them to a state of intellectual acquiescence within his controversial works and moral acquiescence within his sermons. Even Newman's splendid letters, with the possible exception of those to Hurrell Froude, do not repay extensive attention to his correspondents. They make the same demands for unquestioned sympathy of which Harriett complained in his personal relations. Where her letters remain so embedded in context and audience as to be almost indecipherable to an outsider, John's more often read as the transparent unwinding of his own skein of thought. Names of the recipients could frequently be switched with only minimal changes to the opening and closing paragraphs. Newman's scrupulous collection and copying of these letters make sense when we realize that they do in fact belong more to him than to those who received them.

3. While my methodology downplays historical context, it may seem to play fast and loose with textual context. The frequent ellipses within

my Newman quotations may look innocent, but a source check will show that they conceal sometimes only a few words, sometimes sentences, sometimes paragraphs, occasionally even whole pages. Many of my Newman quotations are indeed taken—or, more accurately, pried—out of context. Some such liberty, as Macheray points out (3–19, 75–101), underlies any interpretive reading; being faithful to Newman's context in its broadest sense would produce only a celebration of the Church Catholic as he strove to instantiate it during his Tractarian period. Newman's context is particularly insidious, however, not just because he demands intellectual, emotional, and moral submission, but because his rhetoric enforces these demands by the sheer weight of his periods. Quoting him in full, giving him the space he originally took to develop a given idea, would not only triple the length of this book, it would swamp my project with his own. In making my cuts, I have tried to follow the main thread of his argument, omitting many of the examples and the nervous qualifications. Occasionally these qualifications can initiate a dialectic; more often they only hedge his more innovative thoughts. My précis may make his prose sound anachronistically modern, but they also bring his public style closer to the more assured, emphatic style of his letters, the medium in which he remains, for me at least, simply without equal.

4. While I originally grew interested in Newman because of his educational theories, I soon had to acknowledge that these remained incomplete and misleading when divorced from their religious context. DeLaura ("Prophecy" 494–98) even challenges those critics who claim that our only viable response to Newman is an aesthetic one achieved through a willing suspension of our disbelief. This may, in fact, be a necessary position for some; it is certainly one which all but the most devoted disciples must adopt toward Newman's more arcane convictions. While we might assume that this aesthetic distance has been forced upon us by a shift in the Zeitgeist, I would suggest three cautions: first, Newman's agenda was not creditable to most of his contemporaries; second, it was not as alien to his age as he thought it was; third, our age may not be as different from his age as we think it is. What I can affirm is the futility of trying to distill from Newman's writings some secular, non-sectarian core which would secure his status as a man of letters. To quote G. B. Tennyson: "One must search sedulously in those forty volumes for a piece of writing that is not more or less explicitly on religious matters" ("Removing" 10).

While trying to engage Newman as a religious thinker and writer, I have also tried to engage the aesthetic power of his writing. Newman may not be a poet (even a prose poet) in that he works with and not through figure, yet because of his aesthetic sensitivity and his sheer intelligence he shows more awareness of—and more control over—the metaphoricity of his language than any other essayist of the period. His visionary passages in particular, while they invoke the hermeneutic strategies originally developed to interpret Scripture, remain equally susceptible to strategies employed in secular criticism—even to some of the tamer versions of postmodern critique. As a test case for the rival claims of sacred and secular interpretation, Newman's visions offer criticism a chance to acknowledge its religious roots and religious studies a chance to explore some contemporary extensions of its own hermeneutic tradition.

Ongoing Romanticism

So stated, my project may not sit any better with modern critical opinion than Newman's self-defense did with the prejudiced Kingsley. Dressed out as a Romantic, Newman may not seem any more sympathetic to his admirers or any more central to nineteenth-century studies. Newman spent his life insisting that he need not buy into Romanticism; our postmodern age has proudly or regretfully acknowledged that it has already bought out of Romanticism. Newman's claim would destroy the credibility of my project; the postmodern one would undermine its relevance. In response to both, I can only second the conclusions of Robert Sayre and Michael Lowy: *"far from being a purely nineteenth-century phenomenon, romanticism is an essential component of modern culture,* and its importance is in fact growing as we approach the end of the twentieth century" (23; italics theirs).[20] Their sociological assessment repeats one which Philippe Lacoue-Labarthe and Jean-Luc Nancy draw from the Jena Circle's fusion of literature and critique: "[W]hat interests us in romanticism is that we still belong to the era it opened up. The present period continues to deny precisely this belonging, which defines us. . . . Not the least result of romanticism's indefinable character is the way it has allowed this so-called modernity to use romanticism as a foil, without ever recognizing—in order not to recognize—that it has done little more than rehash romanticism's discoveries" (15).[21] As further evidence, I could point out some otherwise anomalous flickers of continued Romantic vitality: the frequency with which theorists are driven to untenable, or at least unlivable, positions to avoid what they perceive as Romantic essentialism or foundationalism; the frequency with which they recuperate the darker, "negative" formulations of the Romantic agenda; the frequency with which they invoke Kant and Hegel, not so much to support their own positions as to attack those of their opponents. Turning to poetry, we find that here too the English Romantics keep resurfacing, no matter how often they are dismissed as naive in their subjectivity, or sexist in their personal relations, or escapist in their politics. They still constitute a lost golden age of creative energy or an unreachable standard (Byron's Great Horse) by which modern poets covertly measure themselves and each other. If my readers will entertain, at least provisionally, the premise that we all remain more uncannily and uncomfortably bound to Romanticism than we might like, they may also entertain this study of a thinker who was himself uncannily and uncomfortably Romantic, though on very different grounds and for very different reasons.

CHAPTER 1

Parents, Mentors, Siblings, and Friends

❀

LIKE SOME other important figures in any history of Romanticism, Newman has two childhoods: one pieced together by scholars, the other created within his own project of retrospective self-construction. In the latter, examined in chapter 5, he exploits his religious variant of the Wordsworthian epiphany; the former, explored here, suggests why he refused to see himself as Romantic, why he fought to establish a position that transcended this or any other contingent engagement with his age. This chapter will trace Newman's childhood as one common for a precocious first-born, an ongoing effort to please and emulate his parents. Yet because the father exhibited no firm values which could discipline his eldest son, because the mother increasingly turned to John for counsel and support, the adolescent John turned to Evangelical Christianity for the discipline, counsel, and support he could not find elsewhere. In what he interpreted as a divine voice speaking through his conscience, he heard articulated goals, values, moral imperatives which not only abrogated parental authority but challenged all other claims upon him as partial, contingent, and hence idolatrous. Even though his parents' inadequacy taught him to distrust any relationships, he perforce remained involved with mentors, with his siblings, and with friends he made as a student in college, a fellow at Oriel, and a leader within the Tractarian movement. With almost all these people, Newman developed a progressive strategy of transference, appropriation, confrontation, and ultimate rejection. Although this strategy seems highly destructive by any interpersonal norms, it reinterprets intersubjectivity itself as a temptation encountered within his own quest for spiritual transcendence.

Mother and Father

The Newman family itself was happier than most. The father prospered in banking until the financial crash at the end of the Napoleonic wars. His wife, from an old Huguenot family, brought with her both business connections and a sizable dowry. Of their six children, John was born in 1801, Charles in 1802, Harriett in 1803, Frank in 1805, Jemima in 1807, and Mary in 1809. The first four siblings were extremely headstrong, and Charles soon manifested more severe psychological problems. Yet because the parents were loving, nurturing, and supportive, "the surviving records of kindly banter belong to a childhood secure in its affections and delightful in its setting" (Gilley 9). The three most extended accounts of the young John Henry[1] reconstruct him from his sister Harriett's book of children's tales, *Family Adventures*. These, according to Sean O'Faolain (25–29), show him buying his mother a netting box and replacing it after it was stolen, or pleading with his already-wayward younger brother Charles to show "respectability" and "moderation," or leading the family along a cliff-side path which soon degenerated into a sheep-walk, "but he kept silence, as he was a little boy who had very great respect for the feelings of elders, and especially of his parents, and he feared distressing his mamma at that moment."[2]

Maisie Ward goes on to link the young Newman with a somewhat older figure in another of Harriett's books, *The Fairy Bower:*

> George, aged about thirteen, condescends to play with the younger children, likes to "take off the company" when his parents have visitors, "quizzes" his sisters and cousins. He was a young gentleman who "believed he was clever enough to persuade anybody to do anything he chose." . . . Compare all this with the living boy who recited poetry on his birthday as a child, who led a large group at school . . . , who composed comic operas and dramas and led his family in acting them, . . . and I think you will see it comes pretty close to a portrait. (13–15)

These scenes reveal a clever first-born who focuses heavily on pleasing and imitating his parents and adopting a parental role toward his siblings.[3] Even his brother Frank's scurrilous *Early History of the Late Cardinal Newman* admits that John, "in my earliest youth, had more influence with me than my father" (6). Because of John's deference to and assumption of the parental role, his relations with both parents become indices of his religious development.[4]

Until her death when Newman was thirty-five, his mother was unquestionably closer to him than any other member of his family. She seems to have been as flawlessly a loving parent as he was a flawlessly obedient child; yet the very absence of conflict posed a problem for his own self-definition. In 1823, for example, he writes her, "When I rise, I sometimes think that you are lying awake and thinking—and only such reflections make me uncomfortable" (*LD* 1: 167). But at least eight years earlier, the failure of his father's bank had initiated the seamless shift from his dependence on her to her dependence on him. In 1822, after the second financial collapse, he writes to reassure his father about Frank's position at Oxford: "As to Francis, . . . I have arranged all that. He will be thrown out of nothing. Let me alone, and I shall do all very well. . . . Every thing will, I see it will, be very right, if only you will let me manage" (*LD* 1: 156). It is his mother who answers: "I fully accord with you. . . . This is just the text I have preached from, whenever your father and I have discussed the subject. For many months I always begin and end by saying, 'I have no fear, John will manage'" (*LD* 1: 156–57). Robbins notes Mrs. Newman's bias in attributing her third son's brilliant college career to John's influence: "The mother's letters to her favourite son are interesting for . . . the careful adjusting of the spotlight" (16).

As late as 1828, she reverses yet another role: "[W]here I may seem too sensitive, impute it to my earnest desire to possess your esteem as well as affection" (*LD* 2: 54). But her most revealing admission comes on John's twenty-first birthday: "And now that we have no more the dear child, we may boast instead, a companion, counsellor and friend. To your dear brothers and sisters it has given a second father, to whom they are much indebted for the improvement and cultivation of their minds" (*LD* 1: 122). The most interesting relation here must be inferred: if John is her children's second father, he has become her second husband. Charles Reding, the autobiographical hero of *Loss and Gain,* is given a father who "had left his family well provided for" on his sudden death; yet Charles, like Newman, "wished to supply to [his mother] the place of him she had lost" (156, 158). This place, in Freudian terms, marks the ultimate victory in a boy's Oedipal fantasy. In Lacanian terms it marks the indefinite perpetuation of an imagined universe in which the Mother's adoring gaze, which has originally granted coherence to the infant, continues to shape an unbroken unity of subject and object, unthreatened by any intrusion of paternal power and paternal language.

This bond may have marginalized the father just as successfully as the father managed to marginalize himself. Analyzing his portrait, O'Faolain concludes: "Nothing could be less aristocratic, less troubled, less intellectual than this genial extrovert's face. . . . [H]e was much less interested in religious notions than in good music, in good beefsteaks, . . . in Benjamin Franklin, in Thomas Jefferson" (30, 32). In what he describes as "the first Letter your Papa ever wrote to his [five-year-old] Son," the still successful Mr. Newman does assume the role of loving authority figure. He even oversees the first of John's countless efforts to inscribe himself in writing: "I mean to examine you as to your Multiplication Table and if I find you improve I intend after a time to buy you a nice Copy Book and teach you to write" (*LD* 1: 3).

After the failure of his bank in 1816, his son dutifully fights to keep this authoritative paternal image alive. During a return visit to his adolescent home at Alton in 1834, he writes his mother:

> Especially I remember that first evening of my return from Oxford in 1818, after gaining the scholarship at Trinity, and my Father saying, "What a happy meeting this!" Often and often such sayings of his come into my mind, and almost overpower me; for I consider he did so very much for me at a painful sacrifice to himself—and was so generous and kind; so that whatever I am enabled to do for you and my sisters I feel to be merely and entirely a debt on my part, a debt which he calls me to fulfil. (*LD* 4: 331)

But the debt, I suspect, was more emotional than financial—guilt overlying a shame which he could neither reveal nor forget. As late as 1874 he wrote a memorandum, marked "most private," notifying posterity that "I wish no reference to be made, in any Memoir of me, to my or my family's residence" at this same Alton (*LD* 1: 27). Presumably Alton must remain thus shrouded in silence because of his father's failed attempt to manage a brewery there.

In an 1833 letter to his mother, he rationalizes a similar omission: "I have regretted constantly, as you say *you* have, that my book of Memorials [*Memorials of the Past*] contained no direct mention of my dear Father. . . . [B]ut some how, I could not do it—I felt I was not equal to it" (*LD* 3: 274).[5] The humiliation John shared with the rest of the family may have broken through in the delirious nightmares brought on by his fever in Sicily: "I had some miserable nights—the dreamy confusion of delirium—sitting on a staircase, wanting something, or with some difficulty—very wretched—& something about my Mother & Sisters" (*AW* 131). Similar family scenes even reappear within a sermon where he compares a Christian's "disquiet" during Holy week to "a bad dream, restless and dreary; he . . . could not master his grief, could not realize his fears, but was as children are, who wonder, weep, and are silent, when they see their parents in sorrow, from a feeling that there is something wrong, though they cannot say what" (*PS* 4 [23]: 336–37).

It would be tempting to attribute all this shame to the father's successive business failures. Both O'Faolain and Maisie Ward, however, cite another revealing episode from a time well before the bankruptcy. In it the father makes one of his few significant remarks within *Family Adventures:*

> "I do not wish you ever to cease to esteem your own family as your choicest society[," replied the father to Harriett,] "but in order to secure its being worthy this esteem, you should be willing at the same time, to mix, in a simply, good-humoured manner, with any you may happen to fall in with."
>
> "It is a great bore," remarked [John] Henry. . . . "I can be civil enough when I like people." (quoted in O'Faolain 29; M. Ward 12; Svaglic, "Charles" 373)

Even here John displays an undisguised contempt for his father's easy social affability. He showed a similar refusal to compromise in 1820 when he refused to side with his father in excusing the sexual conduct of the beleaguered Queen Caroline. Frank says he "concluded that, after all, my father's argument was *more Christian* than my brother's. . . . My father was so irritated that he ended with a sharp sarcasm: 'Well, John! I suppose I ought to praise you for knowing how to rise in this world. . . .' Years afterwards, I discerned that my father had mistaken fanaticism for self-seeking" (9). In 1822, however, Mr. Newman himself accuses John of a similar fanaticism:

> You are encouraging a nervousness and morbid sensibility, and irritability, which may be very serious. . . . I know it is a disease of mind. Religion, when carried too far, induces a softness of mind. . . . Depend upon it, no one's principles can be established at twenty. . . . Weak minds are carried into superstition, and strong ones into infidelity. . . . Many men say and do things, when young, which they would fain retract when older, but for shame they cannot. I know you write for the Christian Observer. My opinion of the Christian Observer is this, that it is a humbug. You must use exertions. That letter was more like the composition of an old man, than of a youth just entering life with energy and aspirations. (*AW* 179)

Here, unlike Newman's mother, his father asserts himself vigorously and criticizes him for failing to assert his own masculinity. Yet, as we have seen, the assertion and the criticism come from a man bankrupt and broken in health, a man whose temporal authority is being ceded to his son by his wife and whose spiritual authority has already been usurped by his son's new mentor, Mr. Mayers.[6]

This dilemma, I believe, shapes the religious dilemmas Newman will encounter for the rest of his long life. Even without mastering the niceties of Lacanian psychology or accepting its structuralist base, we should acknowledge the importance of someone who can offer a boy both the No and the Name of the Father, both phallic prohibition and a linguistic introduction into the symbolic order which will compensate for it.[7] Instead we have in Newman a first-born who has dedicated his young life to following and identifying himself with his parents, who has shaped the voice of his own conscience on their advice and example, who, when asked why he loves and respects them, offers their "unhesitating assumption of authority over him (*Ari.* 144)." And this boy now finds himself encumbered with a mother who insists on following him and a father who counsels a worldly wisdom which he has failed to follow. Denied any discipline backed by real threat or real power, John must begin his own search for an authority rigorous enough to demand all that he is capable of giving and powerful enough to guarantee that these efforts will be rewarded. As we shall see, the construct which he will christen "the Church Catholic" serves as a partial replacement for his mother; his quest to find some replacement for his father shapes and complicates his image of God.

Conversion

While I, like other critics, have been assuming a causal link between his father's bank failure and his own conversion a few months later, Newman's late-written *Grammar of Assent* describes conversion as a seamless extrapolation from filial to religious duty:

> If, on doing wrong, we feel the same tearful, broken-hearted sorrow which overwhelms us on our hurting a mother; if, on doing right, we enjoy the same serenity of mind, the same soothing, satisfactory delight which follows on our receiving praise from a father, we certainly have within us the image of some person, to whom our love and veneration look, in whose smile we find our happiness, for whom we yearn, towards whom we discover pleadings, in whose anger we are troubled and waste away. These feelings in us are such as require for their exciting cause an intelligent being. (76)

Such a progression—from instinctive filial obedience to loving reverence for one's parents, to a focus on the voice of conscience, to an investigation of its source—deserves some credence. Newman insists that his conversion was not precipitated by the wrenching conviction of sin demanded in the Evangelical literature which Mr. Mayers urged upon him.[8] According to this interpretation, his conversion merely enabled him to recognize the source and nature of the inner voice which he had been obeying all along; to quote Louis Bouyer, "into a mind rendered mysteriously receptive," the advent of Evangelical doctrine "would only reawaken . . . what, in the child was merely a passive impression" (19).⁹

In a late journal entry, however, Newman confesses that he "was more like a devil than a wicked boy, at the age of fifteen" (*AW* 250). This seemingly outrageous claim may refer to an earlier confession in the *Apologia* that "I read some of Hume's Essay; and perhaps that on Miracles. So at least I gave my Father to understand; but perhaps it was a brag" (17). This link between his skepticism and his father's worldliness may suggest that in converting, John was growing deaf to the parental voice rather than listening for some transcendent echo of it. This characteristically negative definition of Newman's Voice as *not* parental undercuts the reductively Freudian approach of Geoffrey Faber. Newman himself, to be sure, sanctions some claims for the unconscious: "[C]ritical disquisitions are often written about the idea which this or that poet might have in his mind . . . , not implying . . . that the author . . . knew what he was doing; but that, in matter of fact, he was possessed, ruled, guided by an unconscious idea" (*US* [15]: 321–22).¹⁰ Ignoring both Newman's caution and his own demurrals,¹¹ Faber invokes thin biographical evidence to portray Mrs. Newman as so domineering that she warped her son's sexual development and drove him toward a repressed homosexuality.¹² From this perspective Faber can collapse Newman's spiritual progress into a frustrated effort to return to the womb: a sense of sin "drove him, like a child running from the terror of the dark to be comforted by its mother, into the consolations of religion—into, finally, the arms of his adopted Mother, the Church of Rome, and his Father, St. Philip Neri" (172).¹³

In a sermon preached when both his mother and Hurrell Froude were still alive, however, Newman seems to anticipate their deaths as essential to his own spiritual growth: God "plucks off some of the promise of the vintage; and they who are left, mourn over their brethren whom God has taken to Himself, not understanding that it is no strange providence, but the very rule of His government, to leave His servants few and solitary" (*PS* 3 [17]: 240).¹⁴ O'Faolain even suggests that instead of passively accepting such isolation as God's rule, Newman actively engineered it: "[I]t is clear . . . that he drew away from [his family] and from everybody else for one main reason, that he was one of those fiercely intolerant men who cannot love where they do not agree" (163). When Harriett enquired about his health after their mother's death, John actually set the beginning of this alienation much earlier: "Years ago, from 1822 to

1826, I used to be very much by myself. . . . Indeed, ever since that time I have learned to throw myself on myself" (*LD* 5: 311–12).[15] To her younger sister, Jemima, five days later, he raises the spiritual ante by attributing inclination to duty:

> God intends me to be lonely. He has so framed my mind that I am in a great measure beyond the sympathies of other people, and thrown upon Himself. . . . I have some sort of dread and distress, which I cannot describe, of being the object of attention. . . . I recollect about two years ago, after I had fainted away, my Mother most kindly stooping down to take up my feet and put them on the sofa. I started up—I could not endure it. I saw she was hurt, yet I did not know how to put things right. (*LD* 5: 313–14)[16]

If after his conversion he "rest[ed] in the thought of two and two only absolute and luminously self-evident beings, myself and my Creator" (*Apo.* 18), he could do so because the second being was conceived as the exclusion of all others.[17] Only such a God could save him from being again disappointed in promises made to him or claims made upon him by family, friends, school, church, or society. Only devotion to such a God would let him expose these promises and claims as contingent, stifling, and idolatrous.

While such exclusion informs his treatment of mentors, family, and friends, the compromises he makes identify his conversion as specifically adolescent. Had his spiritual intensity been fostered from early childhood, the figures, symbols, and narratives of Christianity might have remained as unprobematic for him as they seem to have been for the Rossetti sisters. Had he converted as an adult, the decision would have been made from a lived experience of the secular world. For Newman, however, this secular world remains neither unknown nor fully experienced. Voltaire's verses denying the immortality of the soul, for example, appear to him both "dreadful" and "plausible" (*Apo.* 17). The Enlightenment heritage of early nineteenth-century England could thus represent both heightened threat and heightened temptation. At a time when most adolescents, even nineteenth-century adolescents, would be looking past their parents' horizons, Newman sought to deny himself an intellectual breadth which had never been denied him but which he had experienced only vicariously. Within his quest, moreover, maturity itself became a vehicle for ever greater self-denial.

As a nineteenth-century Anglican, the adolescent Newman possessed no viable model for an ascetic life, no means and little real inclination to withdraw into hermit-like isolation. He also knew, from his mentor Mayers if no one else, that he needed the advice and support of those more spiritually advanced than he. If he was to remain in the world but not of it, however, he had to find a way of interacting with others without being corrupted by them or by the emotions they awoke in him. In practice, he developed three characteristic, though probably unconscious, strategies: (1) by separating others' theological insights from their persons, he could retain the insights while severing the relationships themselves; (2) when others' secular attitudes struck a disturbing chord within him, he could distance the attitude by transferring it to and denouncing it in them; (3) if a relationship became overwhelmingly important, he could subsume it within a shared religious quest or (the other being absent or dead) subsume him or her within his own personality.

In tracing these behavior patterns, I am admittedly following one subtext among many: in so doing I am slighting (1) the graciousness and tact which Newman displayed in most of his personal encounters, (2) the fervor which made him loved by his friends, admired by his congregations, and venerated by his disciples, and (3) the example of his sister Jemima, who by seeming to agree with John more than she really did, maintained a mutually supportive dialogue with him throughout their lives. Nor is my own argument impervious to cultural or temporal parochialism. In an age that prizes intersubjectivity as the basis for value and truth, Newman's behavior may easily be dismissed as destructive and probably self-destructive. According to Thomas Gornall, this behavior remained baffling to those around him but invisible to Newman himself: "The things he did and said at those [stressful] times have all the same characteristic: excessive self-protectiveness. The positions he then took became knotted and remained so for the rest of his life; even when he looked back he could not see what was wrong."[18] But it is the primacy of such intersubjective norms that Newman is challenging. The great thinkers of Christendom—Paul, Augustine, Aquinas, Luther, Calvin—have rarely qualified as hale fellows well met; nor have they sought to do so. It was, we remember, such conviviality in Newman's father which originally vitiated his authority with his son. Hence even charges brought against Newman from other religious perspectives risk slighting the power of his God to order and direct his life, to subordinate the welter of personal and social experience, to stand as both source and goal without being subsumed within any intellectual or theological system.

Mentors

While Newman encountered this God as negation, he remained paradoxically dependent on others to learn its nature and its demands upon him.

This paradox, in turn, complicated his search for a series of older men, men who were both temporary surrogates for his own inadequate father and partial custodians of the spiritual power which he spent his Anglican years trying to capture and internalize. The *Apologia*, subtitled *A History of My Religious Opinions,* is organized around the series of positions which he studied, assumed, tested, and discarded in favor of yet closer approximations to Catholic truth. The same sequence, however, can also be read as Newman's selection, idealization, and subsequent rejection of a whole series of spiritual mentors: to quote Robert Pattison, "Newman defined himself by separating himself from everyone else" (*Dissent* 60). This pattern may be seen as neurotic repetition and a return of the repressed, Newman's endless deferral of the crisis in which he would finally renounce all surrogates and acknowledge himself an adult. The same pattern, however, may also be seen as a means of continual growth. While the Anglican Newman constantly reaffirmed his duty as fidelity to an enshrined and internalized parental legacy, in practice he legitimated growth as progressive rebellion, a redefinition of his spiritual identity as separate from his parents, their successive surrogates, and the social contexts they inhabited. He continued to insist that he dropped these mentors in response to an ever more clearly heard voice of God; yet as we shall discover, the source of this voice, heard only as the negation of an ever-wider net of contingencies, grows ever harder to place or identify.

As the agent of his conversion and its guide, Walter Mayers is always treated with the greatest reverence. Newman's first letter to him claims that he was sent by the Holy Spirit,[19] and at his death in 1828, Newman uses a similar encomium: "[H]ad it not been for my intimacy with him, I should not have possessed the comfort of that knowledge of God which (poor as it is) enabled me to go through the dangerous season of my Undergraduate residence" (*LD* 2: 58). Mayers's brand of Evangelical fervor, however, comes in for increasing criticism; finally, in a canceled passage from the *Memoir,* Newman placates his father's memory by reinterpreting his own earlier "fanaticism": "had [Mr. Newman] known his son's character thoroughly, he would have had a still greater right to anticipate a change in the religious views of the youth. . . . [E]vangelical religion had never been congenial to him. . . . Its emotional and feverish devotion and its tumultuous experiences were foreign to his nature" (*AW* 82). Frank even accuses his brother of unfairness to Mayers's good name and memory: "I thus know Mr. Mayers much better than did my brother, whose few words have been interpreted as though Mr. Mayers were a high Calvinist" (15).

Where Frank complains that John has willfully reduced one mentor to a straw man, he laments that the premature death of another has left his brother theologically benighted: Dr. Charles "Lloyd was the Regius Professor of Divinity as well as Bishop [of Oxford]. . . . [H]e was learned in German theological literature, and felt it a scandal that in Oxford there was a total absence of solid learning as to the origin and history of the separate books of our Scriptures. He was bent to remedy this by promoting classes of Scriptural study after taking the Bachelor's degree" (39). John's resistance to these foreshadowings of the higher criticism, however, could not be blamed on lack of exposure. In a letter of 1823 to his mother, he writes, "I am beginning to attend some private lectures in Divinity . . . which [Lloyd] has been kind enough to volunteer to about eight of us" (*LD* 1: 167).[20] The *Memoir* claims that this class left him unimpressed:

> [Lloyd] had more liking for exegetical criticism, historical research, and controversy, than for dogma or philosophy. He employed his mind upon the grounds of Christian faith rather than the faith itself. . . . [H]e was not the man to exert an intellectual influence over Mr Newman or to leave a mark upon his mind, as Whately had done. To the last Lloyd was doubtful of Newman's outcome, and Newman felt constrained and awkward in the presence of Lloyd. (*AW* 71)

Yet Newman's account of the sessions themselves suggests that his attitude might be better described as disconcerted:[21]

> [Lloyd] was free and easy in his ways . . . [with] an indulgence of what is now called *chaffing* at the expense of his auditors; and, as he moved up and down his room, . . . taking snuff as he went along, he would sometimes stop before Mr Newman, on his speaking in his turn, fix his eyes on him as if to look him through, with a satirical expression of countenance, and then make a feint to box his ears or kick his shins before he went on with his march to and fro. (*AW* 71)

We are left wondering how much of Newman's discomfort came from Lloyd's manner and how much from his matter. If the former, it was a poetically just reprisal for the "quizzings" which the young Newman administered to his friends and siblings. If the latter, Lloyd's approach, however much discredited here, will reappear in Newman's essays on Holy Scripture and on ecclesiastical miracles.

Edward Hawkins, unlike Lloyd, offered Newman a model for carrying out an academic and ecclesiastical agenda.[22] In 1827–28 Newman was instrumental in having Hawkins chosen over Keble as Provost of Oriel because "we are not electing an Angel, but a Provost" (*LD* 2: 45). But when Newman, Froude, and Wilberforce redefined the role of tutor without

Hawkins's prior consent, Newman found his pragmatism far less admirable. Reassessing their conflict some twenty-five years later in a private memorandum of 1860, Newman attributes it to a "coldness, dryness, and donnishness on his part, and [a] provoking insubordination and petulance on mine. We differed in our views materially, and he, always mounting his high horse, irritated me and made me recoil from him. In my innermost heart I have always loved, as well as respected him" (*LD* 2: 202). Some fifteen years later still, the *Memoir* admits that the two shared many academic goals: "The Provost loyally and energetically backed up his tutors in their measures for the enforcement of discipline and the purification of the College. He inflicted severe punishments on offenders; he showed no hesitation in ridding the place of those who were doing no good there either to themselves or to others. It began to be the fashion at Oriel to be regular in academical conduct, and admission into the Tutors' set became an object of ambition" (*AW* 92). But in the mass of letters with which Newman obsessively documents the tutorship controversy, Hawkins sounds a bit pompous, perhaps, but painstakingly accommodating. The tone of Newman's replies, by contrast, David Newsome describes as "imperious and aloof" (*Convert* 66): "Retire of my own accord, I think I never can—for . . . I feel it no point of *honor* to resign on finding my views of its duties differ from yours" (*LD* 2: 237).[23] In the *Idea,* Newman will be able to champion an intellectual rigor very much like Hawkins's, but in the early 1830s Newman's quarrel may be transferring to him secular values which he does not wish to acknowledge in himself.

It was with Richard Whately that Newman had the most mutually painful falling out. Yet both the *Apologia* and the *Memoir* are uniformly generous in their praise of Whately and poignant in their grief over the subsequent estrangement. Of the Oriel Fellow who virtually adopted him after his election, Newman writes:

> If there was a man easy for a raw bashful youth to get on with it was Whately—a great talker, who endured very readily the silence of his company,—original in his views, lively, forcible, witty in expressing them . . . singularly gracious to undergraduates and young masters, who, if they were worth anything, were only too happy to be knocked about in argument by such a man. And he on his part professed to be pleased at having cubs in hand whom he might lick into shape, and who, he said, like dogs of King Charles's breed, could be held up by one leg without yelling. (*AW* 66)

If this animal image seems harsh, the *Apologia* tempers it with another: "[A]ll his geese were swans. While I was still awkward and timid in 1822, he took me by the hand, and acted towards me the part of a gentle and encouraging instructor. He, emphatically, opened my mind, and taught me to think and to use my reason" (*Apo.* 23). Significantly, the power Whately held for Newman and over him included discourse and symbolic reasoning: "Whately's great satisfaction was to find a layman who had made a creed for himself, and he avowed that he was *prima facie* well inclined to a heretic, for his heresy at least showed that he had exercised his mind upon its subject matter" (*AW* 70).[24]

By the early 1830s, however, Newman had grown less inclined to tolerate heretics; in 1834 he seized on the opportunity of formally disengaging himself.[25] When Whately, by then Anglican Archbishop of Dublin, asked him to deny the rumor that "you absented yourself from chapel on purpose to avoid receiving the Communion along with me," Newman accused him of encouraging secularism and infidelity.[26] In reply Whately quoted Newman's own letter of 1826 thanking him because he had "taught me to think correctly, and—strange office for an instructor—to rely upon myself." But Newman answered, "I recollect well that the words . . . were intended to convey to you that . . . even then I did not fall in with the line of opinions you had adopted" (*Apo.* 326–31). Newman is clearly writhing here under some theological version of Harold Bloom's anxiety of influence. The evident pride with which he assimilates, rejects, and coopts the paternal figure of Whately should not blind us to the irony that he is laying claim to Whately's intellectual freedom *in order* to deny its authority.[27] Only in the late *Memoir* is he ready to acknowledge this anomaly: "[H]e had . . . no license at an after date to forget, that, if he was able to assert his own views in opposition to theirs [the other Fellows], it was, in truth, they who had put him into a position, enabling him to do so" (*AW* 65).

Newman himself acknowledges his conflicted behavior toward these last two mentors in a letter of 1836: "[I]t has . . . got me into scrapes, my looking up to those who happened to be just over me. Thus for a while Whately and Hawkins beguiled me. Really, I boast . . . that I was never taken in by an equal, continually by a superior" (*LD* 5: 304). Donald Capps interprets both relationships through Hjalmar Sunden's theory of role taking, in which an interaction with spiritual mentors can be overlaid by a scriptural interaction with other humans and with God.[28] Focusing on the typology of two sermons, each following a dispute with a mentor, Capps argues that by playing David to Hawkins's Saul, Newman can script their curricular debate as one between his nascent spirituality and his mentor's soon-to-be-punished worldliness ("Sunden" 62–65). By playing the elder son in the parable of the Prodigal, on the other hand, Newman receives both chastisement and forgiveness for coveting the preferment which he thought Whately, as newly elected Archbishop, would bestow on him (66–69). While Capps sees these sermons as re-negotiating Newman's troubled relations with his mentors, I would argue that the relations had grown troubled because Newman, having appropriated their limited access to the divine, had *already* ceased to regard them as mentors. The fluid interaction of human and divine within biblical narrative, in other words, may have offered him, not just a medium for interpreting human relationships, but a master script for making and breaking them.

This series of relationships thus helps to explain Newman's paradoxical attitude toward authority. On the one hand, many Anglican contemporaries besides Kingsley felt that Newman had sold his honor and his honesty to gain the security of the Catholic Church. Even O'Faolain claims that "He nourished, from the womb, a great many tightly-wound, inborn ideas which . . . he would spend many years and much spiritual sweat in unwinding. . . . One of his ideas was an inordinate respect for authority" (53–54). We can see this, for example, in his repeated assertions that the word of his own Bishop represented for him the word of God. Yet when Bishop Bagot of Oxford gently reprimanded him for Tract 90, his vaunted obedience grew suddenly hedged: "[W]hile I will pay unlimited obedience to the Bishop set over me while he comes in Christ's name, yet to one who comes in the name of man, in his own name, in the name of mere expedience, . . . I should not be bound to pay him any at all" (*KC* 186).[29] And as Wiseman and Manning were to discover to their sorrow, this same recalcitrance stayed with him through his conversion and down to his famous toast "to Conscience first, and to the Pope afterwards" in 1875.

Siblings

Newman's experience of God's voice as negation thus brings him to see life as a series of encounters that can only dramatize God's command to transcend all such encounters. While he came to acknowledge that his mentors had offered valuable, if partial religious insights, he could never fully reconcile himself to his siblings. Although his treatment of them is often seen as willful, inflexible, or unfeeling, Newman claimed a deep love for his whole family[30] and backed up his claim in action: as he promised his parents, he paid Frank's expenses at Oxford, even tutoring additional pupils in order to do so. He supported all his sisters, their mother, and her scatterbrained sister, Aunt Betsy, who incurred sizable losses in trying to run a girl's school. He helped arrange the marriages of Harriett and Jemima to the brothers Mozley. He bailed the wayward Charles out of countless scrapes and shared with Frank the burden of supporting him when he proved unable or unwilling to work.

When his youngest sister Mary died suddenly in 1828, probably of a burst appendix, John poured out his hopeless love in one encomium after another: "All that happened to her she could change into something bright and smiling like herself" (*LD* 2: 49-50). His grief even drove him to question, not just his faith, but his sense of self. His early encounter with temporal flux is poignantly recapitulated two decades later in a dialogue between Charles Reding and his sister, also named Mary:

> "What I mean is," continued Charles, "that we can rely on nothing here, and are fools if we build on the future."
> "We can rely on each other," she repeated.
> "Ah, dear Mary, don't say so; it frightens me. . . . [I]t seems presumptuous to say so." (*LG* 103-4)[31]

Immediately after his own sister's death, Newman tries unconvincingly to cut his emotional losses: "[I] rejoice again, because whom God loveth He chastiseth, and because I feel I am especially honored by him and cared for" (*LD* 2: 50).[32]

Subsequent letters, however, suggest that he is indeed devastated. As he writes Jemima, "On Thursday I rode over to Cuddesden. . . . The country too is beautiful—the fresh leaves, the scents, the varied landscape. . . . I wish it were possible for words to put down those indefinite vague and withal subtle feelings which quite pierce the soul and make it sick. Dear Mary seems embodied in every tree and hid behind every hill. What a veil and curtain this world of sense is! beautiful but still a veil" (*LD* 2: 69). Here Newman's appeal to his longstanding doubts about physical reality only turns Mary's troubling spirit loose in the natural world. His next reference to his grief, in a letter to Robert Wilberforce refusing to seek comfort in travel, stands as one of his most candid confessions of how deeply the fact of her death has shaken his usually adamantine faith: "One thought alone has occupied my mind these 6 months—never ½ hour together out of it. . . . I cannot reconcile my imagination to the *fact*—and when I am from home this irrational incredulity, this involuntary scepticism gains its hold upon me, and makes me seem to myself in a dream. . . . I really think I feel God most good and am quite and wholly convinced and satisfied His will is right wise and merciful" (*LD* 2: 82).[33] Anticipating the famous mirror passage in the last chapter of the *Apologia* (216), this incredulity leads to imperfectly suppressed doubts, first about God's purposes and then about his own existence.

Because Mary's loss leads to an internal loss of control, John comes to practice upon her memory the same strategies of appropriation he attempts with his living siblings. Specifically, he concentrates less on invoking her than on delimiting her influence upon him. Four months later, he is able to project her spiritualized presence onto the surrounding natural world, simultaneously resuscitating her and consecrating it: "My ride of a morning is generally solitary; but I almost prefer being alone. . . . I have learned to like dying trees and black meadows—swamps have their grace, and fogs their sweetness. A solemn voice seems to chant from every thing. I know whose voice it is—it is her dear voice. Her form is almost nightly before me, when I have put out the light and lain down. Is not this a blessing?" (LD 2: 108).

Although Jemima was almost as accommodating as her younger sister Mary, the fact that she remained alive makes John's efforts at appropriation seem more obvious. A patronizing early letter to her concludes, "What a gossiping letter this last half has been! It is quite a girl's letter—ah, I feel ashamed" (LD 2: 91). When he converts to Catholicism, Jemima alone refuses to judge him or his decision; yet she also refuses to deny that she finds both his reasons and his new faith unconvincing: "I have so much sanguineness in my composition that I always hope the worst misfortunes may be averted till they are irremediable. And what can be worse than this? It is like hearing that some dear friend must die. . . . Our poor distracted Church seems to me in pieces, and there is no one to help her, and her children's sympathies seem all drawn off another way. And how sad it is to me that I cannot say these things to you without your thinking me in error" (Moz. 2: 409-10). By maintaining their correspondence within this painful yet loving tension, she maintains her own theological commitment to the apparently incompatible values of interpersonal relationship and personal integrity: "I know . . . how little I ought to assume I am right in any one thing. Yet there are some things one dare not doubt, and some things it is one's highest happiness to believe and try to realize. So, however unworthy I am, I feel we must in some measure go by our own faith and our own light, though that light be little better than darkness" (Moz. 2: 414).

While Newman came to appreciate, and appropriate, his two youngest sisters, the other three siblings—Charles, Harriett, and Frank—could offer him little besides temptation and threat. He felt intuitively, almost viscerally, the biblical injunction which concludes his first Tract: "HE THAT GATHERETH NOT WITH ME SCATTERETH ABROAD."[34] Those who could or would not further his spiritual pilgrimage could only threaten it. First, as the eldest child, he had so identified himself with adults that he never seriously entertained the possibility of learning from his juniors. Second, they were simultaneously too like and too unlike him. The first four children were equally self-assured, self-assertive, and self-centered.

Mrs. Newman is surely right when she complains that Charles "is as earnest in Mr Owen's plans as Frank can be in his 'good cause,' yet it is very striking how similarly self-willed they each are. They each consider that they *alone* see things rightly" (*LD* 2: 263). To be fair, however, she should have included her eldest son and daughter in the bargain. Harriett, Frank, and Charles, moreover, all reflected John's own nature in a way that impugned some of his cherished opinions. At the age of nine, for example, he wrote in a copy-book, "Train up a child in the way he should go, and, when he is old, he will not depart from it." As we will see in the next chapter, his obsession with early spiritual influences amounted to a moral determinism. His siblings had all had the same training which he had—better, if anything, because he has been there to guide them. And yet they used this training to shape lives different from one another and, worse yet, different from his.

Harriett in particular had a well-earned reputation as a wit; after an early visit to the British Museum, she wrote her sister, "As to the Elgin Marbles, they do not improve by laying by" (quoted in D. Mozley 7). According to O'Faolain, hers "are by far the most graphic of all the Newman letters, and the most human. They alone give us hard, bright thumbnails of days and people" (79–80). Glorying in this reputation, she savages one prospective suitor in conversation: "I could hardly keep him down though I several times wounded him enough to extort a cry of 'Miss Newman, you insult me!'; 'Mrs. N., your daughter insults me.' . . . Absurd little person, why did he stay?" (quoted in O'Faolain 129). Later, she playfully warns her fiance, Thomas Mozley, of what *he* can expect in marriage: "You don't know perhaps that by some near connexions I have been voted a 'vixen.' . . . You will have discovered there is something more frightful before you than the long winter evenings—it is quite cheering to me to think how I might worry and torment you—you poor dear creature" (quoted in D. Mozley 58). Despite John's protestations that "of all my brothers and sisters . . . you alone know my feelings and respond to them" (*LD* 2: 55), she refused to be convinced: "I hoped you loved me, dear John, whenever I thought of it—but I could never persuade myself that there was any thing in me that could inspire the same feeling towards me that I feel for other, much more you. I cannot persuade myself so now" (*LD* 2: 55–56).

John paid lip-service to this independence: "Harriet thinks and judges much more dispassionately and rationally than I do" (*LD* 2: 6); but he had already found his feminine ideal epitomized in the cheerful, pliant Mary.[35] Hence, long before their father's death, he feels justified, even compelled, to assert paternal authority over Harriett, particularly when he detects within her desires and hostilities which he would deny in himself. Just after the bank failed and the family had to move, he wrote his aunt: "Why should Harriett be sorry at leaving Norwood? . . . I hope I shall hear of her with Stoical front disdaining to feel any affection for the place in which she has delighted these last eight years. . . . [John,] when he left Norwood on one Monday morning . . . must have been conscious to himself, he would never see it (as his home) again; let her ask herself, whether he was in the least unwilling to leave it, tho he liked it; perhaps as much [as] she did" (*LD* 1: 26). A decade later, his criticisms of her social life pass beyond chauvinism into mere crochet: "I meant in my last [letter] . . . invitations to places where there will be *many* people, a most irrational mode of spending time. If I had my will, no lady should go where she could not take her work. . . . See as many persons as you can—though *not all at once*" (*LD* 2: 7). Kathleen Tillotson sums up this attitude with his remark, "There is that in Harriett which I will *not* permit" (187).

Harriett tries to take all this hectoring in good humor; in one letter, according to O'Faolain, she makes merry "because John wanted to bury a couple who would have preferred to get married; and then tried to marry the wrong couple, who would thereby have been twice married; and then tried to marry the right couple in the wrong name" (81). Next she tries banter: "[Y]our letter . . . was certainly penned with the quill of a wild goose. I long to expose you, and to read it to some of the sober folk here who are so deluded still with the belief of your wisdom" (quoted in M. Ward 162). Next she is driven to sarcasm: "I wish you had some one with you, poor fellow—but a monk deserves no compassion. Don't tumble off your horse—give my love to Klepper [the horse]—if you see no objection" (*LD* 2: 254).[36] Later she vents more overt hostility: "[F]irst, is your own manner, which I am sure you must know is sometimes very trying to me, and which I cannot always understand. . . . Another difficulty I have felt in speaking to you freely, is the great difference I see in our opinions on many points" (*LD* 3: 107). She, like Frank, seems to have been waiting for some opportunity to retaliate; learning of John's conversion, she compared it to "a disgraceful marriage," domesticating her brother's spiritual quest by comparing the advent of a new church in the family to the appearance of a new and thoroughly disagreeable in-law (D. Mozley 163). While she cut him off immediately, she had already admitted that the split within her church had torn the fabric of her own life: "I long to be writing again, and yet I feel pretty sure I have lost the power. I believe the Oxford folks have helped to put me in this state, for I feel as if every thing were about to be pulled to pieces and could cry 'cui bono' to every project" (116).

Of Frank's continued hostility to his eldest brother, the *Early History* offers abundant proof; but such impetuosity was no new thing. A decade after their father had accused John of fanaticism, Frank fell under the influence of John Nelson Darby, joined the radical Plymouth Brethren, and set out on an incredibly ill-conceived missionary trip to Persia. On this trip, several of the party died and Frank himself returned very ill. John, however, found his brother's actions less foolish than ungrateful. If his sisters were supposed to represent otherness, Frank was supposed to imitate the course of his own life, with the failures and wrong turns eliminated. Newman outlines this agenda in *Loss and Gain:* "Youngest sons in a family, like monks in a convent, may remain children till they have reached middle age; but the elder, should their father die prematurely [or, we might add, become otherwise ineffectual], are suddenly ripened into manhood, when they are almost boys" (159). From the burdens of paying for and supervising Frank's college education (*LD* 1: 155) came the natural urge to identify with his success: "The class list came out on Friday last, and Frank was in both first classes. How I have been led on! how prospered! . . . I went before, failing in the Schools, to punish and humble me. Then, by gaining a fellowship here, I was enabled to take him by the hand. And now he is my 'Avenger of thy father's bloody death [Gr.]'" (*AW* 209).[37]

Hence, beneath the condescending humor of his note announcing Frank's homecoming lurks the complaint that he has not been given due credit for this triumph:

> I hereby send you a young person from Oxford, to whom I hope you will be kind for my sake. . . . You must indulge him in some things poor young gentleman—he has got some odd ideas in his head of his having been lately examined, of his having been thanked for the manner in which he acquitted himself. . . . [Y]ou must not thwart him in these fancies, but appear to take no notice of them and gently divert his attention to other subjects. . . . He is to eat no breakfast or dinner while with you. Deluge him with gruel, of which he is fond. (*LD* 1: 290-1)

Besides raining on Frank's parade, the note cruelly describes him in the very terms usually reserved for the errant Charles. Frank, as expected, remembers his brother's coaching as more degrading than helpful: "If my brother had shown me as much courtesy as did my *tutors* at Worcester College, or my senior Fellows at Balliol, instead of tormenting me by chidings as if I were a young child, he might have known me better" (63). John, for his part, finds Frank ungrateful: "Frank has offered Froude some of his books as not needing them more [on his missionary journey to Persia]. *He has made no such offer to me.* One would think I had a prior claim" (*LD* 2: 227; italics Newman's).

Frank's zeal was itself a threat. Just as John was leaving Evangelicalism for the Church Catholic after a brief flirtation with the Noetics, Frank's commitment to Darbyism embarked him on the missionary vocation which John had invoked to justify his own commitment to celibacy. Then, after following out a road which John had examined and rejected as a dead end, Frank fell into the skepticism which John had prophesied as the inevitable result of Protestant private judgment. A prophetic scorn suffuses his reaction to Frank's announcement that he had renounced the doctrine of the Trinity: "As to your still holding regeneration etc. I value it not a rush. Such doctrines . . . may remain on your mind awhile after you have given up the High Mysteries of Faith—but will not last longer than the warmth of a corpse" (*LD* 5: 167). Conversely, Frank insists that he could have predicted the inevitable result of his brother's idolatry from its beginnings: "While I was arranging furniture in my new rooms (1824), I suddenly found a beautiful engraving of the 'Blessed Virgin' fixed up. I went to the print-shop and begged its immediate removal, and then learned that my brother had ordered it" (18). As Robbins's book attests, this spiteful bickering continued all their long lives and, in print, even after John's death.

John's problems with Charles stemmed not just from Charles's madness but from the fact that it, like Frank's religious progress, offered a cruel and threatening parody of his own beliefs. As O'Faolain sums up this unfortunate creature: "On one tenet of Owenism Charles was always crystal clear: namely, that since character is made by circumstances no man is responsible for his actions and should, therefore, not be punished for them. . . . In the end he declared that he had been born under such disadvantages that he might as well give up all attempts to support himself, and informed his family that he had as much claim in justice on them to support him as if he were bedridden or a cripple" (75). On one famous occasion, for example, he demanded his whole inheritance in a lump sum and was found soon after, living in London with a woman who had spent his money, pawned his clothes, and confined him to a room in his underwear. While John was once again obliged to rescue him, initially Charles proved less a monetary threat than a psychological one. On the one hand, his denial of personal responsibility rebuts John's celebration of conscience as the only admissible evidence for the existence of God. On the other, Charles's whole argument is an inadvertent parody of John's own moral determinism.

Without denying that Charles did have severe psychological problems, we need to heed Svaglic's note that the family was "assured by medical advisers that . . . he was at least technically sane" ("Charles" 371). After citing Harriett's opinion "that we are all bewitched," Charles himself confesses to John that "The family of the Newmans is as mad a family as perhaps can be found in th[is] mad country. Frank, the moment he gets out of his line, is the maddest person I am acquainted with. Next to him I rate either you, or I, or Owen of Lanarck" (quoted in Svaglic, "Charles," 380, 382). Mad or sane, he wins some credence for his insistence that his family had made him what he was.[38] Reading John's letters to him calls up Foucault's claim that a society labels as mad those whose opinions most disturb it.[39] George Levine (235) sees the sudden madness which visits the freethinking Juba in *Callista* as dramatizing Charles's lack of both intellectual and emotional restraint. Yet we may wonder whether John felt his brother held Owenite opinions because he was deranged or was deranged because he held Owenite opinions.[40]

While Newman's intellectual approach to skepticism needs a separate discussion, the tone of these letters is sufficiently overdetermined to suggest that he may again have been transferring unwanted emotions and opinions to Charles.[41] In 1825, after Charles has refused to sit at the knee of his elder brother, John breaks out: "[F]ar from suffering me [to help], you bid me keep my distance and prepare for action—Be it so. . . . I am not allowed to *convince* you, I must now attempt to *confute* you" (*LD* 1: 246). Yet his approaches before and after this challenge remain equally aggressive. When Charles renews the contest, Newman jubilantly describes its course to his sister Jemima as something between a fraternal brawl and a rescripted narrative of Christian versus lion:

> I am amused, entre nous, at C.'s perplexity and indignation. Five years ago, when our correspondence took place, I recollect having a strong feeling on my mind that unbelievers took an unfair advantage in always *assailing* Christians. . . . Directly [as Charles] had fully committed himself, I pounced upon his neck and held him down "Now" I said, "as you value your life, answer me these questions directly—you shall not rise nor breathe till you do—." . . . So puzzled, surprised and angry, he ducked about for some time in all directions, and then gave in. Now, having recovered himself and having put his dress in order, he is naturally indignant; and *not yet* seeing *his own* absurdity, accuses me of *perverseness and obstinacy!* . . . [I]t was perfectly fair in me to commence on the offensive. He *challenged* me. (*LD* 2: 285–86)

His mother receives a different version of the same encounter: "My head, hand, and heart are all knocked up with the long composition I have sent Charles. I have sent him 24 closely written foolscap pages, [sheets?] all about nothing. He revived the controversy we had five years ago. I have sent him what is equal to nine sermons" (*LD* 2: 284). While diligence has replaced jubilation here, questions remain about why he should write the equivalent of nine sermons about "nothing" or, even more basic, why he should become so emotionally entangled with someone whom he and the whole family acknowledge to be not in his right mind. Yet even as we smile at the threat John discovers in his brother's skepticism, we need to appreciate the spiritual zeal which drove him to drive other consciousnesses, particularly those of his siblings, to positions at some clearly defined distance from his own.

Friends

In seeming contrast to his treatment of his siblings, Newman's deep attachment to a select circle of kindred souls stands out as one of his most endearing qualities.[42] Chief among these was Hurrell Froude, whom O'Faolain describes as "a completely unconventional thinker, impish, mischievous, daring, . . . hard as nails on himself, yet tender too, and playful and elastic, a fastidious high-tempered aristocrat" (149). In 1832 Newman accompanied him and his father to the Mediterranean in a vain effort to arrest Froude's consumption. Quarantined on Malta because of their earlier exposure to cholera, Newman invokes a Gospel sanction of friendship, as if in prophetic anticipation of Hurrell's death: "I wonder how long I should last without any friend about me. Scripture so clearly seems to mark that we should not [be] literally solitary (the apostles being sent 2 and 2 and having their attendants) that I suppose I should soon fail" (*LD* 3: 209). Newman's deepest friendships as an Anglican—those with Froude, Bowden, Keble, and Pusey—seem to have met several unstated but very rigorous conditions.[43] The friends had to be encountered during the 1820s and 1830s, when he was most confident that his changing opinions were only progressively closer approximations of the truth; they had to seem his equals in intellect, conviction, and religious sensitivity; and finally they had to be fellow questers, whose varied talents, insights, and energies were furthering a project which had sprung from Newman's own psyche.[44]

Geoffrey Faber, to be sure, suggests that these friendships owed their intensity to a repressed homosexuality. In addition to the cautions already raised, however, we should acknowledge the precision with which Newman delimits his emotional involvement. His numerous letters to these friends during the early and mid-1830s remain affectionate and informal, but hardly intimate. Even during his Mediterranean trip with Froude and his father, his letters home, while ecstatic about the scenery, remain cool toward his travelling companions. Where he compares himself and Froude to a pair of disciples in one letter to his mother, he writes her from Rome that "I had expressed a wish to be quite alone as the only remedy of my indisposition [a cough]. I had withdrawn to my bedroom . . . and quite excluded him [Froude] and his father; and in answer to his many sollicitations [*sic*], and his offer to sit with me or read to me, had assured him all I wanted to recruit myself was perfect solitude" (*LD* 3: 272).[45]

O'Faolain speculates that although "An old Oratorian father, now gone to his rest, once said: 'Newman's secret was simply that he didn't give a damn about this world' . . . , his [real] weakness was that he would always love most passionately when all was gone, always speak his love too late" (49). Bremond concurs: "[T]he very friends whom he retains in the present Newman loves in the past" (37).[46] His warmer feelings for these friends thus find expression only when the relationship itself is in peril. Just as the heartbreaking testimonials to his friendship with Keble appear only after Newman's conversion is inevitable,[47] so the long tender letters beginning "Carissime" pass between Newman and Froude only after the progress of Froude's consumption has made his death inevitable and imminent. He writes Jemima that God "is teaching me, it would seem, to depend on Him only—for, as perhaps Rogers told you, I am soon to lose dear Froude—which, looking forward to the next 25 years of my life, and its probable occupations, is the greatest loss I could have. I shall be truly widowed, yet I hope to bear it lightly" (*LD* 5: 240–41). A few days later, Froude metamorphoses from a mate to the reincarnation of Newman's undergraduate roommate Bowden: "I was from time to time confusing him with you and only calling him by his right name . . . by an act of memory" (*LD* 5: 249).

If even Froude can become not just expendable but interchangeable, we may conjecture that Newman can appropriate his friends just as surely as he did his mentors and siblings. And if he succeeds better with his friends, it is by exploiting their mortality as he has earlier exploited Mary's. In a letter to Keble on Froude's death, Newman longs, like a modern Elisha, to take over his friend's prophetic mission: "I do earnestly trust it will be granted to me, who have most claim on it, so to say, to receive his mantle—most claim, as having most need— . . . but I would fain be his heir" (*LD* 5: 253). And a few weeks later Newman records in his diary: "[R]ead one of Dear H. F.'s sermon[s] (on his birthday) being the first not my own I ever read in my life" (*LD* 5: 267).

When Bowden died, also of consumption, in 1844, a letter to Keble carries this conflation of identities even further: "In losing him I seem to lose Oxford. We used to live in each other's rooms as Undergraduates, and men used to mistake our names and call us by each other's. When he married, he used to make a similar mistake himself, and call me Elizabeth and her Newman" (*KC* 333). Such involvement is not conventionally sexual except as a Romantic identification with the beloved as a mirror of the self, the kind of identification which drives Cathy to cry out, "I *am* Heathcliff!" While Newman was engaged with these friends in furthering the Oxford Movement, such individual identifications were subsumed in their common identification with the Church Catholic. Once the friends' lives or courses faltered, then the relationship itself became simultaneously more precious, more fragile, and more dangerous. But with the impending deaths of Bowden and especially Froude, the same losses which threatened to carry off part of Newman's identity allowed him to subsume their identities into his own.

The necessarily one-sided nature of such relationships has led me to describe them as appropriations. Yet Newman, as we shall see, interprets them as mutual fusions within the spiritual realm, a realm which these deaths have both necessitated and made credible.[48] Unlike his Protestant contemporaries, however, he finds the historical incarnation of this realm, not in the Apostolic church of the New Testament, but in the Patristic church of fourth-century Alexandria. Early on he envisioned his God as above definition, categorization, or prediction; now—as Alexandria's best living custodian—he can envision it as above, beyond, or before any possible modern appropriation. From these two ineffable perspectives, theological and historical, he can confront his own world from outside its ideological horizons.

CHAPTER 2

The Parallel Realms
of Patristic Spirituality

❁

AS WE HAVE SHOWN, the young Newman comes to hear the voice of his conscience directing him to transcend his own age. While the source of this directive remains mysterious, the cogency of its rationale is not far to seek. While the emerging Victorian age worked to deny any grounds for such transcendence, it simultaneously embraced the moral and social chaos into which this denial was leading it. Specifically, as Robert Pattison has convincingly shown, Newman spent his adult life fighting what he saw as an inevitable slide into liberalism and its consequences: skepticism, increasing distrust of Scripture, acceptance of pluralism as a given, smug identification with the Victorian progress myth, reliance on distasteful emotionalism, and finally the abandonment of history as evidence, of theology as a system, and of the church as an institution. To oppose this seeming inevitability, however, Newman had nothing but an inner voice which, like Goethe's Mephisto, identified itself only as denial. As we will investigate in chapter 11, he eventually came to safeguard his spiritual ideal within institutional Catholicism, but during the 1830s the price seemed too high to pay; there the individual seemed reduced to a polity, emotion to manipulative spectacle, and history to the celebration of thinly veiled power. During this same decade, however, the two bastions of contemporary Protestantism stood closed to him: His image of Christ remained so transcendent that it qualified Christianity's claims as an incarnational religion. Simultaneously, his faith in the Bible, particularly the New Testament, grew so troubled that it qualified Christianity's claims as a historical religion.

Both as a historical epoch and as a spiritual model, however, fourth-century Alexandria offered a home for the glorified Jesus, a codification of the doctrines strewn throughout the Gospels and Epistles, and an organized church towards which the diverse churches within Apostolic

Christendom could only feel their way. Within this perspective, according to the carefully balanced synopsis of H. S. Holland: "[T]he two worlds of Nature and Grace, of Experience and Spirit, of Reason and Revelation, are seen to be of one piece, of one type, of one purpose, illuminated by correspondences, interpreted by reiteration of a common theme, knit together into coherent sequence by kindred analogies, and delicate refrains, and responsive corroborations, and intimate resemblances, and recurring parallels" (cited in Harrold, "Alexandrian," 284). Within these parallel worlds the individual believer is both immersed and empowered within a spiritual context, a theological system, and a universal church. Thus sheltered, New Testament anomalies are bolstered by Patristic witness; spiritual aspirations are shielded from the Pelagianism of Romantic quests to grasp imaginative reality through the senses;[1] the idolatrous present is measured against eighteen-hundred years of Christian tradition;[2] the visible church is bolstered by spiritual powers without the embarrassing burden of political institutions; emotional longings are satisfied through biblical figures, now given symbolic dominion over material nature and human history.[3] Within these parallel worlds, the Anglican Newman could justify the impression which J. C. Shairp gives of him in the pulpit: "The look and bearing of the preacher were as of one who dwelt apart, who, though he knew his age well, did not live in it" (247).[4]

Newman's Christ

It is just this protection from the age which Newman wishes to afford the figure of Christ. Convinced that High-and-Dry Anglicanism could no longer speak to the Victorian present, liberal theologians like Jacob Abbott turned to a newly "naturalized" image of Jesus. Attacking this image as one made in their own image and likeness, Newman betrays a personal, almost visceral disgust: "The more ordinary and common-place, the more like vulgar life, the more carnal the history of the Eternal Son of God is made, the more does this writer exult in it." Although Abbott, as Thomas points out (122–23), was writing for adolescents, Newman refuses to acknowledge any such extenuating circumstances. Thus the comparison of Jesus with Napoleon (whom Newman will later identify as a type of the Antichrist [*Tracts* 5 [83]: 30]) he labels as one of this author's "most unclean and miserable imaginings": "One seems to incur some ceremonial pollution by repeating such miserable words" (*Tracts* 3 [73]: 48). He sees this naturalism as undermining Abbott's Christology: "[I]s Christ God, or is He not? if so, can we dare talk of Him as having 'a taste for nature?' . . . The Incarnation was not 'a conversion of Godhead into flesh, but a taking of the manhood into God.' . . . [W]e must never speak . . . of the Person of the Eternal Word as thinking and feeling like a mere man, like a child, . . . which is Mr. A.'s way" (3: 46).[5]

Newman's way, however, is to impart to Jesus his own abhorrence of material reality: "He . . . lived alone, the immaculate Son of a Virgin Mother; and He chose the mountain summit or the garden as His home. . . . [L]ike the first Adam, solitary,—like the first Adam, living with His God and Holy Angels" (*PS* 5 [8]:104–5).[6] Although Newman takes Abbott to task for putting words in Jesus' mouth, he often appropriates the same technique for a very different end: "His discourse seems to run thus: . . . I Myself, who speak, am at this moment in Heaven too, even in this My human nature" (*PS* 3 [18]: 265).[7] And Heaven is clearly where Newman's Jesus wants to be:

> He did not implicate and contaminate Himself with sinners. He came down from heaven, and made a short work in righteousness, and then returned back again where He was before. . . . He went, before men knew that He had come, like the lightning shining from one side of heaven and unto the other, as being the beginning of a new and invisible creation, and having no part in the old Adam. . . . [A]nd, as well might fire feed upon water, or the wind be subjected to man's bidding, as the Only-begotten Son really be portion and member of that perishable system in which he condescended to move. (*PS* 5 [7]: 93–94)

Newman's presuppositions here are nicely summarized by Colin Gunton: "In his rebuttals of Abbott, Newman uses many phrases which can be taken in an orthodox manner, but which do appear to make the humanity of Jesus a cipher" (320); for Thomas, "He was a happy Trinitarian theologian, but at times a somewhat uneasy Christological thinker" (101).[8] Brilioth adds, "the equipoise of [Christ's] natures seems in danger of being abolished. . . . Newman can, though with reservations, touch on the figure of one who acts a part, . . . can venture to say that, 'though man, He was not, strictly speaking, in the English sense of the word, *a* man. . . . As He had no earthly father, so has He no human personality'" (*Anglican* 224, quoting *PS* 6 [5]: 62). And Roderick Strange reluctantly acknowledges the force of Gabriel Daly's judgment: "Put in Newman's own later terminology, his Christ is really divine and notionally human" (quoted in "Mystery" 323–24).[9] In this context, even Bremond's condescension seems warranted: "If, in spite of himself, he fashions Christ in his own image, we shall be able to judge how far Christ is familiar to him" (242). The very rigor of Newman's injunction "never [to] speak . . . of the Person of the Eternal Word as thinking and feeling like a mere man" thus produces a Christ as "familiar" to him as the naturalized Jesus was to Abbott. But if this familiar to him, Jesus cannot speak except as the subjective voice of Newman's conscience, cannot stand as either the historical or theological ground of that subjectivity.

Scripture as Natural Language

Scripture, in its turn, proves equally vulnerable, but for different reasons. The Anglican Newman works doggedly to protect it from nineteenth-century skepticism; yet because this skepticism is at least partially his own, his defense slides imperceptibly toward critique. Acutely susceptible to the authority of the biblical narrative and the immediacy of biblical imagery, he initially tries to claim them as some form of natural language, one that is simultaneously too deep for interpretation and too transparent to need it.[10] His Anglican writings explore a dichotomy, not between Scriptural fact and human reason, or writing, or history, but between Scriptural language and all other kinds. Robert Pattison exemplifies the tenuousness of this dichotomy in the implicit relativism of Newman's nemesis at Oriel, Rene Hampden. His relativism encompassed all reason, all language, everything except the "fact" of Scripture: "All that is left of revelation is the New Testament, which Hampden characterized as a 'sacred enclosure'" (*Dissent* 90).[11] As Pattison goes on to point out, Hampden's "'sacred enclosure' is either empty or nonexistent. . . . The gospel is a philosophical black hole in the firmament of nature" (*Dissent* 93).[12] Newman saw more quickly and clearly the hermeneutic problems in such claims. Borrowing his conclusions from the still-fledgling higher criticism, he replaced Scripture first with codified doctrine and later with the Fathers who codified it.

Newman's most forceful claims for biblical authority appear, curiously enough, in the rather late *Prophetical Office:* "Scripture has a gift which Tradition has not; it is fixed, tangible, accessible. . . . We can argue only from a text; we can argue freely only from an inspired text" (*PO* 304). Here, to quote Valentine Cunningham, "the truth of the text and the truth of the real presence the text contains reside in the metaphoric essence of the text—the essence suspicious deconstructionists dismiss as logocentrism, or even theologocentrism" (247). Instead of becoming a hermeneutical object, this text can remain the touchstone of all other interpretation: "Thus Scripture is in itself specially fitted . . . to be a repository of manifold and various doctrine, a means of proof, a standard of appeal, an umpire and test between truth and falsehood in all emergencies. It thus becomes the nearest possible approach to the perpetual presence of the Apostles in the Church" (*PO* 304).

Figure as Inescapable

In one extended sermon passage of 1834, however, Newman acknowledges that the immediacy of scriptural fact sounds to the modern ear like figure: "[A]n additional difficulty occurs, on minutely considering the [Ascension]. Whither did He go? beyond the sun? beyond the fixed stars? . . . Again, what is meant by *ascending*? Philosophers will say there is no difference between *down* and *up*, as regards the sky; yet . . . we can hardly take upon us to decide that it is a mere popular expression, consistently with the reverence due to the Sacred Record" (*PS* 2 [18]: 208). What do we do "when we have deduced what we deduce by our reason from the study of visible nature, and then read what we read in His inspired word, and find the two apparently discordant" (208)? Denying our need or our ability to interpret, Newman insists that we should maintain "a sense of the utter nothingness of worms such as we are, of our plain and absolute incapacity to contemplate things *as they really are*, . . . a conviction, that what is put before us, in nature or in [Scripture] . . . is but an intimation . . . , as two languages, as two separate approximations towards the Awful Unknown Truth" (209). The language of science, he continues, "must not dare profane the inner courts [of the Temple], in which the ladder of Angels is fixed for ever, reaching even to the Throne of God, and 'Jesus standing on the right hand of God'" (209).

Here, however, instead of standing against the deconstructionists, Newman is himself playing defer the referent. Both scientific and biblical languages are "approximations," but that of science must not aspire to the "reality" of a tableau pieced together from what he has already acknowledged to be biblical figures. As figures, moreover, these stand only as vehicles to some tenor beyond them: "Instead of explaining, Scripture does but continue to awe us in the language of the type." "Shall we therefore explain away its language as merely figurative," he asks rhetorically— rhetorically because for him to describe something as figurative, "(as the word is now commonly understood) is next to saying it has no meaning at all" (211). His alternative exploits the "awe" Scripture should evoke in us, simultaneously renouncing, obviating, and transcending interpretation in a passive reception of vision: "Clouds and darkness are round about Him. We are not given to see into the secret shrine in which God dwells. Before Him stand the Seraphim, veiling their faces. Christ is within the veil. We must not search curiously what is His present office. . . . And, since we do not know, we will studiously keep to the figure given us in Scripture; we will not attempt to interpret it" (211). Here the deferral, the gesture of veiling which simultaneously hides and constitutes the object veiled, is built into the secret shrine and into the response of the Seraphim. But Newman's deferral paradoxically interprets the "sacred enclosure" in the very act of holding it sacred: "We will hold it as a Mystery, or (what was anciently called) a Truth Sacramental" (211).

As we will see in chapter 4, this appeal to economy as a privileged hermeneutic brings problems of its own, both as hermeneutic and as privilege. If we focus instead on the vexing discrepancies between biblical language and its referent, we find Newman accounting for them differently, in new circumstances and for a new audience, in the essay on Scripture of 1838:

> Scripture then, treating of invisible things, at best must use words less than those things; and, as if from a feeling that no words can be worthy of them, it does not condescend to use even the strongest that exist, but often take[s] the plainest. The deeper the thought, the plainer the word; the word and thought diverge from each other. Again, it is a property of depth to lead a writer into real contradictions; and it is a property of simplicity not to care to avoid them. Again, when a writer is deep, his half sentences, parentheses, clauses, nay his words, have a meaning in them independent of the context, and admit of exposition. (*DA* 174)

If Hampden's relativism turned scriptural truth into a black hole, the gap opened here between signifier and signified looms equally dark and equally voracious. The inspired writers are pictured as hurling paradoxes, inconsistencies, incompleteable gestures toward an otherwise unknowable reality.

Newman's Higher Criticism

On the surface, the remarkable and undervalued essay on Scripture seems a perceptive, devout, yet honest response to the still limited skepticism of the English Enlightenment. Newman delivered his twelve "Lectures on the Scriptural Proof of the Doctrines of the Church" between 8 May and 7 August of 1838 (*LD* 6: 241).[13] When the first eight of these were published as Tract 85, Tom Keble wrote to his brother, Newman's friend John, "[A]mongst us privately, [it] caused a good deal of discussion and uneasiness: because . . . many passages occur which may too easily be made a very bad use of" (*LD* 6: 356). When the letter was forwarded to Newman, he replied, "[I]t is with great scruple and much uneasiness that I published the Tract in question. . . . And yet, if I *am* to speak, I cannot speak otherwise than I do" (*LD* 6: 353–54).

Derek Holmes suggests that "Newman possibly overstated the [skeptical] position . . . , which did not necessarily represent his own views about scripture" ("Criticism" 23), but the views are spelled out so rigorously as to sound almost inexorable:

> [P]erhaps it would be said that the Old Testament altogether was not inspired, only the New— . . . and so men would proceed giving up first one thing, then another, till . . . they would come to consider [Christianity] mainly as an historical event occurring eighteen hundred years since, . . . influencing us in the improved tone of the institutions in which we find ourselves. . . . The view henceforth is to be, that Christianity does not exist in documents, any more than in institutions; in other words, the Bible will be given up as well as the Church. (*DA* 232-33)[14]

He insists that the opponents of Scripture are all "out there," that he is simply raising these troubling issues to keep them from beating him to the punch: "I would predict . . . that minds *are* to be unsettled as to what is Scripture and what is not; and I predict it that, as far as the voice of one person in one place can do, I may defeat my own prediction by making it" (*DA* 198-99).[15] Yet as we saw in the Introduction, when Keble sent him his brother's demurrals, Newman hinted that the spirit of critical inquiry was already within him, that he too was caught up within its inexorable chain of inference: "My constant feeling when I write is, that I do not realize things, but am merely drawing out intellectual conclusions— which, I need not say, is very uncomfortable" (*LD* 6: 353-54).[16] He thus implicates himself within his own unflattering portrait of the liberal historian Milman, trapped within his own ideological cage:[17] "None of us can go a little way with a theory; when it once possesses us, we are no longer our own masters. It makes us speak its words, and do violence to our own nature. . . . Where is theory to stop, if it is once allowed?" (*Ess.* 2: 222-24).[18]

Though written before he had had the opportunity to read Strauss, the essay on Scripture echoes many of the German's challenges to biblical historicity:

> [T]hough the Bible is . . . in one sense, written by God, yet very large portions of it . . . are written in as free and unconstrained a manner, and (apparently) with as little apparent consciousness of a supernatural dictation or restraint . . . as if He had had no share in the work. . . . [W]e may speak of the history or the mode of its

composition, as truly as of that of other books; we may speak of its writers having an object in view, being influenced by circumstances, being anxious, taking pains, leaving things incomplete, or supplying what others had so left. . . . It is as if you were to seize the papers, or correspondence of leading men in any school of philosophy or science, which were never designed for publication, and bring them out in one volume. (*DA* 146)[19]

Later in the essay, the anguish aroused by this quandary breaks through his matter-of-fact tone in a set of Job-like questions: "We have reason to believe that God, our Maker and Governor, has spoken to us by Revelation; yet why has He not spoken more distinctly? He has given us doctrines which are but obscurely gathered from Scripture, and a Scripture which is but obscurely gathered from history" (*DA* 244).[20] Cunningham notes that Newman "confronts [his] readers rather often with a dizzying bottomlessness rather resembling what deconstructionists have heralded as the linguistic and textual *mise en abime*" (249–50).

Although Cunningham seems surprised that Newman avoids such a fall into nihilism, Newman has already found a new, non-scriptural means of support.[21] Implicit in his anguished repetition of "obscurely," Newman's desperate need for distinctness, consistency, and doctrine has led him to base his faith "elsewhere": "I own it seems to me, judging antecedently, very improbable indeed, that [Scripture] *should* contain the whole of the Revealed Word of God. . . . I am naturally led to look not only there, but elsewhere, for notices of sacred truth. . . . Till we prove that Scripture does contain the whole Revealed Truth, it is natural, from its *prima facie* appearance, to suppose that it does not" (148).[22] As we will see in chapter 10, his subsequent investigations of Patristic tradition will show it to be just as anarchic as Scripture; here, however, he works to put the two on an equal footing: "[D]id the account of the feeding of the 4,000 with seven loaves rest on the testimony of Antiquity, most of us would have said, 'You see how little you can trust the Fathers; it was not 4,000 with seven loaves, but 5,000 with five'" (*DA* 166–67). To Chadwick, the "kill-or-cure" argument Newman borrowed from Butler "harmed him both as a controversialist and a Christian thinker" by simply abandoning to his Protestant audience the now-formidable task of protecting the "weaker" case from Scripture (*Bossuet* 124). To me, Newman may be indicted less for an outdated strategy than for an unacknowledged preference.[23] He shows himself very willing to tie the credibility of the New Testament to that of Patristic forms and traditions, willing even to abandon both rather than salvage the first at the expense of the second.[24]

Patristic Spirituality

This preference for the Patristic church is not casually bestowed; the Anglican Newman finds within it a spiritual exaltation that he is not afraid to identify as inspired. His *Arians,* where first, the *Apologia* tells us, "The broad philosophy of Clement and Origen carried me away" (36), vests these mystics with an extension of that natural language which he tried to posit for Scripture itself, a necessary, one-for-one correspondence between word and reality:

> [T]here are minds so gifted and disciplined as to approach the position occupied by the inspired writers, and therefore able to apply their words with a fitness, and entitled to do so with a freedom, which is unintelligible to the dull or heartless criticism of inferior understandings. So far then as the Alexandrian Fathers partook of such a singular gift of grace . . . , not incited by a capricious and presumptuous imagination, but burning with that vigorous faith, which, seeing God in all things, does and suffers all for his sake, . . . they stand not merely excused, but are placed immeasurably above the multitude of those who find it so easy to censure them. (*Ari.* 63–64)

As this envelope of quasi-scriptural inspiration shields these Fathers from modern criticism, it also safeguards their expanded vision of revealed truth from any need for historical or doctrinal mediation: "If I avow my belief, that freedom from symbols and articles is abstractly the highest state of Christian communion, and the peculiar privilege of the primitive Church, it is . . . because when confessions do not exist, the mysteries of divine truth, instead of being exposed to the gaze of the profane and uninstructed, are kept hidden in the bosom of the Church . . . for those, that is, who are diligently passing through the successive stages of faith and obedience" (*Ari.* 36–37).

The resulting mystical bent of Newman's theology was early apparent to his contemporaries. In 1832 Archdeacon Lyall, evaluating a draft of his *Arians,* objected to "those places where he speaks of the disciplina arcani. . . . Mr Newman's notions about tradition appear to me directly adverse to that which Protestant writers of our own church have contended for— according to them a 'secret tradition' is no tradition at all" (*LD* 3: 105). Harrold notes that as early as 1835 Newman's colleague Frederic Faber suggested that his "nature and habits no doubt encouraged in him 'that mystical allegorizing spirit of Origen and the school of Alexandria'" ("Alexandrian" 286). A review of his *Justification* further objected that "once or twice, his imagination seems to have seduced him a little way into the realm of shadowy and mystical fancies" (quoted in *LD* 6: 253n).[25]

In response, Newman presents the Patristic Church as more varied yet more coherent than commonly granted by his critics or by their unacknowledged source, Edward Gibbon.[26] His *Arians* makes painstaking theological distinctions among the participants in fourth-century councils, and his popular essays emphasize the range of personalities and vocations within the orthodox ranks: the contemplative Basil, his militant uncle Gregory, the genial visionary Antony, the questing, self-tormenting young Augustine, the passively heroic Ambrose.[27] Yet all these diverse men, Newman argues, agree in affirming the coherence and credibility of a mysterious universe that Gibbon dismisses as the product of fear and fantasy.

Avoiding any philosophical response to such criticism, Newman argues that the ability to perceive spiritual evidences is itself evidence of inspiration:[28] "[E]asiness to believe Him interposing in human affairs, fear of the risk of slighting or missing what may really come from Him; these are feelings not natural to fallen man, and they come only of supernatural grace" (*US* 10: 193).[29] Newman accuses Milman of a similar blindness, on the apparent assumption that employing Occam's razor would endanger one's own throat: "Such persons cannot enter into the possibility of a visible and an invisible course of things going on at once. . . . Were the electric fluid ascertained to be adequate to the phenomena of life, they would think it bad philosophy to believe in the presence of a soul; and, sooner than believe that Angels now minister to us unseen, they deny that they were ever seen in their ministrations" (*Ess.* 2: 230).[30] Any evaluation of these different criteria thus reduces to an evaluation of their moral consequences: "[I]f I must choose between the fashionable doctrines of one age and of another, certainly I shall prefer that [exemplified in the stories of Antony] which requires self-denial, and creates hardihood and contempt of the world, to some of the religions now in esteem which . . . excuse self-indulgence by the arguments of spiritual pride, self-confidence, and security" (*HS* 2: 125).

Recuperation of Personal Loss

Other passages, in contrast, suggest that retrieving a lost age of Patristic spirituality may allow Newman to retrieve much more recent and more personal losses. The letters written after the death of Mary in 1828 presuppose some embryonic faith in a parallel spiritual realm as the grounds of his consolation. If Newman could best relate to others only after they had been taken from him, as O'Faolain maintains, such a relation requires not some future reunion but the continued presence of the loved one.[31] These speculations, however, could lead to pantheistic nature worship or to the secular spiritualism which so fascinated Elizabeth Barrett Browning and so annoyed her husband. A sermon written during Froude's last illness wrestles with these problems in trying to anticipate his station after death: "Where is that spirit gone, over the wide universe, up or down, which once thought, felt, loved, hoped, planned, acted in our sight, and which wherever it goes, must carry with it the same affections and principles, desires and aims? . . . [W]e know that beloved mind, and it knows us, with a mutual consciousness;—and now it is taken from us, what are its fortunes?" (PS 3 [25]: 370). Such questions, more sectarian but no less anguished than those Tennyson asked of Arthur Hallam in *In Memoriam,* lead Newman to a similar, equally primitive sense of the spirit's ghostly, almost magical presence: "There is a peculiar feeling with which we regard the dead. . . . We cannot tell what he is now,—what his relations to us,—what he knows of us. We do not understand him,—we do not see him. He is passed into the land 'that is very far off'; but it is not at all certain that he has not some mysterious hold over us" (PS 5 [2]: 25).

Amid his anguished uncertainty, Newman's belief in parallel realms offered him the consolation of this reflection to Keble: "It was an idea of Bowden's the other day (whom I saw in town under great affliction at the sudden loss of his brother's wife) that as time goes on and more and more saints are gathered in, fewer are needed on earth—the city of God has surer and deeper foundations day by day" (LD 5: 253).[32] The same doctrine accounts for the apparent callousness with which Newman anticipates the loss of others' loved ones. He claims that the spirituality of Rogers' sister has sealed her death: "[S]carcely do you hear of some especial instance of religious excellence, but you have also cause of apprehension how long such a one is to continue here. . . . The more we live in the world that is not seen, the more shall we feel that the removal of friends into the unseen world is a bringing them near to us, not a separation. I really do not think this fancifulness. I think it attainable" (LD 6: 76).[33] One might even assume that the dissention between Newman and Manning began with this response to news of his wife's terminal illness: "[T]hey who seek God do (as it were) come for afflictions. . . . [I]f in His great wisdom and love He take away the desire of your eyes, it will only be to bring her really nearer to you. For those we love are not nearest to us when in the flesh, but they come into our very hearts as being spiritual beings, when they are removed from us" (LD 6: 95). Yet Manning replied with apparent sincerity, "If you could know how much comfort your letter gave me. . . . I feel something in the way you deal with my sorrows, particularly soothing and strengthening" (*LD* 6: 102).

The Invisible Church

Having won this consolation for himself and his friends, Newman begins applying it to an ever-widening circle of situations. To Robert Wilberforce he implies that the psychological benefits of prayers for the dead speak for their spiritual efficacy: "It is so very natural, so soothing. . . . And it is so great a gift, if so be to *be able* to benefit the dead, that I sometimes am quite frightened at the thought how great a talent our Church is hiding in a napkin" (*LD* 5: 260). Conversely, if prayers of the living can reach the dead, it is through prayer that the influence of the dead can reach the living: "Blessed indeed, is the power of those formularies, which thus succeed in throwing a sinner for a while out of himself, and bringing before him the scenes of his youth, his guardian friends now long departed, their ways and their teaching, their pious services, and their peaceful end" (*PS* 1 [20]: 268). Although this early parochial sermon is careful to posit a naturalistic means of transmission, successive volumes will show the dead assuming an ever more active role.[34]

Within the first volume of *Parochial and Plain Sermons,* churchyards grow holy as the repositories of what will be resurrected at the Last Judgment: "The dust around us will one day become animate. . . . A great sight will a Christian country then be, if earth remains what it is; when holy places pour out the worshippers who have for generations kept vigil therein, waiting through the long night for the bright coming of Christ!" (*PS* 1 [21]: 278). Within volume two, "it may be, that Saints departed intercede, unknown to us, for the victory of the Truth upon earth. . . . Yea, doubtless, they are keeping up the perpetual chant in the shrine above. . . . [S]o much light as this is given us by the inspired pages of the Apocalypse, that they are interested in the fortunes of the Church" (*PS* 2 [18]: 214). By volume three Newman can rebuke modern men who "give up a most gracious means divinely provided for their entering into 'that which is within the veil,' and seeing beyond the grave" (*PS* 3 [25]: 384–85). Revelation, fused now with Exodus, allows him to refine both on the thoughts of the dead and on their state: "They are 'under the Altar.' Not in the full presence of God, seeing His face, and rejoicing in His works, but in a safe and holy treasure-house close by,—like Moses 'in a cleft of the rock,'—covered by the hand of God, and beholding the skirts of His glory. . . . And in some unknown way, that place of rest has a communication with this world, so that disembodied souls know what is going on below" (373–74). Later in the same sermon, this knowledge is hesitantly enlarged to influence: "Few now alive may understand or sanction us; but those multitudes in the primitive time, who believed, and taught, and worshipped, as we do, still live unto God, and, in their past deeds and their present voices, cry from the Altar. They animate us by their example; they cheer us by their company; they are on our right hand and our left, Martyrs, Confessors, and the like" (385–86).[35] Finally, by volume four, this host of the dead have virtually drained the present church of its reality:

> Fifty times as many Saints are in the invisible world sealed for immortality, as are now struggling on upon earth towards it. . . . This *invisible* body is the *true* Church, because it changes not, though it is ever increasing. What it has, it keeps, and never loses; but what is visible is fleeting and transitory, and continually passes off into the invisible. . . . [The Church Catholic] is not on earth, except so far as heaven can be said to be on earth, or as the dead are still with us. . . . The Ministry and Sacraments, the bodily presence of Bishop and people, are given us as keys and spells, by which we bring ourselves into the presence of the great company of Saints. (*PS* 4 [11]: 172–76)[36]

By bringing ourselves into this company, however, we can find meaning and pattern within the otherwise senseless burden of suffering. If Bowden's sister was marked for death by her piety, then, by extension, the massacre of the Holy Innocents "had in it the nature of a Sacrament; it was a pledge of the love of the Son of God towards those who were included in it. All who came near Him, more or less suffered by approaching Him, just as if earthly pain and trouble went out of Him, as some precious virtue for the good of their souls" (*PS* 2 [6]: 62). Even for the living, for one like Newman whose friends and loved ones are being carried off daily by consumption, loss can be converted into—and literally compounded as—spiritual wealth: "There is a Treasury in heaven stored with such offerings as the natural man abhors; with sighs and tears, wounds and blood, torture and death. The Martyrs first began the contribution, and we all may follow them; all of us, for every suffering, great or little, may, like the widow's mite, be sacrificed in faith to Him who sent it" (*PS* 3 [11]: 154).

Much more imposing (because much less anal), is the visionary sublimation of suffering into a celestial performance evaluated on aesthetic terms, a drama in which the sufferer participates in a cosmic harmony almost Dantean in its range and grandeur:

> It is as though all of us were allowed to stand around His Throne at once, and He called on first this man, and then that, to take up the chant by himself, each in his turn having to repeat the melody which his brethren have before gone through. Or as if we held a solemn dance to His honour in the courts of heaven, and each had by himself to perform some one and the same solemn and graceful movement at a signal given. Or as if it were some trial of strength, or of agility, and, while the ring of bystanders beheld and applauded, we in succession, one by one, were actors in the pageant. . . . Our brethren have gone through much more; and they seem to encourage us by their success, and to sympathize in our essay. Now it is our turn; and all ministering spirits keep silence and look on. (*PS* 6 [16]: 230–31)

One of the most original and fully developed of Newman's visions, this one remains characteristic in that the successive vehicles—singing, dancing, competing, acting—are interchangeable, all of them transparent signs of an otherwise invisible, inaudible reality behind them. Our most sensuous experience, in fact, comes not from any of the details but from the rhythms of Newman's prose as it reenacts the cosmic rhythm here imposed on our otherwise random encounters with human suffering.[37]

The Heavenly Court

For all these pictures of the heavenly court, Newman may have been indebted to a passage from Clement included, presumably by him, among the "Records of the Church" within *Tracts for the Times:*

> This is the mountain beloved of God, not like Cithaeron the subject of tragedies. . . . The chorus are the righteous, the song is the hymn of the King of all things, Virgins are singing it, Angels are heralding it, Prophets are repeating it. The sound of music arises, they run to the gathering, they that are called, hasten, longing to reach their Father. . . . I am lighted into the heavens, and by seeing God I become a holy partaker in the rites, and the Lord is the chief instructor, and seals the initiate, lighting him on." (XVI: "Clement to the Heathen"; *Tracts* 2: 35–36).

But Newman is just as likely to have gone back to the same scriptural sources used by Clement. Revelation gives him the following sermon passage: "We are told that the Angels of God are very bright, and clad in white robes. The Saints and Martyrs too are clad in white robes, with palms in their hands; and they sing praises unto Him that sitteth upon the Throne, and to the Lamb" (*PS* 7 [14]: 201). And Ephesians gives him this passage: "A Temple there has been upon earth, a spiritual Temple, made up of living stones . . . with God for its Light, and Christ for the High Priest, with wings of Angels for its arches, with Saints and Teachers for its pillars, and with worshippers for its pavement. . . . This unseen, secret, mysterious, spiritual Temple exists every where, . . . perfect in one place as if it were not in another" (*PS* 6 [20]: 280). But in the sequel to this passage and in several others, Newman returns again and again to the passage from Hebrews 12 which underlies the quotation from Clement. Here we discover "that blessed privilege which, as the Apostle assures us, is conferred upon us Christians! 'Ye are come unto Mount Zion, and unto the city of the Living God, the heavenly Jerusalem, and to an innumerable company of Angels, to the general assembly and Church of the first-born, which are written in heaven, and to God the Judge of all, and to the spirits of just men made perfect, and to Jesus the Mediator of the New Covenant'" (*SD* [13]: 171).[38]

This court can be invoked as the scene of the Last Judgment in order to humble sinners: "You fear shame; well, and will you not shrink from shame at the judgment-seat of Christ? . . . You fear the contempt of one small circle of men; what think you of the Saints of God, of St. Mary, of St. Peter and St. Paul, of the ten thousand generations of mankind, being witnesses of your disgrace?" (*PS* 7 [4]: 55). The same prediction, conversely, can comfort the oppressed righteous: "That indeed will be a full reward of all our longings here. . . . Then we shall see how the Angels worship God. We shall see the calmness, the intenseness, the purity, of their worship. We shall see that awful sight, the Throne of God, and the Seraphim before and around it, crying, 'Holy!'" (*PS* 7 [13]: 189).

Newman's vision of parallel realms can also bring this court into his congregation's immediate experience. In *Tracts for the Times,* he attributes to Justin Martyr the claim for a dual or simultaneous existence as the principal gift bestowed by God upon the New Covenant: "In every foreign country [Christians] recognize a home; and in their home they see a place of their pilgrimage. . . . They live in the world, but not according to its fashion; they walk on earth, but their conversation is in heaven" (Records of the Church XV: "The Epistle to Diognetus"; *Tracts* 1: 1). A later sermon elaborates on Justin's words: "Such is the mysterious state in which Christians stand. . . . They are in Heaven, in the world of spirits, and are placed in the way of all manner of invisible influences. 'Their conversation is in heaven'" (*PS* 3 [18]: 263–64). This contingent apotheosis, as a still later sermon makes clear, actually brings us "into that invisible kingdom of Christ which faith alone discerns . . . which flows in upon us . . . in a starry host or (if I may so say) a milky way of divine companions, the inhabitants of Mount Zion, where we dwell" (*PS* 4 [15]: 229).[39] In Tract 83, Scripture becomes the means of our apprehending this dualism: "[T]he Book of Revelation . . . lift[s] up the covering which lies over the face of the world, and make[s] us see day by day, as we go in and out, . . . the Throne of God set up in the midst of us" (5: 27). But similar visions may be no farther away than the nearest church: "The very disposition of the building, the subdued light, the aisles, the Altar, with its pious adornments, are figures of things unseen, and stimulate our fainting faith. We seem to see the heavenly courts, with Angels chanting, and Apostles and Prophets listening, as we read their writings in due course" (*PS* 3 [17]: 251).

Cosmic Warfare

As it expands, this vision of the heavenly court flows over into a vision of the Lord of Hosts. Even in his early sermons, Newman is not shy of invoking divine vengeance: "May God arise, and shake terribly the earth, (though it be an awful prayer,) *rather* than the double-minded should lie hid among us, and souls be lost by present ease!" (*PS* 2 [16]: 181). Nor does he question whether this prayer will be answered: "Even though He is silent, doubt not that His army is on the march towards us. He is coming through the sky, and has even now His camp upon the outskirts of our own world. Nay, though He still for a while keep His seat at His Father's right hand, yet surely He sees all that is going on, and waits and will not fail His hour of vengeance" (*PS* 2 [10]: 115). We are even counselled to glory in the coming destruction: "We must . . . be content to wound as well as to heal, to condemn as well as to absolve. . . . We must learn to acquiesce and concur in the order of God's Providence, and bear to rejoice over great Babylon and her inhabitants, when the wrath of God has fallen upon her" (*PS* 2 [22]: 268).

As we move from the second to the fourth volume of sermons, however, Newman comes to focus on Revelation (passim),[40] on Isaiah (2:2), and especially on 2 Kings (6:17) for more militant visions of his Invisible Church: "Isaiah prophesies that 'it shall come to pass, that the Mountain of the Lord's House shall be established in the top of the mountains, and shall be exalted above the hills; and *all nations* shall flow into it.' And it was shown . . . to Elisha's servant when 'the Lord opened the eyes of the young man . . . and behold, the mountain was full of horses and chariots of fire round about Elisha'" (*PS* 4 [12]: 193). In a passage quoted earlier, the sermon just before this one measures the vast size of the Invisible Church, then invokes the ministers and liturgy as "keys and spells," and then goes on to reveal to us, as to Elisha's servant, the power of this invocation:

> When we pray in private, we are not solitary; others "are gathered together" with us "in Christ's Name," though we see them not, with Christ in the midst of them. . . . When we are called to battle for the Lord, what are we who are seen, but mere outposts, the advanced guard of a mighty host, ourselves few in number and despicable, but bold beyond our numbers, because supported by chariots of fire and horses of fire round about the Mountain of the Lord of Hosts under which we stand? (*PS* 4 [11]: 177)[41]

Although Newman often glories in his spiritual isolation (as we saw in chapter 1), his invocation of parallel realms here compensates for it with visions of invincible support.[42]

Within this spiritual cosmology, the Church needs such militancy because war is being waged against it; in a remarkable essay on Antony, primitive Christians are praised for their belief "that visible things are types and earnests of things invisible. The elements are, in some sense, symbols and tokens of spiritual agents, good and bad. Satan is called the prince of the air" (*HS* 2: 107–8). In the last of his university sermons Newman will poke fun at the Evangelicals' penchant for populating the vast spaces outside their intellectual horizons with demons; in his vision of suffering as a cosmic drama he uses sound and rhythm to avoid reifying the heavenly court or reducing his vision to a crude mythopoeia. In his defense of Antony, however, he insists that if "the Church is a supernatural ordinance," then conversely the powers arrayed against it remain equally vigorous—and even more territorial: "This earth had become Satan's kingdom; our Lord came to end his usurpation; but Satan retreated only inch by inch. The Church of Christ is hallowed ground, but external to it is the kingdom of darkness. . . . I see Satan frightened at the invasions of the Church upon his kingdom; I see him dispossessed by fasting and prayer, as was predicted; I see him retreating step by step; and I see him doing his utmost in whatever way to resist" (*HS* 2: 110–11). Newman concludes his *Arians* with this celestial conflict: "[W]e may rest in the confidence, that, should the hand of Satan press us sore, our Athanasius and Basil will be given us in their destined season, to break the bonds of the Oppressor, and let the captives go free" (394). Nor is this mere pulpit rhetoric; to Henry Wilberforce he attributes the political vicissitudes of the Tractarian cause, not just to diabolical agency, but to Satan's own long-term strategy: "O that we had one Bishop for us! what a net we are in—this is what Satan has been toiling at this 300 years, gradually bringing it about—and now his day is coming" (*LD* 4: 312).

Within his sermons, however, we can trace a progression in Newman's use of this spiritual warfare. In the earlier sermons, his references parallel the attacks on secularism which we will study in chapter 9. Those who refuse any master have actually chosen one by default: Free speakers seem to acknowledge "the Author of Evil to be their great master and lord. Yes! he *is* a master who allows himself to be served without trembling. It is his very art to lead men to be at ease with him, to think lightly of him, and to trifle with him. He will submit to their ridicule, take (as it were) their blows, and pretend to be their slave, that he may ensnare them. *He has no dignity to maintain*" (*PS* 1 [23]: 306). Newman next denies their claims to intellectual freedom by denying it physical room within his increasingly crowded cosmos: "We cannot possibly be in a neutral or intermediate state. Such a state does not exist. If we will not be Christ's servants, we are forthwith Satan's. . . . Satan's kingdom touches upon Christ's, the world touches on the Church" (*PS* 4 [1]: 3).[43] Within volume seven, the moral blindness of tempted sinners stems from their visionary blindness to these parallel realms:

> Could you see, what God sees, those snares and pitfalls which the devil is placing about your path; could you see that all your idle thoughts . . . are inspired by that Ancient Seducer of Mankind, who stands at your side . . . , not able to laugh at his own jests, . . . doubtless you would tremble, even as he does while he tempts you. But this you cannot possibly see. . . . You cannot see the unseen world at once. They who ever speak with God in their hearts, are in turn taught by Him in all knowledge. (*PS* 7 [15]: 215)

Finally, by volume eight, this increasingly Manichean conflict has reduced the individual to near passivity: "God does His part most surely; and Satan too does his part: we alone are unconcerned. Heaven and hell are at war for us and against us, yet we trifle" (*PS* 8 [5]: 73).

Intermediate Beings

The incongruity of such a momentous conflict being waged for a trivial human prize may have led Newman to fill his spiritual canvas with intermediate beings, neither God nor Satan but partaking of the grandeur of both.[44] Because his portraits of angels and demonic powers will reappear in chapter 10 with other evidence of his latent animism, here we need establish only that he believed in these beings and that he felt uncomfortable about it. His reconstruction of his Anglican years within the *Apologia,* for example, both acknowledges and displaces the visionary theology within his *Arians* by tying it to his adolescence: "It is evident how much there was in all this in correspondence with the thoughts which had attracted me when I was young" (37). His account of angelic influence grows even more confessional:

> It was, I suppose, to the Alexandrian school and to the early Church, that I owe in particular what I definitely held about the Angels. . . . I considered them as the real causes of motion, light, and life, and of . . . what are called the laws of nature. . . . [I]n my Sermon for Michaelmas day, written in 1831, I say of Angels, "Every breath of air and ray of light and heat, every beautiful prospect, is, as it were, the skirts of their garments, the waving of the robes of those whose faces see God." (37)

As he works down the spiritual hierarchy, his theology becomes increasingly visionary: "Also, besides the hosts of evil spirits, I considered there was a middle race, . . . partially fallen, capricious, wayward; noble or crafty, benevolent or malicious, as the case might be. These beings gave a sort of inspiration or intelligence to races, nations, and classes of men" (38). Once again, however, he anticipates—almost encourages a skeptical reaction: "I am aware that what I have been saying will, with many men, be doing credit to my imagination at the expense of my judgment— 'Hippoclides doesn't care'; I am not setting myself up as a pattern of good sense or of any thing else: I am but giving a history of my opinions" (39). By thus confining all these beliefs to his first chapter, Newman distances them, not just from his present position as a Catholic, but from the high-Anglican position he adopted after 1833.

Within this Tractarian period, however, he rather defensively appeals to Scripture for support: "Surely we, as we well as our Divine Lord, are 'seen of Angels;' nay, and ministered unto by them, much as they excel us in strength! St. Paul plainly tells us, that it is God's purpose that 'His manifold wisdom should be known to the heavenly principalities and powers, through the Church'" (*PS* 2 [1]: 10). The *Church of the Fathers* cites Basil's letter to Gregory: "Pious exercises nourish the soul with divine thoughts. What state can be more blessed than to imitate on earth the choruses of Angels?—to begin the day with prayer, and honour our Maker with hymns and songs?" (*HS* 2: 64).[45] Next, the *Prophetical Office* affirms this blessed state against the incredulity of the world: "Should a man . . . profess to regulate his conduct under the notion that he is seen by invisible spectators, that he and all Christians have upon them the eyes of Angels, especially when in church; . . . would not what he said be certainly met with grave, cold, contemptuous, or impatient looks, as idle, strained, and unnatural?" (14).

Nor does Newman shrink from such affirmations in his letters. To Pusey in 1836 he maintains that "St Antony is bright and cheerful, and Athanasius particularly insists on this—and he looks on evil spirits as utterly contemptible and weak to the *believer in Christ*—as powerful only towards the timid, and cowards towards the bold" (*LD* 5: 198-99). To Wood a year later, however, he confesses his fear that some spiritual forces may be powerful enough to control the destiny of their whole movement: "Daniel speaks as if each nation had its guardian Angel. I cannot but think that there are beings with a great deal of good in them, yet with great defects, who are the animating principles of certain institutions, etc etc. . . . That *we* are under the superintendence of some supernatural power, I cannot doubt for an instant—we have a game to play, a course to run. But then comes the question, is it not something short of God?" (*LD* 6: 112-13). And in a letter to Keble five years later, the forced resignation of a friend provokes the fear that their angelic protectors, uncomfortably like rats in a sinking ship, may be deserting them: "If we have, as it were, minute guns, to tell us that our Angels are going from us, to a certainty we shall lose our members too" (Moz. 2: 344).

The danger in these conjectures only comes home to Newman after they have been taken up by the more naively mystical of his followers in the late 1830s: "What does [Morris of Exeter] do on St. Michael's day but preach a Sermon, not simply on Angels, but . . . [saying] Angels fasted on festivals, to make the brute creation fast on fast days" (*KC* 37). Newman is driven to an uncharacteristically earth-bound curse: "May he (*salvis ossibus suis*) have a fasting horse the next time he goes steeple chasing." Morris's surmises, however, while much sillier than Newman's, are neither more daring nor more imaginative.[46] If the fully elaborated, vividly realized universe Newman offers us seems alien, anachronistic, irrelevant to our experience, it may have seemed only slightly less so to his congregation at St. Mary's. As I have been arguing, moreover, it was intended to seem so, to stand against the entire modern world both in judgment and, more conditionally, in hope. For it to stand so, however, Newman must be able to stand with it and in it. His ingenious, convoluted, and ultimately self-defeating efforts to do so we will trace in the following chapter.

CHAPTER 3

Bridging the Gulf of the Enlightenment

❖

THE LAST CHAPTER outlined Newman's appeal to a Patristic vision of parallel realms. If this vision has a solid historical basis and if it remains immediately available, then the modern, post-Reformation world shrinks to a temporary aberration and the Enlightenment becomes a tardy acknowledgement that the reformers' original project was bankrupt from the beginning. To establish this continuity, however, Newman's own etiological project must make good on two claims: (1) that the Patristic period was a faithful witness to the spiritual fullness of the Apostolic Church, and (2) that he and his disciples can indeed return to it. The labyrinthine complexities and contradictions he encounters suggest that he cannot so easily turn back the millennial clock, specifically that he cannot vault over the gulf opened in Western history by the Enlightenment. The spiritual fullness which he posits as simply neglected, Friedrich Schiller had already described as a naivete available only to primitive cultures.

The Anglican Newman thus shares his spiritual agenda with liberal contemporaries for whom the gap between the ancient naive and the modern sentimental reinscribed itself as an analogous gap between the ancient sacred and the modern secular. Compared with their formulations, Newman's parallel realms appear far more arcane and anachronistic, but they offer some unforeseen homologies with postmodern attacks on Enlightenment subjectivity. Where Hegel interpreted the Fall as a past stage within an irrevocable historical continuum, Newman insists that evil cannot be fully subsumed, that such historical determinism is itself evidence of our fallen condition. Hence his invocation of spiritual realities retains an ontological thickness that his contemporaries abandoned when they internalized human meaning within figure. Because his dual realms resist any imaginative (or, as he would call it, pantheistic) interaction of tenor and vehicle, they anticipate the deconstructive preference for allegory over symbol. At the same time, his premonition of a spiritual reality lambent over the material world parallels the diverse invocations of "otherness" by competing critical schools, be they feminist, Marxist, or Lacanian.

Patristic Witness

The last chapter saw Newman granting to the Alexandrian Platonists an inspired status: "[T]here are minds so gifted and disciplined as to approach the position occupied by the inspired writers, . . . burning with that vigorous faith, which, seeing God in all things, does and suffers all for his sake" (*Ari.* 63–64). In so doing, he also grants them a double authority, both as conduits of an immediate revelation and mediators of an earlier one. As witnesses to the spirituality of the Apostolic age, they retain this spirituality in a form realized, harmonized, even institutionalized, but not rationalized: "[W]hen confessions do not exist, the mysteries of divine truth, instead of being exposed to the gaze of the profane and uninstructed, are kept hidden in the bosom of the Church" (*Ari.* 37). O'Faolain notes how "he develops tenderly the notion of the instinctive conscience . . . as a plant so frail as to flourish best in the warm shelter of the unenquiring heart: . . . something so ineffable as to be assaulted by words" (190). An early sermon spells out with even greater emotional intensity both the joy of this unmediated immediacy and the pain of losing it:

> [I]n the Church there was light and peace, fear, joy, and holy meditation. Lawless doubtings, importunate inquirings, confident reasonings were not. An heartfelt adoration, a practical devotion to the Ever-blessed Son, precluded difficulties in faith, and sheltered the Church from the necessity of speaking. . . . Sight and hearing superseded the multitude of words. . . . But when the light of His advent faded, and love waxed cold, then . . . Christians were forced to speak against their will, lest heretics should speak instead of them. (*PS* 2 [3]: 27–28)

Such visions of spiritual plentitude overwhelmed by cold and darkness prompt Rowan Williams to remark that because of Newman's "admiration for the ante-Nicenes . . . , the advance of dogma is something almost tragic, a poignant ideological puberty. . . . Newman comes close to a *Verfallstheorie* of dogmatic language, the notion of formulation itself being a kind of betrayal of some richer truth; but it is a necessary fall, a *felix culpa*" (270).[1]

While the happiness of this fall is far from evident in Newman, its necessity is painfully so. The most obvious, but perhaps least interesting evidence for such a fall would include suspicions about the historical accuracy of the Patristic witness. Such suspicions are seized upon by the anonymous reviewer of *Arians* in the *Edinburgh:* "It is impossible to form a right judgment of the Alexandrian Christians without enquiring into their contemporaneous history. Mr Newman most blamably neglects to do this. He assumes, throughout his long account, that the system of the Alexandrian fathers proceeded from an independent, unbiassed conviction. . . . [A]t once identifying the system with that of the earlier church, [he] proceeds to explain it as if it were the only true and legitimate one" ("Newman's *History of the Arians*" 60). Newman cavalierly dismisses another such attack: "As to Mr Osburn, he is so insufferably profane, that I cannot help thinking that if that . . . be put before well disposed people, they would eschew him and his opinions." But this confidence is belied by subsequent hedging: "'[W]e take [the Fathers] simply as *witnesses* to an existing state of things—and we do not go by the testimony (much less the opinion) of *one,* but the joint witness of *all*—' thus Tertullian schismatized, Lactantius was heterodox, Origen extravagant—what is this to the purpose? . . . [T]hat men so different as Origen, Basil, Jerome, and Augustine should agree together one should have thought was a good argument, in proportion to their peculiarities" (*LD* 5: 348–49). Here Newman pulls back from his assertions on the inspired status of Clement and Origen and appeals instead to the Vincentian canon of *quod semper, quod ubique, quod ab omnibus.*

Even within *Arians,* however, the acknowledgment of a similar fall from spiritual plenitude lies implicit within the allegorical mode through which the Fathers transmit their scriptural insights. There only the heretics interpret Scripture literally; in orthodox hermeneutics, according to Valentine Cunningham, "The parable of the grain of mustard seed, full of hidden, secret potential for great growth, is just one self-referential emblem of textual copiousness, interpretative potential and pleromatic expansiveness. A figure illustrates, a figure carries, the developmental life of the text; the metaphorical plenitudes of Scripture are ripe for interpretative expansion; metaphor is reality, becomes reality" (243). As Williams paraphrases Newman's own justification, "'Allegory' is not a heathen importation, but rooted in 'the operation of a general principle of our nature,' the desire to speak of overwhelmingly significant vision in terms that somehow articulate the way in which it informs other perceptions—that is, to speak in figure and metaphor, lest the scope of the vision be narrowed" (267). Though he replaces traditional descriptions of figurative language with their modern, subjective counterparts, Williams here remains surprisingly faithful to the sophisticated hermeneutic which continues to undermine Newman's most passionate etiological assertions:

> When the mind is occupied by some vast and awful subject of contemplation, it is prompted to give utterance to its feelings in a figurative style; for ordinary words will not convey the admiration, nor literal words the reverence which possesses it; and when, dazzled at length with the great sight, it turns away for relief, it still catches in every new object which it encounters, glimpses of its former vision, and colours its whole range of thought with this one abiding association. . . . Such are the feelings under which a deeply impressed mind addresses itself to the task of disclosing even its human thoughts; and this account of it . . . applies to the case of a mind under the immediate influence of inspiration. . . . [T]he divinely-instructed imagination of the writers is ever glancing to and fro, connecting past things with future. (*Ari.* 57–58)

As the creation of religious allegory becomes a sub-division of the Romantic sublime, Newman's concept of biblical typology expands into a never-ending process of refiguration: "No prophet ends his subject: his brethren after him renew, enlarge, transfigure, or reconstruct it; so that the Bible, though various in its parts, forms a whole" (58).

Newman here explores in practice what Pusey alone would admit in theory: "[D]estitute of the key which would have opened to him the fuller riches of Scripture, [Ernesti] forgot that every new religion must form to itself a new language, that in order to convey new truths, . . . [words] must be recast, remoulded" (1: 133). Focusing on Newman's conception of economy, Williams finds him engaged in a similar progression, a progression which locates the principle of development, supposedly a product of the next decade, buried within *Arians* itself.[2] Williams concludes,

> [H]is refusal to identify a single moment or epoch as *fully* crystallizing that [doctrinal] content already suggests that the continuity or identity of belief can only appear *in* the interaction of the diverse articulations of belief through history. . . . [U]ltimately, the *unity* of Christian theology is not capable of being articulated in abstraction

from the particularities of its history. . . . Only in the activity of conversation do we find what the depths and what the limits are of our common language, what it is that holds us together as sharers in one world. (283)

Here, Newman's methodology is being invoked in support not just of Romantic subjectivity but of an intersubjectivity often appealed to by his opponents within the Broad Church Movement. He insisted that any ecumenical discussions with such opponents take place within the physical confines of an Anglican Church, "not on neutral ground, or rather an enemy's, the open inhospitable waste of this world, but within that sheltered heritage whose land-marks have long since been set up" (*PS* 3 [14]: 202). He appealed to the Fathers as an equally non-negotiable premise; yet here Williams cites his interpretation of the Fathers as sanction for just this kind of negotiation.

To escape seeing the Fathers as an arbitrarily chosen link within some endless hermeneutic chain, Newman needs to invoke an ongoing spiritual witness immediate enough to render interpretation unnecessary. The *Prophetical Office* posits just such a witness. For the Patristic Church, the Apostolic tradition constitutes

> a vast system, . . . pervading the Church like an atmosphere, irregular in its shape from its very profession and exuberance; . . . at times melting away into legend and fable; partly written, partly unwritten, partly preserved in intellectual expressions, partly latent in the spirit and temper of Christians; poured to and fro in closets and upon the housetops, in liturgies, in controversial works, in obscure fragments, in sermons, in popular prejudices, in local customs. This I call Prophetical Tradition . . . what St. Paul calls "the mind of the Spirit," the thought and principle which breathed in the Church, her accustomed and unconscious mode of viewing things, and the body of her received notions. (*PO* 268–69)[3]

However powerful, this evocation raises more questions than it answers. First, it reformulates Newman's quest for origins into one of continued, and possibly continuous, deferral; the intuitive intensity of one past age is posited upon the intuitive intensity of a yet prior one. Second, it diffuses, rather than focuses, both the search for causes and the tracing of effects; tradition surfaces in all aspects of religious life and it moves in every direction, heterodox as well as orthodox. Finally, the passage recapitulates the very Romantic turn to the self Newman has tried to avoid; because the tradition may appear in every experience of every individual believer, distilling it from its subjective source becomes an exercise in futility.[4]

Chadwick indirectly offers one reason why Newman felt obliged to blur the Patristic witness. While Brilioth claims that "The gulf that divided the old Catholic Church from the Apostolic was to him hidden" (*Anglican* 118), Chadwick suggests that Newman's unspoken, unspeakable motive throughout the late 1830s was the growing realization that the Fathers were in fact *not* reliable witnesses, that their age and the Apostolic age were radically different. According to Chadwick, Newman turned to development reluctantly because "the effort to justify Anglicanism by the Vincentian Canon seemed to have collapsed" (121); he invoked it only as "a hypothesis to account for a difficulty" (144).[5] At least one of Newman's letters from this period acknowledges such a gap: "Surely the Episcopal System is an accident. . . . I may believe that first of all *all* Ministers were made Apostles, that next, as in the Epistles, there were an indefinite number of orders" (*LD* 5: 205). The awkwardness of such acknowledgments is most bluntly summarized by Jonathan Loesberg: "To accept that perfection in religious doctrine must result from historical change rather than seeing such change as a process whereby the original revelation may become deformed or degraded, we must begin with the assumption that revelation is like any other historical occurrence, a natural event subject to natural laws" (101). From this perspective, Newman's theory initiates the progressively broader conception of development which Livingston traces through Matthew Arnold and into the turn-of-the-century Modernists (*Arnold* 54–58). It even comes to resemble a more dangerously secular post-Enlightenment movement: "[I]t looked, after all, suspiciously like the kind of historical theory that Mill, influenced by the distinctly un-Catholic Comte, was trying to spread in England" (Loesberg 102).[6]

For Loesberg, Newman circumvented this conclusion by reinscribing revision, both compositional and doctrinal, as erasure, the restoring of what was always already there. As I argued in chapter 2, however, I am not convinced that Newman found the distance between Fathers and Apostles as distressing as modern commentators believe. As we shall see in chapter 10, when he reread the Alexandrians in a new "Catholic" sense in the late 1830s (*Diff.* 1: 371–72), he certainly interpreted them as proto-medieval instead of post-Apostolic; yet even here, within his earlier "Anglican" interpretation, he found the Patristic church not just different from the Apostolic one, but better. Even Paul, himself not overly interested in the earthly Jesus, becomes in Newman a sort of spiritual supply house for the edifice completed by the Fathers: "He was not allowed to build the House of God, for He was, in figure, like David, a 'man of blood.' He did but bring together into one, the materials of the Sacred Building. . . . [T]ill a time of peace came, and by the end of four hundred years the work was accomplished" (PS 3 [22]: 330).

Within this context neither Jesus, nor Paul, nor the Apostles could be truly efficacious in saving souls: The Apostles

> roused and inflamed their hearers into enthusiasm, till "the Kingdom of Heaven suffered violence, and the violent took it by force." . . . [M]any of them, doubtless, would wax cold in love, and fall away; for many had entered only on impulse; many, with Simon Magus, on wonder or curiosity; many from a mere argumentative belief, which leads as readily into heresy as into the Truth. . . . [Yet t]he examples of meekness, cheerfulness, contentment, silent endurance, private self-denial . . . , the sublimity and harmony of the Church's doctrine,— the touching and subduing beauty of her services and appointments, — . . . the simplicity of her ascetics, the gravity of her Bishops, the awful glory shed around her Martyrs,— . . . these . . . turn[ed] the whisper of their hearts into an habitual conviction. (Jfc. 271–72)

Exactly what violence the Kingdom has suffered and where the violent are bearing it has been in dispute from Mark's time to that of Flannery O'Connor. It is indisputable, however, that Newman's first-century converts here find themselves in company, not just with simonists, but with the spiritual ancestors of the argumentative, heretical Gibbon and the sensation-seeking Evangelicals. No such converts could be saved unless they won a "habitual conviction" born of repeated encounters with harmonious doctrine, lavish church services, simple ascetics, grave bishops, and glorious martyrs. To take the passage literally, a first-century Christian's best hope of salvation lay in somehow managing to survive until the fourth century.

This strategy may seem to cut right through the Gordian knot of spiritual belatedness, to reinstate the Fathers as *the* locus of spiritual fullness. In actuality, however, Newman's Patristic Church maintains its centrality by exploiting its own belatedness, by positing a spiritual power as past and then assuming ritualized control over it, a control that keeps it distant enough to be safe but available enough to be powerful.[7] In a note to his Cicero article, Newman quoted Samuel Johnson: "It is not uncommon for those who have grown wise by the labour of others, to add a little of their own, and overlook their master" (HS 1: 300). Here Newman presents the Fathers themselves as "strong" theologians, overcoming their anxiety of influence by a calculated, if covert, process of appropriation.[8]

Patristic Availability

The same immediate spiritual intuitions which supported Patristic witness also support Newman's access to Patristic Christianity. And if an active participation in Patristic spirituality demanded something more than
imaginative recuperation, Newman was ready to expend all his considerable visionary powers in that effort. Principal Shairp, for instance, recalls
"the tone of voice with which he uttered the [following] beautiful passage about music as the audible embodiment of some unknown reality
behind, itself sweeping like a strain of splendid music out of the heart of
a subtle argument" (250). Newman begins here on aesthetic grounds
with the musical variety inherent in a diatonic scale: "[I]s it possible that
that inexhaustible evolution and disposition of notes . . . should be a
mere sound, which is gone and perishes? Can it be that those mysterious
stirrings of heart, and keen emotions, and strange yearnings after we
know not what, and awful impressions from we know not whence, should
be wrought in us by what is unsubstantial, and comes and goes, and begins and ends in itself?" (*US* [15]: 346–47). At this point, however, the
spiritual tenor subsumes its vehicle: "It is not so; it cannot be. No; they
have escaped from some higher sphere; they are the outpourings of eternal harmony in the medium of created sound; they are echoes from our
Home; they are the voice of Angels, or the Magnificat of Saints" (347).
And if mere music can constitute an invitation to return to this spiritual
home, the shared aspirations of the Tractarians enable Newman to argue
in the *Prophetical Office* that the Movement itself offers "a providential
window in time" (20). In Tract 83 he takes the next and last logical step;
instead of claiming that the gap is bridgeable or transforming a temporal
gap into a spatial one, he actually superimposes past and present, matter
and spirit upon one another: "What we want, is to *understand* that we are
in the place in which the early Christians were, with the same covenant,
ministry, sacraments, and duties;—to realize a state of things long past
away" (5: 27). Surrounded by such opportunities, the Church, "as it actually has become in these dark and secular days," exemplifies not the
post-Enlightenment condition but a cowardly failure of spiritual vision:
"Do not we hover about our ancient home, the home of Cyprian and
Athanasius, without the heart to take up our abode in it, yet afraid to
quit the sight of it . . . ? Alas! is not this to witness against ourselves,
like coward sinners who hope to serve the world, without giving up God's
service?" ("Records of the Church" XXV; *Tracts* 2: 2–3).

At this point, however, we must repeat Chadwick's questions: Was he
asking from history "not so much objective truth as the moral example

which would help him? . . . [D]id he live with the Fathers as they were or with them as he wanted them to be?" ("Bremond" 189). Even within *Arians,* Newman has to admit that the same "fall" into controversy and dogmatism which corrupted Patristic Christianity threatens his own mission as its privileged interpreter:

> [S]o perplexed is the present state of things that the Church is obliged . . . unwillingly to take part in the theological discussions of the day, as a man crushes venomous creatures of necessity, powerful to do it, but loathing the employment. This is the apology which the author of the present work . . . offers to all sober-minded and zealous Christians, for venturing to exhibit publicly the great evangelical doctrines . . . in an historical and explanatory form. And he earnestly trusts, that, while doing so, he may be . . . wrapping [the Truth] in reverent language, and so depositing it in its due resting-place, which is the Christian's heart; guiltless of those unutterable profanations with which a scrutinizing infidelity wounds and lacerates it. Here, again, is strikingly instanced the unfitness of books, compared with private communication, for the purposes of religious instruction. (*Ari.* 137)

These complex parallels claim the achievement of an unmediated truth and then immediately acknowledge its impossibility. Newman becomes one with the Fathers, but only because both are trapped in the conflicting goals of transmitting their spiritual bequest and preserving it undefiled. For Newman, as for the Fathers whose books he treasures, books are simultaneously the best means of "depositing" the truth within "the Christian's heart" and a public, controversial medium which does inevitable violence both to the truth and to its eventual "resting place."

In his essay on ecclesiastical miracles, the Fathers have been moved to the relative safety of a pre-controversial age: they "wrote for contemporaries, not for the eighteenth or nineteenth century, not for modern notions and theories, for a degenerate people and a disunited Church. They did not foresee that evidence would become a science, that doubt would be thought a merit, and disbelief a privilege" (*Mir.* 226). But this move only reopens the gap between them and Newman himself, a gap which he can bridge only by reinvoking the same hermeneutical approaches toward them which they invoked toward Scripture. Justifying to Hugh James Rose the Patristic researches which eventually produced his *Arians,* he asks rhetorically, "What light would be thrown on the Nicene Confession *merely* by explaining it article by article? to understand it, it must be prefaced by a sketch of the rise of the Arian heresy, the words introduced by Arius, . . . etc" (*LD* 2: 352).[9] He argues that "Texts have their illuminating power, from the atmosphere of habit, opinion, usage, tradition, through which we see them" (*US* [10]: 191); yet he must also admit that Augustine's writings remain the sole memorials, not only of him but of African Christendom. Recapturing his own recent musings on board the *Hermes,* he writes that Africa's "five hundred churches are no more. The voyager gazes on the sullen rocks which line its coast, and discovers no token of Christianity to cheer the gloom. Hippo has ceased to be an epis-copal city; but its great Teacher, though dead, yet speaks; his voice is gone out into all lands, and his words unto the ends of the world" (*HS* 2: 140-41). By the last of his university sermons, this conflation of the Fathers with their texts has progressed so far that their "resting place" is no longer "the Christian's heart" but the library: "To see [Faith's] triumph over the world's wisdom, we must enter those solemn cemeteries in which are stored the relics and the monuments of ancient Faith—our libraries. Look along their shelves, and every name you read there is, in one sense or other, a trophy set up in record of the victories of Faith" (*US* [15]: 315).

This repository function of both libraries and churches also casts doubt on the claims, quoted earlier, that modern believers possess the same unmediated access to the spiritual as that enjoyed by the Fathers. After picturing the pathetic solipsism of the contemporary Lutheran, who "sits amid the ruins of human nature, and . . . indulges a pensive meditation over its misery" (*Jfc.* 335-36), Newman offers the alternative of Patristic worship:

> [T]hey went out of their own minds into the Infinite Temple which was around them. They saw Christ in the Gospels, in the Creed, in the Sacraments and other Rites; in the visible structure and orna-ments of His House, in the Altar, and in the Cross. . . . Unwaver-ing, unflagging, not urged by fits and starts, not heralding forth their feelings, but resolutely, simply, perseveringly, day after day, Sunday and week-day, fast-day and festival, week by week, season by season, year by year, in youth and in age, through a life, thirty years, forty years, fifty years, in prelude of the everlasting chant before the Throne,—so they went on, "continuing *instant* in prayer," after the pattern of Psalmists and Apostles, in the day with David, in the night with Paul and Silas, . . . still they had Christ before them; His thought in their mind, His emblems in their eye, His name in their mouth, His service in their posture, magnifying Him, and calling on all that lives to magnify Him, joining with Angels in heaven and Saints in Paradise to bless and praise Him for ever and ever. (*Jfc.* 337-39)[10]

This impressive passage, capturing in its prose rhythms the life rhythms he is describing, bonds the individual worshiper with nature, with the cycles of the day, the week, and the year, with both the physical and liturgical dimensions of the church, with both Old and New Testament models, with the heavenly court, and—above and within all—with a very cosmic manifestation of Christ. In an 1842 sermon Newman maintains that this Patristic consensus can still foster a vital community of the spiritually awakened within his own time:

> Hitherto, it has seemed as if . . . men of more correct and more orthodox views seemed to be of a cold and forbidding school—nay, the less fervent, the less spiritual for their very exactness: but all this is gone by. A more primitive, Catholic, devout, ardent spirit, is abroad among the holders of orthodox truth. The piercing, and thrilling, and kindling, and enrapturing glories of the kingdom of Christ are felt in their degree by many. Men are beginning to understand that influence, which in the beginning made the philosopher leave his school, and the soldier beat his spear into a pruning-hook. (*SD* [9]: 115)[11]

A contemporary letter to Stephen rejects the Evangelical hermeneutic of subjective identification, but again Newman's alternative, the recuperation of the past through ritual, simply replaces one hermeneutic with another: Butler "caught the idea which had actually been the rule of the Primitive Church, of teaching the more Sacred Truths ordinarily by rites and ceremonies. No mode of teaching can be imagined so public, constant, impressive, permanent, and at the same time reverential. . . . In this way Christians receive the Gospel literally on their knees" (*LD* 5:46). The very smoothness of these transitions—from the Fathers, to Butler, to the present—raises the additional suspicion that in "returning" to the Fathers, Newman may not be going anywhere. Just as they, in his account, projected their own needs upon the Apostolic past, so he may be projecting his own modern (re)vision of the Church Catholic upon a fourth-century screen.[12] "There was," claims Brilioth, a "romantic interest in the past which made the dreary pages of Church history open enchanting vistas for the eye of faith. . . . And yet . . . appealing to the standards of Christian antiquity and Caroline Anglicanism was profoundly unhistorical, and doomed to failure" (*Evangelicalism* 40, 61).[13] Inge challenges Newman's supposed recuperation on both historical and philosophical grounds: "To deny the existence of universals [as Newman does], to regard them as mere creations of the mind, is rank blasphemy to a Platonist; and the Alexandrines [*sic*] were Christian Platonists" (189).[14]

The Gulf of the Enlightenment

Newman's religious contemporaries, certain that the Patristic cosmos had passed beyond even his power to resurrect it, were equally unwilling to let him escape so easily from their midst. His claims for ongoing angelic intervention provoked Connop Thirlwall to remark in private: "[N]o mind could attempt to realize it without feeling itself in danger of losing its senses. Surely it is one thing to believe that all is regulated by a Supreme Will, and quite another to believe that this Will employs machinery like that of the 'Rape of the Lock'" (269). Thomas Mozley caricatures a similar critique of Newman's system-building: "Newman is fully aware that he has nothing to stand upon, and . . . must descend to the common abyss. . . . [But he] has laid planks across this abyss, and standing upon them invites us to share his basis as if it were everlasting, though he knows it to be only a mechanism of his own" (2: 436). Mozley dismisses this portrait as unfair to Newman's veracity, but in defending Newman's faith he implicitly reinstates it: Because "faith is an imaginative and creative power . . . , it has no choice but to fill the void with what may be called its own forms and outlines. . . . It will always be building castles and cities, and filling the heavens with the most glorious conceivable counterparts of all that earth can show" (2: 442).

All these critiques, I believe, rest upon an insistence that Newman remain subject to the contextualization which he himself will come to demand of other "great writers": "[T]he history of their works is the history of their fortunes or their times. Each is, in his turn, the man of his age, the type of a generation, or the interpreter of a crisis. He is made for his day, and his day for him" (*Idea* 257).[15] Newman himself must abide by Leslie Stephen's maxim: "No one can quite cut himself loose from the conditions of the time" (178); in particular, he cannot be allowed to circumvent the Enlightenment. Thomas claims that in his Tract 73 against rationalism, "Newman caught what has since been called the 'turn to the subject'—the post-Enlightenment atmosphere in which religion was perceived as being about how human beings understand themselves, rather than about what God has revealed" (108). I would suggest that he had indeed "caught" this atmosphere—much as Matthew Arnold, unlike his Scholar-Gypsy, would find himself infected with "this strange disease of modern life" (203).[16]

The distinction between pre- and post-Enlightenment thinkers has never been more incisively drawn than in John Keats's thumbnail sketches of Wordsworth and Milton: In the Reformation, the remaining Dogmas and superstitions . . . constituted those resting places and seeming sure points of Reasoning. . . . Milton . . . appears to have been content with these by his writings—He did not think into the human heart, as Wordsworth has done—Yet Milton as a Philosop[h]er, had sure as great powers as Wordsworth—What is then to be inferr'd? O many things—It proves there is really a grand march of intellect—, It proves a mighty providence subdues the mightiest Minds to the service of the time being, whether it be in human Knowledge or Religion. (To Reynolds, 5/3/1818 [*Letters* 1: 282])[17]

Echoing the Keats letter, M. H. Abrams specifies the "time being" to which Newman's mighty mind rendered its involuntary service: "[S]ince they lived, inescapably, after the Enlightenment, Romantic writers revived these ancient matters with a difference: they undertook to save the overview of human history and destiny, the experiential paradigms, and the cardinal values of their religious heritage, by reconstituting them in a way that would make them intellectually acceptable, as well as emotionally pertinent, for the time being" (*Natural* 66).

Itself a cornerstone of the Enlightenment, Schiller's *On Naive and Sentimental Poetry* foreshadows Abrams's own theory: "All poets . . . will belong, according to the time when they flourish, . . . to the order of the *sentimental* poetry or to *simple* [naive] poetry" (281). For Abrams, "Schiller's emphasis is on the primary split in the mind's unity with itself which converts unself-consciousness into self-consciousness—the awareness of the self as a subject distinct from the object it perceives, and the intervention of reflection and choice between instinct and action" (*Natural* 213–14). In Schiller's words,

We see, then, in nature, destitute of reason, only a sister who, more fortunate than ourselves, has remained under the maternal roof, while in the intoxication of our freedom we have fled from it to throw ourselves into a stranger world. We regret [losing] this place of safety, . . . and in the totally artificial life in which we are exiled we hear in deep emotion the voice of our mother. . . . [Yet] your heart ought to plunge into these troubles with joy, and to find in them the compensation in the liberty of which they are the consequence. . . . This nature which you envy in the being destitute of reason deserves no esteem: it is not worth a wish. You have passed beyond it; it ought to remain for ever behind you. (275–77)[18]

Newman's effort to rehabilitate the Fathers could thus come under Schiller's judgment on modern recreations of the bucolic idyll: "By the very fact that the idyll is transported to the time that precedes civilization, it . . . finds itself in opposition to itself. . . . [I]t places *behind us* the end *towards which it ought to lead us,* and consequently it can only inspire us with the sad feeling of loss" (314).

We have been emphasizing Newman's more inspired, ecstatic, sanguine claims for the continued availability of Patristic spirituality. In his soberer moments, however, he tacitly admitted that the power of the Zeitgeist remains just as strong in religion as in literature: "[T]his age is a practical age: the age of the Fathers was more contemplative. . . . No good could come of merely imitating the Fathers for imitation's sake. . . . We cannot, if we would, move ourselves literally back into the times of the Fathers: we must, in spite of ourselves, be churchmen of our own era, not of any other, were it only for this reason, that we are born in the nineteenth century, not in the fourth" (*Ess.* 1: 286–88). And this caveat is supported by an anticipation of Heideggerian thrownness: "To murmur and rail at the state of things under which we find ourselves, and to prefer a former state, is not merely indecorous, it is absolutely unmeaning. We are ourselves necessary parts of the existing system. . . . [I]n wishing for other times we are, in fact, wishing we had never been born" (*US* [4]: 67). In both these passages, he offers his own acknowledgment of the difference Schiller remarks between ancient naivete and modern sentimentality, between ancient fullness and modern belatedness, between a comfortable, unselfconscious existence within myth and an uncomfortable, very self-conscious effort to recreate it.

The Primary Poetry of Inspiration

This acknowledgment, in its turn, brings Newman all unwilling into the company of other, usually more liberal, religious thinkers who reinterpreted these larger temporal dichotomies as one between the ancient sacred and the modern secular. According to Prickett, for example, Coleridge's disciple Maurice translated Schiller's gap into religious terminology but refused to abandon his effort to bridge it: "Our religious language is that of another age, and of a different world-view, resting on different and outmoded cultural assumptions, yet it is, partly for that very reason, the vehicle of a different kind and *quality* of consciousness without which the sophistication of philology and Historical Method is drained of meaning and becomes lost in a sterile relativity" (*Romanticism* 136). Although Newman complained to Hook that Maurice, as Coleridge's disciple, speculated with what he should simply receive,[19] he could bring no such charge against Keble; and Keble, while he acknowledged the same gap, so privileged the naive, or "primary," poets as he called them, that nothing was left for the moderns but a wan nostalgia.[20] As Prickett summarizes his *Lectures on Poetry:*

> The Primary [poets, for Keble] consist in "those who, spontaneously moved by impulse, resort to composition for relief and solace of a burdened or over-wrought mind"; the Secondary are "those, who, for one reason or another, imitate the ideas, the expression, and the measures of the former." . . . [F]or Keble there is no question that the Primary poets are the more important. . . . [They] are analogous to the founders of the Church—the prophets, Apostles, and early Fathers who have shaped the development of our religious sensibility through the tradition of the Church; like the Fathers, they bring catharsis and soothing out of the intolerable tensions of the human predicament. The Secondary poets are, as it were, the army of saints and ecclesiastics who have kept pure the tradition of the Church. (*Romanticism* 111, 116-17)[21]

From Keble's sacramental conception of nature and his invocation of it within *The Christian Year,*[22] we might assume that religious epiphanies would be equally available in the present, but Goodwin argues that Keble

> would have us conclude that Protestant attempts to minimize the deposit of faith and Romantic attempts to maximize it are both wrong in neglecting the manner in which the divine hieroglyphs of Scripture were pursued by the Fathers. . . . [I]f there were such a developing tradition, it was not the contemporary tradition of private inquiry or what we have since learned to call the Romantic tradition. The making of religious symbols took place in the Church and only there . . . : "Let an uninspired poet or theologian be never so ingenious in his comparisons between earthly things and heavenly, we cannot build anything upon them; there is no particular certainty, much less any sacredness in them; but let the same words come out of the mouth of God, and we know the resemblance was intended from the beginning." (485, quoting *Tracts* 5 [89]: 167)

Curiously enough, the contrast Keble draws here between sacred and secular resembles that drawn by Hampden in his effort to box Scripture into a "sacred enclosure." We will discuss in the next chapter the influence of Keble's quasi-Romantic aesthetics on Newman; here we need only point out that Newman's essay on Scripture dramatizes the folly of constructing any such artificial stay against relativism. While his claims for spiritual recuperation may seem to throw Keble's caution to the winds, he shows himself more aware than Keble that identifying the sacred is often more difficult than compassing it.

Newman's Challenge to Rationalism

What lasting value, then, has Newman's spiritual construct? It is, as we said, far more arcane and anachronistic than the rear-guard efforts of his contemporaries to privilege Scripture as history or poetry. Yet it retains, I think, a curious relevance for an age which has come to challenge the Enlightenment project much as that project challenged the religious epochs before it. In distinguishing Newman's universe from Keble's, both Goodwin (485 ff.) and Stephen Finley (155–66) describe it as darker and more obviously fallen. A similar distinction, I think, renders it proof against the vaunting rationalism of Enlightenment critique. In his analysis of Kant's *Religion within the Limits of Reason Alone,* for example, Donald Marshall finds him "particularly withering on the slavish temperament to which pietism gives rise. Every traditional religious symbol is hermeneutically stripped down to bare reason" (80). In the last chapter of the *Apologia,* Newman charts the incursions of this "all-corroding, all-dissolving scepticism of the intellect in religious inquiries" (218). Anticipating this same "prophet's scroll" of unbelief, however, an early sermon can claim that when religious liberals extrapolate from any "natural" order to God, they deny the contingency of our human condition: "They lay much stress on works on *Natural Theology,* and think that all religion is contained in these. . . . Religion[, however,] is something *relative to us;* a system of commands and promises from God *towards* us. But how are we concerned with the sun, moon, and stars? . . . [H]ow will they speak to *sinners?* They do not speak to sinners at all. They were created *before* Adam fell. They 'declare the *glory* of God,' but not His *will*" (*PS* 1 [24]: 317). The Philosophes dismissed the Fall as a self-serving priestly fable; Hegel reinstated it as a historically delimited consequence of self-conscious action; here Newman replies that both moves constitute inadvertent evidence for the Fall itself.

In his first important foray into theology and Church history, *Arians* shows him already tracing modern rationalism back to what he saw as the Judaizing sect within Christian Antioch. As Robert Pattison has pointed out, the Arian heresy spawned from this sect drives a wedge between the physical and spiritual realms. After showing the sequels to Arianism in the apostasy of Julian and the fulsome praise bestowed upon him by Gibbon, Newman asks rhetorically: "Who does not recognize in this old philosophy the chief features of that recent school of liberalism and false illumination, political and moral, which is now Satan's instrument in deluding the nations, . . . the cold, scoffing spirit of modern rationalism?" (*Ari.* 106).[23] In the increasing emphasis on cosmic struggle which we found within the parochial sermons, Newman saw this depersonalization of reason as itself the strategy of a fully personified evil: "[C]ould you see that all your idle thoughts . . . are inspired by that Ancient Seducer of Mankind, who stands at your side . . . , not able to laugh at his own jests" (*PS* 7 [15]: 215). In Tract 83, he even identifies "enlightenment" as the most dangerous of these temptations: Satan "promises you illumination,—he offers you knowledge, science, philosophy, enlargement of mind. . . . He bids you mount aloft. He shows you how to become as gods. Then he laughs and jokes with you, and gets intimate with you; he takes your hand, and gets his fingers between yours, and grasps them, and then you are his" (*Tracts* 5 [83]: 13–14).[24]

While Newman's defiantly personal spirituality resists Enlightenment abstraction, it also resists deconstructionist challenges to any Enlightenment faith in historical progress. According to Rajan, Derrida attacks Schiller's postulate of a naive poetry by pointing out that "signification, which reveals the separation between signs and things, is always already a feature of language. Naive cultures are always already sentimental" (33).[25] We have been arguing that Newman's attempts to transcend historical change are self-defeating and even ingenuous, but when he invokes a spirituality whose narratives are ordered and harmonized by doctrine, he anticipates Derrida's claim that mythic immediacy cannot exist unmediated.

The uneasy relation of this universe to that of nineteenth-century England anticipates yet another postmodern challenge, de Man's attack upon the synthetic power of the Romantic imagination. When he championed Alexandrian efforts to allegorize the Old Testament, Newman may have subverted his claims for some Patristic natural language, but he also assured that his borrowed spiritual universe would avoid some of the cozy, post-Wordsworthian sacramentalism of Keble's *Christian Year*. As part of a realm that remains parallel rather than immanent, Newman's heavenly court—his angels, his devils, his intermediate beings, even his God— define themselves by their very irrelevance to the limited ideological horizons of modern society.

In their marginality, these figures even appear homologous to those seen as "other"—or not seen at all—by this same society. Within Lacanian psychology, for example, the other (lowercase "o") represents the part of the inevitably divided subject vested in the object of desire; the Other (uppercase "o") represents the fantasy of a universe held together by some controlling consciousness; perhaps even closer to Newman's universe, the Real represents the unknowable "outside" the subject which manifests itself by refusing to go away. For feminist critics, by contrast, the other is woman herself, already marginalized by a patriarchal culture, who uses her role to embody what this culture has chosen to deny. For the neo-Marxist Marjorie Levinson, by contrast, materialism is the other, invisible within even a late-capitalist ideology "insofar as matter is not, for Marx, ultimately reducible to the category of the human and its operations" (32). Newman's universe is neither materialist, nor feminist, nor even psychological. And yet his angels wearing the vesture of a spring day, his devils insinuating themselves within apparently abstract thought, his scores of saints hiding within churchyards, his heavenly hosts fighting unseen alongside the beleaguered believer, his heavenly court veiling itself within the dark recesses of the sanctuary—all these figures escape immanence by an apparent irrelevance. And it is their irrelevance, like that of other postmodern "marginalia," which calls the age itself to judgment.

CHAPTER 4

The Romantic Realignment of Self and God

☼

AS WAS SUGGESTED at the end of the last chapter, the Anglican Newman's spiritual universe presents a troubling counter-vision to the Victorian age and to our own; yet the source of his vision remains very much in doubt. If his arguments for its ontological autonomy never escape self-contradiction, the vision itself survives as an epiphenomenon of the post-Enlightenment subjectivity which Newman identified as the most pernicious legacy of the Reformation. For me, however, this vision seems more closely identified with another movement—at once an off-shoot of the Enlightenment and a reaction to it—Romanticism. Even though the term and its referents have been defined largely in retrospect, and even then with considerable disagreement, Newman's reaction to its various manifestations may appear more than a little obtuse. And yet most modern commentators are willing to acknowledge Newman's participation in at least some of the competing Romanticisms which swept across nineteenth-century Europe.[1] John Coulson's account is representative: "In one respect the Oxford Movement does for England what Schleiermacher did for Germany: it provides the theological programme of Romanticism, if we interpret Romanticism as restoring a conception of Nature, not as dead and exploitable, but as a divine sacramental language. But there are two differences. . . ." (35).[2]

These "differences," these qualifications, which appear as an almost obligatory second sentence, usually relegate Newman, along with Novalis, the later Schlegel, and Chateaubriand, to what Colin Falck calls the "second face of Romanticism, which looks backwards for its inspiration to religion, and which encourages us not towards mastery but towards submission. . . . [T]his second side of Romanticism is also its darker side" (2). John Beer's qualification also differentiates Newman from this "first face": "There was another tradition of romanticism, more vitalistic in tendency, which, seeing man as a child of the earth and an involuntary disciple of his own imagination, sought to use those resources for the renewal of humanity. . . . Newman had little feeling for that tradition" (213–14). D. G. James suggests that "We cannot understand the narrow ways into which, in [late] Coleridge and Newman, Romanticism came . . . if we do not first discern the scope and range of the Romantic imagination in its original exposure to the world" (165).[3] Robert Pattison is still more specific: "The Oxford Movement mounted an attack on the leading ideas of Romanticism—the religious awe of selfhood, the sacramental value of art, the divine inspiration of individual vision" (*Dissent* 44).[4]

If we want to argue that the early Newman did participate in what Harold Bloom would call high Romanticism, that he did at times value selfhood, art, and individual vision, then we face formidable problems even beyond his predictable hostility.[5] For one thing, he tends to encounter such phenomena from a perspective decentered from the original author's stated purpose; for another, he consistently reinscribes Romantic phenomena within a pre-Enlightenment, specifically theological vocabulary; for yet another, he undermines the conflation of imaginative and religious perspectives characteristic of the more overtly Christian Romantics. Despite these incongruities, however, we will find that Newman's efforts to ground his own subjectivity rest upon and often parallel the progress of German Idealism from Kant through Hegel.

While the English Romantic poets enter and exit this progression at very different points, Newman shares their implicit, pragmatic recognition that subjectivity is not a philosophic right but a victory of inspired utterance. In many of these visionary moments within Newman's prose, he wrestles with what Sacvan Bercovitch, following Augustine, has identified as a "trial of the center," a contest for dominance between the human subject and God. While for Bercovitch the eventual victor identifies the work itself as either Romantic or pre-Romantic, Newman's "trials" retain links with both periods. His visions grow from and remain grounded within an ongoing dialogue between self and God, a dialogue in which the identities of both parties are continually renegotiated. As both Romantic and anti-Romantic, Newman escapes subsequent efforts to reduce Romantic claims into their psychological or sociological counterparts; he also anticipates some of the more recent post-structuralist challenges to these same claims.

[81]

Newman's Encounter with Romantic Thought

Newman's most searching portrait of a Romantic comes, appropriately enough, from an early sermon:

> [T]here are others of a mystical turn of mind, with untutored imaginations and subtle intellects, who follow the theories of the old Gentile philosophy. These, too, are accustomed to make love the one principle of life and providence in heaven and earth, as if it were a pervading Spirit of the world, finding a sympathy in every heart, absorbing all things into itself, and kindling a rapturous enjoyment in all who contemplate it. They sit at home speculating, and separate moral perfection from action. These men either hold, or are in the way to hold, that the human soul is pure by nature; sin an external principle corrupting it; evil, destined to final annihilation; truth attained by means of the imagination; conscience, a taste; holiness, a passive contemplation of God; and obedience, a mere pleasurable work. (*PS* 2 [23]: 288)

This passage, fascinating for the amalgam of discrete traits included within it, denies Romanticism its novelty by identifying it with a "Gentile philosophy," possibly pantheism. It then gives an adequate summary of Wordsworthian and Coleridgean nature worship, only to weigh it (finding it, of course, wanting) against a militant Christianity. Rather than meet Coleridge on his own terms, Newman makes him and his movement play by theological rules. Even more explicitly hostile, the essay on Scripture identifies the movement as another phase of the diabolical plot we saw him tracing in chapter 3. It becomes "the spread of a Pantheistic spirit, that is, the religion of beauty, imagination, and philosophy, without constraint moral or intellectual, a religion speculative and self-indulgent. Pantheism, indeed, is the great deceit which awaits the Age to come" (*DA* 233).[6]

In their cogency, both these critiques suggest that Newman's conception of high Romanticism, either English or German, was far more coherent than it may have actually been. Mark Pattison betrays the spite of a lapsed disciple in his famous comment, "A. P. Stanley once said to me, 'How different the fortunes of the Church of England might have been if Newman had been able to read German'" (210); the comment does, however, point up Newman's self-imposed provincialism. After extensive effort to establish Newman's debt to German theories of development, Chadwick falls back on the claim that such ideas were simply "in the atmosphere which surrounded Newman at Littlemore. . . . [They were] part of the environment and helped to condition the expression and the vocabulary [of development], but no more" (*Bossuet* 119, 122).[7] We should, however, keep in mind Goethe's remark to Eckermann that Kant "has influenced even you, although you have never read him; now you need him no longer, for what he could give you, you possess already" (quoted in Weiskel 38).

To me, the best evidence for Newman's acquaintance with some Romantic theory comes from his benevolent response to Pusey's equally benevolent book of 1828 on German liberal theology.[8] The first volume ends with coherent and sympathetic summaries of Kant,[9] Fichte, and Schelling and includes a guarded appreciation of Schleiermacher. Newman, partly for friendship's sake, offers a remarkably perceptive defense of it to Harriett:

> It is a very valuable sketch, and will do good, but will be sadly misunderstood both from his difficulty of expressing himself, the largeness, profundity and novelty of his views, and the independence of his radicalism. It is *very* difficult even for his friends and the clearest heads to enter into his originality, fullformed accuracy, and unsystematic impartiality—I cannot express what I mean. He is like some definitely marked curve, meandering though all sorts and collections of opinion, boldly, yet (as it seems) irregularly. (*LD* 2: 74)[10]

More publicly, to Robert Wilberforce, he hides the intellectual nervousness evident here by sacrificing the book to the man: "[T]ell [Rickards] that, if ever he was a week with Pusey, he would be quite ashamed of the false judgment he has passed upon his mental condition from the phaenomena of his book" (*LD* 2: 97). To Froude, his praise is, rather characteristically, for those of Pusey's ideas which approximate his own.[11] And throughout the 1830s, his recorded response to German thought confines itself to a series of guilty, half-hearted promises to learn the language[12] and to the ebullient expectation that the Germans will be open-minded enough to learn from *him*: "The Edition of Dionysius, I am engaged in . . . may be of use elsewhere. In Germany they eagerly read every thing —the Germans are making their way to the light—One may suggest views" (*LD* 4: 274).

These examples of what Bremond calls Newman's lack of curiosity support Prickett's claim that Newman "had a tendency to avoid reading things that might weaken his faith" (*Romanticism* 156)—perhaps even the quip that his originality could be measured by the number of important books he had not read. Pusey's scattered remarks on Schleiermacher, whom he had met in person (Faber 135),[13] may help explain why Newman felt justified in not reading further. According to Pusey the German theologian, "whatever be the errors of his system, has done more than . . . any other, to the restoration of religious belief in Germany, . . . [The *Kurze Darstellung,*] with a few great defects, is full of important principles and comprehensive views, and which will form a new era in theology whenever the principles which it furnishes for the cultivation of the several theological sciences shall be acted upon"(1: 115n).[14] The Anglican Newman, however, measured the value of a position by an intuition of the ends to which he saw it taking him; to quote Robert Pattison: "Liberalism wants to discuss knowledge; Newman prefers to talk about dogma. Liberalism wants to discuss behavior; Newman prefers to talk about justification. The modern world wants to examine rationality; Newman would rather investigate Socinianism" (*Dissent* 54).

Within this paradigm, Schleiermacher, like other liberals, offered only a speedy and irreversible journey into infidelity. Newman gloats knowingly over the liberal Milman's distressed discovery that Schleiermacher is more dangerously liberal than he is. Then, having distanced his own distress, Newman is free to acknowledge the German's reputation:

> [T]he rationalizing principles which [Milman] has adopted do not necessarily secure even to this doctrine [of the immortality of the soul] a place in the idea of Christianity; and that, in the judgment, not of any mere paradoxical minds, but of one of the most profound thinkers, as fame goes, of his age. Mr. Milman writes: "The most remarkable evidence of the extent to which German speculation has *wandered away* from the first principles of Christianity, is this, that one of the most religious writers, the one who has endeavoured with the most earnest sincerity to reconnect religious belief with the philosophy of the times, *has actually represented Christianity without, or almost without, the immortality of the soul;* and this the ardent and eloquent translator of Plato! . . . *Schleiermacher is silent, or almost silent, on the redemption from death.*" (*Ess.* 2: 244; italics Newman's)

Newman's other reference is also drawn from a source in English,[15] but Thomas points out that "the document in Newman's hands was a weighty and detailed translation of, and commentary upon, Schleiermacher's treatise upon the Sabellian heresy. . . . When one turns to Newman's use of Schleiermacher's treatise, [however,] one is struck by the perfunctory quality of his remarks" (133–35). He focuses exclusively on Schleiermacher's rationalistic, anthropomorphizing use of economy: "The personality of the Godhead consists in these developments [interactions] made in time, and made to intelligent and rational beings. Strictly speaking, personality is not in [Schleiermacher's] view eternal." Newman concludes: "[I]t is believed that Protestant France, as well as Germany, could be made to afford similar evidence of the Sabellian tendencies of the day" (*Tracts* 3 [73]: 54–56). That similar evidence could be found much closer to home, however, is clear from an earlier letter to Hugh J. Rose: "[W]e cannot form an idea of Personality except as viewed in action, passion, relation etc—ideas inconsistent with the true notion of the Supreme Being" (*LD* 3: 78).[16] Such a confession raises at least the possibility that the other Romantics may also serve as stalking horses for ideas which Newman cannot admit to others, or even to himself.

Romantic and Sacramental Aesthetics

In light of his response to German thought—his tendency to reinterpret it within his own conceptual framework and to reject it in public for ideas which he acknowledged in private—we may suspect a similar duplicity in his reaction to Coleridge.[17] The evidence is equally sketchy but equally intriguing. Beer, for example, seizes on the circumstance that "In 1833, during his Mediterranean tour, he visited Coleridge's friend, John Hookham Frere" (198). Stephen Prickett postulates that "the story of Coleridge's secret heterodoxy was widely enough in circulation for Newman—who disclaimed any close connections with Coleridge—to have heard of it" (*Romanticism* 37). Prickett thus sees Coleridge's influence to be real but covert: Neither Keble, Maurice, or Newman "had direct access to Coleridge's papers or knew him personally; for two of the three [Newman included] his name was an object of the gravest suspicion." Yet in Coleridge's "notebooks is an idea of the Church, of Nature and Faith, and of the development of doctrine that was to foreshadow the[ir] debates and controversies" (68).

The most famous and most curious piece of direct evidence comes from a journal entry of 29 March 1835: "During this Spring, from Christmas down, Acland lending me some of Coleridge's works, I have *for the first time* read parts of them—and am surprised how much I thought mine is to be found there. I believe at Froude's in 1831 I carelessly looked into the Idea of Church and State—and had read two or three sentences in Jemima's [copy of] Aids to Reflection" (*LD* 5: 53; italics Newman's). In support of Newman's claim, his references to Coleridge after this point do become more numerous and more specific, but not any more complimentary. To Rickards Newman now writes that "With all his defects of doctrine, which are not unlike Knox's, he seems capable of rendering us important service. At present he is the oracle of young Cambridge men, and will prepare them (please God) for something higher" (*LD* 5: 27).

Bernard Reardon concludes that "after [Coleridge,] it was impossible to omit the subjective consciousness from any serious discussion of the basic issues of religious belief" (*Coleridge* 72). I would suggest, however, that one measure of Newman's greatness is the near success of his effort to do just that. If Newman's dispute with Schleiermacher boiled down to one between a liberal and a doctrinal theology, his dispute with Coleridge boils down to one between a theology which fused religion and subjective aesthetics and one which strove, however unsuccessfully, to keep them separate.[18] Coleridge's proposed fusion is encapsulated in a quotation offered by Engell: "[I]n the Scriptures God *has* descended to a middle ground. Here the Logos, or 'communicative intellect,' of God employs a poetically imaginative language that expresses the effects of God. From these effects it is possible to infer his presence and affirm our intuition of him. . . . Religion becomes the poetry of mankind" (363–64).[19] Prickett, for one, includes Newman in the list of those who responded to this "poetry": "The influence of Wordsworth and Coleridge on their successors is neither simply theological, nor simply aesthetic, but in their sense of the word, 'poetic'—in other words, an indivisible union of the two. . . . [M]odern theologians often seem curiously unaware of the literary premises from which such men as Hare, Maurice, Keble, and Newman begin. . . . [They all] use a language about the Church that . . . draws its imagery . . . from *aesthetic* criticism" (*Romanticism* 6–7, 37).[20] In one particularly ebullient passage, moreover, Newman himself acknowledges the feasibility of some distinctly modern, distinctly literary forms of religious expression: "[T]he taste for poetry of a religious kind has in modern times in a certain sense taken the place of the deep contemplative spirit of the early church . . . as if our character required such an element to counterbalance the firmer and more dominant properties in it. . . . Poetry then is our mysticism, and so far as any two characters of mind tend to penetrate below the surface of things, . . . so far they may certainly be said to answer the same end, and that too a religious one" (*Ess.* 1: 290–91). This passage, however, comes from his most politically inclusive essay, the one Newman quotes at length in the *Apologia* as "the last words which I ever spoke as an Anglican to Anglicans" (92); it is the same essay in which he tries to enlist the Coleridgeans. But, as McGann points out, Newman must first warn them that their leader has "indulged a liberty of speculation, which no Christian can tolerate, and advocated conclusions which were often heathen rather than Christian" (94).

Prickett offers yet another avenue for Coleridge's influence in the theory and poetry of John Keble; he makes a strong case for Keble's aesthetics from the *Christian Year,* from the Oxford Lectures on Poetry, and from the sacramental vision of nature within Tract 89.[21] Goodwin (483) supports this reading of Keble with a quotation from near the end of the tract: "Poetry traced up as high as we can go, may almost seem to be God's gift from the beginning, . . . the very fact is unquestionable, that it was the ordained vehicle of revelation, until God himself was made manifest in the flesh. And since the characteristic tendency of poetical minds is to make the world of sense, from the beginning to end, symbolical of the absent and unseen, any instance of divine favour shown to Poetry . . . would seem . . . to warrant that tendency" (5: 185–86).[22] That Newman was influenced by Keble's theories is now almost universally acknowledged. Tennyson points out that Keble's vision of poetry as emotional release in essays of 1814 and 1824 anticipated the anti-Aristotelian focus of Newman's 1829 essay (*Victorian* 24–37). There, poetry "provides a solace for the mind broken by the disappointments and sufferings of actual life" (*Ess.* 1: 10). And, later in the same essay: "Poetical eloquence consists, first, in the power of illustration; which the poet uses . . . almost by constraint, as the sole outlet and expression of intense inward feeling" (24).

Keble's use of repression has even been interpreted as proto-Freudian by Abrams in his *Mirror and the Lamp* (147–48), but Tennyson argues persuasively that Keble was talking less about psychological neuroses than about reserve, the inability of the believing mind to capture or express fully its intuitions of a transcendent reality (*Victorian* 59–62). Tennyson finds no proto-Arnoldian tendency "in favor of poetry as an autonomous form or at the expense of religion. The danger in Tractarian poetics was that of religion replacing poetry" (70). As was noted in chapter 3, Goodwin pointed out that Keble's reverence for the ancients in general and for Scripture in particular was so strong that he denied any claims to even imaginative inspiration in modern poetry and reduced the moderns themselves to a "secondary," caretaker, position. Newman, in other words, could buy into Keble without buying into the more radical conflation of secular and sacred inspiration in Keble's master, Coleridge. Newman saw, I think, that the Coleridgeans had bound religion, not just to aesthetics, but to a specifically *modern* post-Enlightenment aesthetics.[23] In 1838 he explodes to Rogers, "What a set they are! They cannot make religion a reality; nothing more than a literature" (*LD* 6: 365).[24]

This critique anticipates in militant terms the thesis of Abrams's *Natural Supernaturalism*—that Romanticism consciously attempted to modernize, and hence secularize, the spiritual values it found tied to what it saw as an outmoded theological system: "[This] working-out of an implicit design in systematic thought, in nature, and in the history of human actions and consciousness is very like the theological concept of the universal but hidden working of divine Providence, transferred . . . to the immanent operation (in Hegel's repeated phrase) of 'the cunning of Reason.' And we find, in fact, that these philosophical systems are, as Novalis said of Fichte's philosophy, 'perhaps nothing else than applied Christianity'" (178). Pusey found religious values even within secular philosophy; he praises the Kantian categorical imperative for indirectly forcing people to acknowledge the impossibility of true moral altruism (1: 164–65), and he claims later that the various branches of German Idealism have demolished the covert premises of "rationalism" (1: 171–72). Newman, however, must refuse the aid of either literature or philosophy if it comes at the price of accepting a modern, subject-centered universe.

Grounding the Romantic Subject

As we suggested in the last chapter, however, Newman's visions, in their subjectively grounded claims to transcend subjectivity, presuppose exactly such a universe. In fact, Newman's own self-description, immortalized within the "two luminous and self-evident beings" of the *Apologia*, actually parallels the quest for an adequate self-description which founds and guides the progress of German Idealism. The origins and nature of Romanticism have exercised critics ever since the early debate between Wellek and Lovejoy; more recent formulations have challenged the coherence of the Romantic position, its claims to be a position, the very notion of progression itself. Yet the Hegel scholar Charles Taylor still seems remarkably cogent in his account of Romantic theory as torn between the incompatible claims of subject and object. Taylor argues that even Descartes' radical suspicion of self and sensation grew from a covert refusal to participate in some prearranged ontological or cosmological pattern. When it objectified nature in the name of intellectual maturity and science, the Enlightenment was simultaneously facilitating another project, the generation of a free, uncontingent subject (6–10). This project, however, confronted the early German Romantics with two equally uncomfortable choices. One path to the uncontingent lay through Kantian moral freedom (29–36): to quote Pusey's summary: "[E]very rational being is conscious of this unconditional unlimited law, and then most strongly, when his inclinations are in contradiction to it" (1: 161). Yet here the subject defines itself against circumstance by acting on a basis which is only formally, logically consistent; here also the noumena, the reality "outside," remains unknowable. Following Isaiah Berlin, Taylor traces the alternative path to Herder (16–25). According to this expressive theory, the subject becomes truly human through an integrated combination of self-conscious introspection and outward self-projection against and into the other. This last move demands some affinity with the other, but every species of affinity raised new problems. Pusey described Fichte's dilemma:

> [I]nfinite thought, coming into existence in finite, places together with thought a something, by which thought may be confined. This is the material world, which appears as something external, so that with each self is necessarily united a not-self, a contrast to self. The life and activity of human thought consists then, in a continued endeavour to break through that by which it is confined, partly theoretically, by penetrating and thinking through the objects, and thus appropriating them to thought. (1: 167–68)

If this goal of full appropriation were reached, however, the self would lose its self-defining activity.

As this philosophical dilemma played itself out in Germany, the English Romantic poets pursued their individual agendas, on their own terms, with their own timetable. Their relation to German thought has been explored by Lovejoy and Wellek, codified by Abrams's *Natural Supernaturalism,* and deconstructed by the Yale school. Their agendas impact the Anglican Newman, but not because he was any more directly influenced by them than by the Germans. In his practice, however, he follows the poets by vesting his subjectivity in privileged moments of imaginative awareness. Newman's visions are indeed moments; as we encounter them in essays or, even more frequently, in sermons, we can feel the context building up to and then falling back from them. Despite the self-acknowledged occasional nature of Newman's writing, these moments usually come near the end of a volume, even if the volume is only a collection of separate pieces.[25] The moments are also privileged in that physical confines drop away and reveal some larger reality beneath or beyond them. Even though Newman may offer them as available to all believers, they remain, as we will see, the exclusive prerogative of the elect. In these respects they resemble the famous spots of time in the *Prelude,* Blake's re-envisioning of Miltonic prophecy, the Mariner's blessing of the water snakes, the fading coal of inspiration in Shelley's "Defense."

When I claim that Newman covertly participated in a subject-centered aesthetics, I may seem to follow postmodern critics in their claims for the subversive nature of Newman's figures. For T. R. Wright, "His suspicion of literature . . . makes him insist on its rigorous control. But the more he insists, the more his writing undoes him with a range of metaphors, similes and other rhetorical figures which elude such discipline. Newman, as Kingsley was to discover, always means more than he says, which is why he remains worth reading and why he is not quite as 'safe' a theologian as is sometimes thought" (182). Cunningham continues in a similar vein: "A wedge cannot with any certainty be driven between his fictions, and his sermons and other apparently non-fictional texts. Both sorts of text . . . continually raise problems as to the nature of story, metaphor, rhetoric" (233). Prickett even argues "that one can treat his images as one might the complex imagery of a Shakespearian play" (*Romanticism* 179); yet Newman's background in Patristic hermeneutics made him very wary of the temptations hidden within metaphorical language. A year before reading Coleridge, he complains to Keble that "Many men have no notion of any meaning of '*mystical*' but that of *figurative*—they have no notion of a *real* presence" (*LD* 4: 217).[26]

Newman used figures, but as Nicholas Lash suggests, he did not think through them or within them: "[E]ven for a thinker of Newman's delicacy and precision, the unit of meaning may be the paragraph or the page, rather than the individual term" (*Change* 84). As the exalted passages from chapter 2 suggest, Newman's real poetry was vision, a genre which does not rely on figure alone. It relies instead on a more pervasive interplay between figure, the supernatural scene being described, and the biblical source being evoked and imperceptibly extended. As Newman's visions embodied his most radical efforts to escape a Romantic subjectivity, they also embody his most radical participation in it. It is only when he trusts the apparent safety of these visions enough to explore their prerogatives that he inadvertently engages in Romantic self-instantiation.[27]

The Trial at Newman's Center

Grounding the self within such a spiritual universe occasions a quandary whose roots run deep into the Judeo-Christian tradition. Abrams, for example, notes "the emergence in Augustine, fully developed, of the distinctively Christian spiritual autobiography. Its moral psychology is very different from representative classical treatments of self-reliance, self-continuity, and the rational weighing of alternatives; it is, however, entirely consonant with the crises, cataclysms, and right-angled changes of the Christian pattern of history" (*Natural* 48). A recent paradigm, however —one formulated by Sacvan Bercovitch and extended by Avrom Fleishman —claims that traditional Christian authors responded to these biographical crises differently than their Romantic descendants. According to the paradigm, such crises culminated in what Augustine himself calls the "trial of the center," in which the subject's encounter with some larger reality confronts it with a choice. Within a Protestant spiritual autobiography, one modelled on Augustine's, the subject surrenders its individuality to gain a closer union with God. In Romantic narratives, on the other hand, the individual spirit rejects such self-transcendence in order to exalt itself in "an all-but-identification [with] deity" (Fleishman 105). The latter response is neatly exemplified in Abrams's portrait of Rousseau, whose heart Newman himself saw as "naturally religious."[28] In this infidel, what had been divine illumination "becomes self-effecting, self-warranting, self-sufficient, and manifests timelessness as a quality of the experiential moment. In certain states of mind during his reveries on the Ile de Saint Pierre, Rousseau tells us, he discovered 'the supreme felicity' in which 'time means nothing' and 'the present lasts forever, yet without indicating its duration and without any trace of successiveness'; and 'so long as this state endures one is sufficient unto himself, like God'" (386).

Newman's practice, at least in the pulpit, would seem a deliberate rejection of such Romantic self-exaltation in favor of an orthodox self-transcendence.[29] As Father Lockhart described his preaching:

> Many men were impressive readers, but they did not reach the soul. They played on the senses and imagination, they were good actors, they did not forget themselves, and one did not forget them. But Newman had the power of so impressing the soul as to efface himself; you thought only of the majestic soul that saw God. It was God speaking to you as He speaks through creation; but in a deeper way by the articulate voice of man made to the image of God and raised to His likeness by grace . . . , a transcript of the work and private thoughts which were in God. (*KC* 391)[30]

Yet Newman himself acknowledged, though he did not accept, Thomas Arnold's allegations "of [my] identifying high excellence with certain peculiarities of my own—i.e. preaching myself" (*AW* 125). The Modernist priest George Tyrrell, in his Introduction to Bremond, agrees with Arnold that Newman's response to Augustine's trial was itself conflicted: "[T]he absorption of God into Self . . . more commonly threatens [one's psychological balance] with destruction; and the personality of a man like Newman is created and developed by the struggle to maintain each member of this unstable system in its due place and relation, and to intensify the spiritual self by subjecting all the forces of conquered egotism to its service" (xiii). While Newman's will pushes him toward orthodox self-transcendence, Tyrrell sees his darker emotions as waiting their chance to erupt in Romantic self-assertion: "It is therefore . . . in moments when distraction, sickness, weariness, or age have relaxed the habitual vigilance and effort of his free and self-determined states [that we see] the nature and measure of those lawless forces escaped momentarily from the control of that will" (xiii).[31] Newman's engagement with his conscience we will treat in chapter 7; his inferences from liminal states we will treat in chapter 10. Here I would suggest only that Newman's conscience may not always protect his orthodoxy, nor his liminal states always threaten it. As befits an implicit Romantic, Newman's "trial," his moral, imaginative, doctrinal encounter between self and God, expands to encompass the larger epistemological encounter between subject and object. Within these visionary moments, I would argue, Newman could envision self and God as engaged in a dialectical process of mutual and ongoing redefinition. And within this new paradigm, in turn, self-transcendence and self-assertion coalesce into two perspectives on the same gesture.

For his part, Newman continually appeals to his conscience to witness that he has sacrificed self to God in all his trials: Like the true Christian, he

> alone admits Christ into the shrine of his heart; whereas others wish in some way or other, to be to themselves, to have a home, a chamber, a tribunal, a throne, a self where God is not,—a home within them which is not a temple, a chamber which is not a confessional, a tribunal without a judge, a throne without a king;—that self may be king and judge; and that the Creator may rather be dealt with and approached as though a second party, instead of His being that true and better self, of which self itself should be but an instrument and minister. (*PS* 5 [16]: 226)

Yet as we will see in chapter 6—and as he hints in the shifty, self-conscious repetition of "self" within this last claim of selflessness—perfect submission comes to offer perfect freedom. Through this strategy Newman can assume what Capps describes as the God-role ("Sunden's" 60), but in a more radical sense than Capps admits. Once the self achieves union with God, God has simultaneously achieved union with self: "[T]he Christian has a deep, silent, hidden peace, which the world sees not,—like some well in a retired and shady place, difficult of access. . . . What he is when left to himself and to his God, that is his true life. . . . He can bear, he finds it pleasant, to be with himself at all times,—'never less alone than when alone.' He can lay his head on his pillow at night, and own in God's sight, with overflowing heart, that he wants nothing,—that he 'is full and abounds'" (*PS* 5 [5]: 69-70). That the Christian here is Newman we can surmise from his translation of Copleston's early compliment to him: "Numquam minus solus, quam cum solus" (*Apo. 27*), but the precise parameters of this relationship he refuses to question: They "are 'secret things with the Lord our God,' things not lightly to be spoken of, not dreams of our own, which, as not existing, have no answer, but such as have an answer one way or the other, though we do not know which way, and it is presumptuous to inquire" (*PO* 137).[32] As we will see, however, Newman comes to suggest that within this relationship all conventional boundaries—contingent and unconditional, active and passive, physical and spiritual—virtually dissolve.

Resilient Romanticism

Within the fluid interactions of this dialogue, Newman's revised Romanticism implicitly escapes many subsequent critiques of early Romantic claims for imaginative autonomy. From Schelling onward, according to Thomas McFarland, Idealism increasingly surrendered the "Ich bin," from which Kant started, to the "Es ist" of a cosmology which grounded the subject at the cost of its subjectivity. In Pusey's enthusiastic summary of Schelling, for example,

> the spirit only becomes conscious of itself, in that it thinks matter through and appropriates it; so that the whole employment of speculation upon external things is only a self-affirmation. God accordingly cannot be considered as a mere unity, but can only be conceived as a living God, in that he has a contrast in himself, the removal of which is his life. The unity of God has consequently continually revealed itself in plurality, spirit in matter, that the plurality may extricate itself into unity, matter be exalted to spirit, and be freed. (1: 168–69)

Here the subject's self-realization through art mirrors and participates in God's self-realization through an ongoing creation. Pusey's summary, however, besides blurring successive stages of Schelling's thought, may even appropriate a philosopher pointedly absent from his book, Friedrich Hegel.

The ghost of Hegel, in turn, raises the even more disquieting prospect that Newman himself, along with the rest of his age, may be acting out a paradigm whose scope and dimensions remain hidden from him.[33] For Hegel, Newman's participation within his visions would have been always already subsumed within a dialectic of radical immanence. There, subjectivity—the self knowing the self—is the definitive action of Spirit, while existence—the self knowing the other—is the self-realization of Spirit. Yet as Hegel himself acknowledged, such an *Aufhebung* need not presuppose any form of co-optation: "Enlightenment that wants to teach faith the new wisdom does not tell it anything new" (cited in Cascardi 67). Coulson, as we saw in the Introduction, finds Newman himself advocating an implicitly dialectical approach to religious paradoxes, urging us to put "ourselves on the guard as to our proceeding, and protest against it, while we do it. We can only set right one error of expression by another. By this method of antagonism we steady our minds . . . by saying and unsaying to a positive result" (64).[34] I would suggest, however, that if we extend this principle from self-regulation to self-realization, we will see that Newman's version of dialectic differs markedly from the totalizing, teleological construct wherein *Geist* realizes itself in history. Just as his cosmology retains a pre-Enlightenment thickness that animates abstractions, so the figures in his Romantic interaction with God bring with them a comparable aura of personality and power. Here, neither the end nor the mechanism is fully specified. Newman's spirit may assume moments of transcendence, God may become manifest in moments of immanence, but neither is fully subsumed within the other; the resolution of Augustine's trial remains always in doubt.

This same fluidity also shields Newman from the far more reductive critique of Hegel's rebellious pupil Ludwig Feuerbach: "Instead of saying that man knows himself in God, [Hegel] says that God knows himself in man" (quoted in Kamenka 36).[35] For this reductive definition of religion as projection, "In every wish we find concealed a god; but in or behind every god there lies nothing but a wish" (43). Within this paradigm, Newman would be seen as positing his God as a collection of desires, fears, and ideals, displaced from their human source and writ large across the universe. The interrelation of self and God Newman would describe as a process of discovery and being discovered, the Romantics as a process of creating and being created, Hegel as one of subsuming and being subsumed; now Feuerbach redescribes it as one of projecting and being projected. If none of these paradigms fully encompasses the relation, it is because at one time or another each party incorporates all of these apparently incompatible interactions.

Newman's God in particular does not submit willingly to Feuerbach's reductive demystification. Newman takes great care to stay within the strictest confines of Judeo-Christian history and theology; yet with his intimate knowledge of that tradition and his unusual selection of materials from it, he thwarts conventional expectations that his God will resemble that of his contemporaries, or even of his mentors. Though we described this God in chapter 1 as Negation, he allows Newman to escape the phenomenal world, not by obviating it, but by subsuming within himself much of the unaccountable contingency Newman found so threatening:

> Should any one attempt here to . . . refer in turn Divine Justice, as seen in the world, to Divine Benevolence . . . let him ask himself, merely as a philosopher, whether there is no difference between re-ferring phenomena to an hypothetical law or system for convenience sake . . . and on the other hand undertaking to assign and fix . . . the acts of a Mind, unknown and infinite, and that, from a knowl-edge of merely one or two characteristics of His mode of acting. . . . [W]e are utterly incapable of conceiving, why a Being supremely blessed in Himself from eternity should ever commence the work of creation. (*US* [6]: 109–10)[36]

Newman even recoils from the prospect of having children because, with-out infant baptism, "no one of any seriousness could bear the thought of adding to this world's 'children of wrath,' except an express divine com-mand obliged him to do so. . . . [W]hat is any sin, say blasphemy, mur-der, . . . to the giving being to a soul intelligent, individual, accountable, . . . immortal, and in due season manifesting a will incurably corrupt, and a heart at enmity with God" (*PS* 3 [20]: 289–90). Here he goes well beyond Bacon's fear of giving hostages to Fortune; he fears instead giv-ing hostages to a Being likely to reject them and just as likely to hold Newman personally responsible for this rejection.

The ferocity of Newman's God has been acknowledged from his time to ours. Alexander Whyte's criticism is among the most outspoken: "New-man's St. Mary's sermons . . . [w]ith all their genius . . . , are not properly speaking New Testament preaching at all. . . . Moses was never dressed up in such ornaments before. . . . [But] he still carries his whip of scorpions hidden away among his beautiful garments. Do and live! Disobey and die!" (90, 97–98). As early as 1835 James Stephen (over-secretary of the Colonial Office and father of Leslie Stephen) complained of these same sermons: "What a Pity that a man of so vigorous an under-standing . . . should contrive to invest Christianity with an aspect so harsh and repulsive" (*LD* 5: 21). Using Samuel Wilberforce as an inter-mediary, Newman replied: "[Y]ou may say that the *impression of the whole* [second] volume is not quickening and encouraging—that it on the whole induces fear, and depression. *I grant it.* It was meant to do so. *We require the 'Law's stern* fires.' We need a continual Ash-wednesday" (*LD* 5: 39–40; italics Newman's).[37] Hence in a parochial sermon Newman broods that at the funeral of a reprobate, friends and relatives too "confidently talk of his being at peace, of his pains being at an end, of his happy release. . . . [W]hereas their duty lies in keeping silence, waiting in trembling hope, and being resigned" (*PS* 4 [6]: 90). His sixth university sermon presents child sacrifice as "man's instinctive judgment upon his own guilt" (116):

> Surely, to be in gloom—to view ourselves with horror,— . . . to wait in miserable suspense, naked and shivering, among the trees of the garden, for the hour of His coming, and meanwhile to fancy sounds of woe in every wind stirring the leaves about us,—in a word, to be superstitious,—is nature's best offering, her most acceptable service, her most mature and enlarged wisdom, in the presence of a holy and offended God. They who are not superstitious without the Gospel, will not be religious with it. (117-18)

As the sternness of Newman's religion keeps him from using it for his own purposes, the sternness of his God keeps him from being vulnerable to at least part of Feuerbach's critique. As Eugene Kamenka summarizes him, Feuerbach claims that because any possible god would remain irrelevant to the human condition, we desire an impossible fusion of the immanent and the transcendent (47, 57). In a letter cited above, Newman shows himself well aware of the philosophical difficulties of such a fusion:

> [W]e cannot form an idea of Personality except as viewed in action, passion, relation etc—ideas inconsistent with the true notion of the Supreme Being—An infinite immutable Mind cannot be realized as a Person—My conclusion is, that it is as difficult to conceive God one Person as Three, the difficulty being deeper than people suppose. The personality of God, in our *notion* of personality, is a *mystery*. . . . His being angry, repenting—or resting—etc. etc.—for these, and such like, *make up* the idea of a Personal God, as distinct from a mere System or Anima Mundi. (*LD* 3: 78)[38]

Newman even anticipates later criticisms of Feuerbach for failing to establish a definitively human perspective, of which the divine would be only the projection. The first university sermon treats any such perspective as merely parochial: "The philosopher has only to confess that he is liable to be deceived by false appearances and reasonings, to be biassed by prejudice, and led astray by a warm fancy; he is humble because sensible he is ignorant, cautious because he knows himself to be fallible, docile because he really desires to learn. But Christianity, in addition to this confession, requires him to acknowledge himself to be a rebel in the sight of God" (*US* [1]: 12–13).[39]

The Viability of the Subject

The paradigm we have been tracing provides an equally cogent defense against still later efforts to formulate the human party in this interchange. Earlier critics celebrated Wordsworth's claims for the unaided power of his imagination as a heroic stand against empiricism. In an interesting analogue to this argument, Marshall sees Wordsworth as exploring what Kant described as unknown and unknowable territory beyond the phenomenal world.[40] Robert Langbaum insists that such claims for the Romantic subject remain viable: "[T]he romanticists were the first literary generation to regard the self as problematical. They asserted the self so extravagantly in order to answer an attack on the self . . . by Locke and the even more radical attack by Hume.[41] . . . The romantic self can withstand de Man's criticism, because it was originally asserted against such attacks" (*Word* 22, 30). For Rajan, however, "What is striking about English theory is an insecurity in its logocentric rhetoric which makes it the prelude to rather than the antithesis of its German contemporary. . . . It is thus to German theory that one turns for a vocabulary which can name the specters that haunt an ideal art" (27, 29). And later: "What German theory progressively brings out . . . is a naivete in the poetics of hope of which the Romantics are always half conscious" (53). Specifically, she finds as early as Schopenhauer a reduction of the subject, not within the more inclusive subjectivity of *Geist,* but within a reductively mechanistic psychology: "Schopenhauer robs the ideal of its legitimacy as a metaphysically independent category, by exposing its psychological substructure. Idealism becomes genetically linked to anxiety, as the conscious mind's way of covering up a latent awareness of anxiety" (36). Whether or not this proto-Freudian invocation is historically viable, it does signal the advent of what Ricoeur calls the hermeneutics of suspicion, the series of efforts to enclose the Romantic subject within the paradigms of language, psychology, sociology, or ideology.[42]

The remainder of this book will evaluate Newman's quasi-Romantic paradigm against those of his predecessors and against the subsequent attacks made upon them.[43] Chapter 5 will show him reappropriating his own childhood and then testing this newly won identity against the disturbing sights, people, and institutions encountered on his grand tour of 1832–33. Chapter 6 will explore his changing sense of himself as elect and elected during his theological transition from Calvinism to Catholicism; chapter 7, the power won from his rigorous conscience to translate subjective encounter into self-defining action; chapter 8, the viability of his acute self-consciousness as implicit self-criticism; chapter 9, the transformation of his reactionary politics into a trenchant probe of Victorian ideological horizons. At this point, however, chapter 10 will explore some progressive incursions upon his tidy dyadic relationship with his God: troubling visions of natural fecundity, ghostly intrusions, Patristic miracle stories, and intimations of pantheistic immanence. Finally, chapter 11 will explore the subsequent revision of his image of God and his search for an institution capable of encompassing its theological consequences.

Very conveniently, most of these successive stages offer us new perspectives on the Romantic movement: the reappropriation of his past revises that of Wordsworth, the vistas on his trip call forth variants on the Romantic sublime, his sense of election parallels the vatic stances taken by secular contemporaries, the militancy sanctioned by his conscience extends that of Carlyle, his self-consciousness anticipates postmodern invocations of critique, his social criticism toys with Marxist appeals to fetishism and ideology. Finally, the incursions which trouble Newman's theocentric Romanticism awake equally troubling intimations of Romantic irony. So described, Newman's quasi-Romantic paradigm succeeds in critiquing the more self-mystifying claims of Romanticism; as we have seen, however, current theories of Romanticism can just as easily be used to critique Newman's paradigm. Since the Romantics themselves were trying to escape what they saw as the shackles of theology, their more radical successors would doubtless reduce Newman's dialogue to an internal conflict within a psyche, or a text, or an ideology. We will return to these critiques at appropriate points in our argument. For now, we will bracket them until we see whether the two different voices within Newman can remain credible as different and as voices.

CHAPTER 5

The Self in Dialogue

❖

AS BREMOND SUMS IT UP: "All the history of Newman, emotional, intellectual, and literary, is in fact, nothing else than the history of his personal relations with God" (16). But these relations, while they define him, allow him to escape from a far more reductive definition suggested by the moral determinism which he saw operating from earliest childhood. In dramatizing these "personal relations with God," the Anglican Newman revisits his own childhood, reinterprets the progression he finds there, and then reappropriates this progression to reshape his own adult identity. As he probes the Romantic implications of childhood, he also toys with Wordsworth's innovative vehicle for recapturing it, the epiphany.[1] While nervous about the self-indulgence in such recuperations, Newman is far more open to exploring the minute particulars of a more recent encounter. On the grand tour he took in 1832 with the Froudes, he exposed his still tentative sense of self to the disconcerting vistas of Orthodox Greece, Catholic Italy, and pagan classical history. In the process, he encountered first what seemed like a window onto the Golden Age in Sicily and then what seemed like a direct visitation from God in the near-fatal fever he contracted there. As this agon of self and God played itself out upon a wider and distinctly foreign stage, Newman's newly-won powers of growth and reappropriation transformed both protagonists.

Escape from Circumstance

While the adolescent Newman describes his conversion as a turning toward God and away from his childish, self-centered obliviousness, his transparently autobiographical reflections on childhood continue to picture it as God-shaped, even God-driven, from infancy. As he matures, these demands grow more insistent and peremptory; yet, just as the self-submission within Augustine's "trial" flowed into self-assertion, so here

[99]

God's demands actually free Newman from the suspicion that a web of circumstance shapes character virtually from birth. Otherwise, early cultural forces can determine, not just a child's adult character, but the fate of its immortal soul:

> Ignorant as we may be when children begin to be responsible beings, yet we are ignorant also when they are not so. . . . We know that two lines starting at a small angle, diverge to greater and greater distances, the further they are produced. . . . A very slight deviation at setting out may be the measure of the difference between tending to hell and tending to heaven. . . . [C]hildren's minds are impressible in a very singular way, such as is not common afterwards. The passing occurrences which meet them . . . rest upon their imagination, as if they had duration; and days or hours, having to them the semblance, may do the work of years. . . . [H]ow miserable is it to reflect . . . that children are commonly treated as if they were not responsible. . . . Things are done or said before them, which they understand and catch up, when others least think it, and store in their minds, or act upon; and thus the indelible hues of sin and error are imprinted on their souls, and become as really part of their nature as that original sin in which they were born. (*PS* 4 [3]: 39–41)²

Early sanctity can produce the fullest embodiment of Newman's religious ideal, the Teacher of Truth: He is one who "never transgressed his sense of duty, but from his earliest childhood upwards has been only engaged in increasing and perfecting the light originally given him. In him the knowledge and power of acting rightly have kept pace with the enlargement of his duties, and his inward convictions of Truth with the successive temptations opening upon him from without to wander from it" (*US* [5]: 80). But Newman broods over the fate of children less spiritually advantaged: "Alas! there are persons . . . whose consciences have been so early trained into forgetfulness of religious duties, that they can hardly, or cannot at all, recollect the time . . . when they acted with the secret feeling that God saw them, saw all they did and thought" (*PS* 7 [4]: 46).³ In an early university sermon, the flexibility of the juvenile twig and the rigidity of the mature trunk betoken a sociological determinism so stifling "that nothing but the knowledge of the Gospel announcements, and above all of the gracious words and deeds of our Redeemer, is equal to the burden of it" (*US* [3]: 53).⁴

To counter this determinism, he attempts to baptize a blatantly Wordsworthian vision in which children are open to spiritual influence and hence shaped all unconscious for God's service: "[C]hildren are baptized before they know what is to happen to them. They sport and play as if there was no sorrow in the world, and no high destinies upon themselves; they are heirs of the kingdom without knowing it; but God is with those whom He has chosen, and in His own time and way He fashions His Saints for His everlasting kingdom: in His own perfect and adorable counsels He brings them forward to fight with Goliath" (*PS* 8 [4]: 58).[5] Only in this last phrase are we jarred from the natural piety of "It Is a Beauteous Evening" and pointed toward militant religious conflict.[6] As the child's "intimations" grow more openly Wordsworthian, they are more peremptorily redirected: "The simplicity of a child's ways and notions, his ready belief of everything he is told, his artless love, his frank confidence, his confession of helplessness, his ignorance of evil, his inability to conceal his thoughts, his contentment, . . . are all evidence of his being lately (as it were) a visitant in a higher state of things" (*PS* 2 [6]: 65). But such Wordsworthian "clouds of glory" do not here invite Romantic retrospection; they are rather "a blessed *intimation,* given for our comfort, of what God will make us, if we surrender our hearts to the guidance of His Holy Spirit,—a prophecy of good to come,—a foretaste of what will be fulfilled in Heaven."[7]

For David Simpson, Romanticism "makes [the child] an 'ironist,' a persona whose exact status in himself is indeterminable, and therefore unassailable, and whose function consists in this negativity, the emptiness, the disruption of institutions and personalities outside himself through being perceived by them as their 'other'" (33). But as Newman strives to make religious obedience the vehicle for the child's progressive transcendence of family, friends, and society, he shifts this ironic stage from childhood to adolescence. Early unselfconsciousness now appears less a blessing than a spiritual void, from which only suffering can awaken us into the self-awareness necessary for religious experience:

[A] frame entirely without painful sensations is (as it were) one whole without parts, and prefigures that future spiritual body which shall be the portion of the Saints. And to this we most approximate in our youth, when we are not sensible that we are compacted of gross terrestrial matter, as advancing years convince us. The young reflect but little upon themselves, they gaze around them, and live out of doors, and say they have souls, little understanding their words. "They rejoice in their youth." This then, is the effect of suffering, that it arrests us; that it, as it were, puts a finger upon us to ascertain for us our own individuality. (*PS* 3 [11]: 147)

Adolescence, by contrast, awakens ideals, longings, and dissatisfaction with the narrow, self-seeking materialism of adult life. While never counseling disobedience to parents or authority figures, Newman suggests that holy men "have kept up the feeling which young people often have, who at first ridicule the artificial forms and usages of society, and find it difficult to conform themselves to its pomp and pretence" (*PS* 4 [10]: 166).

This alienation forms an analogue to Augustinian restlessness:

> Youth, especially, has a natural love of what is noble and heroic. We like to hear marvellous tales, which throw us out of things as they are, and introduce us to things that are not. We so love the idea of the invisible that we even build fabrics in the air for ourselves, if heavenly truth be not vouchsafed us. We love to fancy ourselves involved in circumstances of danger or trial, and acquitting ourselves well under them. Or we imagine some perfection, such as earth has not, which we follow, and render it our homage and our heart. . . . While [youths'] hearts are thus unsettled, Christ comes to them. . . . He does not wait till they have learned to ridicule high feelings as mere romantic dreams. (*PS* 6 [22]: 317–18)[8]

Newman's own adolescent fondness for the safely conservative Romanticism of Scott, so evident here, has been long acknowledged. More recently, however, Marilyn Butler has suggested a more radical political agenda in one of Newman's other, altogether less likely, favorite books. According to Father Ryder, Southey's long quest romance, *Thalaba,* "was particularly attractive to Cardinal Newman as the picture of a life-long vocation[,] with its . . . tremendous catastrophe in which the hero dying achieves his victory, without earthly recompense. It was his picture of what . . . his share in the Movement would have been" (quoted in W. Ward 2: 354–55). If so, however, the Movement may have been less reactionary than usually assumed; Butler argues that within the poem, "Southey the Rousseauist and secularist sees culture as man-made, evolutionary, but also capable of being changed by human will: revolutionary change becomes possible, change itself desirable" ("Repossessing" 77).[9] Southey's "quest already has a goal alien to the transhistorical idealizations of [Romantic] critics" (Butler, "Plotting," 143). She even likens one episode to a yet more radical narrative where "populations are kept quiet by being told religious tales. . . . When the gullible masses cease to be gulled, they will overthrow their rulers" (147–47). Such militancy may seem worlds away from the transhistorical, indeed transcendent religious imperatives awakened in Newman's adolescent. As we saw in chapters 1 and 4, however, the very transcendence of Newman's God negates some of the same social forms which Southey's *Thalaba* is contesting.

Romantic Recapitulation

This same quest for transcendence leads Newman to redirect an other-wise Romantic longing to recuperate himself from his own past. Although homiletic decorum forces him to disguise the circumstances of these shaping encounters and their biographical relevance, evidence for both appears in the midst of this chapter's first extended quotation. There Newman illustrates the heavy moral consequences of seemingly trivial childhood events with a series of transparently personal recollec-tions: "Any one, on casting his thoughts back on his first years, may con-vince himself of this [influence]; the character, which his childhood bears in his memory as a whole, being traceable to a few external circum-stances, which lasted through a very small portion of it, a certain abode, or a visit to some particular place, or the presence of certain persons, or some one spring or summer" (*PS* 4 [3]: 40). Another sermon, illustrating Newman's habit of appreciating people only after they were lost to him, shows similarly Wordsworthian powers of recapitulation:[10]

> Let a person, who trusts he is on the whole serving God acceptably, look back upon his past life, and he will find how critical were mo-ments and acts, which at the time seemed the most indifferent: as for instance, the school he was sent to as a child, the occasion of his fall-ing in with those persons who have most benefitted him. . . . God's hand is ever over His own, and He leads them forward by a way they know not of. . . . Some relic or token of that early time, some spot, or some book, or a word, or a scent, or a sound, brings [such men] back in memory to the first years of their discipleship, and they then see, what they could not know at the time, that God's presence went up with them and gave them rest. (*PS* 4 [17]: 261–62)

In case the autobiographical references here were not already clear, New-man tells us in his *Memoir* that his father waited until the last moment be-fore deciding whether to tell the coachman to take his son to matriculate at Oxford or at Cambridge (*AW* 30). Befitting its gesture at a Words-worthian recollection in tranquility, the whole passage closes with an un-conscious parallel to the stolen boat passage in the *Prelude:*[11] "Great Saints, great events, great privileges, like the everlasting mountains, grow as we recede from them" (263).

As his argument unfolds, however, Newman works to distance his use of the past from Wordsworth's: Religious men only "think that they re-gret the past, when they are but longing after the future. It is not that they would be children again, but that they would be Angels and would see God" (262–63). Any openly Romantic recapitulation Newman sees as dangerously self-indulgent. When he invokes a return to childish wonder, an escape from "the film of familiarity and selfish solicitude," it is only as a God-inspired means of adult conversion: "[W]hen the mind is . . . thrown for a while out of its subjection to habit, as if into that original unformed state when it was more free to choose good and evil, then in like manner it takes impressions, . . . almost unconsciously, after the manner of childhood. This is one reason why a time of trial is often such a crisis in a man's spiritual history. It is a season when the iron is heated and malleable; one or two strokes serve to fashion it as a weapon of God or for Satan" (*PS* 4 [3]: 41–42). Such moments are far more directed than even the "Severer interventions, ministry / More palpable" (*Prelude* 1.355–56) through which Nature chastened the willful young Wordsworth. Where these interventions demanded a wise passiveness, Newman's demand militancy: "He again places you for an instant in that early, unformed state of nature when habit and character were not. He takes you out of yourselves, robbing sin for a season of its in-dwelling hold upon you. Let not these visitings pass away 'as the morning cloud and the early dew'" (*PS* 1 [9]: 122).

All these gestures at Wordsworthian recapitulation, in other words, may be no more than gestures—no more because the self to be rediscovered is always already known by God: "[W]e do not in any sufficient sense believe that [God] is . . . 'about *our* path, and about *our* bed, and spieth out all *our* ways.' . . . [Men] think of [God's presence] as of a flood pouring itself out all through the world. . . . And then, perhaps, . . . [s]ome especial Providence . . . brings it close home to them, in a way they never experienced before, that God sees them" (*PS* 3 [9]: 116, 118).[12] As Bremond puts it, "Newman's autocentricism is not like that of everybody else. . . . Newman is thus absorbed in contemplating the small events of his life only because the eternal Wisdom is itself absorbed in foreseeing them, in preparing them to make them serve for great designs" (298).[13]

Newman's Epiphanies

Yet when Newman finds himself effectively cut off from the Patristic structures which he claims to have recuperated, the "great designs" themselves grow increasingly problematic. God may be seeing him, but because he cannot see either God or his purposes, he is reduced to sifting through his own life for some implicit pattern, static or dynamic, which may have been surreptitiously imposed upon it: "[E]very religious man may be expected to have experienced more or less of wonderful providences, which he cannot speak about to others, but which make it certain to him that, in spite of his own unworthiness, God is with him" (SD [23]: 350–51). As we have already seen, therefore, Newman redescribes a receptivity to divine guidance as a quest for special providences.[14] In this same quest, I would venture, he was shaping a religious parallel to the Romantic epiphany.

In his recent *Poetics of Epiphany,* Ashton Nichols notes its connection with Wordsworthian recapitulation: "[E]piphany involves just such restorative acts of memory. Memory combines with a present perception to produce a heightened sense of the significance of a specific image" (25). While he traces the long Christian history of the term (13–20), however, he seeks to differentiate its modern use from traditional religious vision:

> [T]he epiphanies of the nineteenth century emphasize not the interpretation of the ultimate meaning of the event but the emotional importance attached to certain transformed perceptions. Instead of revealing moments of supernatural manifestation, the new epiphany discloses a state of mind. . . . [It] reveals not an otherworldly spirit but the imaginative essence of experience, an essence which does not demand any particular interpretation. . . . The visible reveals *something* invisible, but the status of the invisible component is left unstated. Its mystery becomes part of the value of the experience. For the Romantic, the imagination produces significance out of the mundane. (14, 16, 21)

Robert Langbaum offers a handy list of six characteristics for the modern epiphany: incongruity, (apparent) insignificance, psychological association, momentousness, suddenness, and fragmentation.[15] While Nichols and Langbaum make room for a modern religious epiphany in Hopkins and Eliot, some of these same qualities are provoked in Newman by the unpredictability of his God. Newman remains uncertain, not just when and how God will appear to him, but what that appearance will reveal about either one of them.

On the most trivial level, this uncertainty provoked behavior which eventually degenerated into crotchet. Among Newman's notoriously compulsive responses to his own writing, his hoarding of papers has been dismissed as anal,[16] his running commentary on these writings as egotistical, his penchant for self-presentation as narcissistic, his republishing of Anglican writings when a Catholic as covertly rebellious. According to the hostile Abbott, he "seldom received religious truth into his inmost being except through indirect avenues, momentary flashes, involuntary recollections, chance utterances of friends, suppressed panics of his own heart" (*Anglican* 1: 319). Even more sympathetic commentators have remarked on Newman's superstitious fascination with dates, anniversaries, and numbers. Svaglic finds this fascination justified in an 1822 sermon which recommended "that we should mark the days or seasons of mercy, and commemorate them in succeeding years by some act of charity"; yet he grants that the sermon only gave "sacred sanction for a congenial tendency" ("Oriel" 1014).[17] In perhaps the most balanced judgment, Brilioth describes this same tendency as "a feeling of unrest, an anxious striving after a maximum as the best possible guarantee for the election of its possessor" (*Anglican* 257).

In its opportunistic reliance on happy coincidence, however, this search for pattern resembles Wordsworth's openness to those spots of time,

> In which the heavy and the weary weight
> Of all this unintelligible world,
> Is lightened
> . . . .
> While with an eye made quiet by the power
> Of harmony, and the deep power of joy,
> We see into the life of things.
> ("Tintern Abbey" 39–41, 47–49)

To be sure, the pattern Newman is awaiting tells him less about his joyful participation within a harmonious, mutually creative universe than about his relation to an aggressively unpredictable God. Yet occasionally Newman's own sense of being lost wins him analogous, compensating moments of spiritual epiphany, moments in which he perceives himself as having been found: "A thick black veil is spread between this world and the next. . . . [B]ut every now and then marvellous disclosures are made to us of what is behind it. At times we seem to catch a glimpse of a Form which we shall hereafter see face to face. We approach, and in spite of the darkness, our hands, or our head, or our brow, or our lips become, as it were, sensible of the contact of something more than earthly" (*PS* 5 [1]: 10). The "Form" here, while recognizably divine, is otherwise not recognizable at all except as the locus of a darkened encounter in which specific sense impressions are transmuted into something beyond sense. In such encounters, most of Langbaum's characteristics for modern epiphany (incongruity, momentousness, suddenness, fragmentation) seem fully met.

Mediterranean Encounters

While we must reserve Newman's most troubling, problematic encounters with his God until chapters 10 and 11, we can turn now to those for which we have the best biographical evidence, those which occurred during his grand tour of the Mediterranean. From it we have not only the summary in the *Apologia,* but a long and remarkably intimate journal, "My Illness in Sicily" (*AW* 111–38). While Bremond claims that Newman's quest for signs ceased with his conversion,[18] for example, this much revised journal reveals that as late as 1874 he was still exploring the interplay of continuity and discontinuity, consciousness and delirium, during his Sicilian fever: "I wonder I have not mentioned how I simply lost my memory as to *how* I came to be ill and in bed—and how strangely by little and little first one fact came back to me, then another, till at length I realized my journey and my illness in continuity" (*AW* 138). We also have the fullest, frankest, most detailed, and I think most undervalued set of letters in his long career. Claiming them as a source for Newman's later novels, Alan Hill describes these "confessional letters" as "blend[ing] poetic self-searching and vivid documentary within a single journey of discovery through pagan and Christian landscapes" (22).

The trip is also important for its position at a biographical, spiritual, and emotional crossroads. Newman had just suffered his first political failure; after leading an effort to reemphasize the religious dimension of Oriel tuition, he was being deprived of any further students by Provost Hawkins. In partial recompense, he was favored with the uninterrupted company of his dearest friend, Hurrell Froude, but the very occasion of the trip—a friendlier winter climate for Froude's diseased lungs—gave Newman an all too accurate premonition that this cure would fail and that his loss would become total. Finally, he had just completed his *Arians,* his first and fullest exploration of Patristic spirituality, only to discover that the Protestant establishment, as we saw, shied away from its grandest claims. Now he was, as it were, testing these claims at their source; he was looking for direction, for vocation, for relationship, for some personal providence. The vast changes which the Mediterranean basin had undergone in the intervening sixteen hundred years challenged Newman's social and ecclesiastical preconceptions in ways we will investigate in chapters 9 and 11. Here I will focus on the challenges to his spiritual preconceptions embedded within the "pagan and Christian landscapes" he encountered.

Not surprisingly in a classical scholar, the ancient locales, historical and fictitious, call up the most disconcerting memories of his own past: "I gazed upon [Ithaca] by the quarter of an hour together, being quite satisfied with the sight of the rock. I thought of Ham and of all the various glimpses, which memory barely retains and which fly from me when I pursue them, of that earliest time of life when one seems almost to realize the remnant of a pre-existent state" (*LD* 3: 172). Here the dissolution of Odysseus' mother in the underworld (Bk. 11) itself dissolves into the Wordsworthian recapitulations cited above. In its use of Platonic transmigration in the service of imaginative creation, this effort to "realize . . . a pre-existent state" anticipates his effort to "realize a state of things long past away" (*Tracts* 5 [83]: 27) in returning the Anglican Church to its Patristic past. An equally Romantic metamorphosis underlies his remarkable claims five days later with Corfu: "I *am on the spot*. If Thucydides were to rise from the dead, he would *recognize* the spot. . . . [A]nd knowing his lines seeing the change, I am in his place, as it were, and see the vision for him. I am Thucydides with the gift of second sight" (*LD* 3: 177). Here the more subtle means by which writers displace their predecessors are abandoned in favor of a bold imaginative usurpation.

Confronting the Sublime

The more disturbing impressions forced on him by this landscape Merritt Lawlis associates with a Johnsonian fear of losing rational control (77–79), but Newman's inner conflict is being waged within more characteristically Romantic parameters. As his response to classical scenery invokes mythopoeia, that to the scenery around Naples wrestles with the Wordsworthian and/or Kantian sublime. Thomas Weiskel places the sublime where Abrams placed Romanticism itself at a point "pervaded by the nostalgia and the uncertainty of minds involuntarily secular. . . . The Romantic sublime was an attempt to revise the meaning of transcendence precisely when the traditional [spiritual] apparatus of sublimation . . . was failing to be exercised or understood" (Weiskel 3–4). This, I would suggest, is precisely the physical, historical, cultural point at which the culture-shocked Newman now stands. As Weiskel segments Kant's definition of the sublime into a sequential process, "the habitual relation of mind and object suddenly breaks down. Surprise or astonishment is the effective correlative. . . . Either mind or object is suddenly in excess. . . . [A] natural phenomenon catches us unprepared and unable to grasp its scale . . . [or] the object (often a memory) is . . . in danger of precipitant attenuation" (23–24). At this point, however, "the mind recovers the balance of outer and inner . . . [when that] very indeterminacy . . . is taken as symbolizing the mind's relation to a transcendent order" (24).

If Newman's account of his ascent up Vesuvius remains less fully developed than Wordsworth's account of Snowdon or Shelley's of Mont Blanc, it explores the same hiding places of sublimity:

When at the top we found an awful sight,—the vast expanse of the true crater, broken into many divisions and recesses, . . . and resplendent with all manner of the most beautiful colours from the sulphur,—clouds of which were steaming [out here] and there from holes in the crust. . . . [T]he imposing effect . . . became quite fearful, when, on putting the ear to a small crevice, [you] hear a rushing sound, deep and hollow, part of wind and part of the internal commotion of the [mountain]. (*LD* 3: 285)

So described, the scene hovers between the Kantian sublime and what Weiskel describes as a "visionary" variant, in which the transcendent order impresses its own animism upon the mind: "the visionary [claims] that the unconditioned can be (and must be) *seen,* realized through perception" (7).[19] As he searches for his own personal version of the "unconditioned," Newman would be happy to find in Vesuvius "types and symbols" of a Patristic spiritual realm, but here the traditional associations of depth, fire, and sulfur with hell overlie a more Romantic inversion of landscape. He is thus torn between the visionary expedient of troping his descent as Asia's quest for some "deep truth" from Demogorgon and the more Kantian alternative of affirming Demogorgon's reply that "the deep truth is imageless" (*Prometheus Unbound* 2.4.116).[20]

When his party reascends to the outer cone, Newman works to escape this Romantic dilemma, to reestablish a more traditional spiritual hierarchy by reassuming a more traditional vantage point: "The view is very striking. The vast plain of Naples, which is covered with innumerable vines, was so distant as to look like a greenish marsh—we could see Pompeii and its amphitheatre very distinctly at a little distance, and in the same direction various streams of lava (their age indicated by their successive <shades of> blackness)" (*LD* 3: 286). Here he becomes, not the prober of the depths nor even the mountain-top recipient of spiritual peace, but the witness and the surrogate agent of a far less comforting providence, the divine retribution poured out upon Pompeii. To Wood a month earlier he bragged that he had fully prepared himself to assume this role:

I had seen ruins enough already to bring before me past time—and all the curiosities of this very place, which are brought together in the Museum at Naples—And what past age did it carry one back to? one of the most profligate and abandoned in history. . . . There is scarce ground for doubting that the fire from Vesuvius was as strictly judicial as that which overwhelmed the cities of the plain. There is a room set apart in the Museum for odious Mosaics etc collected from Pompeii, which they say are atrocious beyond power of words to stigmatize. . . . A Christian can scarce have any feeling but one of a solemn yet remorseful triumph in seeing the dead carcass of human crime. . . . [T]he first thing one hears is that the city was surprised in the midst of revelry, the amphitheatre being crowded—and the bones of a lion were found in the den close to the arena. (*LD* 3: 253–54)[21]

Already, however, this same Naples museum has occasioned an emotional identification with the victims: "I have seen Herculaneum and Pompeii and the Museum at Naples thence enriched and find that the ancients used portable stoves and eat cake—and at Rome there is a mule's head in marble and a group of fighting dogs, as like present nature as one dog is like another" (*LD* 3: 241). And this empathy now prompts a moral iden-tification, moving in its acknowledgment of what it cost him to make it,[22] which tempers his original judgment:

Yet now, at the distance of three weeks from the time, queer relent-ings come across me, and I almost yearn in my mind over this guilty place, with which I would fain persuade myself I have no sympathy. Why this is, I leave to philosophers to say—here I will but suggest as a theory, that the human heart will in spite of itself claim kindred with every thing human—and in the blackest deformity pities its brethren—enters into their feelings and experiences what bad ten-dencies they have developed—and imagines their present fearful re-morse—according to the old saying, "Homo sum, humani nihil etc." (*LD* 3: 254)[23]

As he places himself with the rest of humanity, however, he simulta-neously reduces Providence to the role of inexorable, inexplicable fate. The otherwise tidy dualism of his parallel realms did admit of interme-diate beings, but these guided the fate of nations, preferably foreign na-tions,[24] not that of individuals who "used portable stoves and eat cake." The more he travels, the more he sees, the harder it becomes to place his God, to identify him with—or to exclude him from—particular times, peoples, institutions; the harder also it becomes to know where to place oneself in relation to him. He had just written George Ryder: "I look upon it as one good of travelling, (the same in mind as that of *reading*) that it takes one out of oneself, and reduces in one's eyes both the impor-tance of one's own particular station and of one's own decisions in acting in it" (*LD* 3: 249). Fully as all his experiences have fulfilled this mission, none of them matches those which he encountered on Sicily.

Sicily

Newman's sense of historical, cultural, theological displacement is epitomized in his first sight of the Doric temple at Segesta. This displacement did not enable him to anticipate his astonishment, but it did enable him to experience it:

> [O]n this circular hill was nothing but a single temple.—Such was the genius of early Greek worship, grand in the midst of error; simple and unadorned in its architecture, it chose some elevated spot, and fixed its faith as a solitary witness on heights where it could not be hid. No words can describe the piercing effect of the sight of this temple. It is (I believe) the most perfect remaining—very plain—Doric—six gigantic pillars before and behind—twelve in length—no roof.—Its history is unknown—the temples of classical time, which came after it, have vanished—the whole place is a ruin—this alone remains in a waste solitude—A shepherd's hut is near, surrounded with the mud which accompanies a farmyard—a number of eager dogs—a few rude intrusive men, who would have robbed us, I fancy, had they dared—on the hill of the theatre (which we thought might be the Roman town) a savage looking bull prowling amid the ruins; mountains around us—and Eryx in the distance. The past and the present! I began to understand what Scripture means by speaking so much of cities set upon hills—what a noble but ungodly sight it must have been, like Satan himself, the mockery and imitation of true greatness, when this place was in its glory. (*LD* 3: 219-20)

Geoffrey Faber offers a dramatic recreation of the scene (290-94),[25] but O'Faolain's analysis of it seems the more perceptive: "Every man has his symbol. We must feel that this solitary temple was in some way the image of the heart's desire—a vessel of ancient piety, a tomb of human ambition, a place of worship in retirement from the world, the evocation of a nobility of soul that, though pagan, was not faithless, a form of classic grace. At Segesta all that was thoughtful, devoted and sensuous in John's being faced him as in a shattered mirror" (183). We need add only that, as in other instances of the Romantic sublime, these "opposite or discordant qualities" have been juxtaposed but not reconciled. A gap opens up between "The past and the present," as Newman puts it, with the classic grace and beauty pitted against a squalid and sexually aggressive modern scene. The past itself, as he imaginatively reconstructs it, also takes on biblical colors—Doric piety sliding into the impiety of Eastern fertility worship and, conversely, the evocation of Satan taking on a Dantean monumentality and a Miltonic grandeur of spirit.

Newman later tells Christie that in returning to Sicily, he is "not sorry to go alone, in order, as Wordsworth would say, to commune with high nature" (*LD* 3: 277), and a modern reader hears in his description echoes of "The single sheep and the one blasted tree" or the Gondo Gorge, where

> Tumult and peace, the darkness and the light—
> Were all like working of one mind, the features
> Of the same face, blossoms upon one tree;
> Characters of the great Apocalypse,
> The types and symbols of Eternity
> (*Prelude* 6.635–39)

Wordsworth's gestures toward cosmic synthesis restore the balance between outer and inner which Weiskel posits as the final "reactive phase of the sublime moment" (24). Yet because Newman's imagination is working with and against more intractable materials, the appeal of Greek religion cannot be so easily subsumed within the demands of a Judeo-Christian God. Instead his dilemma recapitulates the fear and awe awakened by mountains and ruins in earlier, overtly Christian forerunners of the Romantic sublime.[26]

As we saw in the preceding section, however, Newman's gradual identification with the original builders of these ruins makes him progressively less willing to stand in the position of a wrathful God. Hence he prefaces the description of Segesta with an appeal to Jemima's pity: "And now [Sicily] lies in desolation under a bad government, not tricked forth in the vanities of modern dissipation or literature, but in mourning over her children all forlorn, yet as beautiful as ever" (*LD* 3: 216).[27] He offers her, and his own conscience, a prototype of the "Prophet's scroll" vision in the last chapter of the *Apologia,* but here the vision lacks any infallible bulwark within which to escape the secular human condition. His immediate difficulty in disentangling "high aims" and "manifold talents" from sin and consequent failure may help account for his return to the island. He had told Henry Wilberforce: "I would not see [Segesta] again if I could—lest I should get familiar with it—as it is I have something for memory to dwell upon—the first impression of things is the poetical one" (*LD* 3: 245).

O'Faolain rightly sees Newman's itch to encounter the rest of Sicily as an anomaly: he "strikes off alone for the mountainous interior of remote Sicily, . . . in the fullest foreknowledge of the beastliness he must endure there. . . . The most moving thing about this return journey is that he himself could never explain it" (180–81). On the Froudes' departure, he admits as much to Jemima: "I had lost too my companions, and that with anticipations for the future too painful for me to mention [F.'s death]. I was going among strangers into a wild country, to live a wild life, to travel in solitudes and to sleep in dens of the earth; and all for what? for the gratification of an imagination—for an idea of the warm fancy, which might be a deceit, drawn by a strange love of Sicily to gaze upon its cities and mountains" (*LD* 3: 282). Our best clue, I think, is an image he repeats, first to her and then to Christie: "Think what Spring is! and in Sicily! it is the nearest approach to Paradise, of which sinful man is capable" (*LD* 3: 266). And two weeks later, "What a country it is! a shadow of Eden, so as at once to enrapture and to make one melancholy" (*LD* 3: 277). Here again we see Newman groping for some imaginative mediation between rapture and melancholy, between an escape from and a testimony to sinfulness, between an approach to and a mere shadow of some unfallen state. To reconcile these contraries within history and landscape instead of within his own mind, he begins to construct an only marginally Christian narrative of the Golden Age.

This same quest, hinted at in the allusions above and codified in his support for Keble's "primary poet," concludes the 1829 essay on poetry: Homer's "is the style of one who rhapsodized without deference to hearer or judge, in an age prior to the temptations which more or less prevailed over succeeding writers—before theatre had degraded poetry into an exhibition, and criticism narrowed it into an art" (*Ess.* 1: 26).[28] Yet in Sicily, this neo-classical identification of the Golden Age with the golden mean metamorphoses into a full-blown etiological quest like those which informed Keats's *Hyperion* poems or Shelley's *Prometheus*. His encounters with paganism—and, as we shall see, with the equally disturbing mores of Greek Orthodoxy and Roman Catholicism—have broken down his clear intimations of the world as fallen, as separate from its spiritual counterpart. Hence he can risk a covert look outside biblical history and Judeo-Christian theology for a distinctly secular source of inspiration.

Newman, like his Romantic predecessors, frames his project in terms of past discovery. Unlike Faber and the other Helio-Arkite mythologists,[29] however, these poets were all engaged in covert mythopoeia, the creation of the mythic reality which they claimed to find. At the turn of the century, Friedrich Schlegel had acknowledged the disappearance of communal beliefs: "The modern poet must create all these things from within himself . . . and each work from its very beginning, like a new creation out of nothing. . . . Our poetry lacks a focal point, such as mythology was for the ancients" (81). To counter Enlightenment instrumentality, to "cancel the progression and laws of rationally thinking reason, and to transport us once again into the . . . original chaos of human nature" (86), he proposed creating a mythology. This "will come to us by an entirely opposite way from that of previous ages, which was everywhere the first flower of youthful imagination. . . . The new mythology, in contrast, . . . must be the most artful of all works of art" (81–82). The conflicting demands of Schlegel's agenda became readily apparent: it must be individual yet communal, vital yet self-conscious, established yet new. Keats implicitly admits the failure of this project when he elects to internalize myth, to shield his Psyche, "latest born . . . / Of all Olympus' faded hierarchy," within "some untrodden region of my mind" (24–25, 51).

Still persuaded that he could live within the fullness of Patristic spirituality, Newman was unwilling to acknowledge that he was seeking any new myth, much less that he was creating it, much less that any such creation must remain a subjective one. Hence he reappropriates for his secular Eden the powers we saw variously attributed to the natural language of Scripture and to the inspired interpretation of the Alexandrian Fathers. Defending both these, he had virtually defined the Romantic sublime as an inevitable series of metaphorical displacements: "[W]hen, dazzled at length with the great sight, [the mind] turns away for relief, it still catches in every new object which it encounters, glimpses of its former vision" (*Ari.* 57–58). Here, as he recalls Segesta for Trower, its Doric architecture also becomes a mute metaphor, testifying to some far fainter but equally ineffable reality:

> There is something mysterious about [the early Greek temples]— their power is prior to the time of history . . . and the simplicity in their architecture seems to imply a corresponding simplicity in their religion. How far had the world then proceeded in the career of irreligion of which Babel was the first instance? What traces of holier principals [*sic*] still lingered amid the wilful inventions of men? . . . —[W]ho can say whether holy ones did not walk the rounds of these primitive temples, till the pride of science and literature extinguished the rays which had been providentially left among them? (*LD* 3: 291–92)

Earlier, Archdeacon Lyall had objected to the manuscript of *Arians* because "you speak of the 'dispensation of Paganism,' and consider it as proceeding from God.—I know this to be a very common view of the matter, in Clemens Alexandrinus—but it is open to very grave objections— You speak at P 103 of the Heathen poets having been 'divinely illuminated'" (*LD* 3: 113). Now, in Sicily, Newman was prepared to meet these objections, to find the *locus classicus* wherein the twin strands of what Arnold would later call Hebraism and Hellenism, pushed back to their sources, would converge. And if he had won access to the Fathers, those earliest witnesses to primitive Christianity, through reverent reading, then perhaps he could win access to this earliest witness to Edenic, unfallen humanity through an equally reverent visitation.

The Fever as Sign

The sequel is well known. Newman got to Sicily, put up with weeks of delay and frustration, finally set off on his trek only to be struck down with the fever which nearly killed him, a fever he saw as God's judgment upon him for his willfulness in going in the first place. He returned, renewed in his commitment to follow God's will and not his own. Yet here again, just as in his efforts to see childhood as God-directed, the self in this divine dialectic merges with God and God's will with self-will. For one thing, John's chastened "willfulness" may have lain not so much in returning to Sicily as in returning with the heterodox agenda we have been tracing. For another, the chastening did not so much crush this agenda as displace it within other, less threatening endeavors and defer it until the traumatic events at the end of the decade. For a third, the account within his correspondence suggests that this interpretation of his fever is in fact a reinterpretation, eventually replacing the more naturalistic ones he offered in earlier letters; O'Faolain suggests: "How much of the *Apologia* records not so much what happened at the time as posthumous rationalizations which had meanwhile merged with the event in his memory" (152). Even "The account of my illness in Sicily," though daring in its recreation of the phantasmagoric stream of his fevered consciousness, was begun a full year later and not completed, Culler tells us, for some forty-three years ("Remembrance" 66).

His earliest identification of the fever as a judgment appears in an earlier quoted letter to Henry Wilberforce on 16 July 1833.[30] But in the letter of 5 June to Rogers from Palermo, a detailed account of the fever explains it very differently: "Now you will say, how was it I alone suffered all this of all Sicilian travellers? Why, to tell the truth, *the* way to avoid it would have been to have taken a Sicilian regular lioniser and purveyor, who would have avoided all difficulties; but this for *one* person is very expensive, and it falls light on several" (*LD* 3: 313). Newman concludes the letter by defending the trip: "And now you will say my expedition to Sicily has been a failure. By no means. Do I repent of coming? Why, certainly I should not have come had I known that it was at the danger of my life. I had two objects in coming—to see the antiquities and to see the country. In the former I have failed. . . . But I have seen Taormini, and the country from Aderno to Palermo" (*LD* 3: 315). Three weeks after the

Wilberforce letter, he confesses to Christie, "I only regret I did not enjoy [the country] more for 3 weeks I was laid up; what a time that would have been for wandering over hill and dale, and rummaging out old places!" (*LD* 4: 27). And three weeks later still he admits to Rogers that he is "beginning to get very dissatisfied with not having done more in Sicily. It was most unlucky to be detained three weeks in Palermo, when I might have been roving over the island" (*LD* 4: 36). I am not suggesting that his interpretation of the fever as judgment was a complete after-thought—only that it was one interpretation among several that he explored and evaluated. Eventually he concluded that this one, while it cast a cloud over his search for any earthly paradise, shone bright upon his quest for a reincarnation of Patristic spirituality in England's green and pleasant land.[31]

What had he actually found on his second visit? The first letter to Rogers reaffirms his earlier description of the island as a secular Eden: "It *is* a country. It passes belief. It is like the garden of Eden, and though it ran in the *line* of my anticipations (as I say), it far exceeded them" (*LD* 3: 315). Amid his stoic and often humorous accounts of dreariness and squalor, only one passage in a letter to Harriett justifies and amplifies upon this claim:

> [When] we mounted to the theatre [at Taurominium], . . . to have seen the view thence was a nearer approach to seeing Eden, than anything I had conceived possible. . . . I felt for the first time in my life with my eyes open that I must be better and more religious, if I lived there. Never before have I brought home to my mind the reality of foreign scenery . . . —long slopes which seem as if they never would end, cultivated to the top—or overhung there with jutting rocks—bold precipitous crags standing, because they choose to stand, independently—range after range of heights, so that you wonder the series does not proceed for ever. (*LD* 3: 303)

The gap here between the scene itself and the religious claims made for it can be brought home if we compare this passage to a celebration of spring from the *Parochial Sermons:* "Then the leaves come out, and the blossoms on the fruit trees and flowers; and the grass and corn spring up. There is a sudden rush and burst outwardly of that hidden life which God has lodged in the material world" (*PS* 4 [13]: 209).

Like most of Newman's landscapes, this one has little color or visual detail. It points instead toward an apocalyptic future: "This earth, which now buds forth in leaves and blossoms, will one day burst forth into a new world of light and glory, in which we shall see Saints and Angels dwelling." Newman seems to fear lest we rest, even momentarily, in nature itself: "Bright as is the sun, and the sky, and the clouds; green as are the leaves and the fields; sweet as is the singing of the birds, . . . they are not [God's] fulness; they speak of heaven, but they are not heaven; they are but as stray beams and dim reflections of His Image; they are but crumbs from the table" (209-11).[32] By contrast, the "range after range of heights" in Sicily frustrate our efforts to comprehend or subordinate them, not just from their seemingly infinite extension but from their seemingly human volition. Unwilling to dwindle into "dim reflexions" of anyone or anything, they stand, "because they choose to stand, independently."

The conclusion of the passage supplements these features of the Romantic sublime with the grandeur Newman earlier bestowed on both height and depth in his description of Vesuvius:

> The theatre is situated in a hollow hill, and the scena forms a screen—through it you see magnificent steeps, falling down and down—and above all, Etna towers. . . . [G]oing out of Taurominium down the hill you have a very novel and striking effect. The slants centre almost in a point, so that you see[m] descending into a pit—they were clad with the bright green of corn when it looks brightest. . . . Etna was magnificent beyond description—The scene around was sombre with clouds, when suddenly as the sun descended upon the cone, its rays shot between the clouds and the snow, lighting upon the latter, and disposing the former about it in vertical curtains—on one side the ascent to the top half showed itself like a Jacob's ladder (it had hitherto been hidden)—I no longer wonder at the poets placing the abode of the Highest upon Mount Olympus. (*LD* 3: 303-4)

Here Newman, bereft, as he tells us (302), of most of his clerical garb, finds no platform for divine judgment upon any surrogate "cities of the plain." In its place, up a cloudy Jacob's ladder, he finds an imaginative approach, not to Eden, but to "the abode of the Highest."[33] Fortunately for the future of English literature and theology, reports of previous travellers dissuaded him from physically attempting the snow-covered ascent (*LD* 3: 305), but his caution left standing the religious ambiguity which ends this passage. Would he have been ascending Sinai or Olympus, and which resident deity would he have encountered at the top? This, baldly stated, is the same ambiguity which informs his whole aborted tour.

By this time, as we shall see in chapter 11, he had already surmised a spirit of place shaping Roman Catholicism, but whether *his* God could be so identified with a particular place and time was a question only resolved by his illness. In the letter to Wilberforce, then in the journal account, then in the *Apologia*, he insisted that the fever was not an interruption but an answer, the self-revelation of a God who struck him down as a wilful man only to raise him up as a trusted servant. Yet the new trust bestowed on him is imaged in scenes of spiritual privilege which recall those encountered on the trip, and the new militancy enjoined upon him grants him the power and the sanction to project his mountain visions onto a larger social world. These defenses hold until the end of the 1830s: by then, however, accounts of increasingly troubling specters appear in his letters; images of an amoral, purposeless natural fecundity appear in his published writings; and from several sources appear supernatural intimations rather like those encountered on the trip—intimations of a God who can no longer be subsumed within the dialogue which has constituted Newman's Romantic faith.

CHAPTER 6

Romantic Election

❖

NEWMAN'S SICILIAN FEVER was only one of a series of crises from which he recovered, always chastened by his religious commitment, but always stronger in the spiritual power that commitment bestowed upon him. In this process, he shaped for himself a religious ideal that both mirrored and masked his transition from a Calvinistic doctrine of election to a Catholic model of sainthood. This ideal encompassed his sense of spiritual exaltation, his ecclesiastical ambition, his need for physical self-discipline, his reliance upon a visionary escape from the mundane, his reverence for Patristic models, and his concomitant need to remodel them in his own self-conscious likeness. As a path where few could follow and even fewer were invited, Newman's ideal abetted the sense of alienation he lamented so poignantly. For those admitted to its rigors, however, it offered a bond, a common purpose, and a privileged station from which Newman could spiritualize his earlier encounters with mythopoeia and Romantic sublimity on his Mediterranean tour.

Crisis, Convulsion, and Control

The whole course of Newman's development, as analyzed by Culler among others (*Imperial* 14–87), falls into cycles very much like Newman's Sicilian odyssey: confident self-assertion, followed by self-destructive crises of confidence, followed by contrition and resubmission to divine guidance, followed by renewed academic or ecclesiastical triumphs. We encountered his first conversion in chapter 1 and will analyze his second in chapter 11; here, focusing on his failure in the Schools, we can test the frequent charge that in each cycle his psychological division betrayed a fear of his own intellectual potential. Does Newman, in other words, exemplify the claim of Vico quoted by Geoffrey Hartman: "'It was fear . . . which created gods in the world, not fear awakened in men by other men, but fear awakened in men by themselves.'"[1] In the same way, continues Hartman, Blake's "visionary poems show . . . the self-astonishment of an imagination which shrinks from its own power and then abdicates it to the priests" (15).

On the surface Newman's academic failure, disrupting the pattern of progressive appropriation we studied in chapter 1, seems provoked by an imaginative failure. Instead of an increasing autonomy from family, friends, and mentors, this crisis produces a violent, almost visceral self-division. His most vivid account, in a letter to Walter Mayers, describes it as an assault upon his "facility of comprehension," taken in its etymological sense as a reaching out and grasping of objective experience: "[S]o great a depression came on me, that I could do nothing. . . . My memory was gone, my mind altogether confused. . . . It was as if a surgical operation was day after day being carried on upon me, and tearing away something precious" (*LD* 1:99).[2]

The *Memoir* acknowledges that "a similar affection . . . overtook him seven years later, on all but the same day . . . when he was exercising his office of University Examiner in the very same Schools in which in 1820 he had failed as examinee, and that attack came on with greater violence, for he was obliged to leave Oxford, and for a time to relinquish his office" (*AW* 48). A contemporary memorandum describes the breakdown in even more violent figures: "[O]n Sunday felt the blood collect in my head; on Monday found my memory and mind gone. . . . It was not pain, but a twisting of the brain, of the eyes. I felt my head inside was made up of parts. I could write verses pretty well, but I could not *count*. I once or twice tried to count my pulse, but found it quite impossible; before I had got to 30, my eyes turned round and inside out, all of a sudden" (*AW* 212–13). He finds himself, not a unified, powerful subject but a skull broken into and a collection of sense organs wrenched out of place.[3] This invasion leaves him, on the one hand, a parody of the fragmented Humean psyche and, on the other, a prefiguration of the Tennysonian self, reduced to a broken machine by the loss of Arthur Hallam:

> Be near me when my light is low
> When the blood creeps, and the nerves prick
> And tingle, and the heart is sick,
> And all the wheels of being slow.
> (*In Memoriam* 50.1–4)

Faber, as we would expect, attributes these crises to a conflict between the master and the slave within Newman:[4] "If he climbed out of the abyss, it was only to fall back into it. If he fell into the abyss, it was only to climb out of it again" (323).[5] Faber, reducing a religious conflict to a psychological one (and a neurotic one at that), simply assumes what he needs to establish. He does, however, acknowledge that Newman's "recovery from these [crises] was always rapid" (51).

This rapidity, I would venture, suggests that by submitting to a power above human comprehension or control, Newman actually won greater comprehension of his world and greater control over it. Shortly after his failure in the Schools, for example, he can still reassure his father not to take his self-deprecating statements at face value: "I assure you that they know very little of me and judge very superficially of me, who think I do not put a value on myself *relatively* to others. I think (since I am forced to speak boastfully) few have attained the facility of comprehension which I have arrived at, from the regularity and constancy of my reading, and the laborious and nerve-bracing and fancy-repressing study of Mathematics, which has been my principal subject" (*LD* 1: 125). Coming hard upon this failure, his success in the Oriel Fellowship would have seemed grounds for celebration for anyone. To his aunt, however, Newman can interpret it as a divinely bestowed reward, a victory within a conflict more prophetic than academic: "I glory in confessing it was God and God alone who accomplished it. . . . And before it took place, I was by God's grace fully persuaded that He *would* save me and preserve me; . . . my bread *would* be sure, I *should* be fed; and see, I was quite right in my opinion" (*LD* 1: 138). These crises can thus be reinterpreted as increasingly successful efforts to achieve that control of his subjective universe which he will celebrate thirty years later in the *Idea*. It is not just a liberal education, but Newman's own spiritual education

> which gives a man a clear conscious view of his own opinions and judgments, a truth in developing them, an eloquence in expressing them, and a force in urging them. It teaches him to see things as they are, to go right to the point, to disentangle a skein of thought, to detect what is sophistical, and to discard what is irrelevant. It prepares him to fill any post with credit, and to master any subject with facility. . . . It shows him how to accommodate himself to others, how to throw himself into their state of mind, how to bring before them his own, how to influence them, how to come to an understanding with them, how to bear with them. He is at home in any society, he has common ground with every class. (*Idea* 154–55)

In this passage, and still more in the definition of the gentleman within Discourse 8, such control manifests itself as accommodation. Throughout his Anglican period, however, Newman measures the same control as the power of self-differentiation.

Spiritual Power, Spiritual Danger

In religious terms, moreover, Newman can dismiss conventional models of Christian piety as inadequate, perhaps not for others, but for his own spiritual life. He remained, to be sure, more sensitive than most to the dangers of spiritual pride. In *Arians* he insisted that although the redeemed "are said to be Christs, or the anointed, to partake of the Divine Nature, to be the well-beloved of God, His sons, one with Him, and heirs of glory," nevertheless "In all these forms of speech, no religious mind runs the risk of confusing its own privileges with the real prerogatives of Him who gave them" (228). To the idolatrous flatteries of a Miss Holmes in 1842, therefore, Newman could reply gruffly,

> I am *not* venerable, and nothing can make me so. I am what I am. I am very much like other people, and I do not think it necessary to abstain from the feelings and thoughts, not intrinsically sinful, which other people have. I cannot speak words of wisdom; to some it comes naturally. . . . No one ever treats me with deference and respect who knows me. . . . [P]eople have never bowed to me—and I could not endure it. I tell you frankly, my infirmity I believe is, always to be rude to persons who are deferential in manner to me. (*PL* 58)

We need to take this denial seriously. It fits with Newman's rock-solid sense of self, his gracious accommodation to the interests of guests and companions, his hearty participation in plays and entertainment at the Oratory. It also fits, however, with his suspicion that people would venerate an image that was not the real Newman.

Intimations of this inner reality surface in a journal account of his visit to a dying girl during his early years as a priest:

> [S]he took the Sacrament again, and about a week after departed, as I may trust, to the Lord who bought her.—The case is very painful —it is like a sword going thro' my heart.—Her mother has since told me she said that when I entered her room she thought of Jesus Christ in the picture. I should not have put this down did not St Paul say to the Gal. 'Ye received me as Jesus Christ'—and tho' ministers now are immeasurably below St Paul, yet Xt is infinitely above Paul as well as us.—I am indeed a sinner. (*LD* 1: 232)

The warring intimations of spiritual power and spiritual danger—so evident here in the relentless alternation of self-exaltation and self-condemnation—suggest a difficulty in adjudicating those rival claims of self and God which constituted Augustine's trial.

In searching for models, Newman is caught between one which he is moving beyond and another which he cannot yet attain. As Newsome suggests ("Evangelical" 17), he held on to a lively conviction of election —the same conviction which motivates and justifies any Calvinist work ethic—long after he claimed to have shed its doctrinal support.[6] In the mean time, the Catholic institution of sainthood was growing increasingly appealing. Newsome again sums up Newman's epistolary debate with Stephen and Wilberforce: "In his quest for a middle way, Newman never failed to find a path; sometimes, however, it was a path which could only be trodden by the saints" ("Justification" 53). When the Catholic Newman describes Charles Reding in 1848, he fuses these two incompatible ideals, cloaking with sacramental theology a belief in final perseverance just as strong as it was at his first conversion: Reding "could not escape the destiny of being one of the elect of God; he could not escape the destiny which the grace of his Redeemer had stamped on his soul in baptism, which his good angel had seen written there, and had done his zealous part to keep inviolate and bright" (*LG* 206).

Even pursued singly, however, both these ideals posed formidable problems. As the following parody suggests, Newman became convinced that Calvinistic quests for evidence of salvation could produce only a debilitating self-absorption: "[S]ee that you feel. If you do not feel, Christ will profit you nothing: you must have a spiritual taste; . . . you must be conscious of a change wrought in you, for the most part going through the successive stages of darkness, trouble, error, light, and comfort" (*Jfc.* 335–56). Sainthood, on the other hand, offered two difficulties of its own.[7] First, as we shall see in the next chapter, Newman had to acknowledge that compared with Rome and High-and-Dry Anglicanism, his Tractarian church existed only "on paper." On these terms, Tractarian sainthood became yet another impotent projection of an idealized human figure upon an indifferent cosmos. Second, although he could write Faber in 1844 that "Observances which may be very right . . . in a Church which creates saints, . . . may be dangerous in a communion which has them not" (*KC* 356), yet the converse held equally true. Unlike election, sainthood was an honor bestowed only after death. Willing one's own canonization would turn one's religion into an exercise in magical coercion. As attempted by Tennyson's near-contemporary creation, St. Simeon Stylites, it produced only what Herbert Tucker has called the "peculiarly doomed genre of autohagiography."

In a later sermon, however, Newman can insist that these difficulties appear as such only from outside; only the worldly misinterpret it as a mark of insincerity, that [religious] persons should profess to know so much about themselves, and yet so little,—that they can hear so much said about themselves, that they can bear so much praise, so much popularity, so much deference, and yet without being puffed up. . . . [T]he Christian ought to be self-conceited, for he is gifted; he ought to understand evil, because he sees and speaks of it; he ought to feel resentment, because he is conscious of being injured . . . ; but not so: his mind and heart are formed on a different mould. (*PS* 6 [18]: 264, 266–67)

Newman's own spiritual mold helps him avoid these same dilemmas, but in the process it recasts both Calvinistic election and Catholic sainthood within an essentially Romantic dialogue between self and God. It is this same remolding which has occasioned the subsequent attacks upon his spiritual ideal. Newman's defenders, in their turn, have accused the attackers of bias, of a refusal to see that his ideal fits within one version or another of Christian orthodoxy. To me, most of these attacks remain justified within their authors' frames of reference—and yet unfair as assessments of Newman's accomplishment. Working through the various facets of his ideal, we will consider his interpretations of celibacy, of separation and communion, of visionary power, and of visionary glory. Each of these stands as an affront to humanistic notions of social decorum, to Protestant notions of religion as opposed to idolatry, to more general Christian notions of humility. If they are seen as baptizing Romantic moments of imaginative power and self-instantiation, however, these ideals constitute a challenge both to Romanticism and to orthodox Christianity.

Celibacy

Newman saw celibacy as part of his effort to set himself apart from the world without setting himself above it. He added and then deleted from the *Apologia* a passage rationalizing his decision to a hostile audience (484n). More recently, critics interested in feminism and the psychology of gender have reformulated the charges made earlier by Geoffrey Faber and still earlier by Charles Kingsley. Detractors can point to Newman's heavy-handed paternalism toward his strong-willed sister Harriett; defenders can point to his concern for his mother, his warmth toward Jemima, and his long-suffering tolerance of his impetuous admirer, Maria Giberne. Gerard Manley Hopkins had the misfortune to leave some confessions of homosexual feelings, and critics have had the good fortune to find and translate them from the Latin. Hoping for similar revelations, Newman's critics have analyzed and reanalyzed promising passages: the distress noted above at being touched by his mother, the hostility to his friends' marrying,[8] the resolution to "make my own mind my wife . . . against that loss of friends which [marriage] makes inevitable" (*LD* 4: 170),[9] Charles Reding's nausea at the sight of a newly married couple in *Loss and Gain*.[10] From such inconclusive evidence, George Levine can conclude only that "The revulsion from the flesh and the fear of self in Newman are . . . deeply rooted" (234). For Fleishman, the issue is less sexual than theological: "[H]ere is an unmistakable deposit of gnostic disdain for the material world. . . . The covert or unconscious homosexuality that has been ascribed to [the 'Oxford Apostles'] makes Newman appear much more gregarious than his writing allows us to believe him. His 'problem' was not men or women but *others*" (158, 160).

As we saw in chapter 2, however, Newman anticipates such incredulity: "Should a man . . . profess to regulate his conduct under the notion that he is seen by invisible spectators, . . . would not what he said be certainly met with grave, cold, contemptuous, or impatient looks, as idle, strained, and unnatural?" (*PO* 69).[11] This hostility, in turn, is shown to betray a spiritual provincialism. Because the elect "are commonly unable to enter into the ways of thought or feelings of other men, . . . to the world they seem like *foreigners*. We know how foreigners strike us; they are often to our notions strange and unpleasing in their manners. . . . [W]e think they mean something unpleasant, something rude, or over-free, or haughty, or unrefined, when they do not" (*PS* 4 [15]: 235–36). By 1840 this mutual alienation had hardened from incidental to deliberate: "Every thing about a clergy man is a warning to men, or ought to be, of the next world, of death, and judgment, heaven and hell. . . . His mode of speech is graver than that of others. . . . His life is given to objects out of sight. All that he does is intended to remind men that time is short, death is certain, and eternity long. And, this being so, do you think that men, being as they mostly are, careless and irreligious, do you think they like this? No" (*PS* 8 [10]: 147).[12]

Sacrificing the world's love, Newman has won something of greater value to him—sexual self-determination. If Newman's contemporaries could not convict him of misanthropy, it was because he redescribed their charges; if we cannot convict him of a repressed homosexuality, it is because he has managed, not just to repress his sexuality, but to redescribe it. Despite Newman's famous gliding walk—with "head thrust forward, and gaze fixed as though on some vision seen only by himself" (Shairp 245)—and despite Charles Kingsley's insinuations of effeminacy, Newman's conception of Christianity was almost as muscular as Kingsley's; Newman may even have been the more vigorous walker. But where Kingsley saw gender as sexually fixed, Newman saw it as asexually open.[13]

This openness, in turn, made yet another aspect of the self available for Romantic reinscription. Others, like Browning, were exploring the possibility of androgyny through sexual union; Newman discovered early that by ridding himself and his human ideal of sexual markers, he could appropriate for himself a specifically spiritual androgyny. He did not seek to use, abuse, reify, or marginalize either specific women or women in general. He sought instead to do without them by appropriating the feminine into himself and a small, already marginalized, group of male friends. Virginity thus became for him a dearly won possession: "O my brethren, make much of your virginal state, if you possess it, and be careful not to lose it. . . . What is passed cannot be recalled. Whatever be the heights of holiness to which repentant sinners attain, yet they cannot have this pearl of great price, *not* to *have* sinned" (*SD* [2]: 24).[14]

Later, discussing such sin with Wilberforce, Newman will "make a cross division of *innocent* and *committed to guilt,* and high and low. I am not sure that the *merely* innocent, as (e.g.) women may be, are therefore the higher saints;—though the innocent *alone* have any right to do without penance." He goes on to claim that sin after baptism "is a *sin against light*" (*LD* 5: 286). In the spiritual clarity of his Sicilian fever, we remember, Newman protested himself innocent of just this sin: "I repeated, 'I shall not die, for I have not sinned against light, I have not sinned against light.' I never have been able quite to make out what I meant" (*Apo.* 43). This letter to Wilberforce may elucidate at least part of his meaning; it may suggest how he can participate in both halves of his "cross division," how he can achieve a sanctity which is both high, like the Fathers of the Church, and innocent, like his unworldly female parishioners. By purging himself of all sensual opacity, he can thus embody both male and female qualities without the need for any sexual intrusion.

Such androgyny enabled him to assume the feminine grace remarked by his contemporaries,[15] the passive tact of the gentleman in the *Idea,* the asexual intimacy with his colleagues. So constituted, he can see himself as widowed after Froude's death, he can appropriate the departed spirits of Froude and his sister Mary, he can so fuse and confuse his identity with Bowden that Bowden, even after his marriage, used to "call me Elizabeth and her Newman" (*KC* 333). As we saw in chapter 2, Newman violently repudiated liberal efforts to humanize the figure of Jesus, but within his *Justification,* the resurrected Christ claims that He has abandoned his flesh *in order* to gain an almost sexual union with the believer: "[W]hen I am ascended, thou shalt see nothing, thou shalt have everything. Thou shalt 'sit down under My shadow with great delight, and My fruit shall be sweet to thy taste.' Thou shalt have Me whole and entire. I will be near thee, I will be in thee; I will come into thy heart a whole Saviour, . . . inward in presence, and intimate in fruition, a principle of life and a seed of immortality, that thou mayst 'bring forth fruit unto God'" (*Jfc.* 217).

Isolation and Communion

Celibacy makes Newman aware of still further private intimations. A passage he quotes from Gregory Nazianzen pleads for retirement as requisite to any such spiritual encounters: "[A] certain love insinuated itself, of the moral beauty of quiet, and of retirement. . . . Accordingly, I did not endure being tyrannized over, and being thrust into the midst of tumult, and dragged forcibly away from this mode of life, as if from some sacred asylum" (*HS* 2: 82). And with this Patristic sanction, Newman can reject the apparent breadth conferred by other relationships as narrow, partial, and hence expendable:

> Love of home and family [may be] sufficient to make this life tolerable to the multitude of men. . . . We may indeed love things created with great intenseness, but such affection . . . is like a stream running in a narrow channel, impetuous, vehement, turbid. The heart runs out, as it were, only at one door. . . . Created natures cannot . . . elicit the ten thousand mental senses . . . through which we really live. None but the presence of our Maker can enter us; for to none besides can the whole heart . . . be unlocked and subjected. . . . We know that even our nearest friends enter into us but partially. . . . If it be not over bold to say it, He who is Infinite can alone be [the heart's] measure; He alone can answer to the mysterious assemblage of feelings and thoughts which it has within it. (*PS* 5 [22]: 317–19)[16]

Newman knew well that this exclusive focus on the "two luminous and self-evident beings" of the *Apologia* exacted a personal cost even heavier than ostracism. Within his "Illness in Sicily," he counts this cost to himself as his only audience: "The thought keeps pressing on me, while I write this, what am I writing it for? For myself, I may look at it once or twice in my whole life: and what sympathy is there in *my* looking at it? Whom have I, whom can I have, who would take interest in it? . . . This is the sort of interest which a wife takes and none but she—and that interest, so be it, shall never be taken in me. Never, so be it, will I be other than God has found me. All my habits for years, my tendencies, are towards celibacy" (*AW* 137). In the apparent anonymity of the *Parochial Sermons,* he even subsumes such isolation within an almost cosmic alienation:

> Men of keener hearts . . . are cast among persons unable to enter into their feelings, and thus strangers to them, . . . or are misunderstood by those around them, and find they have no words to set themselves right with them, or no principles in common by way of appeal; or . . . seem to themselves to be without place or purpose in the world, or to be in the way of others; or have to follow their own sense of duty without advisers or supporters, nay, to resist the wishes and solicitations of superiors or relatives; or . . . have the burden of some painful secret, or of some incommunicable solitary grief! (*PS* 3 [9]: 124)[17]

If such alienation were always and everywhere inevitable, it might be more bearable, but in another parochial sermon, fellowship remains easy and available only for the reprobate; for believers it remains rare, fleeting, and subject to chance and loss:

> Is it not enough to be pilgrims and soldiers all our days, but we must hear the mutual greetings, and exulting voices, of those who choose the way of death, [while we] must walk not only in pain but in solitude? . . . [T]hose who obey Him . . . are sprinkled up and down the world; they are separated the one from the other, they are bid quit each other's dear society, and sent afar off to those who are differently minded. . . . [N]ow and then, as they walk their way, they see glimpses of God's work in others; they take hold of them awhile in the dark, but soon lose them; they hear their voices, but cannot find them. (*PS* 3 [17]: 238–40)

An 1834 sermon, however, written during the exuberant early days of the movement, posits this otherwise lonely pilgrimage as an occasion for respite and a forum for spiritual discourse: "Time was when, even at the most necessary times, we found it difficult to speak of heaven to another. . . . [B]ut now our affection is eloquent, and 'out of the abundance of the heart our mouth speaketh.' Blessed portion indeed, thus . . . to range over the face of the earth pilgrims and sojourners, with winning voices, singing . . . the song of the Lamb; . . . without father, without mother, without abiding place, . . . allowed to bring forth bread and wine to refresh the weary soldiers of the most High God" (*PS* 5 [21]: 309–10).[18] Such accounts suggest that long before setting up the community at Littlemore, Newman had opened his spiritual criteria wide enough to admit a few like-minded souls. As early as 1833, citing again the examples of

Basil and Gregory, he sets their ideal against that of a stereotypical An-glican clergyman:[19] "Somehow, the idea of marrying and taking orders, or taking orders and marrying, building or improving their parsonages, and showing forth the charities, the humanities, and the gentilities of a family man, did not suggest itself to their minds. They fancied . . . that their choice lay between . . . two ascetic disciplines, that of the solitary or hermit, and that of the secular. . . . Midway, however, between these lay . . . the monastic; removed from the world, yet acting in a certain se-lect circle" (*HS* 2: 55–56).

The Criteria for Election

If Newman's circle remained this select, what criteria defined it? Fully aware of the charges of spiritual elitism which would be brought against him, he worked hard to avoid some and to reinterpret others. His various invocations of this communion, while they borrow heavily from Calvinis-tic election and Catholic sainthood, reshape both to fit his individual needs as a spiritual pilgrim and as a friend. Sermons like the following, to be sure, merely dramatize the accepted Christian paradox that earthly titles only prefigure the spiritual potential within everyone:

All Christians are kings in God's sight; they are kings in His unseen kingdom, in His spiritual world, in the Communion of Saints. They seem like other men, but they have crowns on their heads, and glor-ious robes around them, and Angels to wait on them, though our bodily eyes see it not. Such are all Christians, high and low. . . . He came to you first; he loved you before you loved Him. . . . He said not to you, "Obey Me, and I will give you a kingdom"; but "Lo I give you a kingdom freely and first of all; now obey Me henceforth, for you can, and you shall remain in it"; . . . God is looking out now for kings to fill thrones in His Son's eternal kingdom, and to sit at His right hand and His left. . . . Christ's ministers (blessed be His name!) may choose and baptize all whom they meet with. . . . Christ says, "Compel them to come in." (*PS* 8 [4]: 53–55)

While this 1837 sermon seems almost Arminian in its inclusiveness, a much earlier one, though revised for later publication, retains Calvinistic vestiges that thwart any collective human potential: "Men we remain, but not mere men, but gifted with a measure of all those perfections which Christ has in fulness, partaking each in his own degree of His Divine Na-ture so fully, . . . that [his Saints] are all but Divine. . . . Surely in proportion to His glory is His power of glorifying; so that to say that through Him we shall be made *all but* gods . . . is to say, and truly, that we shall be higher than every other being in the world; higher than Angels or Archangels, Cherubim or Seraphim" (*PS* 8 [17]: 253). Here Newman's inner struggle betrays itself in his nervous shifting between the inclusive "we" and the restricted and restrictive vocabulary of spiritual hierarchy.

The sermon on divine calls, analyzed in chapter 11 as a reflection of (and on) Newman's conversion, admits openly that "He really does call some men by His free grace to higher things than others; . . . this man sees sights which that man does not see, has a larger faith, a more ardent love, and a more spiritual understanding" (*PS* 8 [2]: 31).[20] But it is the heat of his diatribe against Peel's Reading Room which provokes a less guarded celebration of this hierarchy: "Faith, viewed in its history through past ages, presents us with . . . an aristocracy of exalted spirits, drawn together out of all countries, ranks, and ages, raised above the condition of humanity, specimens of the capabilities of our race, incentives to rivalry and patterns for imitation" (*DA* 288).[21] Just how literally Newman takes this analogy with social class we can see from a slightly earlier sermon, where his innate class consciousness wars with a conscious effort to transcend and transform it:

What indeed is called "*good* society" is often very worthless society . . . [but just as] the influence of the words there used . . . extends in a most subtle way over all that men do, . . . so a habit of prayer, the practice of turning to God and the unseen world . . . has what may be called a *natural* effect, in spiritualizing and elevating the soul. . . . [Such a one] is as one coming from kings' courts, with a grace, a delicacy, a dignity, a propriety, a justness of thought and taste, a clearness and firmness of principle, all his own. (*PS* 4 [15]: 229–30)

Newman's intimation of parallel realms posited a spiritual aristocracy which both subsumed and stood in judgment on its vainglorious earthly imitation; here, this spiritually conferred social "grace" anticipates that conferred by a liberal education in the *Idea,* a grace otherwise achievable only by birth.

In actuality, however, this company is far more select: "Religion, for instance, may be reverenced by the soldier, the man of literature, the trader, the statesman and the theologian; yet . . . [O]nly one is the truth and the perfect truth; . . . God knows which it is; and towards that one and only Truth He is leading us forward. He is leading forward His redeemed, He is training His elect" (*PS* 8 [2]: 27). The reward for "those who give themselves up to their Lord and Saviour, those who surrender themselves soul and body," is not just inclusion in Revelation's 144,000 saved, but a gift which is pointedly personal, pointedly unique, pointedly secret from everyone save self and God: "[T]hese are they who gain the Lord's secret gift, even the 'white stone, and in the stone a new name written which no man knoweth, saving he that receiveth it'" (*PS* 8 [5]: 74–75). This gift even renders its recipient proof against the refusal of "others" to credit such evidences:

> Care not for the perplexing question which many will put to you, "How can you be sure that you are right more than others?" Others are nothing to you, if they are not holy and devout in their conversation. . . . This way, I say, carries with it an evidence to ourselves of its being the right way. . . . God surely will listen to none but those who strive to obey Him. Those who thus proceed, watching, praying, taking all means given them of gaining the truth . . . shall not be "turned unto fables." "The secret of the Lord is with them that fear Him." (*PS* 8 [13]: 198)[22]

Election as Self-Defined

Newman, I think, needed such gifts; yet he may not have garnered the "white stone," the secret name, the divine assurance against being "turned unto fables" for himself alone. His vision of parallel realms, I argued, helped to explain the loss of other friends and loved ones, but the loss of Hurrell Froude demanded still greater assurance, greater compensation. Newman's proleptic question, "Where is that spirit gone, over the wide universe . . . ?" could only be answered by positing some special destination. In a moving letter from the last year of Froude's life, Newman's forced jocularity disguises a concerted effort to win a cosmic role for his friend's soon-to-be-departed spirit:

> Methought, if your health would not let you come home, you ought to be a Bishop in India—there you might be a Catholic and no one would know the difference. . . . It is quite impossible that in some way or other you are not destined to be an instrument of God's purposes—Tho' I saw the earth cleave and you fall in, or heaven open and a chariot appear, I should say just the same—God has ten thousand post [*sic*] of service. You might be of use in the central elemental fire, you might be of use in the depths of the sea. (*LD* 4: 362)[23]

As we saw in chapter 2, even before his death Froude achieves greater spiritual stature than Mary achieved after hers. Her spirit remained bound to the delusive appeal of the natural world; his spirit, not content with mere sainthood, assumes the angelic nature which it had concealed during its brief earthly sojourn. Natures like his "give token of their immortality, give token to us that they are but Angels in disguise, the elect of God sealed for eternal life, and destined to judge the world and to reign with Christ for ever. Yet they are suddenly taken away, and we have hardly recognized them when we lose them. Can we believe that they are not removed for higher things elsewhere?" (*PS* 4 [14]: 218-19). An earlier sermon passage already cited anticipates the answer: "They are taken away for some purpose surely: their gifts are not lost to us; their soaring minds, the fire of their contemplations, the sanctity of their desires, the vigour of their faith, the sweetness and gentleness of their affections, were not given without an object. Yea, doubtless, they are keeping up the perpetual chant in the shrine above" (*PS* 2 [18]: 214). Given this destination, even "on his death-bed," as Edwin Abbott claims, Froude was able "to 'exhort with authority' and to deliver a message from heaven" (*Anglican* 1: 387).

In tracing the close parallels between Froude and Newman's prerequisites for spiritual election, I do not mean to imply that Newman did not mold them on his spiritual mentors among the Fathers. Apart from his Platonic fondness for the theologically suspect Origen, Newman's appeals to the Fathers are supported by a fifteen-hundred year tradition. Even in his early essay on miracles, however, Newman also acknowledges an even older tradition, the Prophets' expedient for valorizing their own missions: "The respective claims of the Kings and Priests were already ascertained, . . . whereas extraordinary messengers, as Moses, Samuel and Elijah, needed some supernatural display of power to authenticate their pretensions. . . . I might observe upon the unembarrassed manner of the Prophets in the exercise of their professed gift" (*Mir.* 24). Newman's case for Froude is similarly self-authenticating; evidence of his spiritual nature appeals to his personality and evidence for his personality appeals to his spiritual nature. Since Newman's portrait turns in upon itself, traditional distinctions between elected and self-selected simply collapse. And since Froude's true spirituality is initially visible to Newman alone, Newman stands in God's shadow as his friend's revealer and/or creator.

Whether modelled on Froude or for Froude, Newman's more generalized criteria for election partake of a similar reflexivity. Although he values ecclesiastical structure, as we have seen, because it offers clear moral guidelines, he acknowledges that such obedience "cannot be the lot of all; but it is the lot of the many. Thus God pours out His blessings largely, and puts trial on the few" (*PS* 3 [14]: 205). While the path of "the few" will thus be more arduous than that of "the many," it will be

their own path: "We should be very much on our guard, when we are engaged in contemplating the lives of holy men, against attempting just
what they did. . . . Holy men may say and do things which we have no
right to say and do. . . . [C]ommon men have no right to use the prayers
which advanced Christians use without offending; and if they attempt
it, they become *unreal*" (*PS* 6 [3]: 34–35).[24] With such advanced Christians, moreover, even the gap between inclination and religious duty
eventually breaks down: "[A]t first it *is* a kind of servitude, it is a task till
our likings and tastes come to be in unison with those which God has
sanctioned. It is the happiness of Saints and Angels in heaven to take
pleasure in their duty, and nothing but their duty" (*PS* 3 [7]: 92). This
fusion of inclination and duty, here distanced within superhuman natures
in a supernatural existence, reappears in association with unfallen humanity and a romanticized image of childhood: "[T]his gift which sanctified
Adam and saves children, does become the ruling principle of Christians
generally when they advance to perfection. According as habits of holiness are matured, principle, reason, and self-discipline are unnecessary; a
moral instinct takes their place in the breast, or rather, to speak more
reverently, the Spirit is sovereign there. There is no calculation, no struggle, no self-regard, no investigation of motives. We act from love" (*PS* 5
[8]: 109). As Brilioth observes, "It is particularly in his last Anglican
years that the ideal of holiness calls forth these pleasanter feelings in
Newman's preaching" (*Anglican* 234): "The pleasures of holiness are far
more pleasant to the holy, than the pleasures of sin to the sinner. O that I
could get you to believe this!" (*PS* 7 [14]: 197).

Election as Self-Referential

As we might expect from his accounts of Vesuvius and Etna, Newman's
preferred place for such transcendence is the mountaintop. A poem sent
back to his mother early in the tour suggests that well before these encounters he is already anticipating their spiritual significance. In it he
claims that Truth resides only in the select few in their mountain watch-
towers:

> Still is the might of truth as it has been,
> Lodged in the Few, obeyed and yet unseen;
>   Reared on lone heights and rare,
>   His Saints their watch-flame bear
> And the mad world sees the wide circling blaze
> Vain searching whence it streams and how to quench its rays.
>   (*LD* 3: 174)[25]

We have suggested that Newman modelled his criteria for spiritual election on the Fathers or on Froude. When he returns to such scenes in later sermons, however, he reworks these criteria to recuperate the sublimity of his mountain encounters without risking another rebuke for visionary "willfulness." Within these newly spiritualized encounters, the mountain offers a platform for vision, a platform which in turn exalts the visionary: "[O]n their turning to God, . . . the world, instead of being like the stream which the countryman gazed on, ever in motion and never in progress, is a various and complicated drama, with parts and with an object" (US [14]: 285). To interpret this drama, Newman again cites the visionary claims of Antony: "Certainly I believe that that soul which is clean on every side, and established in its highest nature, becomes keen-sighted, and is able to see things more and further than the devils, having the Lord to reveal them to it. Such was the soul of Eliseus, which . . . discerned the heavenly hosts which were present with it" (HS 2: 115). Antony's evocation of Newman's favorite mountain vision from 2 Kings, with its "chariots of fire and horses of fire," establishes them as twin vehicles of divine revelation.[26] Still another passage we will return to as Newman's indictment of his age; in the present context, however, it also presents him as the inspired interpreter of this same revelation: "Wisdom is the clear, calm accurate vision, and comprehension of the whole course, the whole work of God; . . . the deep things of the Creator . . . are, in a measure, 'revealed unto us.' . . . Others understand him not, master not his ideas, fail to combine, harmonize, or make consistent, those distinct views and principles which come to him from the Infinite Light, and are inspirations of the breath of God" (US [14]: 293).

While the identity of this visionary is carefully generalized, it is tempting to compare the mountain height from which Newman confronts a fallen world with the physical, spiritual, intellectual height from which Newman preached at St. Mary's. As Principal Shairp (246–56) and other witnesses have described the scene:

> The sermon began in a calm, musical voice, the key slightly rising as it went on; by and by the preacher warmed with his subject, till it seemed as if his very soul and body glowed with suppressed emotion. . . . There are those who to this day, in reading many of his sermons, have the whole scene brought back before them[: the] great church, the congregation all breathless with expectant attention, the gaslight just at the left hand of the pulpit, lowered that the preacher might not be dazzled. . . . (Whyte 43)

Though he preached most of these sermons in the Oxford University church, Newman strove to make them *parochial:* "I am continually asking such of my Parishioners as attend if they understand them, and not unfrequently am asked for them by them to read and lend afterwards. . . . I certainly do write for my own people" (*LD* 6: 275).[27] Before such a congregation, Newman is virtually driven into a vatic role of near God-like authority. Nowhere else in his writing could he dare assume so powerful (because so carefully generalized) a persona. Jemima indirectly compares this homiletic power to that of Paul: "[H]ow little you know of the estimation in which [your sermons] are generally held. . . . I am sure it is a great gift, that insight you show into human nature. . . . [I]t is a sort of spiritual perception; and I wonder whether it is anything like the gifts in the Corinthian Church" (Moz. 2: 288).[28]

Newman was so uncomfortably aware of this gift that when he tried to relieve Robert Wilberforce's self-doubts in 1828, he only revealed his own: "I cannot bear seeking in any way to influence others, not merely because it is a very great responsibility, but also more especially I feel (I can say without affectation) that I am not worthy to suggest any thing to any one—What am I among the thousands in Israel? arises in my mind continually. . . . I have before now felt in my own mind the distress you speak of about the right mode of preaching—at one time . . . so sorely that I thought I must have given up my curacy, nay have left the Church" (*LD* 2: 84). Subsequently, however, he found it equally difficult to surrender this power. As he attempted to back gracefully out of St. Mary's pulpit in 1843, a woman wrote Jemima that he was betraying a trust, that he could not so easily divorce person from preacher or auditors from flock:

> [H]e has taught and they have striven to be obedient pupils. He has formed their minds, not accidentally: he has *sought* to do so, and he has succeeded. He has undertaken the charge and cannot now shake them off. His words have been spoken in vain to many, but not to them. He has been the means under Providence of making them what they are. . . . If he was silenced, the blame would rest with others; but, giving them up of his own free will, they will have a sense of abandonment and desertion. . . . [O]ur champion has deserted us—our watchman, whose cry used to cheer us, is heard no more. (Moz. 2: 376)[29]

Election as Apotheosis

In her eloquent account of Newman's spiritual power, this follower challenged the use to which he put it. His own most exalted account of this power, contained within his *Justification,* has occasioned even more pointed criticism. The *Apologia* claims that this work "was aimed at the Lutheran dictum that justification by faith only was the cardinal doctrine of Christianity" (74). It may also have been written to protect from Protestant incredulity the personal possession of a righteousness which approaches apotheosis:

> For what in truth is the gift even in this our state of humiliation, but a grafting invisibly into the Body of Christ; a mysterious union with Him, and a fellowship in all the grace and blessedness which is hidden in Him? Thus it separates us from other children of Adam, is our badge and distinction in the presence of the unseen world, and is the earnest of greater good in store. It is an angelic glory which good spirits honour, which devils tremble at. . . . Well then may Prophets and Apostles exult in it as . . . the rich garment of salvation, and the enjewelled robe of righteousness, . . . as "Christ in us," and "upon us," and round us; as if it were a light streaming from our hearts, pervading the whole man, enwrapping and hiding the lineaments and members of our fallen nature, circling round us, and returning inward to the centre from which it issues. (*Jfc.* 160–61)

Despite Newman's seamless interweaving of Patristic mysticism and biblical periods, Joseph O'Leary claims that he here "clutches at the robe almost as at a fetish. . . . The stylization of righteousness as the completion of a circle of self-identity removes the subject from the dynamic interplay of freedoms in history and human relationships and robs the quest for integrity of its elements of risk and uncertainty" (180).[30] O'Leary concludes that "Newman haunts his own text to an uncanny degree" (180) and in consequence loses "that punch or bite which Luther's voice never lacks, and that comes from the *extra nos* (outside ourselves), the idea that salvation consists . . . in a total change of situation whereby the sinner is taken out of himself" (176). Echoing the charges of egotism raised by his own siblings, this critique reverses the more secular ones we encountered in chapter 3. Where literary historians saw Newman as selling his Romantic birthright for religious capitulation, O'Leary sees him as subverting the operations of grace through a covertly Romantic claim to spiritual self-instantiation. On these terms, Newman's whole life would betray an insistence that he alone could determine the criteria for his election, the path of his spiritual journey, the company he chose, the status of his visionary world, his place within it, and finally his role in God's providential scheme. Even this passage, his celebration of perfected Christian freedom, would then seem less a subordination of will to duty than a redefinition of duty in terms of his own individual will.

In its entirety, however, Newman's passage transcends Rousseau's Romantic claim to be "sufficient unto himself, like God." Instead of exalting himself in "an all-but-identification [with] deity" (Fleishman 105), Newman brilliantly coopts the supposedly incompatible responses to Augustine's "trial of the center." As the light continuously turns back upon this center, Newman claims it not for his own unaided spirit but for a visionary fusion of self and Christ so complete that even God the Father cannot tell the two apart: "The Almighty Father, looking on us, sees not us, but this Sacred Presence, even His dearly beloved Son spiritually manifested in us; with His blood upon our door-posts, in earnest of that final abolition of sin which is at length to be accomplished in us" (*Jfc.* 161).[31] Even the first-person plural "us" begins an imperceptible shift in its reference from Newman and his reader to Newman and his Christ. His spiritual ideal borrowed from Calvinistic election and Catholic sainthood without subscribing fully to either; here his righteousness embodies both Christian self-transcendence and Romantic transcendence without submitting to be judged by either.

CHAPTER 7

Action as Romantic Self-Definition

❀

AS WE DESCRIBED the Anglican Newman standing in God's stead within his visions or in the pulpit of St. Mary's, we have shown him coming perilously close to those who "wish in some way or other . . . that self may be king and judge" (*PS* 5 [16]: 226). He seems to resemble in particular those liberal thinkers ridiculed in the *Tamworth Reading Room* because their professed devotion to natural religion masks a subtle idolatry: "[S]elf-conceit may stand proxy for adoration. . . . So, this is the religion we are to gain from the study of Nature; how miserable! The god we attain is our own mind; our veneration is even professedly the worship of self" (*DA* 301). The barrier which Newman opposes to Robert Peel's invitation to self-worship, the faculty through which God can reassert his power over self, is the conscience. This voice, as we have seen, may have empowered him to break away from an ever-widening circle of potential influences, but it revealed remarkably little about its source. Attempting to identify that source with the God he found in the Bible and the Patristic Church, Newman confronts such philosophical and psychological tangles that he comes to affirm action as somehow self-authenticating. As he elaborates his theory, he replicates those responses to a chaotic universe proposed by Goethe and preached in England by Carlyle. As he implements this theory, his new-found militancy wins him individual autonomy, sweeping rhetorical freedom, and power to instantiate his subjective vision within his followers. Judged by its own radical criteria, Newman's redefinition of conscience as militancy deserves greater recognition within both nineteenth-century intellectual history and twentieth-century theology.

The Law Within

Paradoxically enough, these achievements all stem from Newman's acceptance of a lawgiver whose obligations take precedence over all others:

"The essence of Religion is the idea of a Moral Governor, and a particular Providence. . . . Can physics teach moral matters without ceasing to be physics? . . . [W]hich [science] teaches of divine holiness, truth, justice, or mercy? Is that much of a Religion which is silent about duty, sin, and its remedies?" (*DA* 303). To quote Reardon: "Whatever other certainties may in the end have eluded him, the conviction that in the depths of the moral consciousness he truly heard God speak was inexpugnable" (*Coleridge* 139). Here, as Reardon acknowledges, he is paraphrasing Bremond: "The whole of his philosophy has as its end the establishment of a fundamental identity between the voice of conscience and the voice of God. It is always new because he finds an inexhaustible mine in this first experience of his religious life, always human, always convincing, because under each of these words is heard the other of personal recollection and the certainty of experience" (*Coleridge* 191). As Newman generalizes upon his own moral experience in a sermon, the sensations are hardly less immediate: "For a man of religious mind is he who attends to the rule of conscience, which is born with him, which he did not make for himself, and to which he feels bound in duty to submit. And conscience immediately directs his thoughts to some Being exterior to himself. . . . [T]hat inward sense does not allow him to rest in itself but sends him forth again from home to seek abroad for Him who has put His Word in him. He looks forth into the world to seek Him who is not of the World" (*PS* 2 [2]: 18). Because this inner voice remains prior to and beyond the material world, it seems to transcend any empirically derived, sanctioned, or conditioned ethic. Instead, conscience becomes its own continually self-correcting guide: "Our duties to God and man . . . are means of enlightening our eyes and making our faith apprehensive. Every act of obedience has a tendency to strengthen our convictions about heaven" (*PS* 6 [8]: 100).

Bremond maintains, however, that when Newman sends the subject "forth again from home," he is implicitly admitting that he cannot "claim that each perception of a moral truth brings him directly into touch with the Absolute. His conscience says nothing else to him except 'Do this; do not do that'" (334).[1] Because the source of these moral injunctions remains unknown, the self interprets it as fundamentally unknowable: "There is a voice within us, which assures us that there is something higher than earth. We cannot analyze, define, contemplate what it is that thus whispers to us. It has no shape or material form. There is that in our hearts which prompts us to religion, and which condemns and chastens sin. And this yearning of our nature is met and sustained, it finds an object to rest upon, when it hears of the existence of an All-powerful, All-gracious Creator" (*PS* 6 [23]: 339–40). The voice, in other words, does not identify or verify itself but depends upon the set of associations brought to it. And the particular associations which Newman brings depend upon his low regard for unaided human potential: "The grounds of Faith, when animated by the spirit of love and purity, are such as these:—that a Revelation is very needful for man; that it is earnestly to be hoped for from a merciful God; . . . that, if Almighty God interposes in human affairs, His interposition will not be in opposition to His known attributes" (*US* [12]: 239).[2] Newman's argument here threatens to recapitulate the hermeneutic circle: the reality which must be revealed can be identified only by a subject who has prior knowledge of the revelation. He attempts to break the circle by endowing his subject with an "animat[ing] spirit of love and purity," but even this spirit, predetermining the kind of supplement it needs, still binds his image of God to his image of the human.

Newman nevertheless insists and acts on the assumption that the voice of his conscience comes to him from outside. As he will put it in a passage from the *Grammar:* "If, on doing wrong, we feel the same tearful, broken-hearted sorrow which overwhelms us on hurting a mother; if, on doing right, we enjoy the same sunny serenity of mind, the same soothing, satisfactory delight which follows on our receiving praise from a father, we certainly have within us the image of some person. . . . [W]e are not affectionate towards a stone" (*GA* 76). He readily admits that such feelings must be psychologically, and hence historically, conditioned: "[E]ver so many sermons about the inward satisfaction of strict conscientiousness [will not] create in my mind the image of a virtuous action and its attendant sentiments, if I have been brought up to lie, thieve and indulge my appetites" (*GA* 26). Here he anticipates Mitchell's objection: "When Newman says 'On irreligious men evidences are thrown away' he nevertheless lays himself open to the charge of begging all the important questions from the start. It is, apparently, impossible to preach except to the converted" (234). As we saw in chapter 6, however, Newman insists that his upbringing, with its careful protection of a pristine innocence, was objectively better than another's because it opened him to that outside voice and made him transparent to the parental surrogate speaking. Newman's hope amounts to a this-worldly conflation of Corinthians 13. Dispensing with the dim mirror (or the darkening glass of the King James), he would like to know, here and now, as he is known by coming to see face to face. By rendering himself transparent to God, he hopes to see God seeing the Self: "[I]t becomes our comfort to look up to God. 'Thou, God, seest me!'" (*PS* 1 [13]: 173).

The Witness of Conscience

Just as breathtaking as the fusion of the righteous soul with God in the *Justification* essay, this claim opens itself to even more criticism—theological, psychological, and political. Theologically, it was early argued that to deify the conscience constitutes a self-mystifying means of deifying the self. While Newman was accusing the liberals of such self-worship, a letter of Thomas Arnold had already charged Newman with idolatry: "[A] fanatic worships something which is the creature of his own devices, and thus even his self-devotion in support of it is only an apparent self-sacrifice, for it is in fact making the parts of his nature or his mind, which he least values, offer sacrifice to that which he most values. . . . [I]t is clear to me that Newman and his party are idolaters" (quoted in DeLaura, *Hebrew,* 10). Where Arnold anticipated Feuerbach, Dean Inge echoes him, discovering in Newman's claims for conscience a similar psychological self-projection: "[T]o Newman his own nature was a revelation which he called conscience" (183).

Those practitioners of what Ricoeur calls the hermeneutics of suspicion subject Newman's claims for conscience to an even more damaging critique.[3] Even deferring any discussion of Marx and Nietzsche, we can see that in Newman's naive analogy between the judgmental voice of God and the equally judgmental voices of parents, he has virtually defined the Freudian superego. And in wanting to see God seeing the self, he has defined the Lacanian paradigm of the child introjecting the maternal gaze, working out a neurotic desire to stand in subject and object roles simultaneously. Walter Jost, following Küng and Berger, counters that "it is no argument against the evidence for God that we project onto our understanding of the divine our own significant human influences. . . . [O]ur mothers and fathers may rather be seen as *topoi* that open us up to the transcendent" (234). Yet the grotesque manifestations of Victorian repression should convince us that even though Newman's inner voice may deny his conscious desires, this denial cannot by itself guarantee his conclusion that the voice must come from outside himself.[4] The mature Newman's asceticism, for example, retains vestiges of the aggressive self-righteousness which so annoyed his father; for Weatherby, this insistence on privileged intuitions "seems appallingly vain and recalls one of the least savory aspects of evangelical Protestantism. . . . [W]hat appear to you 'weak reasons' or mere 'presumptions' appear to me sufficient grounds for conviction . . . ; for I am 'spiritually minded' and you are not" (182–83).[5]

Working from hints in the *Grammar* and the earlier *Argument from Conscience to the Existence of God,* other recent apologists have suggested that the Catholic Newman moved beyond this untenable position to an argument from personality, an analogy between his intimate interactions with those closest to him and an equally intimate relation with God: "[T]he special quality in our [moral] feelings leads us to a Person" (*Argument* 77).[6] Translated from theological to philosophical terms, this defense would imply that Newman finally acknowledged Hegel's claims for the mutuality of recognition, his insistence that one's sense of self can only be freely awarded by others. Such an apology might well make better theology or philosophy—but not, I think, a better picture of Newman's own practice. As we have seen, Frank had good reason to charge that John continued to conduct even his closest friendships on his own terms.

Action as Incremental

Even if the Anglican Newman does not eagerly engage other individuals, other groups, other institutions, his conscience-based psychology of religious affirmation may yet suggest ways of cutting through the Gordian knot of conflicting ideological claims and achieving a life which is somehow self-authenticating. As we will explore further in the next two chapters, English Romantics and German Idealists have frequently been accused of escapism: escape into self-reflection, escape into primitivism, escape into aesthetic transcendence, escape into an intellectual or artistic elite, escape into disinterestedness and negative capability, escape into the telos of historical progress. To all these various escapes, real or only apparent, Newman opposes an insistence upon action. As Newsome puts it, "he actually lived both his theology and his philosophy (or, conversely, devised a theology and a philosophy out of his own personal experience)" (*Convert* 87).[7] Whether this militant agenda engages the spiritual, psychological, and social realms which the Romantics avoided we will evaluate as we explore the ways he implemented it. Even at the outset, however, we can assert that the agenda itself synthesizes otherwise incongruous phenomena and engages otherwise baffling anomalies in the human condition.[8]

Where Newman appealed to conscience to limit the autonomy of his human subject, he now appeals to action to regain some of its integrity: "[O]n religious subjects we may prove any thing or overthrow any thing, and can arrive at truth but accidentally, if we merely investigate by what is commonly called Reason" (*US* [4]: 55).[9] As Newman continues to devastate Peel's faith in scientific humanism, he echoes the "il faut parier" with which Pascal backed up his wager and anticipates the "ultimate concern" through which Tillich will redefine secular goals as covert objects of worship. Though Newman, as we saw, took pains to deny any direct influence, his argument also parallels that of Coleridge: "To one who asks for proof Coleridge would simply reply, Try it; the truth of the Christian religion is self-testifying. 'Ideas, that derive their origin and substance from the *Moral* Being, and to the reception of which as true *objectively* (that is, as corresponding to a reality out of the human mind) we are determined by a *practical* interest exclusively'" (*Aids to Reflection*; cited in Reardon, *Coleridge,* 65). McFarland quotes an even more emphatic affirmation: "This is the corner-stone of my system . . . the priority . . . of the Conscience to the Consciousness in Man—No I without a Thou, no Thou without a Law from Him, to whom I and Thou stand in the same relation. Distinct Self-Knowledge begins with the Sense of Duty to our neighbor: and Duty felt to, and claimed from, my Equal supposes and implies the Right of a third, superior to both because imposing it on both" (242).[10] All four arguments, as variations on the "*tu quoque,*" claim only that the human condition renders faith more credible as a basis for action than its dubious alternatives:

> [F]irst shoot round corners, and you may not despair of converting by a syllogism. . . . Life is not long enough for a religion of inferences; we shall never have done beginning, if we determine to begin with proof. . . . Life is for action. If we insist on proofs for everything, we shall never come to action: to act you must assume, and that assumption is faith. . . . [I]f we commence with scientific knowledge and argumentative proof, . . . or attempt to make men moral and religious by Libraries and Museums, let us in consistency take chemists for our cooks and mineralogists for our masons. (*DA* 294–96)

Newman's faith in action and his conception of faith as action colored his judgments of others. According to Thomas Mozley: "It never was possible to be even a quarter of an hour in his company without a man feeling himself to be invited to take an onward step . . . ; and Newman was sure to find out in due time whether that onward step had been taken" (1: 39). An early letter to Frank rejects *sola fide* as an unreal basis for either living or evaluating life: "I cannot in a day or a year get at that hidden man of the heart in another which God alone sees constantly. My ground of sure hope as to another's spiritual state is the sight of a consistent *life.* . . . [T]o apply high Christian doctrines as medicines is (in my opinion) but to inflame the disease—the disease, namely, of mistaking words for things" (*LD* 2: 183–84). Three years later, he writes to Williams from Malta that his experiences abroad have "much deepened my conviction of the intellectual weakness which attaches to a mere reading man— his inability to grasp and understand and appropriate things which befal[l] him in life—so that he seems powerless as a child while the action of life is passing and repassing, and tossed about and caught and transmitted on all sides of him" (*LD* 3: 194).[11]

Even as an Anglican, Newman anticipates what the *Grammar* will call the illative sense—reliance on an engaged intuition as the surest path toward religious truth. A justly famous example from the *Prophetical Office* illustrates that engagement does indeed precede intuition:

> When we are not personally concerned, even the highest evidence does not move us; when we are concerned, the very slightest is enough. Though we knew for certain that the planet Jupiter were in flames, we should go on as usual; whereas even the confused cry of fire at night rouses us from our beds. Action is the criterion of true faith, as determining accurately whether we connect the thought of God with the thought of ourselves, whether we love Him, or regard Him otherwise than we regard the existence of the solar system. . . . [T]he greater the uncertainty, the fuller exercise there is of our earnestness in seeking the truth, and of our moral sagacity in tracing and finding it. (*PO* 131)

Yet because this engagement must remain intuitive, Newman can soften his spiritual elitism enough to acknowledge certain species of traditional wisdom:

> [I]n practical matters, when their minds are really roused, men commonly are not bad reasoners. Men do not mistake when their interest is concerned. They have an instinctive sense in which direction their path lies towards it. . . . The same thing is proved from the internal consistency of such religious creeds as are allowed time and space to develope freely; such as Primitive Christianity, or the Medieval system, or Calvinism—a consistency which nevertheless is wrought out in and through the rude and inaccurate minds of the multitude. (*US* [11]: 211)

Within several Anglican works, ideas shape themselves over time much as he will describe the process in his 1845 *Development:* "In a higher world it is otherwise, but here below to live is to change, and to be perfect is to have changed often" (*Dev.* 38).[12] In particular, Newman explores the path of faith as one of continual discovery. Within the *Prophetical Office*, Anglican (as opposed to Catholic) faith advances unselfconsciously in its effort to escape pride: It "does not like to realize to itself what it does; it throws off the thought of it; it is carried on and reaches forward towards perfection, not counting the steps it has ascended, but keeping the end steadily in its eye, knowing only that it is advancing" (*PO* 145). Two years later the journey of faith, here under the inspired guidance of St. Paul, becomes a more tentative process of self-discovery:

> What they already were, was to lead them on, as by a venture, to what they were not; what they knew was to lead them on, upon presumptions, to what they as yet knew not. . . . [Paul] appealed to that whole body of opinion, affection, and desire, which . . . would respond to the Apostle's doctrine, as the strings of one instrument vibrate with another. . . . Such, then, under all circumstances, is real Faith; a presumption, yet not a mere chance conjecture,—a reaching forward, yet not of excitement or of passion,—a moving forward in the twilight, yet not without clue or direction;—a movement from something known to something unknown. (*US* [12]: 248-49)

By 1841 and his penultimate university sermon, the uncertainty of the goal appears to have darkened the journey itself: It "is the act of a mind feeling that it is its duty any how, under its particular circumstances, to judge and to act, whether its light be greater or less. . . . Its knowledge, then, though defective, is not insufficient for the purpose for which it uses it, for this plain reason, because (such is God's will) it has no more" (*US* [14]: 298). Three pages later, however, this stoicism yields to the excitement of genuine discovery:

> Faith, while it is so stable, is necessarily a principle of mental growth also. . . . "I will stand upon my watch," says the prophet, "and set me upon the tower, and will watch to see what He will say unto me;" . . . And as Wisdom only can apply or dispense the Truth in a change of circumstances, so Faith alone is able to accept it as one and the same under all its forms. And thus Faith is ever the means of learning something new, and in this respect differs from Bigotry, which has no element of advance in it, and is under a practical persuasion that it has nothing to learn. (*US* [14]: 303)

Within the full sermon, this passage stands in opposition to the portrait of a fearful, insular bigotry which we will examine in chapter 8; in the context of Newman's current theological and political crises, its enthusiasm may sound like whistling in the dark. Yet earlier essays and sermons have been envisioning faith as just such an inner-directed quest: "I would have every one carefully consider whether he has ever found God fail him in trial, when his own heart had not failed him; and whether he has not found strength greater and greater given him according to his day;

whether he has not gained clear proof on trial that he *has* a divine power lodged within him, and a certain conviction withal that he has not made the extreme trial of it, or reached its limits. Grace ever outstrips prayer. . . . We know not what we are, or might be" (*PS* 5 [24]: 351).[13] Comforting the believer with God's spiritual presence, Newman claims that the less clear the destination and the less solid the evidence, the more ennobling the challenge and the greater the reward: "[I]f we insist on being as sure as is conceivable, in every step of our course, we must be content to creep along the ground, and can never soar. If we are intended for great ends, we are called to great hazards" (*US* [11]: 215). Where Newman earlier wrestled with the paradox of a personal God, "e.g. His being angry, repenting—or resting—etc." (*LD* 3: 78), here he seems to be anticipating a process theology which posits change and response within God's nature: "God's thoughts are deeper than human words; they cannot be exhausted. The more you ask, the higher you aim, the more faithfully you expect, the more diligently you co-operate, the fuller return you obtain" (*PO* 225).[14]

Context and Contingency

Up to this point we have focused on Newman's active response to change, uncertainty, darkness, within a recognizably spiritual quest. When these forces render the quest itself problematical, however, Newman's faith in action leads him to a praxis more radical than he would have freely acknowledged. In one sermon written when his faith in the via media was still firm, Newman acknowledges a proto-Heideggerian sense of thrownness, and acknowledges that he and his congregation cannot justify their position from any stance outside it: "We as little choose our religion as we choose to be born. . . . We find ourselves *Christians;* and our duty is, not to consider what we should do if we were not Christians,—not to go about disputing, sifting the evidence for Christianity, weighing this side or that,—but to act upon the rules given us, till we have reason to think them wrong, and to bring home to ourselves the truth of them, as we go on, *by* acting upon them,—by their fruits on ourselves" (*PS* 4 [4]: 58–59). Mitchell broods over the implications of such contingency: "This strain in Newman's thought anticipates Wittgenstein: there is no appeal from our actual practices, whether in thinking or acting, to any ideal, would-be neutral, standard of rationality. . . . But how, in that case, can . . . Christian faith . . . be rational if, as he seems to be maintaining, it is necessary to have had one's moral and intellectual being shaped by Christianity before one can understand and appreciate the rational case for Christian belief?" (239). Yet Newman's call to action denies not just the possibility but the necessity of any such "standard of rationality."[15] Earlier, no matter how dark their path, the faithful could believe themselves guided by a strong and loving God. Now Newman's contingent universe demands action as the only means of positing either the source or the goal of such action. Distressed by this embrace of contingency, Weatherby argues that within such a universe the only testimony which individual and church can offer for their faith is suffering: "Just as martyrdom [for Newman] proves the individual's apprehension of God to be universally true, so the durability of forms, of doctrines and rites, under stress and persecution proves the Church's apprehensions to be valid" (224).

Another sermon echoes "Lead Kindly Light" in its image of an "encircling gloom": "[W]e are in a world of mystery, with one bright Light before us. . . . Take away this Light, and we are utterly wretched,—we know not where we are, how we are sustained, what will become of us, and of all that is dear to us, what we are to believe, and why we are in being" (*PS* 2 [18]: 215). Where this sermon contemplates the disappearance of the Light, an even earlier one contemplates an existing darkness which threatens to reduce any action to "groping." The final sentence, already quoted above, relies on God's ability to see in the dark: "We are in the dark about ourselves. When we act, we are groping in the dark, and may meet with a fall any moment. . . . [I]n our attempts to influence and move our minds, we are making experiments (as it were) with some delicate and dangerous instrument, which works, we do not know how, and may produce unexpected and disastrous effects. The management of our hearts is quite above us. Under these circumstances it becomes our comfort to look up to God. 'Thou, God, seest me!'" (*PS* 1 [13]: 173).[16] Still another sermon, anticipating the psychological critiques we considered above, suggests that any such illumination may not come from God, may not come from outside at all: "Is not every feeling and opinion, of one colour or another, fair or unpleasant, in each man's own judgment, according to the centre light which is set up in his soul? Is not the light that is in a man sometimes even darkness, sometimes twilight, and sometimes of this hue or that, ting[e]ing every part of himself with its own peculiarity?" (*PS* 2 [14]: 157).

Here the objective reality, the believer's "way out" from this radical solipsism, is the Bible: "It is necessary then that he go out of himself in order to assay and ascertain the nature of the principles which govern him; that is, he must have recourse to his works, and compare them with Scripture." Yet, as we saw in chapter 3, Newman's faith in the consistency and doctrinal coherence of Scripture was eroding throughout the 1830s. In an already-quoted letter from the Mediterranean, the burden is transferred to history:

> I feel more and more the blunders one makes from acting on one's own partial view of a subject, having neither that comprehensive knowledge nor precedents for acting which history gives us.—I am resolved, if I can help, not to move a step without some authority to back me, direct or by fair inference; and I look upon it as one good of travelling, (the same in mind as that of *reading*) that it takes one out of oneself, and reduces in one's eyes both the importance of one's own particular station and of one's own decisions in acting in it. (*LD* 3: 249)

As we will see in chapter 10, however, his faith in the historical witness of the Patristic age had similarly eroded by the end of that decade.

In the twelfth of his university sermons, even the stirring invocation of faith as an adventure goes on to acknowledge that "such a view . . . leads directly to credulity and superstition. . . . It is plain that some safeguard of Faith is needed, some corrective principle which will secure it from running (as it were) to seed, and becoming superstition or fanaticism" (*US* [12]: 232–33). Yet the only safeguard Newman can now muster is an unpromising cadre of virtues: "It is holiness, or dutifulness, or the new creation, or the spiritual mind, however we word it. . . . It is Love which forms [faith] out of the rude chaos into an image of Christ" (234).[17] Fifteen pages further on, this guiding impulse has become both more necessary and more evanescent: "[W]hether merely the awakening and struggling conscience, or the 'affection of the Spirit,' whether as a timid hope, or in the fulness of love, [it] is, under every Dispensation, the one acceptable principle commending us to God for the merits of Christ. And it becomes superstition or credulity, enthusiasm or fanaticism, or bigotry, in proportion as it emancipates itself from this spirit of wisdom and understanding, of counsel and ghostly strength, of knowledge and true godliness, and holy fear" (249).

Action as Self-Defining

Within his tenth university sermon, this double failure of inner and outer authority occasions a remarkable confession: "Controversy, at least in this age, does not lie between the hosts of heaven, Michael and his angels on the one side, and the powers of evil on the other; but it is a sort of night battle, where each fights for himself, and friend and foe stand together"

(*US* [10]: 201). No student of Victorian literature can miss the echoes of both Arnold's "Dover Beach" and the Battle in the Mist from the last of Tennyson's *Idylls*.[18] In fact, both Newman's dilemma and his response to it match those of his Victorian contemporaries. Like these other chastened, belated Romantics, he is haunted by the irrelevance of his imaginative visions to the increasingly oppressive realities of the industrial revolution. Like them also, he seeks to ground these visions not in actions but in action itself.

In this strategy, of course, he is echoing the advice from "The Everlasting Yea" of Carlyle's *Sartor Resartus:* "[H]ere, in this poor, miserable, hampered, despicable Actual, wherein thou even now standest, here or nowhere is thy Ideal; work it out therefrom; and working, believe, live, be free. . . . Produce! Produce! Were it but the pitifullest infinitesimal fraction of a Product, produce it, in God's name!" (2: 9). Newman's comments on Carlyle are as studiously vague as those on the earlier Romantics. In a letter to Jemima, he is described as "a man of first rate ability, I suppose, and quite fascinating as a writer. His book on the French Revolution is most taking (to me)—I had hoped he might have come round right, for it was easy to see he was not a believer, but they say that he has settled the wrong way. *His* view is that Christianity has good *in* it, or is good *as far as it goes*—which when applied to Scripture is of course a picking and choosing of its contents" (*PL* 45). The fact that Newman's own approach to Scripture had become equally selective suggests that this reference may be yet another denial of complicity. Carlyle, with his penchant for self-dramatization, projected his own dilemma onto the cosmic scale of *Sartor;* Newman, with his fear of self-dramatization, scattered his throughout several volumes of sermons. Yet both the dilemmas and the solutions proposed for them remain essentially the same.[19]

This split between subject and object (which "spelt death" to Coleridge) Kant attacked through his distinction between *Vernunft* and *Verstandt,* the English Romantics and Schlegel through imaginative synthesis, and Hegel through the *Aufhebung* of his dialectic. Both Newman and Carlyle seek to escape the same split through an almost blind commitment to action. Carlyle, wrapping himself in pious Victorian reticence, only gestures toward God as the ineffable source of his already hazy Idealism;[20] Newman makes as many claims for God as he can. Carlyle tells us to work at whatever duty lies at hand; Newman tells us to work as if we were following God's will. Yet in practice he projects his image of the divine almost as blatantly as does Odin, Carlyle's "Hero as Divinity" from *Heroes and Hero-Worship:* "With all men reverently admiring him; with his own wild soul full of noble ardours and affections, of whirlwind chaotic darkness and glorious new light; a divine Universe bursting all into godlike beauty round him, . . . what could he think himself to be? 'Wuotan [Movement]?' All men answered, 'Wuotan!'" (5: 25). As Odin actively instantiates his own divinity, the "holy men" of one parochial sermon instantiate their intuitions of the sacred, though without the same communal acclaim: "[They] feel 'the powers of the world to come' as truly as they feel the presence of this world, because they have been accustomed to speak and act *as if* it were real. . . . They take for granted, as first principles, what the world wishes to have proved in detail. They have become familiar with the sights of the next world, till they talk of them *as if* all men admitted them. . . . In consequence such men are called bad disputants, inconsecutive reasoners, strange, eccentric, or perverse thinkers" (*PS* 4 [15]: 234–35; italics mine). Frank disdainfully characterized his brother's position: "[He] summed up with, 'Thus we repeat the Creeds in Church, *not because* we believe them, but *in order* that we may believe them'" (94). Thomas Mozley describes the same strategy more charitably: "having once caught sight of that spectre [of skepticism], and found it for a moment gaining upon him, he . . . resolved never once to abate the speed of his onward progress, never even to look behind [and so] give the foe the least advantage. [Yet] it may be said that a man who has to fly from an object is still its victim, and that it really is his master, and the rule of his life" (2: 438).

When he posits action as a means of authenticating the voice of conscience, when he thus renegotiates the relation between inner yearning and revealed object, Newman must shape himself as an agent through this process of negotiation. In so doing he confronts two quandaries, one internal, the other external. Asserting himself risks setting up the self against God, as he constantly accuses his liberal opponents of doing; yet following the voice of conscience into a clearer vision demands just such fearless self-assertion, demands action as a means of self-definition. Newman dramatizes both these quandaries in his ongoing struggle with the figure of Paul.

Completely opposed to a Pauline theology of unmerited grace, Newman also feared that Paul's commitment to a life of action denied him the self-transcendence achieved by the contemplative Fathers: "He was, in figure, like David, a 'man of blood.' He did but bring together into one, the materials of the Sacred Building" (*PS* 3 [22]: 330).[21] Newman embodies Paul's dilemma within an undistinguished poem (later entitled "Warfare") sent to his mother from Sicily:

> If toilsome Paul had stayed
> In cot or cloister's shade,

With the priests' white attire
And the Saints' tuneful choir,
Men had not gnashed their teeth, nor risen to slay;
But thou hadst been a heathen in thy day.

(LD 3: 318)

Newman's frequent return to the dilemma suggests that it was more than academic or even theological; in a letter to his aunt, he confesses, "I really do think I love peace, yet I am destined to be 'a man of strife'" (*PL* 68).[22] One sermon suggests that he cannot be both: "They who venture much with their talents, gain much, . . . yet surely they have much to be forgiven in all their services. They are like David, men of blood; they fight the good fight of faith, but they are polluted with the contest" (*PS* 5 [15]: 214).[23] Another sermon, however, claims that those vested like David with divine favor are also vested with an immunity to conventional moral sanctions: "We are not at all concerned with [his evident failings] as regards our estimate of David's character. That character is ascertained and sealed by the plain word of Scripture, by the praise of Almighty God, and is no subject for our criticism; and if we find in it traits which we cannot fully reconcile with the approbation divinely given to him, we must take it in faith to be what it is said to be, and wait for the future revelations of Him who 'overcomes when He is judged'" (*PS* 3 [4]: 50–51).

In perilous circumstances like the present, therefore, Newman can claim that an apparently callous militancy is simply Christlike: "What a state we are in, when any one who rehearses the plain threats of our Lord and His Apostles against sinners, or ventures to defend the anathemas of His Church, is thought unfeeling rather than merciful . . . , and those who confess the truth, as it is in Jesus, are said to be bitter, hot of head, and intemperate!" (*PS* 3 [13]: 188).[24] Within just such a "state," as early as 1831 he refuses Harriett's suggestion that he take a living: "[I]f times are troublous, Oxford will want hot headed men, and such I mean to be, and I am in my place" (*LD* 2: 367). A few months earlier, he even proposes to the slothful Henry Wilberforce that endurance and perseverance can go far toward justifying apostasy itself: "I only wish our spiritual governors were more like men and less like cows. . . . Surely the veriest heretic who, as Arius, has learned to bear asceticism, or an infidel as Julian who can bear to neglect himself, claims more respect from us than a professed Christian (much more, minister) who sets out with *purposing* to be *comfortable*" (*LD* 2: 331–32).[25]

The Rhetoric of Militancy

Once we ask what use Newman made of this newly sanctioned militancy, we must admit that his career was not just achieved through writing, it *was* writing. There are few accounts of his engaging in oral debate with an opponent or haranguing a crowd, and while his homiletic power, as we have seen, was legendary, it was not achieved through delivery, nor was it overtly political.[26] This limitation threatens both our case and Newman's contemporary stature; it groups him with other authors who invoked writing to "transcend" (i.e., evade their complicity with) their own historical circumstances. All the Romantics, including the radicals Blake and Shelley, enclosed themselves within self-justifying structures of aesthetic authority. Even the prosaic, politically engaged Mill chose writing as an avocation which would not threaten his filial submission to his father or his tenure within the bureaucracy of the British empire.[27]

As we will see in chapter 9, Newman's militancy can win him only a limited social awareness, but it does "enable" his writing both as an autonomous construct and as a lethal rhetorical weapon. In a late letter to Keble, for example, he denies his responsibility for a piece of satire by instantiating it as somehow coterminous with its ludicrous object: "As to ridicule, to state the doings of _____ is in fact to ridicule them. The ridiculous is a natural principle; it is not *made* . . . —the thing, when stated, thus carrying its refutation with itself" (Moz. 2: 361). When he admits to Froude that his *Arians,* begun as an introduction to the Thirty-Nine Articles, had now grown into a sizable book, he awards it a similar autonomy: "Recollect, my good Sir, that every thought I think *is* thought, and every word I write *is* written—and that thought tells, and that words take room—and that though I make the introduction the whole book, yet a book it is" (*LD* 3: 7).

In justifying his essays on Scripture to Keble's worried brother, Newman finds this autonomy troubling even to him: "My constant feeling when I write is, that I . . . am merely drawing out intellectual conclusions—which, I need not say, is very uncomfortable" (*LD* 6: 353–54). He even draws an unconscious parallel between his struggle with an opponent and his struggle with his own ideas and his own prose: "I write—I write again—I write a third time, . . . I then write it out fair for the printer—I put it by—I take it up—I begin to correct again—it will not do—alterations multiply—pages are re-written—little lines sneak in and crawl about—the whole page is disfigured—I write again" (*LD* 6: 193). In this process, Newman's revisions have grown insidiously alive. His intellectual struggles have metamorphosed into the zoomorphic beasties on an illuminated Celtic manuscript and have begun re-enacting the battle on their own terms. When such revisions are spread over a period of decades, they become, not just a metaphor for his life, but that life itself. To quote Valentine Cunningham: "Newman's writings are a palimpsest of readings and re-readings and re-readings of readings. . . . The text of [his] life . . . comprises [an] archaeological site where readings are layered one upon the other" (241).

Since he sees his life's continuity, even his identity, as trapped within these texts, they come to wield a despotic, even a potentially murderous power. In 1860, rereading Hawkins's side of their earlier conflict, Newman acknowledges even this partial written verdict on his past actions: "It is plain reading [his letters] over at this distance of time, that I had angered and alienated him. He is, when not frigid, hot. . . . But I doubt not, if I could see my own letters, I should be very much ashamed of them" (*LD* 2: 203). When he admits that "To the Allseeing Eye they are all open," he implies that even God, instead of looking into the heart, will find better evidence in the letters. He concludes: "I suppose that, as far as this world is concerned, they have been destroyed long since by the person who received them—*and therefore I destroy his in like manner*" (italics Newman's). In reprisal for this alleged obliteration of his own past, he resolves to retaliate in kind, denying Hawkins any written continuity to his past and any written reassessment for his future. When Newman subsequently relents and saves at least some of these letters, he testifies to the grave consequences he associated with their destruction.

Newman could not fully exploit his rhetorical powers until after Keble's attack on the "National Apostasy" in 1833. After that clarion call, a divinely sanctioned war against liberalism expanded his moral system by encouraging him to exploit the interaction between self-definition and divine witness. Instead of following the classical model of his illustrious mentor Whately, Newman's rhetoric exploits commitment, confrontation, and extravagant self-definition.[28] Frank, as usual, offers a negative definition of his brother's practice: "He knew that he was the real head of a religious party, through whom he hoped to regenerate England. Did this inspire modesty and caution? Was there any mark of Christian tenderness or just humility? Rather it seemed that incipient Power goaded him at once into rash precipitation and recklessness of justice" (91). Chadwick, citing the Anglican Professor F. J. A. Hort, counters: "It is the shallow part of [Newman] that wields the bludgeon, even when at times he deceives you into thinking that the bludgeon is a rapier or a surgeon's knife. The deeper part of him is incompatible with all this banging about. The deeper part of him is tender" ("Bremond" 179). For me, however, Newman's vision of moral contingency renders moot both Chadwick's appeal to tenderness and Frank's appeal to objectivity: "A rationalist is intelligible though very offensive—so is a Roman Catholic—so is a[n Anglican] Catholic—but the piebald system, which at present is thought so delightful and promising, is 'neither fish, flesh, nor good red herring,' and cannot stand the sifting of controversy. Nothing but the State . . . keeps it up" (*LD* 5: 135).

And with the state failing, the only viable alternative is a rhetoric of reaction: "The King has tied his own hands—he has literally betrayed us. . . . Therefore, expect on your return to England to see us all cautious, long-headed, unfeeling, unflinching radicals" (*LD* 4: 44). Reshaping Blake's motto, "I must create my own system or be enslaved by another man's," Newman points out the consequences of such enslavement: "I dined with the Dean of Chester yesterday—who is a kind unassuming man, too little assuming by far for a Dean . . . and (when he is a Bishop) will let a man pull his nose, I feel quite sure. He has no *views,* and in consequence is like a ship without a rudder. . . . I easily bring a person to a stand, and to say 'really I had not considered it in that point of view'; . . . I attribute this, not to any powers of argument which I have, . . . but simply to my having got hold somehow or other of an imposing view, call it right or wrong" (*LD* 4: 337).[29]

Views alone, however, could not prevail in nineteenth-century church politics; the needed supplement Newman may have encountered in fourth-century Antioch: "[I]n every contest, the assailant, as such, has the advantage of the party assailed . . . from the greater facility . . . of finding, than of solving objections. . . . [T]he skill of a disputant mainly consists in securing an offensive position, fastening on the weaker points of his adversary's case, and then not relaxing his hold till the latter sinks under his impetuosity, without having the opportunity to display the strength of his own cause. . . . This was the artifice to which Arianism owed its first successes" (*Ari.* 26). Given the obsession which Newman, according to Pattison, built up around this nemesis during the composition of *Arians,* it is both ironic and plausible that he adopted Arius' confrontational stance: "It is a supreme delight to watch this faculty [Newman's intelligence] springing upon its prey, seize the living principle of a question while tearing to pieces the wrappings of conventionality and verbiage in which so many other minds stick fast for ever" (Bremond 65). Newman's unrepentant recollections suggest that he felt a similar delight at least as late as the *Apologia:* "I liked to make [men] preach the truth without knowing it, and encouraged them to do so. . . . I was not unwilling to draw an opponent on . . . to the brink of some intellectual absurdity, and to leave him to get back as he could. I was not unwilling to play with a man, who asked me impertinent questions" (51). That this recollection was accurate, the letters attest: "As to Chillingsworth, I should consider him a shuffler; but I do not see why we should not use the better sayings of shufflers against their worse. It is a homage they pay to truth, and both exposes them and stultifies their admirers—two worthy ends" (*LD* 6: 333).

As Newman's confession in the *Apologia* continues, we see that this strategy betokened a more pervasive aggression toward his audience: "In one of my first Sermons I said, '. . . it would be a gain to the country were it vastly more superstitious, more bigoted, more gloomy, more fierce in its religion than at present.' . . . In the very first page of the first Tract, I said of the Bishops, that, '. . . we could not wish them a more blessed termination of their course, than the spoiling of their goods and martyrdom'" (52–53).[30] In the present degenerate age, almost any change becomes an improvement, even one gloomy, bigoted, and fierce enough to bring the Bishops "the spoiling of their goods and martyrdom." Hence he need only look out for arbitrary occasions to destabilize the religious establishment; he can even ask others for suggestions if he finds none of his own at hand: "At present however men are *sore;* therefore, having established a raw, our game is to keep it from healing. I am projecting then a pamphlet, not for any specific measure, but generally on Church grievances, to *irritate,* and shall (if so) write it as rhetorically and vehemently as I can. If you can send me any *items* of grievance[,] do" (*LD* 4: 270).

Because he implicitly reduces all men and women to a depraved state for which no punishment could be too severe, the Anglican Newman erodes normal distinctions between friendly and hostile audiences. No religious denomination deserves preferential treatment, and none gets it: "[W]hat can one do? Men are made of glass—the sooner we break them and get it over, the better" (*LD* 4: 52). As he describes a friend's pummeling of the Lutherans, he enters into the occasion with what today seems the warped merriment of an abusive parent: "Have you seen Palmer's book? . . . He takes hold of them as gently and tenderly as if he was ipsissimus Luther—and when he has got them safe on his knee, he fetches them the most cruel and malicious blows" (*LD* 6: 217). As his list of opponents grows, the names upon it become almost as arbitrary as the occasions for attacking them. He counsels a fledgling collaborator, "after sketching [the] contents [of your Tract], pounce upon the unfortunate victims which you select. I send you some I *happen* to have—but you will find much better doubtless" (*LD* 6: 245).[31]

By indulging in such apparent vindictiveness, Newman may seem to sacrifice his cause to his personal gratification. He claims, however, to be inviting retaliation: "My book [*The Prophetical Office*], I expect, will be out next Wednesday. It is an anxious thing. I have to deal with *facts* . . .

which touch people to the quick. . . . I am aware that I deserve no mercy from your Protestants—and if they read me shall find none" (*LD* 6: 34). He sees this retaliation, moreover, as essential to his larger purpose: "Willingly would I . . . be said to write in an irritating and irritated way, if in that way I *rouse* people. . . . [B]y ways such as these alone can one move them" (*LD* 4: 117).[32] To shake his audience from their complacency, he abandons even self-consistency in order to play cheerleader, saint, martyr, goad, and buffoon: "I expect to be called a Papist when my opinions are know[n]. . . . Let others be Doctors of the Church. I do not aim at being such, (*though I think myself right*)—let me be thought extravagant, and yet be copied" (*LD* 4: 118). Then, in the midst of such extravagance, he argues that alienating an audience can be an effective, if paradoxical means of winning it over: "[T]he more you say and the further you go, the further people will follow. They will always lag a little behind in order to be safe and moderate, and to have the satisfaction of abusing you. They will any how make unfortunate you, a sacrifice to their self importance—and will criticize and disown you in order that they may with a good grace adopt (in substance) what you say" (*LD* 6: 320). By playing scapegoat, in other words, he is only assuming the indignities of Elijah along with his mantel: "[T]his is the way of things, we promote truth by a self sacrifice" (*LD* 4: 308). Commitment, confrontation, and self-dramatization thus form part of a complex heuristic through which he shapes not just his writing but his own identity.

Controversy as Formative

In an 1838 letter to Keble, however, Newman suddenly pleads with his audience for understanding, pity, even identification: "People really should put themselves into my place, and consider how the appearance of suspicion, jealousy, and discontent is likely to affect one, who is most conscious that every thing that he does is imperfect, and therefore soon begins . . . to have no heart and little power remaining to do any thing at all. . . . Is such conduct kind towards me? is it feeling?" (*LD* 6: 347).[33] Later he enlarges more candidly upon the power of such criticism, not just to undermine self-confidence, but to awaken opposing voices within the self: "Is it not natural that the questions should rise in my mind 'What business is it of yours? and are you doing it in the best way?' When a man like your brother *does* object, he has my own latent feelings on his side—and he goes just the way, whether he wishes it or not, to reduce me to silence" (*LD* 6: 350).[34] Only a few sentences before these, however, Newman has been arguing that he must speak out in spite of, or better still, because of criticism: "The character of [Oxford] must be considered. . . . One cannot stop still. Shrewd minds anticipate views, anticipate objections, oblige one to say yes or no—oblige one to defend oneself, oblige one to anticipate *their objections*" (*LD* 6: 350).

Taken together, these two contiguous passages encompass the paradox of Newman's complex emotional heuristic. His audience may mock him, vilify him, even reduce him to insecurity, self-division, and silence; yet he needs this confrontation every bit as much as the understanding for which he pleads. To quote Frank again: "[H]e urgently needed a thesis to attack or defend, some authority as the goal of his eloquence, or *concessions* made by another: then he had a start. In his conversation, as soon as he had extracted adequate concessions, he was a powerful reasoner, entangling, like Socrates, the unwary disputant" (44). To some friends Newman recommends this confrontational rhetoric as a pedagogical strategy: "You must recollect this is another benefit of tracts; it *engages staunch men in active warfare*. Miller will kindle, when he begins to write" (*LD* 4: 114). To Hugh J. Rose, he also acknowledges the occasional nature of his writings: "[W]hen I have been more alive, I have written too much as if I was *conversing*" (*LD* 4: 343). In Cunningham's words: "The whole atmosphere of his Oxford life leading up to his conversion to the Roman Church is conversational" (236).

More bluntly, Newman's rhetoric might be described as agonistic, called forth by some position with which he wants to take issue—or by someone upon whom he wants to hone his claws. To Blanco White he admits that he must look for subjects in such circumstances: "I ever find in the case of sermon writing, that the stimulus of an object and proposed hearer is necessary to enable me to write at all with satisfaction or comfort to myself—Without the data of place and time I seem to be working only an indeterminate problem" (*LD* 2:59–60).[35] Another letter even suggests that he cannot learn apart from such confrontation: "It is so difficult to read without an object. . . . [C]ontroversy is like the heat administered to sympathetic ink. [Without it I am] like a sailor landed at Athens or Grand Cairo, who stares about—does not know what to admire, . . . makes random remarks, and forgets all about it when he has gone" (*LD* 5: 133).[36] Like Newman himself, his rhetoric is intensely engaged, unashamedly contingent. Unlike his befuddled sailor, however, he uses his dependence on particular controversies to contextualize others. For an entire decade he defines himself as a reader, writer, and thinker by defining himself against all political, ecclesiastical, and educational institutions except the image of the city of God burning invisibly within his own heart.

The Originality of Religious Genius

For Newman, the figures who turn contingency against itself act with the authority of religious genius. Earlier we saw him invoke Paul and David to justify militancy as the only viable response to an age in chaos; yet he can also celebrate Paul's ability to transcend historical contingency by reshaping this chaos on his own spiritual terms:

> [Paul] wrote at a time when, if at any time, Christians were in lively and incessant agitation of mind; when persecution and rumours of persecution abounded; when all things seemed in commotion around them; when there was nothing fixed; when there were no Churches to soothe them, no course of worship to sober them, no homes to refresh them . . . ; it is well worthy of notice, that . . . he should draw a picture of the Christian character as free from excitement and effort, as full of repose, as still and as equable, as if the great Apostle wrote in some monastery of the desert or some country parsonage. Here surely is the finger of God; here is the evidence of supernatural influences, making the mind of man independent of circumstances! (*PS* 5 [5]: 59–60)

Translating Kant's ethical transcendence of circumstance into theological language, Newman extends the spiritual freedom of God's elect to include a freedom from social or historical contextualization.

Even in the secular context of his essay on poetry, he grants a similar potential to the engaged intellect: "Originality may perhaps be defined as the power of abstracting for one's self, and is in thought what strength of mind is in action. . . . Common minds transmit as they receive, good and bad, true and false; minds of original talent feel a continual propensity to investigate subjects, and strike out views for themselves" (*Ess.* 1: 20). Religious originality, as we saw in chapter 6, is both more powerful and more dangerous: Obedience "cannot . . . be the lot of all; but it is the lot of the many" (*PS* 3 [14]: 205). For the elect, however, the way of faith, so dark and blind for others, becomes a venue for demonstrating their consummate skill.[37] The mind

> passes on from point to point, gaining one by some indication; another on a probability; then availing itself of an association; then falling back on some received law; next seizing on testimony; then committing itself to some popular impression, or some inward instinct, or some obscure memory; and thus it makes progress not un-

like a clamberer on a steep cliff, who, by quick eye, prompt hand, and firm foot, ascends how he knows not himself, by personal endowments and by practice, rather than by rule, leaving no track behind him, and unable to teach another. It is not too much to say that the stepping by which great geniuses scale the mountains of truth is as unsafe and precarious to men in general, as the ascent of a skilful mountaineer up a literal crag. It is a way which they alone can take; and its justification lies in their success. (*US* [13]: 257)[38]

David Shaw analyzes this passage: "Suspense and uncertainty are an effect of the slowly expanding syntactic units and protracted grammar. . . . Only the resourceful but unpredictable hovering of Newman's syntax can make the ranging of mind to and fro, as it 'spreads out, and advances forward,' concrete and intelligible" (239–40).

In a slightly earlier university sermon, Newman claims the converse: not that only geniuses can succeed in such ventures but that no one can claim genius except through such success; he even intimates that only geniuses can determine whether they have succeeded or not.[39] If such self-assertion and self-assurance bring on popular contempt, then the populace becomes so much more the loser:

The most remarkable victories of genius, remarkable both in their originality and the confidence with which they have been pursued, have been gained, as though by invisible weapons, by ways of thought so recondite and intricate that the mass of men are obliged to take them on trust, till the event or other evidence confirms them. . . . [I]n an analogous way, Faith is a process of the Reason, in which so much of the grounds of inference cannot be exhibited, so much lies in the character of the mind itself, in its general view of things, its estimate of the probable and the improbable, its impressions concerning God's will, and its anticipations derived from its own inbred wishes, that it will ever seem to the world irrational and despicable;— till, that is, the event confirms it. (*US* [11]: 216–18)[40]

As we have seen, Newman becomes equally radical when he shifts his focus from the speculations of religious genius to the actions of the spiritually elect: "There is no calculation, no struggle, no self-regard, no investigation of motives. We act from love" (*PS* 5 [8]: 109). Just as Newman's images of Froude and of angelic natures seem to coalesce, so this more generalized portrait may not subordinate will to moral obedience so much as it redefines obedience in terms of individual will.

Individual Apotheosis

Weatherby complains that such subjectivity leads to the privileging of an individual leader over the community (177); it does indeed grant Newman almost unlimited appeal to his own ethos: "[I]ndividual exertions have a force about them, which perishes in the hands of a Committee" (*LD* 4: 120). He finds this force so indispensable that, in the privacy of a letter, he is willing to sanction even Luther's irreverent impetuosity as beyond reproof: "No great work was done by a system—whereas systems rise out of individual exertions. Luther was an individual. The very faults of an individual excite attention—he loses, but his cause (if good, and he powerful minded) gains. . . . So that a man corrects carefully upon his own standard, we must allow him his own standard. A critic must not attempt to mend a poem or a connoisseur a painting" (*LD* 4: 308). Yet he is far less comfortable with Luther or even Paul than he is with a model of his own making and very much of his own make. The fifth of his university sermons illustrates the transmission of religious doctrine with an extended portrait of one portentously identified as the Teacher of Truth. Although Newman offers it as a fictional construct, created as he goes along to support his points, their parallel childhoods suggest how closely the Teacher's life and personality mirror his own. The following "supposition," as we saw in chapter 5, can be taken as one of Newman's frankest reconstructions of his own youthful self-image: "We will suppose this Teacher of the Truth so circumstanced as One . . . as has never transgressed his sense of duty, but from his earliest childhood upwards has been only engaged in increasing and perfecting the light originally given him" (*US* [5]: 80).[41]

Having modeled his character, first on his own life and then on that of Jesus, Newman sends his Teacher out to confront the same incredulity that he and Jesus have confronted: "Let us conduct our secluded Teacher, . . . after his thirty years' preparation for his office, into the noise and tumult of the world; and in order to set him fairly on the course, let us suppose him recommended by some external gift. . . . At best [the multitude] will but admire the religious man, and treat him with deference; but in his absence they are compelled (as they say) to confess that a being so amiable and gentle is not suited to play his part in the scene of life; that he is too good for this world" (85–86).[42] With this multitude, a disembodied truth remains impotent: "Men persuade themselves, with little difficulty, to scoff at principles, to ridicule books, to make sport of the names of good men; but they cannot bear their presence: it is holiness embodied in personal form, which they cannot steadily confront and bear down" (92). Hence the Teacher's power must sanctify an aristocratic authority: "[T]he attraction, exerted by unconscious holiness, is of an urgent and irresistible nature; . . . over the thoughtless or perverse multitude it exercises a sovereign compulsory sway, bidding them fear and keep silence, on the ground of its own right divine to rule them,—its hereditary claim on their obedience" (95). In a roughly contemporary parochial sermon, this ability to cow skeptics is linked with an ability to commune with past, notably Patristic, times:

> [H]e who observes [regular church attendance] will grow in time a different man from what he was. . . . [H]is very voice, his manner, gait, and countenance, will speak of Heaven to those who know him well. . . . In seasons of unusual distress or alarm, when men's minds faint for fear, then he will have a natural power over the world, and will seem to speak not as an individual, but as if in him was concentrated all the virtue and the grace of those many Saints who have been his life-long companions. He has lived with those who are dead, and he will seem to the world as one coming from the dead, speaking in the name of the dead, using the language of souls dead to things that are seen, revealing the mysteries of the heavenly world, and awing and controlling those who are wedded to this. (*PS* 3 [17]: 252)

As the power of Newman's rhetoric conferred an integrity upon his own motives, so the power of this figure's ethos translates its claims into effective action. The claims themselves, as we explored them in chapter 3, remain suspect, and Newman seems to acknowledge as much in his repetitions of "will seem to" and "as if." Entering the lists in defense of Pusey's tract on baptism, however, he admits that he too has experienced the security of invisible Patristic support: "[W]hen one knows one has all the Fathers round one, . . . on the whole one feels secure and comfortable" (*LD* 6: 13). Describing his preaching at St. Mary's, Principal Shairp suggests that such influence bestowed on Newman a power rivaling that of his Teacher: "From his seclusion of study, and abstinence, and prayer, from habitual dwelling in the unseen, he seemed to come forth that one day of the week to speak to others of the things he had seen and heard" (247–48).

To Samuel Rickards Newman acknowledged, with Plato, that "Men live after their death . . . in that 'unwritten memory' [Gr.] exhibited in a school of pupils who trace their moral parentage to them. As moral truth is discovered, not by reasoning, but [by] habituation, so it is recommended not by books b[ut by] oral instruction. Socrates wrote nothing" (*LD* 2: 255).[43] It is thus with his own disciples that Newman's Teacher wields his greatest authority:

And if such be the personal influence excited by the Teacher of Truth over the mixed crowd of men whom he encounters, what (think we) will be his power over that select number . . . [who] feel themselves, as it were, individually addressed by the invitation of his example? . . . [B]y degrees they would discern more and more the traces of unearthly majesty about him; they would . . . still find, whether they looked above or below, that he rose higher, and was based deeper, than they could ascertain by measurement. Then at length, with astonishment and fear, they would become aware that Christ's presence was before them; and, in the words of Scripture, "would glorify God in His servant." (*US* [5]: 95–96)

Even though Newman carefully describes the Teacher's apotheosis from the perspective of his disciples, the ambiguous references make it impossible for them to know whether Christ is being made physically or only spiritually "present" to them. They are put in the unlikely position of God the Father within *Justification* who, "looking on us, sees not us, but this Sacred Presence, even His dearly beloved Son spiritually manifested in us."[44]

A Church Built Up from Vision

This power over individual disciples should be transferable to the political agenda of the Tractarians, and Newman is not shy of effecting such a transfer. Shortly after Keble's apostasy sermon, he describes his role to Thomas Mozley as the modest one of herald: "For myself, I am poking into the Fathers with a hope of rummaging forth passages of history which may prepare the *imaginations* of men for a changed state of things [this was 'the Church of the Fathers'], and also be precedents for our conduct in difficult circumstances" (*LD* 4: 24).[45] He comes to believe, however, that if he can himself "realize" his God-entrusted cause within his own mind, heart, and imagination, he can reshape seemingly objective reality. In urging his fellow Tractarians to acknowledge his "paper" church, he argues that proclaiming it forcefully enough will bring it to life: "I should be much against putting new wine into old bottles; but is it not the first step towards obtaining new bottles to vaunt of our new wine? the demand creates a supply. Hence I am used to think that to write *on the assumption* of a state of things which does not actually exist, i.e. in a manner which men will call rash and injudicious, is the way to realize that state" (*LD* 4: 344).[46] Persuaded that these assumptions are finding a local habitation, he encourages Keble to implement a kind of spiritual capitalism: "I hope you will not forget your promise of a volume of Sermons. I put it on this simple ground. *We are raising a demand for a certain article—and we must furnish a supply.* Men are curious after Apostolical principles, and we must not let the season slip. The seizing opportunities is the beginning, middle, and end of success—or rather, to put it higher, is *the* way in which we cooperate with the providential course of things" (*LD* 5: 279).[47] That his own preaching is performative, he is even more certain: "Truth has the gift of overcoming the human heart, whether by persuasion or by compulsion, whether by inward acceptance or by external constraint; and if what we preach be truth, it must be natural, it must be seasonable, it must be popular, it will make itself popular. It will find its own. As time goes on, and its way extends, those who thought its voice strange and harsh at first, will wonder how they could ever so have deemed of sounds so musical and thrilling" (*PO* 70).

Later, within the *Prophetical Office,* he claims that once his own vision is realized by and within his followers, it can instantiate itself within an ecclesiastical structure: "[D]id we receive the Creed as our Gospel, embrace and act upon the doctrine of our Services, and, if anywhere we differed, differ in silence, we should of ourselves without effort revive all those visible tokens of the Church's sovereignty, the want of which is our present excuse for disobedience. Surely, 'the kingdom of God is within us'; we have but to recognize the Church in faith, and it rises before our eyes" (263). Carlyle scoffed that "the Church of England" had been reduced to "shouting in the marketplace, '. . . I am either miraculous celestial or else nothing'" (cited in R. Pattison, *Dissent,* 21), but if Newman's magic was every bit as self-consciously anachronistic, it also shared the Romantic, mythopoeic exuberance of the young Keats: "What the imagination seizes as Beauty must be truth—whether it existed before or not"— or of the young Schlegel: "Every God not *made* by a man for himself is a mere idol"—or of the still youngish Blake: "All deities reside in the human breast."[48]

Newman, of course, would have literally died rather than assent to such blasphemous claims; yet in his own celebration of faith as action, the pervasive metaphors of personal encounter subsume questions of subject and object and of which is acting upon which. Within these multiple perspectives, Newman presents himself as one empowered by an approving God, but *simultaneously* as one creating the Absolute in the act of realizing it: "[S]o alert is the instinctive power of an educated conscience, that by some secret faculty, and without any intelligible reasoning process, it . . . feels a conviction of its own accuracy which bystanders cannot account for . . . —according to the saying which is parallel to the text 'I know My sheep, and am known of Mine'" (*US* [4]: 66–67). Just as this "test" of divine approbation collapses into an internally sanctioned ethic, so Newman's problematic desires to know and be known shift to the more active, more performative, more Romantic desires to create and thereby (re)create one's self.

Intercession and the Direction of Providence

The doctrine Newman uses to baptize this mutual and ongoing redefinition is intercession: "It is strange, indeed, that weak man should have strength to move God; but it is our privilege to know that we *can* do so" (*PS* 1 [19]: 250). Understandably nervous about its misuse, he insists that the vast majority of Christians, unsure of their own salvation, have no business praying for that of others. The elect, however, have not only the privilege of witnessing God's providence but the religious duty of directing it: "How can we complain of difficulties, national or personal . . . if we have but lightly used the intercessions offered up in the Litany, the Psalms, and in the Holy Communion? How can we answer to ourselves for the souls who have, in our time, lived and died in sin; . . . seeing that, for what we know, we were ordained to influence or reverse their present destiny and have not done it?" (*PS* 3 [24]: 365).[49] This duty, moreover, can expand into a role of cosmic importance: "He whom Christ has illuminated with His grace, is heir of all things. . . . He has a glorious prospect before him. . . . [A]re [the Saints] not in one sense counsellors and confidential servants of their Lord, intercessors at the throne of grace, the secret agents by and for whom He guides His high Providence, and carries the nations to their doom?" (*PS* 1 [20]: 265). Within such visions, a member of the elect, even while living, can stand

in God's presence upright and irreprovable, accepted in the Beloved, clad in the garments of righteousness, anointed with oil, and with a crown upon his head, in royal and priestly garb, as an heir of eternity. . . . [H]e is what Christ is. Christ intercedes above, and he intercedes below. Why should he linger in the doorway, praying for pardon. . . . He recognizes in statesmen, and warriors, and kings, and people, in revolutions and changes, in trouble and prosperity, not merely casual matters, but instruments and tokens of heaven and of hell. Thus he is in some sense a prophet; not a servant, who obeys without knowing his Lord's plans and purposes, but even a confidential "familiar friend" of the Only-begotten Son of God, calm, collected, prepared, resolved, serene, amid this restless and unhappy world. O mystery of blessedness, too great to think of steadily, lest we grow dizzy! Well is it for those who are so gifted, that they do not for certain know their privilege . . . for what mortal heart could bear to know that it is brought so near to God Incarnate? (*PS* 3 [24]: 362–64)[50]

What heart indeed! If Newman's does not know, it has certainly manifested strong intimations of just this kind of privilege. Newman may seem here to transform petition into a kind of Fichtean power of reshaping the cosmos into one's own mirror image. Yet here the most "significant other" is not the outer world where the elect "intercedes below." Just as Jesus defines himself by his relationship as God's son, so the elect must establish a like relationship as Jesus' "confidential 'familiar friend.'" As with the apotheosis of the righteous at the end of the last chapter, Newman's dialogic Romanticism has again preempted Augustine's trial; the power to intercede presupposes and is encompassed by a multifaceted power to interrelate.

CHAPTER 8

Self-Criticism, Self-Consciousness, and the Subject

❖

AT THE END of chapter 7, we implied that Newman's claim not to know his own visionary privilege was transparently ingenuous. The climactic apotheosis of his Teacher of Truth, however, is followed by a precipitous and Romantic fall into visionary doubt. Normally, Newman's assurance of divine support saves him from falling out of vision and back into "this unintelligible world," but here the sheer enormity of the Teacher's claims prompts the spiritual counterpart of Keats's rude awakening from his vision of the nightingale: "Forlorn! the very word is like a bell / To toll me back from thee to my sole self!" "Will it be said," Newman asks, that "This is a fancy, which no experience confirms?" (*US* [5]: 96). In answer he must pull back to a less exalted image of the Teacher as messenger: "[S]ay they are few, such high Christians; and what follows? They are enough to carry on God's noiseless work" (96). If the Teacher's visions and his vision of the Teacher are both upheld only by his own imaginative power, then Newman is trapped—not only in a circular argument but in the vicious circle drawn by Wordsworth in "Resolution and Independence":

> By our own spirits are we deified;
> We Poets in our youth begin in gladness,
> But thereof come in the end despondency and madness.
> (47–49)[1]

In this dilemma, however, Newman recapitulates what recent scholars see as the Romantics' most proleptically modern, self-critical gesture. Bracketing the question of whether such gestures can protect those assertions which *are* made, we encounter throughout Newman's Anglican writings a similar self-critical self-consciousness. This stance, while it threatens to cripple his own spiritual aspirations, allies him with the skeptical empiricists Hume and Gibbon and with their Romantic counterpart, Byron. In his version of their skepticism, however, Newman predicates dialogue with some outside power as the paradigm for his empathy with them.

The first-generation Romantics' turn toward individual imaginative transcendence is usually attributed to their disillusionment with the French Revolution. Recently, however, Jerome McGann and others have identified a similar turn in all the Romantics, a self-critical probing of the bases for this transcendence.[2] Romantic studies are still torn by debates over whether such self-criticism wins them pride of place within postmodern critique[3] or whether it remains another failed, self-deluding effort to escape from history; as McGann puts it: "The polemic of Romantic poetry, therefore, is that it will not be polemical; its doctrine that it is non-doctrinal; and its ideology, that it transcends ideology" (*Romantic* 70).[4] If they failed, their poetry only lures the academic community into an equally deluded flight from social responsibility into aestheticism.[5] If they succeeded, their poetry becomes itself critique—or, better, the boundary between poetry and critique dissolves.[6] The Anglican Newman, I would suggest, may offer a new perspective on this potentially circular pattern of critique undermining poetry and poetry anticipating critique. As Dwight Culler pointed out forty years ago, Victorian prose is characteristically "mediatorial": the Romantic poet "envisions," the Utilitarian "knows," but "the writer of critical prose stands in just that indirect and probable relation with his object which we call belief. . . . It is an impassioned form of knowledge" ("Method" 4).[7] In practice, Newman's more limited, relational version of Romantic transcendence may make good on more of its promises because it promises somewhat less.[8]

Self-Consciousness

First, however, we must establish that Newman questioned his moral, spiritual, aesthetic values fully as much as Blake did in his Satan, or Coleridge in his late lyrics, or Wordsworth in the London Books of the *Prelude,* or Shelley in *The Triumph of Life,* or Keats in his "Epistle to Reynolds," or Byron at almost any time. They posed their questions from outside the confines of religious orthodoxy; the Anglican Newman, for his part, wrenches this orthodoxy into an agonized maze of conflicting demands and prohibitions. In chapter 6 we saw him building his spiritual ideal as a bridge between Calvinistic election and Catholic sainthood. Here, rather more ominously, we find him trapped in self-consciousness, somewhere between an outgrown Calvinistic self-scrutiny and an unconscionable Catholic self-abandonment.

No one, to be sure, could be more self-consciously sensitive than Newman to the dangers of self-recording in the religious life: "[A]s to religious journals, useful as they often are, . . . persons find great difficulty, while recording their feelings, in banishing the thought that one day these good feelings will be known to the world, and are thus insensibly led to modify and prepare their language as if for a representation" (*PS* 2 [15]: 172). Reading fiction can lead to an equally debilitating self-analysis: "[I]f we allow our feelings to be excited without acting upon them, we do mischief to the moral system within us, just as we might spoil a watch, or other piece of mechanism, by playing with the wheels of it" (*PS* 2 [30]: 371).[9] Even Luke and Paul, as "accomplished men [who] evidently took pleasure in their accomplishments," ran a similar danger: "[T]he art of composing . . . has in itself a tendency to make us artificial and insincere. For to be ever attending to the fitness and propriety of our words, is . . . a kind of acting. . . . St. Luke perchance might have been such a Sophist, had he not been a Christian" (*PS* 2 [30]: 369, 374–75). Finally, Lutheran justification, as we saw in chapter 3, can encourage an equally paralyzing self-scrutiny: "[T]he poor and sorrowful soul . . . picture[s] to itself faith, as a sort of passive quality which sits amid the ruins of human nature, and . . . indulges a pensive meditation over its misery" (*Jfc.* 335–36).

Despite all his admonitions to Patristic self-forgetfulness, however, no one could question himself more corrosively than Newman. The best illustration of this obsessive, layered self-regard remains what Henry Tristram calls "an autobiography in miniature," a journal entry not completed until he was eighty-four but begun at eleven: "John Newman wrote this just before he was going up to Greek on Tuesday, June 10th, 1812, when it only wanted 3 days to his going home, thinking of the time (at home) when looking at this he shall recollect when he did it" (*AW* 5).[10] Within an 1820 letter to Frank, this progressive reflection transforms into a much more frightening exploration of the ways in which God may be regarding him: "If I look at the mercies of God, my soul is bright; when I view myself from a different point of view, I wonder how I can dare to assert any growth in grace. I am in dread now, lest, I should have written any thing presumptuous. . . . How in my future life, if I do live, shall I look back with a sad smile at these days!" (*LD* 1: 82–83). The same year he confesses to his then-mentor Walter Mayers: "I often find that I am acting the part of a very hypocrite; I am buoyed up with the secret idea, that by thus leaving the event [examinations] in the hands of God, when I pray, He may be induced, as a reward for so proper a spirit, to grant me my desire. Thus my prayer is a mockery" (*LD* 1: 87).[11] He cannot become transparent enough to be "found" by God until he transmutes self-scrutiny into God's scrutiny of the self.

During the course of the 1830s, however, this quest for transparency threatens to cleanse him of all human feelings. In yet another reminiscence on his Sicilian fever, he likens himself to glass, a medium able to transmit heat and light but unable to retain either. Three years later, when Henry Wilberforce praises his spiritual influence, he develops the metaphor: "[Let] any one who thinks good gained to her from what I have written . . . pray for me. . . . Such [compliments] do not seem to comfort or cheer me; I feel so conscious I am like the pane of glass (to use the common simile) which transmits heat yet is cold. I dare say I *am* doing good—but I have no consciousness that I retain any portion of it myself" (*LD* 6: 57).[12] In an 1839 letter to Rogers, coldness and transparency fuse in the figure of ice: "I doubt whether I should grieve though all that has been done [by the Movement] melted away like an ice palace. . . . I wish I lived as much in the unseen world as I think I do not live in this. The fear is, lest one lives in a world between the two, a selfish heart" (Moz. 2: 249–50).

An Empathy with Relativism

These self-judgments have been perhaps too eagerly endorsed by Newman's critics. According to Edwin Abbott, "[H]e cuts his nature into two parts and makes one part try to listen to another" (1:299); to Faber, "[I]n those private memoranda which he was constantly constructing for his own eye, sometimes even in his letters, he stands back and watches his behavior almost as though it were the behavior of another man" (152); to O'Faolain, "John was the most egocentric of the three [brothers], deeply introspective, constantly self-concerned, tirelessly self-recording" (77).[13] Yet Newman's ability to see himself as object is matched by an equal ability to enter into the subjectivity of other, vastly different thinkers. Hence, while trying to examine God examining the self, he can simultaneously contemplate a universe in which the self remains an object of complete indifference. We explored in chapter 7 the historical relativism which enforced Newman's reliance on action, but even his most famous poem, popularly retitled "Lead Kindly Light," grows out of a similarly dark agnosticism. This perplexity in turn inspired other, equally moving acknowledgments of his identification with the rest of struggling humanity: "[A]ll those who try to form their Creed by Scripture only, fall away from the Church and her doctrines, and join one or other sect or party.

. . . [I]t is one [objection] which before now (I do not scruple to say), I have much felt myself, and that without being able satisfactorily to answer: and which I believe to be one of the main difficulties . . . which God's providence puts at this day in the path of those who seek Him" (*DA* 110). Even more poignant is his account, just before he converted to Catholicism, of reading Blanco White's account of *his* conversion to Unitarianism:

> [T]he thought forcibly comes upon one, Why may not the case be the same with me? I see Blanco White going wrong yet sincere—Arnold going wrong yet sincere. They are no puzzle to me; I can put my finger on this or that fault in their character and say, Here was the fault. But they did not know the fault, and so it comes upon me, How do I know that I too have not my weak points which occasion me to think as I think. How can I be sure I have not committed sins which bring this unsettled state of mind on me as a judgment? (quoted in W. Ward 1: 81)[14]

This position of fallibility and possible sinfulness is no position from which to judge the minds and hearts of others: "Nothing is so difficult as to enter into the characters and feelings of men who have been brought up under a system of religion different from our own; and to discern how they may be most forcibly and profitably addressed" (*PS* 2 [9]: 100). He was far from happy with this situation; as Chadwick points out: "He did not say, this is true for me, I do not care whether it is true for others. . . . He cared very much" ("Bremond" 188). Nevertheless, he flirted with a psychological solipsism throughout his life. It will form the ground of the *Grammar*,[15] but it appears just as forcefully almost a half-century earlier in an 1825 letter to Charles:

> Attempt to convince an uneducated person that in mathematics two lines are conceivable which always converge without meeting at any definite distance, and . . . he looks upon his informant as a fool. . . . Your awkward attempt at explanation increases his conviction of your folly. Thus ignorance is conceited. . . . [You are] assuming that unassisted reason is competent to discover moral and religious truth. If this were the case, I confess it would be a great argument *in limine* against any revelation at all. (*LD* 1: 225, 228)

While these defensive accusations of ignorance and conceit are provoked by Charles's open rationalism, elsewhere John scrupulously avoids claiming for himself the kind of knowledge that would allow him to sit in judgment. To an unknown correspondent before his conversion he pleads, "I never proposed to myself at starting to take another man's views of what is good and what is bad. Each man has his own views; one man may criticize another's; let us leave off this unprofitable labour, let us take each other's opinions as *facts,* when they are not counter to one common profession, and learn to bear each other" (*KC* 176-77). The early sermon quoted in chapter 7, indirectly enjoins such mutual toleration by attributing "every feeling and opinion" only to "the centre light which is set up in [each man's] soul" (*PS* 2 [14]: 157). In a letter to the then still-orthodox Blanco White, he also uses color and light to measure

the incommensurability (so to speak) of the human mind—we cannot gauge and measure by any common rule the varieties of thought and opinion. We all look at things with our own eyes—and invest the whole face of nature with colours of our own.—Each mind pursues its own course and is actuated in the course by ten thousand indescribable incommunicable feelings and imaginings. . . . [O]n no single point do any two individuals agree—no single object do their minds view from the same spot and in the same light. (*LD* 2: 60)[16]

Here we come very close to the almost solipsistic lines sent back to his sisters from the Hermes:

Each mind is its own centre; and it draws
Home to itself, and moulds in its thought's span
All outward things, the vassals of its will.
(*LD* 3: 135)[17]

The Attraction of Skepticism

In contemporary sermons, individualities inaccessible to others come to seem unfathomable in their very nature. One passage is justly famous for its stark contrast between the apparent hubbub of "some populous town" and the "truth" that "every being in that great concourse is his own centre, and all things about him are but shades" (*PS* 4 [6]: 82). Equally significant, however, is Newman's subsequent insistence that "No one outside of [the individual] can really touch him, can touch his soul, his immortality; he must live with himself for ever. He has a depth within him unfathomable, an infinite abyss of existence; and the scene in which he bears part for the moment is but like a gleam of sunlight upon its surface."[18] Passages like this prompt Brilioth's claim that "the Calvinistic Evangelicalism of his youth . . . fostered in him that fundamental individualism which no school or party or Church could change" (*Evangelicalism* 24).[19]

His alienation from "school or party or Church" account both for the apparent skepticism criticized by T. H. Huxley, who claimed he could extract "a Primer of Infidelity" from Newman's writings,[20] and by Connop Thirlwall, who sneered: "[T]he extravagant credulity with which he accepts the wildest Popish legends is, as it appears to me, only another side of his bottomless unbelief" (261).[21] Thomas Mozley insists that "During the whole period of my personal acquaintance . . . , I never had any other thought than that he was . . . more entirely convinced of the truth of what he was saying, than any other man"; yet Mozley also acknowledges that "the dread of unbelief may have given greater activity to belief" (2: 437–38). Such insinuations were abroad well before 1845, and in a letter of that year to Christie, Newman's exaggerated fear for his reputation seems to belie a more personal fear. Christie's rumor of his skepticism, instead of occasioning this struggle, seems to have interrupted one already in progress:

> Generally I am careless about reports, but I cannot let this pass without at once contradicting it. . . . I suppose indeed there are few persons of education to whom sceptical thoughts do not occur, that is from without. . . . I never have felt the temptation for an instant from within. Very likely I have said to some persons, indeed I know I have, that I thought the English system was so inconsistent that [if] a careful thinker . . . did not go forward, he might, as a judgment, be left to fall behind. . . . But to fear a temptation is not to feel it. (*KC* 373–74)

The epigrammatic alliteration of this last sentence cannot hide the contradictions latent within it. Fear is nothing if not a feeling, and a temptation cannot be a temptation without evoking other feelings than fear. As Chadwick puts it: "This bogey of scepticism was no bogey; it was his personal terror, the dead hand which scrabbled at him in the night when his faith was sleeping" (*Bossuet* 126). Newman's critics, early and late, are right when they claim that he had an ongoing attraction to skepticism; they are wrong only when they slight its complexity.

Newman is most likely to admit this attraction when it can be somehow delimited. In the third of his *Tracts for the Times,* for example, he restricts it to matters of liturgy: "A taste for criticism grows upon the mind. . . . I confess that there are few parts of the Services that I could not disturb my self about, feel fastidious at, if I allowed my mind in this abuse of reason" (1 [3]: 2). In a university sermon he hedges the attraction as a condition foreign to him and prevalent only in those not graced with an innate sense of God's presence: "The system of physical causes is so much more tangible and satisfying than that of final, that unless there be a pre-existent and independent interest in the inquirer's mind, leading him to dwell on the phenomena which betoken an Intelligent Creator, he will certainly follow out those which terminate in the hypothesis of a settled order of nature and self-sustaining laws" (*US* [10]: 194). Only with this hedging can he cushion his subsequent admission: "It is indeed a great question whether Atheism is not as philosophically consistent with the phenomena of the physical world, taken by themselves, as the doctrine of a creative and governing Power" (194).

The same "great question" certainly punctures Peel's smug assurance that knowing the physical sciences can make people better, but it puts Newman's own conviction in almost equal jeopardy: "[W]e may refer all things forwards to design, or backwards on a physical cause. . . . Does the sun shine to warm the earth, or is the earth warmed because the sun shines? The one hypothesis will solve the problem as well as the other. . . . I believe that the study of Nature, when religious feeling is away, leads the mind, rightly or wrongly, to acquiesce in the atheistic theory, as the simplest and easiest" (*DA* 299–300). Finally, he questions whether religious evidences, even if found, will square with monotheism. Within a slippery slope argument for the relative coherence of the Trinity, we find hidden the theology which bewitched the young Augustine and held some appeal for the Utilitarian James Mill—a Manichean premise that two gods would be more defensible than either one or three. Unbelievers will argue: "'You tell me that there is but one God; and you tell me to look abroad into the world, and I shall see proofs of it. I do look abroad, and I see good and evil. I see the proof, then, of two gods, a good God, and another, evil. I see two principles struggling with each other.' . . . As in the first case [of arguing from Scripture, the Christian] will, unless he is properly qualified, be in great risk of perplexing himself and denying that God is Three, so will he, in the latter, run great risk of denying God is One" (*PS* 6 [23]: 336–37).[22]

This passage may qualify Newman's cry of "utter consternation" at receiving, "a letter from you [Charles] claiming me as a brother-sceptic, if not a brother-infidel" (*LD* 2: 276). In fact an earlier letter to Charles acknowledges the intoxicating novelty of self-conceived and self-centered system-making:

> Fresh theories of morals and religion are no uncommon thing; every projector flatters himself that now at last he has hit the mark; . . . your mind swells and boils; new scenes are opened to your eye; a new order of things is stretched out before you, and you have now

to choose where you shall plant your foot and where mark out the boundaries of your habitation. Nor are you uninfluenced by an ambitious and vain desire of becoming a champion in the cause of your supposed truth; and you feed your mind with proud imaginations of the moral conquests which your enlightened intellect is to achieve. . . . In spite of the allsufficiency of knowledge, you will find it a cold and bleak state of things to be left carelessly and as it were unkindly by the God who made you, uncertain why you are placed here, and what is to become of you after death. . . . Your greatest peace will be the calm of hopelessness: solitudinem faciunt, pacem appellant. (*LD* 1: 214–15)

The whole passage anticipates the charge in the *Tamworth Reading Room* that natural theologians are only worshiping their own ingenuity; yet once again, as in the sermon on suicide, a subtext intercedes for his rebellious opponent.[23] In the skewed appeal to Galgacus' mordant epigram in Tacitus' *Agricola* (30), the wanton devastation wrought by Roman military power figures forth both Charles's rebellion and God's "careless" and "unkind" judgment upon it.[24] Even in a late university sermon, Newman can find "expansion and elevation" inherent in skeptical ideas: "[W]hen a person for the first time hears the arguments and speculations of unbelievers, and feels what a very novel light they cast upon what he has hitherto accounted most sacred, it cannot be denied that, unless he is shocked and closes his ears and heart to them, he will have a sense of expansion and elevation" (*US* [14]: 284).[25]

Gibbon as Mentor

In trying to trace the skeptical strand in Newman's thought, both J. M. Cameron ("Night") and John Finlay have pointed directly to the Scottish empiricists. As Charles Frederick Harrold stated, "[Gibbon and Hume,] two classic skeptics of the English eighteenth century[,] never ceased to fascinate Newman. . . . Newman is never really harsh with Gibbon." Harrold adds, however, that these skeptics "never, of course, convinced him of the tenability of their position" (*Newman* 14). Harrold's "of course" here may prove a bit premature; Newman's infatuation with Gibbon in particular was planted early and took deep root. In an essay appended to the *Idea*, he confesses that, "when I was seventeen . . . , I fell in with the twelfth volume of Gibbon, and my ears rang with the cadence of his sentences, and I dreamed of it for a night or two" (265). Ten pages earlier, he rather melodramatically opposes Gibbon (along with Milton) to English Catholic literature: "[W]e cannot deny their power; we cannot write a new Milton or a new Gibbon; we cannot expurgate what needs to be exorcised. They are great English authors, each breathing hatred to the Catholic Church in his own way, each a proud and rebellious creature of God, each gifted with incomparable gifts" (255).[26] The opposition defined here evokes an early opposition within Newman's own psyche, one disturbing enough to make him cry out for exorcism within an undergraduate letter: "[W]hen I reflect on [Gibbon's] happy choice of expressions, his vigorous compression of ideas, and the life and significance of every word, I am prompted indignantly to exclaim that no style is left for historians of an after day. O who is worthy to succeed our Gibbon! *Exoriare aliquis!* and may he be a better man!" (*LD* 1: 67).

While Newman claims here to be challenging the whole Anglican establishment, his subsequent choice of *The Arians of the Fourth Century* as his first large-scale work suggests that he was throwing down the gauntlet with the set intention of picking it up himself.[27] His allusion to Book IV of the *Aeneid,* moreover, both intensifies and complicates the metaphor of exorcism. The cry, "Exoriare aliquis" (Arise, someone!), hurled by the abandoned Dido at the departing fleet of Aeneas, casts Gibbon as the unfaithful lover and Newman himself as both the seduced Dido and her future avenger. The paradoxes do not stop even there; Newman does indeed begin as a Hannibal, mounting a powerful attack upon Rome. By converting to Roman Catholicism, however, he implicitly allows himself to be seduced by Rome's founder, Aeneas, and by Gibbon, his unlikely surrogate.[28]

That Newman saw Gibbon and Gibbon's style as seductive is implied both in Mozley's recollection that "he could recite many long passages" (2: 40) and in an early letter to one sister about another: "Harriet [*sic*] has been showing me what she has done of the passage of Gibbon. . . . [T]o imitate Gibbon's style is comparatively easy, for here is a set of words put before one, and the mind is insensibly biassed by the diction of them" (*LD* 1: 90). I would argue that in his own quest for an "answerable style," the young Newman was himself "insensibly biassed," not necessarily toward Gibbon's world view, but toward one which *could be* encapsulated within the balanced clauses of a Gibbonesque sentence. Thus, for both authors style dictated substance. Both sought out an order in experience which paralleled the syntactic order of their written prose. Both saw history in terms of what they could say and how they could say it.

Byronism

Cameron argues that Newman's self-consciousness grows directly out of his empathy with an empiricist, Humean skepticism which will not commit itself to any "reality" beyond impressions because of "the absolute unintelligibility of what lies beyond inwardness" ("Empiricist" 87). Hence Newman's self-critical melancholy would also resemble that of Hume: "[W]hen the empiricist comes to explore the structure of the private theatre [of the self], . . . the darkness is now as much an interior as an exterior darkness" ("Night" 106).[29] This same fusion, however, is even more apparent in the Romantic who maintained the least qualified admiration for his Augustan predecessors, Lord Byron. Indeed, if we try to explain Newman's otherwise anomalous admiration for Byron, we may speculate that Byron's stylistic decorum somehow mitigated the rank skepticism of his content. As Harrold puts it: "Newman as a master of rhetoric took keen delight in Byron's flowing eloquence" (*Newman* 264). In Byron, however, Augustan skepticism is put to more grandiose and more desperate uses as the subject rebels against the straightened universe to which rational critique has exiled him. Byron's response, Riede maintains, is to turn from self-discovery to self-conscious self-construction: "[T]he self moves along in the world, seeking to possess the world," and within this process, "self-making and text-making [become] essentially the same operation."[30] Riede points out, however, that in the midst of this construction, Byron's irony "seems even to deconstruct the authority of the poetic self" (250, 252).

As another Romantic whose life is shaped by textual self-creation, Newman is willing to explain (though not excuse) Byron as a victim of his age. He even implies that natures like Byron's could be salvaged under more favorable circumstances: "those minds, which naturally most resemble the aboriginal chaos, contain within them the elements of a marvellous creation of light and beauty, if they but open their hearts to the effectual power of the Holy Spirit. Pride and sullenness, obstinacy and impetuosity, then become transformed into the zeal, firmness, and high-mindedness of religious Faith" (*US* [9]: 166). Byron's only cultural inheritance, however, was social, and thence psychological, anarchy:

> [W]hen the moral and intellectual principles are vigorous, active, and developed[,] . . . if the governing power be feeble, all the subordinates are in the position of rebels in arms. . . . Then we have before us the melancholy spectacle of high aspirations without an aim, a hunger of the soul unsatisfied, and a never-ending restlessness and inward warfare of its various faculties. Gifted minds, if not sub-

mitted to the rightful authority of religion, become the most unhappy and the most mischievous. . . . We have seen in our own day,
in the case of a popular poet, an impressive instance of a great genius
throwing off the fear of God, seeking for happiness in the creature,
roaming unsatisfied from one object to another, breaking his soul
upon itself, and bitterly confessing and imparting his wretchedness
to all around him. (*HS* 2: 143–44)

Anticipating Arnold's portrait of Byron bearing "Through Europe . . . /
The pageant of his bleeding heart," Newman's portrait dramatizes the
bankruptcy of post-Enlightenment Europe by tracing both its despair
and Byron's to an Augustinian longing for the God whom they both
reject.

After asserting that "I have no wish at all to compare [Byron] to St.
Augustine," Newman proceeds to do just that:

[T]he very different termination of their trial seems to indicate some
great difference in their respective modes of encountering it. The
one dies of premature decay, to all appearance, a hardened infidel;
. . . the other is a Saint and Doctor of the Church. Each makes confessions, the one to the saints, the other to the powers of evil. . . .
At least, there is no appearance in St. Augustine's case of that dreadful haughtiness, sullenness, love of singularity, vanity, irritability, and
misanthropy, which were too certainly the characteristics of our own
countryman. (144–45)

This contrast anticipates even the wording of the contrast between Basil
and Julian which concludes Discourse 8 of the *Idea*. Linda Peterson
argues that, within the *Apologia*, Newman's echoes of the *Confessions* signal an autobiographical shift away from the subjectivity of Protestant
conversion narratives (108–19). Yet most of the traits identified in this
passage as Byronic reappear a page later within Augustine's account of
his own Manichean self-division. Very much like Byron's misery, Augustine's

was that of a mind imprisoned, solitary, and wild with spiritual
thirst; and forced to betake itself to the strongest excitements, by
way of relieving itself of the rush and violence of feelings, of which
the knowledge of the Divine Perfections was the true and sole sus-
tenance. He ran into excess, not from love of it, but from this fierce
fever of mind. "I sought what I might love," he says in his Confessions, "in love with loving, and safety I hated, and a way without
snares. . . . So I fretted, sighed, wept, was distracted; had neither
rest nor counsel. For I bore about a shattered and bleeding soul, im-

patient of being borne by me, yet where to repose it I found not; not in calm groves, nor in games and music, nor in fragrant spots, nor in curious banquetings, nor in indulgence of the bed and the couch, nor, finally, in books or poetry found it repose. . . ." (*HS* 2: 145)

This splendid passage, often seen as a cornerstone of Romanticism itself, is transformed by Newman's context into one of its many reincarnations. What the pre-Christian Augustine escapes through conversion,[31] the Anglican Newman, balanced between one conversion and the implicit threat of another, cannot escape so easily. As Newman's anguished description flows into Augustine's anguished self-description—just as Byron's traits flow into Augustine's—both of their self-obsessed, self-doomed, self-mocking quests seem to pass through at least a corner of Newman's own psyche.

The progression of Byron's influence can be traced in Newman's early notebooks; a journal entry of 3 September 1828 reads "finished Pusey's book—began Sardanapalus (Byron)" (*LD* 2: 94). Instead of closing his Byron and opening his Goethe, as Carlyle recommended, Newman here closes off a potential encounter with German Idealism in favor of more congenial reading. Ten days later he "read 2nd Canto Child Harold." What he found congenial is suggested in his 1829 poetry essay: "The Corsair is intended for a remarkable personage. We pass by the inconsistences of his character, considered by itself. The grand fault is, that whether it be natural or not, we are obliged to accept the author's word for the fidelity of his portrait. . . . Byron had very little versatility or elasticity of genius" (*Ess.* 1: 19–20). Behind the neo-classical commonplaces and the defensive condescension, Newman must acknowledge Byron's assertions, however poorly dramatized, because they build a cosmos almost the mirror image of his own. The hero Conrad is at heart as much a solitary as Newman: "Lone, wild, and strange, he stood alike exempt / From all affection and from all contempt" (1.271–72). Like Newman's, his childhood exemplifies a moral determinism which has literally calcified the rest of his life.[32] Imprisoned, he confesses that he too has had an early and decisive encounter with God, a rejection which God is now reciprocating.[33] This God, remarkably like Newman's, Conrad must acknowledge in the very teeth of his defiance: "I have no thought to mock his throne with prayer / Wrung from the coward's crouching of despair" (2:479–80). As we will see in our next chapter, Newman accosted the religiously complacent with similar threats: "It is very common to speak of our political and social privileges as *rights,* which we may do what we like with; . . . you have the right, that is, you have the power,— (to speak plainly) the power to damn yourself. . . . [B]ut the first who exercised that right was the devil when he fell", (*PS* 3 [15]: 216–18). Byron's heroes thus offer gratifying, though negative, support for Newman's cause; they may damn themselves, but like Satan and unlike the British public, they do so knowingly.

In this acknowledgment, however, in this perpetual antagonism to the divine, Byron runs the same risk he ran in opposing his age. Riede, following McGann, claims that in "undermin[ing] every other possible discourse, [Byron's tone] posits its own ironic mode as the one unassailably authoritative discourse" (253). By fixing his God in the stern Calvinistic mold of his childhood, Byron threatens to fix his own persona in rebellious adolescence: "wenn er dichtet," pronounced Goethe to Eckermann in 1825, "sobald er reflektiert, ist er ein Kind."

Dialogue as Paradigm

By contrast, Newman works to keep open not just the dialogue with God but the nature of both parties. By extension, therefore, he can invoke dialogue as a template both for self-reflection and for human empathy. To this point we have regarded these as separate though complementary means of shoring up his claims and his identity. With increasing frequency during the 1830s, however, Newman's previous alternatives, rejection and appropriation, are supplemented by a more open-ended interaction modeled on his spiritual dialogue. As Newman reincorporates religious issues and religious contemporaries, he reenacts the self-reflection which prompted him to engage them in the first place. This alternating rhythm —positing first self in others and then others in self—falls short of the imaginative transcendence claimed by the Romantics, but it incorporates a thicker, more fully realized description of Newman's own experience.

Curiously enough, Newman criticizes Milman's *History of Christianity* most severely for its uncritical identification with its sources:

[W]e really do not see what the merit is, which he seems to claim for his historical method. Not that we cannot conceive many reasons for contemplating sacred things as they show themselves externally; but there is a broad intelligible difference between throwing one's mind into the feelings of a certain state of society, or into the views of certain persons, for an occasion or purpose, and habitually taking their feelings or views as one's own, and making what is not the true position for surveying them the centre of our own thoughts about them. (*Ess.* 2: 207)

Even here, however, he must endorse part of Milman's project; elsewhere he accuses other rationalists of a similar failure to reach out toward the spiritual phenomena all around them: "To believe in Objective Truth [external to this or that individual mind] is to throw ourselves forward upon that which we have but partially mastered or made subjective; to embrace, maintain, and use general propositions which are larger than our own capacity, of which we cannot see the bottom, which we cannot follow out into their multiform details. . . . Such a belief, implicit, and symbolized as it is in the use of creeds, seems to the Rationalist superstitious and unmeaning" (*Ess.* 1: 34–35).[34]

In fact the Anglican Newman insisted that he habitually entered into the mindset of opposing clerics. During their drawn-out debate over Oriel's tutorial program, he assured Hawkins, "I have not neglected to put myself (as far as I could) into your situation—and it is my belief that the plan I consider necessary would be *permanently* beneficial to the College" (*LD* 2: 242). While Hawkins may have thought that Newman's "as far as I could" was not very far at all, we need to temper our skepticism with Isaac Williams's comment that "Newman had a peculiar power of seizing intellectually the ethos [Gr.] of another and making them his own, as it were, on trial" (cited in Bremond 3; see also Abbott, *Anglican,* 1: 406). This judgment echoes Newman's famous portrait of the gentleman in Discourse 8 of the *Idea:* "[H]e is tender towards the bashful, gentle towards the distant, and merciful towards the absurd. . . . [H]e throws himself into the minds of his opponents, he accounts for their mistakes. He knows the weakness of human reason as well as its strength" (179–80). But Newman proleptically employs similar criteria in 1828, even before the tutorship furor, when he gives Hawkins his reasons for objecting to a particular candidate as Oriel fellow: "He seems to me quite or nearly without, not merely original talent, but the power of making the thoughts of others his own—To me he always appears to speak by rote and rule, not as if his mind worked upon a subject" (*LD* 2: 53).

Conversely, he claims to value the opinions of others on himself: In 1843, when J. R. Hope suggested that his difficulty with Anglicanism constituted an elaborate psychological game, Newman considers "the possibility of unknown biases in *myself,* which, if they exist, I would fain detect. I am not conscious of the one I have just mentioned" (*KC* 313).[35] This rhythmic, antiphonal interchange between subject and object positions may be a product of his religious crisis.[36] In 1841, some months after his publication of Tract 90, a university sermon celebrated faith as just this probing, imaginative identification: "Faith is ever the means of learning something new, and in this respect differs from Bigotry, which has no element of advance in it, and is under a practical persuasion that it has nothing to learn" (*US* [14]: 303). Newman goes on to characterize bigotry as faith's opposite, an intellectual tunnel vision:

[I]t disowns Faith, and makes a show of Reason against it. It persists, not in abandoning argument, but in arguing only in one way. It takes up, not a religious, but a philosophical position. . . . [Bigots] expect to be able to argue others into a belief of the[ir doctrines], and are impatient when they cannot. . . . They profess that the inspired writers were precisely of their particular creed, be it a creed of today, or yesterday, or of a hundred years since. . . . Words of parties or politics . . . are as much a portion of the Truth in their eyes, as if they were the voice of Scripture or of Holy Church. . . . Narrow minds have no power of throwing themselves into the minds of others. They have stiffened in one position, as limbs of the body subjected to confinement, or as our organs of speech, which after a while cannot learn new tones and inflections. (*US* [14]: 300, 305–7)

Newman here mounts an attack on sectarianism far more trenchant than any of the similar attacks mounted against him. His Evangelical contemporaries, of course, would align the voice of "Holy Church," not with that of Scripture, but with the "words of parties or politics" venerated by bigots. For once, however, Newman refuses to distance the threat of divergent opinions by denouncing them in opponents. Analyzing this same defensiveness within bigots, he describes graphically those "reptiles of the mind" which it breeds within them:

[Bigots] grow giddy amid cross divisions; and, even if they make the effort, cannot master them. They think that any one truth excludes another which is distinct from it. . . . They are soon persuaded that another agrees with them, if he disagrees with their opponents. They resolve his ideas into their own. . . . [N]o knowledge can be submitted to [true philosophy] with which it is not commensurate, and which it cannot annex to its territory. But the theory of the narrow or bigoted has already run out within short limits, and a vast and anxious region lies beyond, unoccupied and in rebellion. Their "bed is shorter than that a man can stretch himself on it; and the covering narrower, than that he can wrap himself in it." And then what is to be done with these unreclaimed wastes?—the exploring of them must in consequence be forbidden, or even the existence denied. (*US* [14]: 307, 309)[37]

Apparently belying Newman's sectarian uncertainties, the passage foreshadows his claim in the *Apologia* that "Ten thousand difficulties do not make one doubt" (214).

Religious Inclusiveness

Yet before Newman can rest safe from those rebellious regions feared by his Evangelical opponents, he must find ways of engaging the "unre-claimed wastes" of nineteenth-century pluralism.[38] In a contemporary sermon, he does indeed come to an "understanding" (to use his word) with anti-erastianism: "When a man (for instance) says that he takes part against the King or against the Church, because he thinks kingly power or estab-lished Churches contrary to Scripture, I think him as far from the truth as light is from darkness; but I understand him. He takes a religious ground, and, whatever I may think of his doctrine, I praise him for that. I had rather he should take a religious ground (if in sincerity) and be against the Church, than a worldly selfish ground, and be for it" (*PS* 3 [15]: 213). And with this "understanding" of the differences inherent in religious experience, he can invoke his godlike discretion to refrain from judgment: "[I]t does not become us, who . . . [know] definitely where are the paths and dwelling-places of God in the visible world, to despise those who were 'seeking Him, if haply they might feel after Him and find Him.' Superstition is a faith which falls below that standard of religion which God has given, whatever it is. . . . [W]e have no right to apply this standard, in particular cases, to other men whose circumstances are different from our own" (*US* [12]: 244).[39]

Since he refused any permanent refuge in negative capability, Newman revered Froude because he could encompass the controversies threaten-ing their Church within a more productive synthesis: "When I look around and see others carried away [from orthodoxy], I sometimes say, . . . 'he has not the mental power for what is called mysticism—' but now in dear H[urrell] F[roude]'s case, we see the strong temptation fairly met and overcome. We see his mind only breaking out into more original and beautiful discoveries, from that very repression which seemed at first likely to be the utter prohibition of his powers" (*LD* 6: 87). Yet this letter was written to Keble in the process of editing Froude's manuscripts after his death. An earlier sermon transparently describes him as if he were al-ready dead, and here Newman can only measure his friend's spiritual powers, much as Shelley measured the "fading coal" of his own imagina-tive powers, by their present unavailability: "Men there are, who, in a single moment of their lives, have shown a superhuman height and ma-jesty of mind . . . ; and who by such passing flashes . . . give token to us that they are but Angels in disguise. . . . Yet they are suddenly taken away, and we have hardly recognized them when we lose them" (*PS* 4 [14]: 218–19).

At the beginning of this chapter, I juxtaposed the self-conscious turn in Newman's envoi to his Teacher with the same turn in Keats's envoi to the nightingale. I would like to close with Newman's envoi to Anglicanism, the conclusion to his sermon, "The Parting of Friends." In this justly famous passage, Newman returns to Romantic self-criticism under the most trying circumstances. As we have seen, he extended his own dialogic model in response to other, potentially dangerous perspectives. At this point, however, these new perspectives have robbed him of his doctrinal certainty, his historical foundation, his ecclesiastical structure, his institutional position, rank, and title. The passage thus invokes Romantic power and simultaneously laments its passing, it appeals to its audience and simultaneously denies the bases for these appeals, it assumes superhuman gifts and simultaneously acknowledges the manifold evidence of God's anger:

> And, O my brethren, O kind and affectionate hearts, O loving friends, should you know any one whose lot it has been by writing or by word of mouth, in some degree to help you thus to act; if he has ever told you what you knew about yourselves, or what you did not know; has read to you your wants or feelings, and comforted you by the very reading; . . . remember such a one in time to come, though you hear him not, and pray for him that in all things he may know God's will, and at all times he may be ready to fulfil it. (*SD* [26]: 409)

In the amazing indirection of his self-reference, his use of conditional, third person, indefinite pronoun ("should you know anyone"), Newman shows himself more daring in his claims and more hesitant in making them. His characteristic power Father Lockhart described as self-effacement (*KC* 391) and Chadwick as disappearance: "The more overwhelming the reality, the more th[is] preacher's personality started to hide. Popular preachers create their effect by making their personality large. Newman created his effect by disappearing in the reality of which he spoke, as though he must get out of its way. . . . Yet the kind of man preaching comes through" (*Newman* 21, 24).[40] Here, however, forced to instantiate himself as a spiritual leader without either a church or a flock, Newman has nowhere left to hide.[41]

In response, he fuses the two supposedly incompatible genres which Mill defined ten years earlier in his defense of the Romantic lyric, "Thoughts on Poetry": "[E]loquence is heard, poetry is *over*heard. Eloquence supposes an audience; the peculiarity of poetry appears to us to lie in the poet's utter unconsciousness of a listener. Poetry is feeling confessing itself to itself" (348). Here Newman plays for a departing audience, his congregation, the poet that neither he nor they can be alone; he overhears and articulates what they cannot hear within themselves and what he can no longer articulate within himself. Imitating the voice of his conscience speaking to him from without, Newman claims to have been that voice within his congregation, telling them both what they knew and did not know about themselves. Like earlier Romantics, however, he can only identify a faculty which he no longer possesses; as Culler puts it: "He felt that the springs of his power were associated with persons and places and experiences in the past" ("Remembrance" 64).[42] By denying the Church's authority over him, he has simultaneously denied his authority over his audience. Even his self-asserted identity as a voice breaks up, much as Freud and Lacan would have it, into a chorus of internalized voices ever receding into the past.

If the passage thus reenacts the unravelling of Romantic identification and Romantic power, the dialogue and the participants within it cannot be so unravelled because they remain the agents of the unravelling. And as it mourns one set of relationships, the passage interweaves new ones. Through the offices of memory and prayer, the friendship of "kind and affectionate hearts" must compensate for the disappearance of structure, position, authority, and voice. In this invitation, Newman identifies the agent of his fall from power, but instead of invoking God directly, he falls back on a now-chastened power of intercession. At the end of the last chapter, we saw the elect helping to direct the course of the entire world; here Newman must plead with friends to intercede for him before he can reopen what has been an intensely private dialogue with his God.

CHAPTER 9

Social Criticism: Religious and Secular

❖

WHEN WE MOVE from self-criticism to social criticism, the Anglican Newman appears more vulnerable than even the more conservative of his Romantic predecessors. He did nothing to hide his reactionary Tory politics, and although Pattison claims this as a trenchant dissent from modern relativism, his claim seems compromised, in the Anglican Newman at least, by Newman's complicity with Romanticism. The very subjectivity of his spiritual transcendence opens him to the postmodern critique of imaginative transcendence in the Romantics. Yet when Newman differentiates himself from his Protestant contemporaries, his portraits of Evangelicals may be fraught with class bias, but those of the Anglican establishment and their liberal counterparts caricature these same biases within them. Although Newman, as we have seen, cannot avoid manipulating his image of God, he does avoid the self-serving, plea-bargaining religiosity he finds around him.

Newman confronts the secular world, on the other hand, through two specifically theological strategies. The first, his dark vision of a fallen universe, offers him a religious analogue to Marxist critique. Exposing the Victorian appeal to progress as ideological false consciousness, he invokes a norm even more deeply hidden from his age than economics or social class. This norm makes manifest the inevitable contingency and suffering vitiating any secular utopia. His second strategy, the dialogic model we have been tracing, augments his critique from without with a simultaneous stance at the center. As his personal dialogue reshapes his being from within, his appeal to a similar core within individuals, institutions, and nations allows him to reinterpret their apparently random motions as errant and centrifugal. This relational, value-laden center also allows Newman to avoid a critique which instantiates negativity as its own culturally and historically contingent norm.

No analysis of Newman and the Romantics can circumvent their own relation to the social world they inhabited. Early critics saw their internalization of political ideals as justified by the Reign of Terror; slightly later critics celebrated the revolutionary implications latent within the later Blake's iconoclasm, the mature Wordsworth's populism, Shelley's ongoing radicalism, and Byron's trenchant social satire. Yet more recently, as we saw in chapter 8, postmodern criticism has exposed both the self-mystification of their imaginative transcendence and the structures of aesthetic authority which disguised the material conditions of their writing. This ever-increasing critical severity cannot bode well for Newman. Because he finds less to value in his age than any of his contemporaries—Mill, Ruskin, Arnold, even Carlyle—he may deserve to be grouped with his more socially alienated Romantic predecessors. Yet because his alienation, like theirs, grows from subjective norms, we find within his writings and his life the same willful blindness to causes and conditions of social injustice.

Within Valerie Pitt's quasi-Marxist contextualization, for example, both Newman's mysticism and the self-scripted dramas of his spiritual life conspire to overwrite the otherwise painful lives all around him: "[I]n spite of his best endeavours to shut himself away from the common concerns of his time, that is where [his life] belongs. . . . The substance of his dilemma was a nineteenth-century phenomenon" (23). The dilemma to which she alludes is that of winning a "guarantee" for religious certitude. In this effort, she implies, Newman and his generation went astray by divorcing themselves from their believing community and its obligations to the society around it. According to the otherwise sympathetic Prickett: "The Oxford 'ethos' as envisaged by Keble, Arnold, and Newman . . . was one of an organic Christian culture forming a commonwealth of intellectual and spiritual aristocrats" (*Romanticism* 103). O'Faolain agrees: "From the whole range of [Newman's] books and letters one could not extract a single graphic image . . . of the common life of the century he all but spanned; just as nobody would gather from him that the loathed Whig reformers had anything to reform. . . . By comparison with the dynamite of his religious conscience, Newman's social conscience was a squib" (172-73).[1] Invoking J. C. D. Clarke's connection between religious orthodoxy and political conservatism, Thomas explains that "what in Newman, Rose, and Keble appear to the modern reader as protests verging on the hysterical . . . would have been bound up with allegiance to the *ancien regime*. . . . [Newman] had himself gained access only, as it were, by adoption, in his election to the Oriel Fellowship, to the benefits of that world of deference, patronage and privilege. . . . [H]e would defend to the last the establishment which made him" (60). At times, as we might by now expect, the Anglican Newman lies vulnerable to this social critique; at other times, however, he proleptically engages in it, and at still other times he anticipates potential weaknesses within it. His responses, first to his religious contemporaries and then to his society as a whole, comprise a fascinating tissue of blindness and insight.

The Evangelicals

The measure of critical acumen Newman showed toward nineteenth-century institutional Protestantism varies inversely with the threat which its various sects posed to him. He saw Protestantism itself as an amorphus continuum with the High-and-Dry Anglicans on one extremity and the Evangelicals, or peculiars, or "X's" (as he and his friends encoded them), on the other. Within this continuum, the Evangelicals evoke his most defensive snobbishness, the Anglican establishment his sharpest social criticism, and liberalism his most trenchant exposure of the secular norms underwriting apparently religious controversy. Writing to Rickards shortly after the publication of his third volume of sermons in 1836, Newman attributes his distaste for the Evangelicals to their want of system: "I intended [the volume] to be milder and more affectionate than the others. . . . Else I should have been taken for an Evangelical (so called) by the Evangelicals. . . . [They] would have dropped what they did not like, and have incorporated the mangled fragments they chose to admit in their own hodge-podge" (*LD* 5: 247). Throughout the 1830s, Newman maintained that his distaste for effusive Evangelical preaching was objectively, even morally, justified; yet the bases for his justification kept changing. To Stephen he dismisses such preaching as futile and maintains he could do better, should he choose to. It "is but a blaze among the stubble. Does a (so called) Evangelical Preacher do more than melt a number, and persuade one of them? . . . It is *after all*, but a question of number, for that preaching such as mine does persuade, I know" (*LD* 5: 32-33).[2] In a subsequent letter he invokes his superior religious taste and admits (even while deprecating it) his superior education: "What I shrink from is their rudeness, irreverence, and almost profaneness; the profaneness of making a most sacred doctrine a subject of vehement declamation, or instrument of exciting the feelings. . . . I conjecture you will consider this in me fastidiousness in education. I cannot think it so—i.e. it ought not to be so, it need not be so."[3]

Yet, as with his efforts to conceal his father's term as a brewer, so here his "fastidiousness in education" may be as much an effect as a cause of his distance from them. One soul-searching letter to Samuel Wilberforce acknowledges his past emotional involvement: "[I]f Mr Stephen knew more of me or of my doctrine, he would not think that I despised the so-called Evangelicals. . . . When I was a youth of 19 and 20, I held their opinions myself, as far as I had any. I have friends among them, and revere some of them" (*LD* 5: 31–32).[4] In the 1820s and early 1830s, as both T. C. F. Stunt (71–72) and David Newsome ("Justification" 33–37) have pointed out, Newman joined forces with the Evangelicals to resist both Peel's erastianism and the incipient rationalism of the Noetics.[5] An 1837 letter to Maria Giberne, however, reduces Evangelicalism to a phase of his childhood by reducing the Evangelicals themselves to children: "The Christian Observer too has attacked [Pusey] and I am to take up the cudgels in its pages—and, if they will but stand up, I will do my utmost, they may rely on it, to use them in true yeoman fashion. It amuses me beyond measure to see how angry these people are made by their very incapacity. They put me in mind of a naughty child put atop of the bookcase, very frightened, but very furious" (*LD* 6: 13). In a canceled passage from the late-written *Memoir,* Newman further claims that "the critical peculiarities of evangelical religion had never been congenial to him, though he had fancied he held them. Its emotional and feverish devotion and its tumultuous experiences were foreign to his nature, which indeed was . . . incapable, as if physically, of enthusiasm, however legitimate and guarded" (*AW* 82).[6] Yet just as Calvinistic election retained its hold on his visions, Thomas Mozley finds that "the traditions of the Low Church still held their ground in his heart and soul, even side by side with the Saints, Fathers, and Councils" (1: 392). All these demurrals, in other words, may themselves conceal a belated effort to divorce himself completely from a mindset which had once been all too congenial to him, a group close to his own suddenly-reduced economic level, and an "emotional devotion" which sanctioned his exclusive attention to self and God.[7]

High-and-Dry Anglicans

On the Anglican establishment, Newman's critique remains less conflicted and hence far more pointed; overall, he supports Thomas Mozley's retrospective judgment: "Every party, every interest, political or religious, in this country, was pushing its claims to universal acceptance, with the single exception of the Church of England, which was folding its robes to die with what dignity it could" (1: 273). To E. M. Rudd, as early as 1830 he implies that the Church's power, focused in the past, may render the Church itself a thing of the past: "[A]ssociations connected with the Liturgy and affection for it is the great hold of the Church in the minds of the multitude. . . . [T]he influence she exerts in the hearts of her people is chiefly by a reverential attachment to those prayers which they have heard from childhood and have been their solace often in their most trying seasons, and have shed a grace on the high solemnities of marriages and births.—Should we not dread disturbing this feeling?" (*LD* 2: 191). Writing to his mother nearly a year earlier, however, he has already questioned both the real nature of this "feeling" and the wisdom of leaving it undisturbed: "[T]he talent of the day is against the Church. The Church party . . . is poor in mental endowments. It has not activity, shrewdness, dexterity, eloquence, practical powers. On what then does it depend? on prejudice and bigotry" (*LD* 2: 130).[8] If the aspiring churchman sought to grow more tolerant and "modern," he was condemned to banality:

> You may hold the most fatal errors or the most insane extravagances, if you hold them in a misty, confused way. . . . In the present day mistiness is the mother of wisdom. A man who can set down half a dozen general propositions, which escape from destroying one another only by being diluted into truisms, who can hold the balance between opposites so skillfully as to do without fulcrum or beam . . . ,—this is your safe man and the hope of the Church . . . to guide it through the channel of No-meaning, between the Scylla and Charybdis of Aye and No. (*Ess.* 1: 301–2)

It was just such safe men who could be expected to rise to the episcopate. Although Newman's frequently-avowed fealty to his bishop remained open to question, he was always personally gracious to Bishop Bagot of Oxford. His portraits of the rest, however, only confirm the satirical definition of them as the "Tory Party at Prayer." In a passage repeated with some pride in the *Apologia,* his first Tract pronounces that "we could not wish them a more blessed termination of their course, than the spoiling of their goods and martyrdom" (52–53). The gap between ideal and reality he measures in a near-contemporary letter to Jemima: "Mr Dodd . . . is a very episcopal looking man—(was he always so?) and might easily be made an Archdeacon or Dean. Some men have to grow into those things. I mean by the episcopal shape, height f. 5.11—slimness—firmness of step, uprightness, and length of legs—roundness, or rather ovalness of head, or rather ovalness by roundness, height of forehead, and prominence of eyebrow.—and I mean by the episcopal air, gravity, decision, self possession, a certain dryness of manner, and a reserved courteousness" (*LD* 3: 82). By 1841, when the hierarchy lobbied for a Protestant bishopric in Jerusalem, Newman's image of the episcopate had degenerated from the pompous to the ludicrous. Instead of complaining privately to his sister, he sent this letter to the *Times:*

> Why must the successors of Augustine and Anselm become superintendents of a mixed multitude of Protestants, and, what is more likely, of men of no Profession whatever? . . . Why send out a Boy Bishop or an Abbot of Unreason, or Pope of fools, or Monk of Misrule, to . . . disgrace, defile, uncatholicize ourselves? . . . What is the Church worth if she is to be nice and mealy-mouthed when a piece of work is to be done for her good lord the State. . . . Surely it is an evil great enough to find Bishops heretics, without going on to make heretics Bishops. (*KC* 150–51)

Liberalism

The critique which Newman directs toward liberalism fuses his defensive bias toward the Evangelicals and his Olympian disdain of the Anglican establishment. This tension arises because it is critique itself, so successful in all other inquiries, which liberalism employs upon those sacred subjects Newman finds most precious and most vulnerable.[9] In his most daring illustration of this blasphemous assault, the liberal Protestant spirit is first caricatured and then followed out to its destruction in the revolt of Korah. In Newman's retelling of Numbers, Korah and his followers complain to Moses in an anachronistic pastiche of low-church slogans:

> [W]e are not mere dull, brutish, superstitious bigots, to crouch before a priest, and submit to his yoke of bondage; we can reason, we can argue, we are resolved to exercise our free unfettered private judgment, and to determine (candidly indeed and dispassionately), but still to determine for ourselves before we act. . . . [W]e will not go by instinctive feeling, by conscience, by mere probabilities; but everything shall be examined in a rational and enlightened way, everything searched, and sifted, and scrutinized, and rigidly tested, before it is admitted. The burden of proof lies with you. . . . We are "jealous with a godly jealousy," (alas! for men do so speak!) of any encroachments on our spiritual liberty. (*PS* 4 [18]: 275–76)

While this analogy might suggest that God will avenge the liberal blasphemy on his own initiative, Newman's study of early heresies in *Arians* forced him to admit that militant conflict with liberalism had become both increasingly necessary and increasingly compromising: "Now, we allow ourselves publicly to canvass the most solemn truths in a careless or fiercely argumentative way. . . . Then, they would scarcely express in writing, what is now . . . circulated in print among all ranks and classes of the unclean and the profane" (*Ari.* 136–37).

Because Newman sees liberal Protestantism as an interlocking set of rival parties, he can attack each party as though it were fully embodied in the person of its clerical leader: He identifies the higher criticism with Milman and Abbott, noetic nominalism with Hampden, and the reduction of dogma to morality with Thomas Arnold. His conflicted response to the first two individuals we have analyzed as part of his conflicted response to the New Testament. While his attacks on the remaining two remain equally *ad hominem,* he manages to justify his overdetermined responses so trenchantly that they expose unguarded presuppositions within his adversaries.

Acknowledging "Newman's almost pathological detestation of Hampden" (77n), Pattison attributes it not just to Hampden's nihilistic relativism (*Dissent* 79–95) but to Newman's failure in their contest for the professorship of moral philosophy (64–65).[10] In a letter to Pope several years later, Newman admits the personal nature of his antipathy, an admission as shrewd as it is telling:

> There is no doctrine, however sacred, which he does not scoff at—and in his Moral Philosophy he adopts the lowest and most grovelling utilitarianism as the basis of Morals—he considers it is a sacred duty to live to this world—and that religion by itself injuriously absorbs the mind. Whately, whatever his errors, is openhearted, generous, and careless of money—Blanco White is the same, though he has turned Socinian—Arnold is amiable and winning—but this man, *judging by his writings,* is the most lucre loving, earthly minded, unlovely person one ever set eyes on. (*LD* 5: 251)

Newman suggests here that by abandoning the integrity of religious language, Hampden has sunk, not just into skepticism with Milman and Abbott, but into laissez-faire acquisitiveness. Thus corrupted, Hampden has been denied his appeal to "gentlemanly" norms against the personal tone of Newman's attacks: "[Y]ou have no other ground of your assault on me but a fanatical persecuting spirit. I have done no wrong or unkindness to you, but on the contrary have always treated you with civility and respect. Have you (to take the lowest ground) acted towards me in the manner due from one gentleman to another? Would you have dared to act in such a way, had you not taken the advantage of the sacred profession?" (*LD* 5: 83). In his reply, Newman denies him this "ground," rejects any specifically social code as a means of adjudicating theological conflicts. Challenging Hampden's insistence that he had not "done any thing to hurt the feelings of a single person," Newman counters "that Dr Hampden's published statements of doctrine, running counter to received opinions, have much distressed a number of religious persons" (*LD* 5: 85).

Thomas Arnold, here described after a lapse of two years as "amiable and winning," did not fare so well in 1833 during an infamous after-dinner conversation in Rome. As a participant reported it, presumably in the form in which it reached Arnold: "They were speaking of Niebuhr and of some passages in his History seeming to imply sceptical opinions. Neale remarked that 'Arnold considered him to be a Christian'; and Newman's reply was, 'But Arnold must first show (or prove, I forget which) that he is one himself'" (*LD* 4: 107). By the time of the *Apologia*, Newman pared the reply down to "But is *he* a Christian?" (42). The hostility latent in this query may once again defend against the presence of Arnold's doubts in himself. In an unpublished fragment on his conversion, Newman acknowledges, "I cannot make out about the separate books of the Canon—why I receive e.g. Esther and not Ecclesiasticus or Wisdom, or (as the late Dr. Arnold speaks) part of the Book of Daniel. . . . *[H]ow far* going into extreme of believing at all, lest one should be sceptical as Arnold puts it" (*KC* 22–23). These jottings acknowledge his complicity with Arnold on the very issue which occasioned his initial challenge to Arnold's status as a Christian.

Arnold's demand for an apology, directed through this same participant, is both indignant and cogent:

> [W]here misapprehension is so inevitable, and its consequences so serious, is Newman justified in using a common word ["Christian"] in his own fantastic sense. . . . Let N. say or write or print, any where or every where, that in his view I do not understand what Christianity is. People will then know what he means. . . . We must not throw about fire carelessly; and whether he or I am right in our opinions is a question; but it is no question at all, whether evil speaking, imputation of motives, and claiming a monopoly of Christian knowledge and Christian humility, be or be not offenses against Christian charity. (*LD* 4: 107–8)[11]

Arnold shows himself well aware that the Tractarians contested his views on Church governance, his rejection of the priesthood (see *LD* 5: 97n), and his advocacy of a national church uniting most Protestant sects. The letter, with apparent magnanimity, attempts to bracket those issues as debatable and to substitute the common ground of motives and action.

In his reply through the same intermediary, Newman seems discomforted, but as the *Apologia* hints, he remains too proud of his original query to apologize for it. More important, he realizes that Arnold's appeal to Christian conduct, like Hampden's appeal to gentlemanly con-duct, does not invoke any middle or common ground. Both assume as incontrovertible fact the cultural and religious pluralism Newman is try-ing to challenge. While Newman must acknowledge that "to be formally and outwardly a Christian, it is sufficient to be baptized and to assent to certain revealed doctrines," he refuses to acknowledge that his own nar-rower definition entails "using a common word in his own fantastic sense." For Newman, "the word is very commonly restricted to those whose temper and conduct evidence a Christian mind; that faith includes reverence . . . for the declarations and usages of His Church" (*LD* 5: 106). While denying the label "fantastic," Newman implicitly admits and glories in Arnold's charge that the Tractarians "talk and write . . . as if they alone were humble and devout followers of Christ."[12]

At its most trenchant, Newman's critique of Protestant institutions and personalities parallels his larger critique of Protestant theology. As Tho-mas has established, Newman traces contemporary penchants for emo-tional intensity and self-absorption back to their origins—proximately within doctrines of *sola fide* and private judgment but ultimately within Patristic eclecticism, erastianism, and Pelagianism. By borrowing from ancient religious controversies and the equally ancient heresies which they defined, he can redefine and re-contextualize the contemporary sects which claim to have put all such controversies far behind them. From the perspective of these theological norms, modern Protestantism's irrevoca-ble descent into skepticism seems merely the latest in an age-old progres-sion of heresies.[13] From this same perspective, Newman can speak from within institutional Christianity without ever identifying himself with any one sect. By standing outside Protestantism (and at this point Catholi-cism) without standing outside Christendom, he can appeal to religious values in his audience while he simultaneously denies these values to them as believers.

Social Attitudes

Turning from his religious to his ostensibly secular criticism, we again find Newman most vulnerable in his responses to specific individuals and groups. Even here, however, he occasionally anticipates his critique of the underlying contradictions within his society. On one level, examples of the young Newman's social bias are so obvious as to make comment seem cheap; the early stages of his grand tour abound in a defensive, middle-class, English provincialism. At Gibraltar, though he could not possibly have understood them, he smugly remarks on "the native coalmen loudly jabbering in that surprising way which distinguishes all races perhaps but the Saxon and German, about nothing at all" (*LD* 3: 144). In Naples he is horrified by "the fashion of spitting about to an excess perfectly incredible to an Englishman. . . . I have seen an elegantly dressed lady on the fashionable walk on the Pincian, spit manfully; or rather I heard her and looked round" (*LD* 3: 297). With the Neapolitan street urchins, he is equally shocked but more forgiving: "Just now a ragged boy persecuted me in a miserable whining tone for coppers. . . . [W]hen he found that would not do, he tried another mode, beginning suddenly to play a tune on his chin with great dash and effect" (*LD* 3: 294).

As this sequence implies, the same growth in moral tolerance which we traced in chapter 5 carries over into Newman's social attitudes, but here as there, he sees this growth as a potential threat. Culler, in fact, explains the whole trip "as a deliberate experiment in the effect which foreign travel would have in broadening—and perhaps unsettling—his mind" ("Remembrance" 65). The self-doubt which such identification awakened can be measured in the ambivalence of his mocking self-portrait to Woodgate on the eve of his departure for Sicily:

> Can there be a greater proof that I am become a liberal . . . than my refusing to return home with the Froudes and running down to Sicily instead? . . . Thus I am now fairly a man of mind, and have already overcome many prejudices. . . . I habitually desecrate the Sabbath by travelling and visiting; . . . I visit the theatres, and am glad to accept invitations from the wealthy English adulterers here, who are the attraction of the place. I am indeed quite polished, as you prayed I might be—and on my return shall be rational and dispassionate enough to defend the Irish Church spoliation Bill, and to join hand and glove with Dr Arnold in his views of Ecclesiastical Reform in England. (*LD* 3: 297–98)

Newman has no intention of supporting either Arnold or the "National Apostasy," as he makes clear in a satirical recommendation that first the churches and then Oxford itself be divided up among various sects. But it is far less clear whether he has not already become complicit in the liberal cause by Sabbath-traveling, theatre-going, and associating, however unwillingly, with adulterers. He concludes by drawing the line at post-revolutionary France: "I suppose I must stop a day in Paris, which will be much against my will—for in spite of my recent conversion, I have not overcome old prejudice long enough to bear the sight of what I used to think an impious city—so I shall lie in bed all day, I suppose—you know, all things come by degrees—one must not force oneself too hard" (*LD* 3: 299). And by degrees he did come to acknowledge to Jemima on his return from Sicily that "France . . . is truly 'La Belle France'—in all externals. I am enchanted with it" (*LD* 3: 311).

This growing self-awareness makes it progressively harder to catch Newman in moments of blindness, social or otherwise. And within the welter of conflicting opinions surrounding his family, any such slip is sure to be challenged. In 1834, for example, Frank charges that through John's stipend, the family is "keeping up 'the lust of the eye and the pride of life.'" From the length and direction of John's reply, he sees the charge, not as a conventional attack on vanity, but as a religious anticipation of Marxist critique:

> Every one has his place in society—there is a difference of duties, and of persons fitted for them. 'High' and 'low' are mere names, and invidious ones. I would rather speak, if I could of right hand and left hand ranks, all being on a level. When I engage servants, it is a mutual engagement, for the good of all. They do what they are fitted to do, and which I, from want of training, cannot do, and I in turn do good, first to them, then to others—or at least ought to do. . . . Now I must think [Mother] is thus making herself more useful, than if she threw herself out of her place in society. . . . [S]he and my sisters are doing their duty "in their state of life in which it has pleased God to call them,"—are spreading God's glory far more than if they lived simply on their own means, and gave away what they have beyond those means in the lump in charity. They are the instruments of temporal good to 200 people in Littlemore—they teach the children, set an example to the Parents, and . . . make people better who otherwise would become worse. . . . What could I do better with the money? Give it to some Religious Society, to be spent by strangers in whom I had not reason to feel confidence? . . . You know little either of my principles or practice, if you think I go by the mere fashion of society. (*LD* 4: 329–30)[14]

From these "principles," he does seem to "go [more] by the mere fashion of society" than he would have Frank believe; he simply assumes that social station is indeed God-given and that religious instruction can be partly compassed by learning one's place. Yet he implicitly acknowledges some tension when he turns a Tory social hierarchy on its side to accommodate the spiritual hierarchy he is constructing in contemporary public writings.

Instead of preaching equality and practicing privilege, moreover, Newman preaches privilege and then does remarkably little with it. Days after the letter to Frank, he writes of his visit to a rich friend: "I could not (I think) live in so beautiful a place—I should destroy the conservatory, and turn the inner drawing room into a chapel. . . . [E]xotic plants, foreign gems and marbles, rare viands, statues and paintings, seem as out of place as to be waited on by slaves" (*LD* 4: 333). Indeed, he lived quite simply and used most of the royalties from his sermon volumes to provide for his family. If we added to his possessions those which Bourdieu defines as cultural capital, we would have to include his proficiency in music and his stature as a writer. In fairness, however, we should include spiritual capital as well, and then our inventory would merely duplicate those treasures which Newman was seeking to lay up in heaven. Newman's dialogue with God, like anyone else's, can be read as an internalized accommodation between duty and desire; his dialogue, nevertheless, remains relatively free of the rationalizing which passed for conscience among most of his religious contemporaries.

A Stance Beyond Secularism

It may thus be more profitable to focus on Newman's more theoretical—and theological—critique of his society. Robbins speaks of Newman's "protecting his unfolding vision of the Church, of proclaiming Divine Authority by challenging established authority" (36). For Thomas, however, the converse holds true as well: "Newman is, in his own Romantic way, a revolutionary, challenging the cherished assumptions of an increasingly Bourgeois culture" (33). As we have seen, Newman's God was not easy to stay on good terms with; the criteria for spiritual election were stringent and often paradoxical. Yet he offered an invaluable *pou sto* and, given Newman's penchant for defining himself against others, a place to stand grew synonymous with a place from which to judge.[15] As Newman critiqued Protestant theology by appropriating religious norms without adopting a particular sect, he here appropriates the strategies and perspectives of secular rationalism while standing just beyond its ideological horizons.

Simultaneously, moreover, Newman's dialogue with God formed and informed a spiritual center, around which nineteenth-century England was aimlessly drifting. Concealed within the religious equivalent of Bentham's panopticon, the elect can scrutinize a secular world imprisoned by its own spiritual blindness:

"[H]e that is spiritual judgeth all things, yet he himself is judged by no man." Others understand him not, master not his ideas, fail to combine, harmonize, or make consistent, those distinct views and

principles which come to him from the Infinite Light, and are inspirations of the breath of God. He, on the contrary, compasses others, and locates them, and anticipates their acts, and fathoms their
thoughts, for, in the Apostle's language, he "hath the mind of Christ,"
and all things are his, "whether . . . life, or death, or things present,
or things to come." (*US* [14]: 293)

Confronting liberalism, rationalism, secularism, and Utilitarianism with a
proleptically modern set of charges, Newman accuses them, with Hegel,
of denying *Sittlichkeit*, with Heidegger, of refusing to acknowledge their
"thrownness," with Tillich, of setting up their ultimate concerns as so
many petty idols and, with Marx, of accepting capitalist ideology as inevitable and natural.

Marx in particular was tireless in imputing conventional attitudes to
false consciousness, in standing Hegel back on his feet, in trying to
change the world rather than explain it, in discovering the economic bases
for various theoretical superstructures, in redescribing natural desires as
fetishes and natural constructs as ideologies. Newman's transcendental
perspective gives him a similar distance on his society, distance enough to
see its members as ideologically conditioned in ways more insidious than
either the Comteans or Benthamites could imagine. He can see, for example, that the current Pelagian faith in human perfectability remains the
product of a temporary social calm: "When the laws of a country are upheld and obeyed, and property secure, . . . [then h]uman nature appears
more amiable than it really is, because it is not tried with disappointments;
more just, because it is then its interest to respect the rights of others;
more benevolent, because it can be so without self-denial" (*US* [6]:
102-3).[16] In a sermon of 1836 he echoes Carlyle and anticipates Ruskin,
portraying Victorian England as so enslaved by capitalism and the cash
nexus that it is drifting toward a Hobbesian state of nature:

> I do not know any thing more dreadful than a state of mind which
> is, perhaps, the characteristic of this country, . . . that low ambition
> which sets every one on the look-out to succeed and to rise in life, to
> amass money, to gain power, to depress his rivals, to triumph over
> his hitherto superiors, to affect a consequence and a gentility which
> he had not before, . . . —this most fearfully earthly and grovelling
> spirit is likely, alas! to extend itself more and more among our
> country-men,—an intense, sleepless, restless, never-wearied, never-
> satisfied, pursuit of Mammon in one shape or another. (*PS* 8 [11]:
> 159-60)

Unlike Carlyle and Ruskin, however, Newman's stance at these ideological horizons gave him access to the prophetic voice that they had to win through unaided rhetoric.

This stance resembles those of his Romantic predecessors, who "tended to wage war with the ideologies of the times, with the mind-forged manacles, more than with the social conditions or economic structures that nurtured them" (Ferber 78). This focus, as recent Marxist critics have pointed out, cannot protect them or Newman from performative contradictions between theory and praxis; any such theoretical superstructure, no matter how enlightened, rested solidly on a capitalist base.[17] The rise of Western, neo-Marxist thought, however, is tacit admission that some of Marx's own ideals and strategies remain bound to his age.[18] To quote Ferber again: "It was not perverse of Simone Weil to describe Marxism as 'the highest spiritual expression of bourgeois society'; it may have been the utopian and romantic side of Marx that kept him revolutionary, not his analysis of capitalism" (82).

For its part, Newman's theory challenges some of these utopian preconceptions in both Hegelian and positivistic Marxism. Where his attack on Mammon bristles with prophetic, proto-Marxist scorn, another sermon anticipates a darker, Weber-like vision: "[W]e argue that a certain animal is the work of God; why? because its parts fit in together and sustain one another. We bring it as a proof of design. . . . Now human society, or this world our enemy, seems in like manner to bear about it marks of design, and therefore to come from God" (*SD* [7]: 88–89). Here capitalism is so pervasive that it refuses to dwindle into an ideology and stands stubbornly inevitable like some phenomenon of the natural world. The passage goes on to analyze the economic base and basis for this design:

Men may or may not have the fear of God before their eyes, yet they seem to go on equally well either way. Each has his own occupation, his own place; he may be an irreligious and immoral man, a scoffer, or covetous, or heartless, or he may be serious and correct in his conduct, yet none of these things interfere much one way or the other with the development of our social state, the formation of communities, the provisions for mutual protection, the interchange of good offices, and the general intercourse of man with man. Punctuality, honesty, business-like despatch, perseverance, sobriety, friendliness, trust in each other, steady co-operation, these are the sort of virtues which seem sufficient for carrying on the great empires of the world; what a man's character is besides seems nothing to the purpose. (89–90)

Theologically, Newman must choose between a Manichean denial of the good of creation and a servile accommodation with "this world our enemy." Politically, he faces an irrefutable vision of human society as fully brokered by the production and exchange of capital; any other value "seems nothing to the purpose."

Pattison defines Newman's quarrel with his liberal opponents as one between his dogmatic, neo-Scholastic, sacramental parallelism and a relativism so pervasive that it encompasses Marxism as well (*Dissent* 103–16). Within Pattison's critique of twentieth-century reactions to the Arian controversy, for example, "the modern response begs the fundamental question . . . : to ignore dogma is not to rise above the quibbles of Alexander and Athanasius, but to take side with Arius and Asterius. . . . Marxism cannot talk about Arianism without talking about itself. It cannot objectively examine the Arian dispute without taking the Arian side because the Arian premises are the Marxist premises" (*Dissent* 115, 127). Frequently, it is true, Newman secularizes his earlier strategy of rereading Protestant "progress" as heretical degeneration. Where positivists saw history as an evolution from superstition to science, he reinterprets the entire modern agenda as a contingent and hence temporary aberration:

> Then . . . as now, the minds of speculative men were impatient of ignorance, and loth to confess that the laws of truth and falsehood, which their experience of this world furnished, could not at once be applied to measure and determine the facts of another. . . . Hence, canons grounded on physics were made the basis of discussions about possibilities and impossibilities in a spiritual substance, as confidently and as fallaciously, as those which in modern times have been derived from the same false analogies against the existence of moral self-action or free-will. (*Ari.* 33–34)

The modern mind-set thus becomes an anomalous consequence of intellectual and psychological weakness: "[W]here Knowledge is limited, and Reason active . . . there is much need of wariness, jealousy of self, and habitual dread of presumption, paradox, and unreality, to preserve . . . our guesses from assuming the character of discoveries" (*US* [14]: 295).

Spiritual Opportunism

Even as spokesman for an anachronistic worldview, however, Newman may yet participate in what Pattison would see as a modern agenda. As Sayre and Lowy define Romanticism, for example, "in its principal manifestations throughout the key European countries," it is an "*opposition to capitalism in the name of precapitalist values.* . . . It is *because* [the Romantics] turn their gaze toward the past that they are able to criticize the present with such acumen and realism. . . . [I]t is a prejudice—inherited from the Enlightenment—that existing social reality can be criticized only from a 'progressive' perspective" (26, 28; italics theirs).[19] If Newman's anachronism remains more conflicted and complicit than Pattison will admit, his critique of his age looks less like dogmatic dissent than like spiritual opportunism. Hunting out reductive, yet unquestioned refusals to acknowledge non-material phenomena, he appeals to any evidence available to him. In his essay on rationalism, for example, he does not focus on the center of modern thought but on positions just beyond the field of its intellectual tunnel vision. In rationalism,

> The notion of half views and partial knowledge, of guesses, surmises, hopes and fears, of truths faintly apprehended and not understood, of isolated facts in the great scheme of Providence, in a word, the idea of Mystery, is discarded. . . . [T]he Rationalist . . . consequently confines Faith to the province of Subjective Truth. . . . That is, he professes to *believe* in that which he *opines.* . . . [Faith, therefore, lies] in what he calls that candid pursuit of truth . . . which is most natural according to the constitution of our own minds, and, therefore, divinely intended for us. (*Ess.* 1: 34–35)

This passage contains, in germ, most of Newman's case against the nineteenth century—its relativism, subjectivity, disinterestedness, moral smugness, naturalism; but he ties all of them to a reductive itch. Then he searches out fields like history where the "scientific" methodology of *wie es eigentlich gewesen ist* lay just over the English horizon.[20] Within these fields, he can indict his opponents for not considering all the evidence available to them: "To trust to anything but sense in a matter of sense is irrational. . . . But it is otherwise with history, the facts of which are not present. . . . We must do our best with what is given us, and look about for aid from any quarter; and in such circumstances the opinions of others, the traditions of ages, the prescriptions of authority, antecedent auguries, analogies, parallel cases, these and the like, . . . sifted and scrutinized, obviously become of great importance" (*Dev.* 103).[21]

Here and elsewhere, to avoid being dismissed as an advocate for superstition, Newman switches roles with his opponents. Playing the skeptic, attacking the credulous modern acceptance of scientific "fact," he accuses his opponents of intellectual laziness for preferring the comforting predictability of science to the troubling uncertainty of theology. Confronted with some bizarre Patristic miracles, he turns Hume's famous argument on its head, warning that any *a priori* dismissal may reflect an addiction to system for its own sake: "There is so much beauty, majesty, and harmony in the order of nature, so much to fill, satisfy, and tranquillize the mind, that by those who are accustomed to the contemplation, the notion of an infringement of it will at length be viewed as a sort of profanation, and as even shocking, as the mere dream of ignorance, the wild and atrocious absurdity of superstition and enthusiasm" (*Mir.* 159–60).[22] Many of Newman's most trenchant and original critiques are grounded in this prototypically modern acknowledgement of human and historical contingency.

Even earlier than Newman, this proto-Heideggerian insistence on our thrownness appears within Hegel's *Sittlichkeit,* his insistence that a stoic individualism cannot ground itself because our deepest intuitions of self come we know not whence. Simultaneously, Hegel's colleague and rival Schleiermacher was defining religious feeling as total dependency, the acknowledgment that our real freedoms cannot determine how, where, when, and why we came into being.[23] Like these early claims for cultural and historical contextualization, Newman's spiritual opportunism seems an apt response to the problem of self-reference which has plagued critique ever since Kant. With depressing regularity, recent critics have attacked their society from a position as foreign to it as possible, while simultaneously attacking their immediate predecessors for choosing positions more complicit with this society than they had naively imagined. Such strategies, however, involve a performative contradiction: "[I]n a[ny] discourse modeled after the figure of Nietzsche's hammer in *The Twilight of Idols,* ideology finally eludes the hammer of analysis because the instrument itself is idolized, with no one empowered to name the forces that wield it" (Crowley 84). Anticipating the *Grammar*'s argument that we should consider *all* the evidence available, Newman plays instead the proto-pragmatist, renouncing all such efforts to stand outside religious tradition as chimerical: "Let us take things as we find them: let us not attempt to distort them into what they are not. True philosophy deals with facts. We cannot make facts. All our wishing cannot change them. We must use them. If Revelation has always been offered to mankind in one way, it is in vain to say that it ought to have come to us in another. . . . Let us attempt to understand it. Let us not disguise it, or explain it away" (*US* [12]: 231–32).

A Stance at the Center

As this passage suggests, Newman refuses to camp indefinitely on his society's ideological margins. As his God can reject all rivals and yet include the individual subject, so the centrifugal movement of Newman's social critique alternates with a centripetal movement modeled on his own sense of election. Indeed this alternation repeats that of intimacy and mutually defining contention within his own spiritual dialogue. While seeming to stand with the moderns, choosing among the few spiritual alternatives still available, Newman subtly invokes the personal interaction within faith as the implicit goal of any choice. He can thus anticipate Tillich's inclusion of rationalism as another, albeit skewed, form of religious experience:

> We must believe something; the difference between religious men and others is, that the latter trust this world, the former the world unseen. Both of them have faith, but the one have faith in the surface of things, the other in the word of God. Men of the world . . . readily allow that in sciences of the world, the appearance is contrary to the truth of things. They quite understand that the great agencies in the material system are invisible, and that what is visible is deceptive. They are not loth to admit that the stars do not move, though they seem to do so . . . ; yet they think it folly to distrust the face of the world in religious matters, or to search amid the perishable shadows of time for the footsteps and the resting-places of the Eternal. (*SD* [6]: 65–66)

Even with faith thus attenuated into the "folly" of a quest for the invisible, Newman can still redescribe it as the only program which can offer tangible evidence (footprints) amid shadows and stasis (resting-places) amid flux.

The skeptic's faith in surfaces, by contrast, is redescribed in religious terms as a far more incongruous idolatry. Sometimes the object of worship is the world: "[S]uch persons as prefer this world to the leadings of God's Spirit within them . . . lean upon the world as a god" (*PS* 2 [2]: 19). More typically, however, the god is none other than self.[24] As we saw in chapter 4, "others wish in some way or other, to be to themselves, to have a home, a chamber, a tribunal, a throne, a self where God is not" (*PS* 5 [16]: 226). When he describes himself in this passage as merely an "instrument and minister," he oversimplifies his multifaceted interaction with God. Yet as a metaphor for the self-imposed emptiness at the center of secular life, the passage suggests that the skeptic works hard to vacate pre-existing psychological structures and avoid possible psychological interactions.[25]

From this perspective, Newman can expose the unchallenged, unsupported arrogance beneath the skeptics' apparent disinterestedness: "[T]he mind is often compared to a tablet or paper: a state of it is contemplated of absolute freedom from all prepossessions and likings for one system or another, as a first step towards arriving at the truth; and infidelity represented as that candid and dispassionate frame of mind, which is the desideratum. . . . [But i]nfidelity is a positive, not a negative state; it is a state of profaneness, pride, and selfishness" (*Ari.* 84–85).[26] In his twelfth university sermon, Newman argues that while rationalists claim to be constrained by principles, they are actually constrained, like everyone else, by prejudices: "[U]nbelievers call themselves rational; not because they decide by evidence, but because, after they have made their decision, they merely occupy themselves in sifting it. This surely is quite plain, even in the case of Hume" (*US* [12]: 230–31).[27] In an earlier university sermon of 1839, he further accuses these rationalists of cutting off the limb they sit on; their vaunted intellectual freedom leads to a moral determinism that vitiates its own truth claims: Unbelievers "persist in saying that a man is as little responsible for his faith as for his bodily functions: that both are from nature; that the will cannot make a weak proof a strong one; that if a person thinks a certain reason goes only a certain way, he is dishonest in attempting to make it go farther; that if he is after all wrong in his judgment, it is only his misfortune, not his fault; that he is acted on by certain principles from without, and must obey the laws of evidence, which are necessary and constant" (*US* [10]: 192–93).

In much the same way, moral determinism undermines its own efficacy. In an 1832 letter to Wood, Newman argues that when private judgment degenerates into Comtean positivism, the social architect is left with no appeal to free will, with no expedient beyond sociological manipulation:[28]

Men see that those parts of the national system . . . which really depend on personal and private virtue do not work well—and . . . they imagine they can put things right by applying their scientific knowledge to the improvement of the existing system—Hence political economy is to supersede morality. . . . [I]t is the fashion of the day to consider the human mind as a machine and to think that education will do any thing for it; —in fact that *it is not responsible.* . . . Indeed I find a French man has written a book to prove that society has courses of action independent of the will of individuals, and moves (irresponsibly of course) by laws as necessary as those of matter. (*LD* 3: 90–91)

In Newman's case against secularism, any lapse in personal morality generates a collapse in national coherence, direction, and purpose. The same letter correlates the growing political power of the lower classes with the decreasing power of any appeal to them as fallen, and hence fallible, creatures: "[W]hat will happen, when that opinion [the masses' discovery of

their own power] happens to be in favor of their doing without government, or governing themselves? If men could be brought to *know their
weakness* in proportion as they learned what is called their strength, then
of course knowledge would not be dangerous—but this is impossible"
(90). When the theologically liberal Whigs refuse to acknowledge their
constituents as fallen, they render their task "impossible" and their whole
party morally (and thus politically) impotent:

> When good and evil fight together, Tories and Radicals come into
> the field—but Whigs are neither fish, flesh, nor fowl—and have no
> resting place—their whole view is a supercilious theory—their policy
> is liberalism, and their basis Socinianism—they have no root in the
> heart. Superstition may last for ages, and true religion, and Mani-
> cheeism, and fanaticism—any thing that has depth and reality in it—
> but as to that cold and scoffing theory, which says there is no great
> evil in the world, affects non-chalance, and says all religions are
> about the same, nothing can come of it—it is a shortlived dream.
> (*LD* 3: 42)[29]

Reading-Room Morality

In 1841, working from these political, moral, and theological presuppositions, Newman is ready to take on Robert Peel and his putative mentor,
Lord Brougham. Although his political base had badly eroded and his religious opinions were in turmoil, his faith in his own spiritual center
grounded some of the most trenchant satire of the century. The seven letters to the *Times* which comprise the *Tamworth Reading Room* challenge
any attempt to set up a secular morality based on glory and knowledge:
"The Knowledge School does not contemplate raising man above himself. . . . It finds him, like the victims of the French Tyrant, doubled up
in a cage in which he can neither lie, stand, sit, nor kneel, and its highest
desire is to find an attitude in which his unrest may be least. . . . You
must go to a higher source for renovation of the heart and will. You do
but play a sort of 'hunt the slipper' with the fault of our nature, till you
go to Christianity" (*DA* 272, 274). When it denies the power of Christianity, the reading-room mentality must also deny the Fall; when it denies the Fall, it must also deny the bleak reality of the human condition.
Seeking in vain for a substitute, Lord Brougham "feels that man has affections and aspirations which Bentham does not take account of, and he
looks about for their legitimate objects. Christianity has provided these;
but, unhappily, he passes them by. He libels them with the name of dog-

matism, and conjures up instead the phantoms of Glory and Knowledge; *idola theatri*, as his famous predecessor calls them" (277).[30] By the time of the *Idea*, Newman will admit a limited moral efficacy for "the pursuit of Knowledge";[31] here, however, he claims that these socially constructed idols remain even less effectual than the individual idols which he saw intruding into modern secular thought:

> [W]hat is it that th[is] School of philosophy . . . purposes to accomplish? Not a victory of the mind over itself . . . but the mere lulling of the passions to rest by turning the course of thought. . . . Digestive pills half an hour before dinner, and a posset at bedtime at the best; and at the worst, dram-drinking and opium,—the very remedy against broken hearts, or remorse of conscience, which is in request among the many, in gin-palaces *not* intellectual. . . . Strong liquors, indeed, do for a time succeed in their object; but who was ever consoled in real trouble by the small beer of literature or science? (*DA* 264, 266)[32]

Where Newman focuses on individual moral crises, Peel resorts to the same mechanistic social tinkering Newman observed a decade earlier in Comte. Hence the whole reading room project manifests a pusillanimous craving for social efficiency and harmony: "He tells us that his great aim is the peace and good order of the community, and the easy working of the national machine. With this in view, any price is cheap, everything is marketable; all impediments are a nuisance. . . . The old bond, he seems to say, was Religion; Lord Brougham's is Knowledge. . . . [L]et us not hang over our dead, but bury it out of sight. Seek we some young and vigorous principle, rich in sap, and fierce in life, to give form to elements which are fast resolving into their inorganic chaos; and where shall we find such a principle but in Knowledge?" (*DA* 284–86).[33] Here Newman's send-up of Romantic organicism remains as caustic as anything in any post-modern critique, but he also manages to savage Utilitarianism and the Victorian progress myth. What he refuses to do, much like Swift in the *Modest Proposal*, is to argue systematically for his own alternative:

> People say to me, that it is but a dream to suppose that Christianity should regain the organic power in human society which once it possessed. I cannot help that; I never said it could. I am not a politician; I am purposing no measures, but exposing a fallacy, and resisting a pretense. Let Benthamism reign, if men have no aspirations; but do not tell them to be romantic, and then solace them with glory; do not attempt by philosophy what once was done by religion.

The ascendancy of Faith may be impracticable, but the reign of Knowledge is incomprehensible. (*DA* 292)

Newman's bold admission that "the ascendancy of Faith may be impracticable" might imply that his own via media had failed; more likely it reflects Dean Inge's shrewd judgment that he "is like a man fighting with magic impenetrable armour. He enjoys a bout of logical fence; but it will decide nothing for him: his 'certitude' is independent of it" (192–93).

It is Newman's insistence on the Fall, the gulf between secular theory and social practice, which wins him a stance outside the ideological horizons of his age. But it is his inner religious life which establishes structures—"a home, a chamber, a tribunal, a throne"—standing vacant at the age's spiritual center. Because Peel and his followers could join the conversation animating these psychological structures, Newman's critique escapes the implicit nihilism which has infected its secular counterpart ever since Nietzsche. It also escapes Matthew Arnold's discovery, too often forgotten in this century, that the more critique denounces its age, the more it situates itself within an age of critique.[34] Arnold felt that he and his culture had been trapped within this imaginative retrenchment by the *Zeitgeist*.[35] Newman could not succeed in turning the ecclesiastical clock back fifteen-hundred years, but he did succeed in establishing a dialogue, at once imaginative and spiritual, which let him engage the rest of his world in dialogue. Because it can call forth spiritual desires concealed within an apparently secular world, this dialogue transforms Newman's social criticism into a Romantic plea for renewed powers of vision.

CHAPTER 10

Incursions

VALERIE PITT tasks Newman severely with what she sees as the self-scripted, self-dramatized account of his religious pilgrimage. Even in the landscape, the "moor and fen, . . . crag and torrent," over which his Kindly Light will lead him, she sees

> a metaphor for the troubles, his sister's death, his own dangerous ill-ness in Sicily, through which "Thy power" was leading Newman to the ardour of the Tractarian campaign. The metaphor was trans-muted, perilously, into real time in the famous, crucial episode, of Newman's reception into the Roman Church. . . . Here is New-man . . . , within walking distance of a Roman Catholic church in St Clements, . . . "begging" Fr Dominic, still sopping wet from a night journey through a great storm, to hear his confession and re-ceive his submission. It's a marvellously melodramatic scene, and in-deed the whole history of Newman's conversion was conducted with precisely that degree of self-awareness which, inevitably, makes for psychological theater. (18)[1]

Against her criticism, I would suggest only that by this point Newman was no longer the principal author of this script—that he had even relin-quished his role as protagonist. During the 1830s and 1840s, natural and preternatural intruders were barging in upon Newman's interior melo-drama and breaking up the cozy dialogue between him and his Creator.[2] While these intruders arise from a welter of incidents and experiences throughout his Anglican career, many of them revolve around an unlikely pair of events which frame his most productive decade. They have their genesis in the unresolved tensions of the Mediterranean trip in 1832–33, but they do not find their fullest expression until his composition of *Ec-clesiastical Miracles* in 1843. This collection of marginally Romantic vis-itants includes ironic visions of an anarchic nature, preternatural specters,

Patristic miracle stories, Old Testament savagery, and intimations of an immanent, pantheistic Deity. Insinuating themselves between Newman and his God throughout the intervening decade, these eventually force him to redefine both parties.[3]

Liminal States

While most of these intruders come unbidden, Pitt's accusations of self-scripting remain cogent; Newman's Romantic predilection for liminal states and experiences sets his interior stage for the intruders' arrival. In his preference for twilight visions, he may be borrowing uncritically from incidents like the Ancient Mariner's blessing of the water snakes, the death of Alastor, "She Walks in Beauty like the Night," and Wordsworth's visions of Lucy.[4] Yet as with his celebrations of childhood glory, his search for personal epiphanies, and his Wordsworthian recapitulations, Newman works here to bend Romanticism to the service of orthodox sanctity. In all of the above poems, for example, darkness reduces the particularity of objects in order to bring out their organic interaction. When Newman reduces *his* landscapes to increasingly tenuous gradations of light and dark, he conflates this Romantic twilight with its Patristic counterpart. Here the material world is valorized and validated only because it is over-shadowed, point for point, by a spiritual world ready to break through at unforeseen moments. Here each twilight becomes the transition, not just to night, but to some much more numinous advent: "Earth and sky are ever failing; Christ is ever coming; Christians are ever lifting up their heads and looking out, and therefore it is the evening. . . . The evening is long and the day was short; . . . and this last age, though ever-failing, has lasted longer than the ages before it" (*SD* [1]: 10).

Even the landscape of Newman's beloved Sicily, we remember, was figured as "a shadow of Eden" (*LD* 3: 277). For him, as for Carlyle in *Sartor Resartus,* matter simply clothes the spiritual reality behind it, but for Newman these clothes are neither changeable nor subject to the vaga-ries of fashion. The reader is asked to reach back for an archetypal, not a personal, memory—is asked to see the present scene, however bright, as its "shadow." Here again earthly brightness becomes a patch of relative darkness cast by an opaque but still brighter reality. "It is as though God blinds him," claims Cameron, "so that whatever is not God is flickering, ambiguous, open to doubt" ("Tractarian" 92). Hence, in chapter 9 we saw skeptics chastised for refusing "to search amid the perishable shad-ows of time for the footsteps and the resting-places of the Eternal" (*SD*

[6]: 66). Even in revelation, these shadows are the only hints of spiritual reality available to us. Its visions "are but shadows cast, or at best, lines or portions caught from what is unseen, and they attend upon it after the manner of the Seraphim, with wings covering their face, and wings covering their feet. . . . I see herein a deep mystery, a hidden truth, which I cannot handle or define, shining 'as jewels at the bottom of the great deep,' darkly and tremulously, yet really there" (*PS* 3 [25]: 368).[5]

In his last university sermon Newman insists on the reality of spiritual encounters within dreams and other liminal states: "How common is what is called vacant vision, when objects meet the eye, without any effort of the judgment to measure or locate them; and that absence of mind, which recollects minutes afterwards the occurrence of some sound, the striking of the hour, or the question of a companion, which passed unheeded at the time it took place! How, again, happens it in dreams, that we suddenly pass from one state of feeling . . . to another, without any surprise at the incongruity" (*US* [15]: 322).[6] And in his journal for 1821, he describes the sort of experience he wants to valorize, a conversation with an angelic visitant:

About a week ago I dreamed a spirit came to me, and discoursed about the other world. I had several meetings with it. Dreams address themselves so immediately to the mind, that to express in any form of words the feelings produced by the speeches, or the speeches themselves of my mysterious visitant were a fruitless endeavour. Among other things it said that it was absolutely impossible for the reason of man to understand the mystery (I think) of the Holy Trinity, and in vain to argue about it; but that every thing in another world was so *very, very plain,* that it there was not the slightest difficulty about it. (*AW* 166)

In their fluid, "dreamlike" interplay, message and medium reinforce one another. The dream's immediacy reflects the spiritual clarity of the beatific vision, while Newman's inability to repeat the dialogue establishes the ineffable nature of its subject. Even Newman's reaction, though still within the dream, forms an appropriate response to the dream itself: "I thought I instantly fell on my knees, overcome with gratitude to God for so kind a message. It is not idle to make a memorandum of this, for out of dreams often much good can be extracted." Not surprisingly, the "good" which validates dreams encompasses not just their spiritual message but their witness to the divine favor here bestowed on the recipient.[7]

Sickness and Fasting

When Newman transforms physical sickness into spiritual transcendence, he invokes an equally Romantic paradigm. Culler among others claims that he saw his major illnesses, including the Sicilian fever, as God's rebuke for his worldly aspiration (*Imperial* 4, 20–21, 31–32, 85–87).[8] In an 1835 letter to Froude, however, Newman notes that with a recurring symptom of this fever, "a field of pain opened upon me, which has thrown a new light upon the whole subject of Martyrdom etc." (*LD* 5: 9).[9] The longer account given to Henry Wilberforce interprets the experience as both judgment and election:

> I had once, doubtless when I felt myself lonely, quite a revelation come upon me of God's love to His elect, and felt as if I were one. . . . Then again I was much relieved next day, by being able to discover, (as I thought) sins in my conduct, which led God thus to fight against me. . . . But after all . . . I said "I have not sinned against light—" and repeated this often. And then I thought I would try to obey God's will as far as I could, and, with a dreamy confused notion, which the fever (I suppose) occasioned, thought that in setting off the fourth day from Leonforte, I was *walking* as long as I could in the way of God's commandments, and putting myself in *the way* of His mercy, as if He would meet me (Is. xxvi, 8) and surely so He did. (*LD* 4: 8)

Throughout this passage, delirium proves more cogent than normal consciousness. Bridging the gap between material and spiritual worlds, it redescribes an apparently senseless misfortune as a mutually fulfilling dialogue between God and his elect. Summoning a faith unavailable to his "healthy" consciousness, the delirious Newman acts on its bidding; he sets out "as if" God would meet him and thus prompts God to respond in kind. As so often with Newman, a slightly later sermon generalizes upon the visionary potential he has found in sickness: "[T]he mind wanders from things that are seen into the unknown world, it turns back into itself, and is in company with mysteries. . . . It sees the skirts of powers and providences beyond this world, and is at least more alive, if not more exposed to the invisible influences, bad and good, which are its portion in this state of trial" (*PS* 4 [23]: 335–36).

If sickness can offer such a providential conduit to vision, similar results can be induced voluntarily through self-imposed fasting. The journals reveal details of Newman's fasting from the end of January 1837, but as early as 1834 he admits, "I would not say this aloud lest I perplexed people; but let it never be forgotten that the genius of the gospel leads not to *one* fast, but *continual* fasts; and to tell people to fast on this one day, is a tacit permission to neglect the duty *except* on such stated days of humiliation" (*LD* 4: 324). To Froude in 1835 he takes tongue-in-cheek pride in his reputation for asceticism: "Some Head of a House, seeing me (!) pass, said a short while since, 'I wonder how often he has flagellated himself this morning.' Alas he does me too much honour" (*LD* 5: 90).[10] Only the sermons, however, explore the visionary potential of fasting to the point of psychological dislocation: "[I]n some wonderful way [exercises of fasting] open the next world for good and evil upon us, and are an introduction to somewhat of an extraordinary conflict with the powers of evil. . . . [I]f we knew the secret history of men's minds in any age, we should find *this* (at least, I think I am not theorizing,)—viz. a remarkable union . . . on the one hand of temptations offered to the mind, and on the other, of the mind's not being affected by them" (*PS* 6 [1]: 7–8).[11] While Newman claims here to be analyzing "Stories . . . of hermits in deserts," that revealing parenthesis—"(at least, I think I am not theorizing)"—gives his own involvement away.

Natural Anarchy

Within each of these liminal experiences, we see Newman probing the limits of normal experience while pursuing a Romantic journey of discovery and self-discovery. While these journeys carefully restrict the number of participants, some involuntarily raise up more sinister specters. A decade after his Mediterranean tour, for example, his Sicilian quest for some secular Eden takes a sinister turn in his essay on ecclesiastical miracles. Here, Newman compares biblical and Patristic miracle stories by comparing pre- and post-lapsarian landscapes: "Scripture is to us a garden of Eden, and its creations are beautiful as well as 'very good;' but when we pass from the Apostolic to the following ages, it is as if we left the choicest valleys of the earth, the quietest and most harmonious scenery, and the most cultivated soil, for the luxuriant wilderness of Africa or Asia, the natural home or kingdom of brute nature, uninfluenced by man" (*Mir.* 150–51). Newman seems to have reverted to a pre-Romantic stance: "Where man is not, Nature is barren." Yet the apparent distinction between Eden and the secular wilds dissolves in the next sentence when this wildness confronts Adam in the as-yet-unknown and unnamed animals: "Adam might much more justly have been startled at the various forms of life which were brought before him to be named, than we may rationally presume to decide that certain alleged miracles in the Church are not really such" (151).[12]

Five years later, within the aggressively Catholic *Difficulties Felt by Anglicans,* Newman finds his Edenic landscape still more problematic. Arguing that all non-Catholic claims to Patristic Christianity are illusory, he images this landscape itself as a similar illusion:

> Students of the Fathers, antiquarians, and poets, begin by assuming that the body to which they belong is that of which they read in time past, and then proceed to decorate it with that majesty and beauty of which history tells, or which their genius creates. . . . But at length, either the force of circumstances or some unexpected accident dissipates it; and, as in fairy tales, the magic castle vanishes when the spell is broken, and nothing is seen but the wild heath, the barren rock, and the forlorn sheep-walk: so it is with us as regards the Church of England, when we look in amazement on that which we thought so unearthly, and find so common-place or worthless. (*Diff.* 1: 6-7)[13]

Prickett sees the metaphor as an echo of Keats's "La Belle Dame" (*Romanticism* 178), which raises interesting questions of who is seducing whom; he groups it with Newman's new claims for Catholicism as the sole guarantor of imaginative truth.[14] Yet it may also represent a new attempt to bifurcate his original impression of the temple at Segesta. The "disenchanted" setting here—with its heath, rock, and sheep-walk—remains just as stubbornly and savagely real as the modern setting at Segesta—with its bull, dogs, shepherd's hut, muddy farmyard, and would-be robbers. The temple's pristine, Edenic, imagined splendor may thus be threatened with dissolution—and Newman with disillusion—unless he can translate it into some sanctuary within the past of institutional Catholicism.

When Newman's attention shifts from flora to fauna, we realize that the dichotomy which troubles him is not between spiritual reality and material illusion but between two visions, one controlled and the other uncontrollable. A sermon on "The Invisible World," for example, argues *a fortiori* that our dealings with angels are much more straightforward than our dealings with animals. We can

> as little know their state, or can describe their interests, or their destiny, as we can tell of the inhabitants of the sun and moon. . . . [W]e familiarly use, I may say hold intercourse with creatures who are as much strangers to us, as mysterious, as if they were the fabulous, unearthly beings, more powerful than man, yet his slaves, which Eastern superstitions have invented. . . . We inflict very great sufferings on a portion of them, and they in turn, every now and then,

seem to retaliate upon us, as if by a wonderful law. . . . Cast your thoughts abroad on the whole number of them, large and small, in vast forests, or in the water, or in the air; and then say whether the presence of such countless multitudes, so various in their natures, so strange and wild in their shapes, living on the earth without ascertainable object, is not as mysterious as any thing which Scripture says about the Angels. (*PS* 4 [13]: 205-6)[15]

In the *Apologia* Newman admits that as a child he wished the *Arabian Nights* were true (15-16). Here his reference to jinns and genies suggests that this riot of strange forms and habitats can still evoke a lingering love of romance. In *The Church of the Fathers,* however, he comes to find nothing "absurd in considering certain hideous developments of nature as tokens of the presence of the unseen author of evil. . . . [T]he sight of a beast of prey, with his malevolent passions, savage cruelty, implacable rage, malice, cunning . . . awakens very awful and complicated musings in a religious mind" (*HS* 2: 108). By the time of the *Ecclesiastical Miracles,* these visions of brute nature threaten to pass beyond any religious frame of reference. Like the crater of Vesuvius or the crags at Taurominium or the slopes of Etna, they defy the mind's attempt to take them in:

> When an eye thus habituated to certain forms, colours, motions, and habits in the inferior [native] animals, is suddenly brought into the full assemblage of those mysterious beings, with which it has pleased Almighty Wisdom to people the earth, a sort of dizziness comes over it, from the impossibility of our reducing all at once the multitude of new ideas poured in upon us to the centre of view habitual to us; the mind loses its balance, and it is not too much to say, that in some cases it even falls into a sort of scepticism. Nature seems to be too powerful and various, or at least too strange, to be the work of God. (*Mir.* 148-49)

While romance is here exchanged for the Romantic sublime, this disorientation occasions neither a Wordsworthian transcendence nor a Christian self-transcendence. Instead the "dizziness" again mimics the psychological trauma he experienced when taking and administering the Schools.[16]

The same disorientation also subverts Newman's mutual understanding with his God.[17] The problem is not simply that his failure to find any moral purpose in this fecundity tempts him to attribute it to a causal agent other than God. It is also that as these grotesque creatures invade his own "centre of view," they may also body forth some disconcerting aspects of God:

Religion we know to be a grave and solemn subject. . . . And then we are suddenly brought into the vast family of His works, hardly one of which is a specimen of those particular and human ideas with which we have identified the Ineffable. First the endless number of wild animals, their independence of man, and uselessness to him; then their exhaustless variety; then their strangeness in shape, colour, size, motions, and countenance, . . . tempting us to view the Physical Cause of all as disconnected from the Moral. . . . [N]othing we see in this vast assemblage is *religious* in our sense of the word 'religious.' . . . One [anomaly] is that principle of *deformity*, whether hideousness or mere homeliness, which exists in the animal wor[l]d; and the other . . . is the *ludicrous*. (*Mir.* 149–50)

Newman's imaginative zoo is proleptically Darwinian in its random variations, but his response to this variation is nothing like the conclusion of the *Origin of Species*: "[W]hilst this planet has gone cycling on . . . , from so simple a beginning endless forms most beautiful and most wonderful have been, and are being created." We hear instead the nihilism of a Hume: "Look round this universe. What an immense profusion of beings. . . . The whole presents nothing but the idea of a blind nature, impregnated by a great vivifying principle, and pouring forth from her lap, without discernment or parental care, her maimed and abortive children!" (78–79).[18]

Spectral Visitants

Similar specters—furry, figurative, and fantastic—lay siege to Newman's consciousness throughout the Tractarian decade. In the first chapter we found Mary's ghost haunting his twilight landscapes; in chapter 6 we found Froude's spirit assuming angelic form even before his death; in chapter 2 we even found Newman positing a set of preternatural beings intermediate between human and divine. Though these last flabbergasted Connop Thirlwall—and probably terrified the more impressionable within Newman's congregation—they fit tidily within his vision of parallel realms. He quotes with approval Anthony's advice on how to control them without fear: "[E]vil spirits, since they can do nothing, are but as actors in a play, changing their shapes and frightening children by their tumult and their make-belief" (*HS* 2: 119).[19] Yet even with these spirits' angelic counterparts, even in the famous sermon, "The Powers of Nature," such animism raises disquieting questions. Keble certainly would have sanctioned a vision of nature as sacramental as this one: "Every breath of air and ray of light and heat, every beautiful prospect, is, as it were, the skirts of their garments, the waving of the robes of those, whose faces see God in heaven" (*PS* 2 [29]: 362).

Newman goes on, however, to imagine that some amateur scientist, "when examining a flower, or a herb, or a pebble, or a ray of light . . . suddenly discovered that he was in the presence of some powerful being who was hidden behind the visible things he was inspecting, . . . whose robe and ornaments those wondrous objects were, which he was so eager to analyze" (364). Here, I think, we are not too far from the kind of magical anarchy Coleridge offered to the reader who requested a stronger moral for his *Ancient Mariner*: "It ought to have had no more moral than the *Arabian Nights*' tale of the merchant's sitting down to eat dates by the side of a well and throwing the shells aside, and lo! a genie starts up and says he *must* kill the aforesaid merchant *because* one of the date shells had, it seems, put out the eye of the genie's son" (1: 272–73). As "God's instrument," Newman's angelic being should prove more benevolent; yet when anyone claims that "there are Spiritual Intelligences which move those wonderful and vast portions of the natural world which seem to be inanimate" (*PS* 2 [29]: 361), he is not just introducing an element of freedom into a mechanical system; he is inserting a form of demiurge between God's providence and his creation.[20] The *Apologia* may dismiss both angelic and intermediate beings as early, almost adolescent, beliefs but the later passages quoted in chapter 2 suggest that these spiritual loose cannons threatened to sink the whole Tractarian Movement.[21]

On a more personal level, Newman's spectral encounters form a continuum from familiarity through control to something approaching terror. While he rejoiced in his dream of the spiritual world and gradually accustomed himself to his haunting intimations of Mary, other visitants were not so sympathetic. Off Malta he suggests to Harriett that their communication within and through dreams seemed to excite the envy of evil spirits: "I dream about you all, and letters are brought me, but, when I begin to read, they are either illegible, or I wake—as if some beings were trying to tell me, and others prevented it" (*LD* 3: 184).[22] Two weeks later, however, it is Newman who thwarts a much more intrusive ghost in the Lazaretto at Malta:

Do not tell people of course, but we have had mysterious night visitants in the Lazaret. . . . F[roude] recurred (to what he had told me before) to a most shocking dream he had had the first night we slept there, like Coleridge's Christabel. . . . I fancy it was that of an evil spirit seated over against his bed, or something of the sort. On Sunday night last (the 20th) I was awakened by a noise in room 2. . . . The fourth time it occurred, I hollowed out lustily "Who is there" and sat up in my bed ready to spring out—a deep silence followed. . . . You may theorize that the accustomed evil tenants of the place were obliged, when christians were there, to skulk behind real earthly noises and to cease when interrogated. (*LD* 3: 190–92)

Yet Newman can boast that this specter left him undaunted: "I had comfort in feeling, that, whatever was the need, . . . I should have protection *equal to it,* rising *with* the occasion, and I was quite rejoiced to find my faith strong enough to hinder me from fearing" (192).

By the time he wrote his *Church of the Fathers,* Newman had identified the ghost, not with Coleridge's sexually dangerous Geraldine, but with Satan himself. We previously quoted his claim that the "earth had become Satan's kingdom," from which he "retreated only inch by inch." The conclusion to this passage seems to point directly at Newman's Lazaretto encounter: "Many serious persons think that the evil spirits have, even now, extraordinary powers in heathen lands. . . . How unaccountable to him who has met with them are the sudden sounds, the footsteps, and the noises which he has heard in solitary places, or when in company with others!" (*HS* 2: 110). The same encounter may also be an autobiographical source for other passages. Tract 83 claims that "the world is impregnated with unearthly elements, which ever and anon, in unhealthy seasons, give lowering and muttering tokens of the wrath to come!" (5: 21); but a late sermon awards us the requisite protection: "[H]enceforth evil spirits, instead of having power over us, tremble and are affrighted at every true Christian. They know . . . that he may, if he will, laugh them to scorn, and put them to flight" (*PS* 6 [1]: 13–14).[23]

The Lazaretto ghost, while localized, is not a full-fledged spirit of place. Because the *genius loci* at Oxford has been his familiar companion, Newman welcomes a corresponding spirit on his first visit to Cambridge: "[W]hen I saw at the distance of four miles, . . . the Alma Mater Cantabrigiensis lying before me, I thought I should not be able to contain myself, and . . . seemed about to cry out, 'Floreat in aeternum!' Surely there is a genius loci here, as in my own dear home—and the nearer I came to it, the more I felt its power" (*LD* 3: 66).[24] Later, however, the spirit inhabiting his adolescent home at Alton arises so unexpectedly that he cannot summon up the faith which protected him in the Lazaret. He responds with fear, then with denial, and finally with self-disgust:

There was something so mysterious too in seeing old sights, half recollecting them, and doubting. It is like seeing the ghosts of friends. Perhaps it is the impression it makes upon one of God's *upholding* power, which is so awful—but it seemed to me so very strange, that every thing was in its place after so long a time. As we came near, and I saw Monk's Wood, the Church, and the hollow on the other side of the town, it was as fearful as if I was standing on the grave of some one I knew, and saw him gradually recover life and rise again. . . . And then the excitement caused a re-action, and I got quite in-sensible and callous—and then again got disgusted with myself. (*LD* 4: 332)

The very durability of this past landscape brings it back to life. Assuming a known but unnamed human form, it rises from its grave to haunt him.[25]

In another vision, this time an actual nightmare, Newman is betrayed by the insubstantiality of a childhood refuge: "First a sort of weight and horror fell upon me—after a while I found myself in the Tower at Oriel" (*LD* 3: 295).[26] A colleague interposes,

"[L]et me introduce you to our two new fellows," pointing to two men who stood on his right round the table—And, casting my eyes on them, I saw two of the most clumsy awkward looking chaps I ever set eyes on—and they had awkward unintelligible names. . . . When I got away at length, I could find no means of relief. . . . I wished to retire to the shrubberies, which were those of Ham [his family's summer home]—there, thought I to myself, on this seat or in that arbour which I recollect frequenting as a boy, I shall recover myself. But it was not allowed me. I was in my rooms or in some rooms—and had continual interruptions. . . . Then came in a brace of Gentlemen Commoners with hideous faces. (295)

Horrified by these uncouth harbingers of the "new" Oxford, the tutors replacing him and Froude, he is "driven back into childhood, into the time when defeat was synonymous with safety and the settled heavenly order of his father's garden. But he is denied that means of escape. . . . Barred from the shrubberies of Eden, he doubles back into manhood. He would be alone in his rooms" (Faber 313-14). But there too, students impervious to his spiritual direction become intrusive specters who break down every barrier he can put up against them.[27]

His impressionability may grow from the early confusion of fact and fancy which he describes in the *Apologia* (16). In his *Early History,* Frank observes the same tendency but interprets it as pathological: John's "early zeal for ghost stories may have been at the bottom. I remember that at Brighton one year he kept us all agog by a tale of ghosts which seemed inexplicable except by believing in the spirits; then, after two or three weeks, he suddenly told us he had found it all to be false" (45). Though suspect, Frank's memory is anticipated by an early reviewer of Newman's

Justification: "[O]nce or twice his imagination seems to have seduced him a little way into the realm of shadowy and mystical fancies" (quoted in *LD* 6: 253n).[28] The phantoms invoked, not in his writing but by it, remained particularly disturbing. Having sent off the manuscript of his *Arians,* he confesses,

> [I] have been in suspense till yesterday about the fate of my MS. . . . Nothing ought to have alarmed me—but I had been near faint- ing more than once, and altogether (fear being more imaginative at night time—did you never find this? it partly accounts for the fear of ghosts.) I must confess I played the fool. Continuing however indis- posed, I was obliged to leave my work. . . . [I] have all manner of absurd spectres dancing before me, the nephews of mauvais honte (I cannot make out who their father is) which is more painful than guilt. (*LD* 3: 71–73)

In this rather forced effort at jocularity, Newman here describes himself as being driven from his writing by fears about his writing, fears which become embodied as specters whose lineage he queries but cannot es- tablish.

Ecclesiastical Miracles

These specters, in turn, help condition Newman's response to the incon- gruous figures and forces he encounters within Patristic miracle stories. His first essay on miracles remains so indebted to Paley that it finds clear evidence for God in the orderliness of nature: "Were a being who had experience only of a chaotic world suddenly introduced into this orderly system of things, he would have an infinitely more powerful argument for the existence of a designing Mind, than a mere interruption of that system can afford" (*Mir.* 11). Following the accepted Latitudinarian strat- egy, Newman authenticates miracles in the Bible by comparing their power and decorum with the folk-tale quality of their Patristic counter- parts. Some miracles "are unworthy of an All-wise Author. . . . Such are most of the Miracles recorded in the apocryphal accounts of Christ: *e.g.,* the sudden ceasing of all kinds of motion at His birth, birds stopping in the midst of their flight, men at table with their hands to their mouths, yet unable to eat, etc. . . . Under this head of exception fall many of the Miracles related by the Fathers" (*Mir.* 28–29).[29] As late as 1840, New- man can argue that when skeptics refuse to use Scripture as a touchstone to distinguish belief from superstition, they are driven to much baser forms of credulity: "Hence it is a common remark, that irreligious men are most open to superstition. For they have a misgiving that there is something great and divine somewhere: and since they have it not within them, they have no difficulty in believing that it is anywhere else. . . . Scripture is the key by which we are given to interpret the world; but they who have it not, roam amid the shadows of the world, and interpret things at random" (*PS* 6 [17]: 251–52).

As Newman continues to read the Fathers, however, he encounters the opposite problem, an increasing strain put upon his own credulity. As early as the *Arians,* he has to account for the sudden death of Arius himself at the height of his power: "On the evening before the day of his proposed triumph, Arius passed through the streets of [Constantinople] with his party, in an ostentatious manner; when the stroke of death suddenly overtook him, and he expired before the danger was discovered" (269). As Pattison points out, Gibbon offered the twin explanations of miracle and poison and left the choice to the relative gullibility of his readers. Newman resolutely makes his choice: "Under the circumstances, a thoughtful mind cannot but account this as one of those remarkable interpositions of power, by which Divine Providence urges on the consciences of men in the natural course of things. . . . It is remarkable too, that the similar occurrences, which happen at the present day, are generally connected with some unusual perjury or extreme blasphemy" (269).[30]

With the publication of the *Church of the Fathers,* he is growing yet more nervous about yet more insistent claims for the miraculous: "[T]he question of the Fathers is getting more and more anxious. For certain persons will not find in them just what they expected. People seem to have thought they contained nothing but the doctrines of Baptismal Regeneration, Apostolical Succession, Canonicity of Scripture, and the like" (Moz. 2: 261–62). Three months later, he specifies what readers will find: "My 'Church of the Fathers' is now finished. It is the prettiest book I have done. . . . I have no notion how it will take, as I have been obliged to give out the Fathers' views about celibacy and miraculous power" (Moz. 2: 267). Writing to Hope in 1843, he claims that miracles cannot be omitted from any edition of saints' lives:

Church History is made up of these three elements—miracles, monkery, Popery . . . unless, indeed, one adopts Milner's or Neander's device of dropping part of the history, praising what one has a fancy for, and thus putting a theory and dream in the place of facts. . . . Take missions, take Bishops, the Pope comes in everywhere. Go to Aldheim and his schools; you have most strange miracles. Try to retire into the country, you do but meet with hermits. No; miracles, monkery, Popery, are too much for you, if you have any stomach. (*KC* 282–83)

But Newman has even less stomach for the fancy, theory, and dream of rationalized history than for even the strangest miracles. The Fathers entered his life in *Arians* as sources of doctrine, were transformed within *Church of the Fathers* into models of piety, and were transformed again within the *Breviary* into patterns of devotion. Now, however, they have become privileged interpreters of Newman's entire religious universe. A month later he admits to Hope that "to find that the English Church cannot bear the Lives of her Saints . . . does not tend to increase my faith and confidence in her" (*KC* 287).

What this burden cost him his critics have been quick to point out.[31] Thirlwall, as we saw in chapter 8, assumed that Newman found all supernatural claims equally absurd. He attributed "the extravagant credulity with which he accepts the wildest Popish legends" to Newman's "bottomless unbelief" (260). Bremond falls back on psychology and self-hatred to explain the otherwise inexplicable: "[E]ach miracle preserved by the tradition of the Church offers him an opportunity of a fresh sacrifice of intellect, of one of those humiliations and mortifications of the mind which have become so dear to him" (Bremond 105).[32] Within the last of his university sermons, Newman's explanation displays enough concentrated casuistry to justify any such criticisms: "If the alleged [miraculous] facts did not occur, they ought to have occurred (if I may so speak); they are such as might have occurred, and would have occurred, under circumstances; and they belong to the parties to whom they are attributed, potentially, if not actually; or the like of them did occur; or occurred to others similarly circumstanced" (*US* [15]: 343). Just as heinous is the question-begging which pervades the *Ecclesiastical Miracles,* a work Chadwick dismisses as "a jumble of twisted dialectic about historical evidence, which it is not too strong to describe as repellent" (*Mind* 42):[33] "[I]f it be asked, whether, after all, such miracles are not suspicious, whatever be the consequence of admitting it, I answer, that they are suspicious to read of, but not to see" (*Mir.* 207).[34] The argument closest to Newman's heart, I think, grows out of the immense power and sanctity with which he invests his own spiritual heroes:

When, then, controversialists go through the existing accounts of ecclesiastical miracles, and explain one after another on the hypothesis of natural causes; when they resolve a professed vision into a dream, a possession into epilepsy or madness, a prophecy into a sagacious conjecture, a recovery into the force of imagination, . . .

they are consistent in denying [the Church's] outward triumphs, when they have no true apprehension of its inward power. Those, on the other hand, who realize that the bodies of the Saints were in their lifetime the Temples of the Holiest, and are hereafter to rise again, will feel no offence at the report of miracles wrought through them. (*Mir.* 188)

In the context of this chapter, however, the beginning of this passage speaks more to Newman's condition than the end. He rejects any reduction of Patristic miracle because the preternatural forces threatening him are not themselves subject to such reduction. He readily admits that these later miracles remain an historical, moral, and ethical mixed bag: "Miracles posterior to the Apostolic age, are on the whole different in object, character, and evidence, from those of Scripture on the whole" (*Mir.* 99). And several pages later: "The Miracles of Scripture are, as a whole, grave, simple, and majestic: those of Ecclesiastical History often partake of what may not unfitly be called a romantic character. . . . [They] often are only floating rumours, popular traditions, vague, various, inconsistent in detail" (*Mir.* 116–17). As such, I would argue, they align themselves with very personal incursions of the 1830s. The variety and fecundity Newman encountered in animals, for example, rationalize similar qualities in these later miracles: "There is far greater difference between the appearance of a horse or an eagle and a monkey, or a lion and a mouse, as they meet our eye, than between even the most august of the Divine manifestations in Scripture and the meanest and most fanciful of those legends which we are accustomed without further examination to cast aside" (*Mir.* 151).

Buried within a footnote, the most perceptive passage in the 1826 essay on miracles anticipates Barth's warning that no limited human criteria can delimit the locus, nature, and scope of the divine:

There is an appearance of doing honour to the Christian doctrines in representing them as *intrinsically* credible, which leads many into supporting opinions which, carried to their full extent (as they were by Middleton), supersede the need of Miracles altogether. It must be recollected, too, that they who are allowed to praise have the privilege of finding fault, and may reject, according to their *a priori* notions, as well as receive. . . . It is one thing to infer from the experience of life, another to imagine the character of God from the gratuitous conceptions of our own minds. (*Mir.* 51n–52n)[35]

Germinated within the animism of the 1830s, this seminal idea reaches full bloom in the *Ecclesiastical Miracles* of 1843. There, one particularly dense passage invokes the sublime, Edenic vistas of Sicily, the grotesqueness of foreign animals, even the intimations of an indifferent God. Newman implicates all of nature within a plea for abolishing all *a priori* criteria for divine intervention:

> "He hath made every thing beautiful in His time." . . . [F]or those other and manifold objects which the economy of the Gospel king-dom may involve, a more hidden and intricate path, a more complex exhibition, a more exuberant method, a more versatile rule, may be essential; and it may be as shallow a philosophy to reject them merely because they are not such as we should have expected from God's hand, or as we find in Scripture, as to judge of universal na-ture by the standard of our own home, or again, with the ancient her-etics, to refuse to admit that the Creator of the physical world is also the Father of our Lord Jesus Christ. Nay, it may even be urged that the variety of nature is antecedently a reason for expecting variety in a supernatural agency. (*Mir.* 152)[36]

Here the parallel realms, which Newman has so carefully kept separate, begin to intermingle: "There are two providential systems in operation among us, the visible and the invisible, intersecting, as it were, each other, and having a certain territory in common . . . and in many cases we do not know the exact boundaries of each" (*Mir.* 186–87).[37]

We can neither stand outside these systems nor comprehend them from within:

> Christianity is a supernatural gift, originating and living in the unseen world and only extending into this. It is a vast scheme running out into width and breadth, encompassing us round about, not embraced by us. No one can see the form of a building but those who are ex-ternal to it. We are in the Divine Dispensation; we cannot take it in with the eye, ascertain its proportions, pursue its lines, foretell their directions and coincidences, or ascertain their limits. (*PO* 133)

"Religious Truth," he claims in Tract 73, "is like the dim view of a coun-try seen in the twilight, with forms half extricated from the darkness, with broken lines, and isolated masses. Revelation . . . consists of a num-ber of detached and incomplete truths belonging to a vast system unre-vealed" (3: 9). In this twilight we can no longer distinguish God the creator from God the redeemer; even worse, we cannot distinguish the physical order from the spiritual reality which it was to shadow forth. If nature here fails to be as sacramental as Keble would have liked, it fails not just because it remains fallen (as Prickett, Goodwin, and Finley all suggest), but because we no longer know which is the sign and which the signified. The "more hidden and intricate path" recommended in the *Ecclesiastical Miracles* circles back to Newman's earlier quest for Eden; yet now, if "Scripture is to us a garden of Eden," we can no more return to Scripture than to Eden. We have indeed "left the choicest valleys of the earth," have left Scripture itself, not just in "pass[ing] from the Apostolic to the following ages," but in assuming our fallen nature. "The luxuriant wilderness of Africa or Asia" is no longer just "the natural home or kingdom of brute nature" (*Mir.* 150–51); it is our home (or at least Newman's home) as well.

Irony and Autonomy

As "an infinite universe in which flux, change, and growth were the norms" (Furst 43), this home fostered yet another manifestation of Romanticism. In Anne Mellor's summary:

> The burning question for Schlegel and his contemporaries, who were all convinced by Spinozistic pantheism . . . that an objective, external reality exists, was "How can the finite world of sensible knowledge (the phenomenal realm) and the infinite world of pure being (the noumenal realm) be brought together?" . . . By defining essential reality or the noumenal realm as becoming, Schlegel relegated the principal of identity and contradiction to the phenomenal realm. . . . [He] asserts that reality *is* contradiction or, more precisely, becoming. (26–27)

As Clyde Ryals puts it: "Once the doctrine of becoming, eternal change without telos, was embraced, it followed as the night the day that . . . a romantic ironic world was the result" (14).[38]

Ryals's "embraced" is clearly too strong even for the late-Anglican Newman; "sidled up to" or "glanced at furtively" or "contemplated with consternation" might be more accurate. Newman seems far from eager to fill the role which Lilian Furst offers the Romantic ironist: "His irony is the instrument for registering the obdurate paradoxicality of a universe in eternal flux" (229).[39] Yet some of Newman's more daring passages— particularly when taken together—repeat a pattern which Mellor describes in the far more sanguine Schlegel: "[T]he ironic artist must constantly balance or 'hover' . . . in a mental state that he calls *Selbstbeschränkung,* a rich term variously translated as self-determination, self-restraint, or self-restriction. . . . [H]e simultaneously projects his ego or selfhood as a divine creator and also mocks, criticizes or rejects his created fictions as limited and false" (14).⁴⁰ Such ironic play, I will argue later, informs Newman's account of his conversion; used far more hesitantly, the same strategy informs his problematic images of his God.

The Anarchic Image of God

As we have seen, Newman intimates that exotic animals and equally exotic miracles may both reveal disconcerting traits in their divine author. As the decade progresses, he projects onto his God many of the otherwise anomalous forces which intrude into the mutually supportive dyad of "myself and my Creator." He could not ask so much of this dialogue without asking just as much of both parties. And as his God plays increasingly contradictory roles, Newman must invoke a religious analogue to Schlegel's *Selbstbeschränkung* to affirm and deny these contradictions. Through this strategy he can celebrate his visionary power and simultaneously denigrate the vision itself as a limited gesture at the infinite. To Hugh J. Rose, as we saw in chapter 4, Newman anticipates process theology in the face of its philosophical difficulties: "The personality of God, in our *notion* of personality, is a *mystery*. . . . His being angry, repenting—or resting" (*LD* 3: 78). Even harder than conceiving of such a God is guessing what to expect of him: "Laws are stable; but persons are strange, uncertain, inexplicable. 'Ex pede Herculem'; if I know one fact about the physical world, I know a million others; but one divine act and no more carries me but a little way in my knowledge of 'Summum illud et aetermun, neque mutabile, neque interiturum.' There is some chance of our analyzing nature, none of our comprehending God" (*Ess.* 1: 38–39).

Perhaps *because* Newman feels he has outgrown his early Calvinism, he explores these implications of God's sovereignty with uncompromising rigor. Absent any defensible ground for human judgment, the prospect of divine judgment can seem frighteningly arbitrary: "It is certainly quite beyond our understandings, that all we should now be living together as relatives, friends, associates, neighbours, . . . and yet after all that there should be a bottomless gulf between us, running among us invisibly, and cutting us off into two parties . . . so that every person we meet is in God's unerring eye either on the one side or the other, and, did He please to take him hence at once, would find himself either in paradise or in the place of torment" (*PS* 4 [6]: 87–88). From this perspective, even acknowledged sinners seem guilty of only mixed, human, finite evil. As such, therefore, they call up the same compassion Newman felt towards the guilty inhabitants of Pompeii, the same discovery "that the human heart will in spite of itself claim kindred with every thing human" (*LD* 3:

254): "If [one] has any particular tie connecting him with any such [sinner], then will he feel how hard a saying it is that any one, even the most wicked of men, can be destined to eternal punishment. There is no man ever so bad but to our erring eyes has some redeeming points of character. . . . [A]t times, perhaps when in pain or weariness, he shows something to excite our interest and pity. And if not, then his . . . capability of pain, and his showing that he feels it, seem to connect him with us" (*SD* [6]: 75). One sermon even recreates the existential outrage of being trapped within a body throughout life and then trapped within a soul throughout eternity: Modern skeptics

> beat and break themselves fruitlessly against the destiny to which they are chained; and since they cannot annul their creation, they think to revenge themselves by blasphemously rising against their Creator. "Why am I made? why cannot I annihilate myself? why must I suffer?" . . . sometimes even rushing out of life by self-inflicted violence, from the frantic hope that perchance they have power over their own being. And when they have committed that fatal deed, . . . who can imagine the horror that possesses them in that their new state of existence? . . . —without bodies, yet living, living without aught of power over the principle of their life, which rests upon the will of Him alone, who called them into being, and whom they have blasphemed! (*PS* 4 [4]: 56–57)

Newman endows these renegades with his own frustration at being ethically contingent but ontologically unmediated. He shares their frantic efforts to achieve some ground and integrity for the self. Hence, when he foregrounds the power of God and the impotence of the creature, he tends to soften their blasphemy and aggravate the divine reprisal.

This same incommensurability between human and divine informs Newman's vision of the Old Testament, a vision far more literal than we might have expected from his essay on Scripture.[41] In a footnote to his first essay on miracles, Newman warns that "many have rejected the miraculous narrative of the Pentateuch, for an unfounded and an unwarrantable opinion, that the means employed in settling the Jews in Canaan were in themselves immoral" (*Mir.* 52n). By the time of an 1834 sermon, he has quieted his own historical and moral scruples by rationalizing the invaders' mindset:

> Doubtless, while the servants of God executed His judgments, they still could bend in pity and in hope over the young and old whom they slew with the sword—merciful amid their severity—an unspeakable trial, doubtless, of faith and self-mastery, and requiring a very

exalted and refined spirit successfully to undergo. Doubtless, as they slew those who suffered for the sins of their fathers, their thoughts turned, first to the fall of Adam, next to that unseen state where all inequalities are righted, and they surrendered themselves as instruments unto the Lord, of mysteriously working out good from evil. (*PS* 3 [13]: 187)[42]

In Coleridge, such literalism and such carnage inspired equal outrage: "[W]e need not suppose, that the Hebrew Nation set to work a cold-blooded carpentry of Terrors like the Bard or the Vision of Judgment. In those times and in that country men reasoned with the organ of Imagination, and vivid Images supplied the place of words" (cited in Prickett, *Romanticism*, 46). Rather than the God of the soft-hearted Coleridge, however, Newman's anarchic God resembles the divine source of all physical, logical, and moral contradictions in Coleridge's mentor, Jacob Boehme.[43] Anticipating Philip Gosse's *Omphalos*, Newman posits a God who "frames the worlds in a moment, and creates generations by the breath of His mouth, and melts, and hardens, and deluges, and dries up the solid rocks in a day, and makes bones to live, grow, and die, and buries them in the earth, and changes them into stone, apart from time and at His mere will" (*PS* 5 [4]: 51–52). Within Newman's cosmos, therefore, divinity manifests a power beyond physical and ethical limitations: "Mysterious as it is, the very prison beneath the earth, its chains and fires and impenitent inmates, the very author of evil himself, is sustained in existence by God, and without God would fall into nothing. God is in hell as well as in heaven, a thought which almost distracts the mind to think of. . . . He is intimately present *with* evil, being pure from it—and knows what it is, as being with and in the wretched atoms which originate it" (*PS* 8 [18]: 257–58).[44]

Whenever Newman assumes what Sunden calls the God-role, he can avoid confronting this divine omnipresence as its victim. Amid the rather smug invocations of taste and sensibility in his early essay on poetry, we find a mordant appreciation of the brutal Dionysian epiphany in Euripides' *Bacchae:*

[I]t exhibits the grave irony of a god triumphing over the impotent presumption of man, the sport and terrible mischievousness of an insulted deity. . . . Perhaps the victim's first discovery of the disguised deity is the finest conception in this splendid drama. His madness enables him to discern the emblematic horns on the head of Bacchus, which were hid from him when in his sound mind; yet this discovery, instead of leading him to an acknowledgment of the divinity, provides him only with matter for a stupid and perplexed astonishment. (*Ess.* 1: 6–7)[45]

Perhaps anticipating Juba's madness in *Callista* (264–65), the passage anticipates even more closely this sermon comparison of sinners to cattle: "[T]hey would walk close to the throne of God; they would stupidly gaze at it; they would touch it; they would meddle with the holiest things . . . , till the avenging lightnings destroyed them. . . . Miserable beings! . . . that they should be like the cattle which are slaughtered at the shambles, yet touch and smell the very weapons which are to destroy them!" (*PS* 4 [16]: 247–48). In both passages Newman stands, not with the blundering victim, but with the "terrible mischievousness of an insulted deity."

The Spirit of Pantheism

Newman's God, however, does not remain forever angry, does not remain long in any one emotion, posture, or configuration. Within the *Ecclesiastical Miracles,* Newman's probing, inductive methodology leads him from the variety and incongruity of these miracles, to the grotesque and ludicrous within animals, and finally to a new vision of their author. Working to contain the Romantic irony latent within this seemingly directionless universe, he succeeds only in deferring the problem by transferring the irony to his God. In Tract 73 he attacked Jacob Abbott for "speak[ing] of God in pantheistic language, as an Anima Mundi, or universal essence" (3: 81). In the essay on Scripture he prophesied that "Pantheism, indeed, is the great deceit which awaits the Age to come" (*DA* 233). Yet as his own God grows more inclusive, his vision of God's nature and will grows ever more inconclusive:

> What ecclesiastical history rather inculcates is the doctrine of an abiding presence of Divinity such as dwelt upon the Ark, showing itself as it would, and when it would, and without fixed rules; which was seated primarily in the body of Christians, and manifested itself sometimes in persons, sometimes in places, as the case might be, in saintly men, or in "babes and sucklings," or in the very stones of the Temple; which for a while was latent, and then became manifest again; which to some persons, places or generations was an evidence, and to others was not. (*Mir.* 214)

Despite his references to the Ark and "the body of Christians," Newman's evidences and epiphanies point more directly toward some indwelling, pantheistic spirit. In the diffusion of its manifestations and the variety of its witnesses, this vision recalls his earlier vision of the Apostolic Tradition: "[A] vast system, . . . pervading the Church like an atmosphere, . . . poured to and fro in closets and upon the housetops, in liturgies, in controversial works, in obscure fragments, in sermons, in popular prejudices, in local customs" (*PO* 250). A subsequent passage even repeats the earlier comparison with air: "The supernatural glory might abide, and yet be manifold, variable, uncertain, inscrutable, uncontrollable, like the natural atmosphere; dispensing gleams, shadows, traces of Almighty Power, but giving no such clear and perfect vision of it as one might gaze upon and record distinctly" (*Mir.* 217). While far too smug, Edwin Abbott's account invokes these same figures: "[T]he Image of God became for [Newman] the image . . . of a dread-inspiring Holiness; a dazzling Splendour, dark with excess of light; practically a darkness; before which he could prostrate himself in abject awe, prepared for what ever lightnings and thunderbolts might come forth, and prepared to *call* them just" (*Philomythus* 39).

The Apostolic tradition, as I argued in chapter 3, threatens to reformulate Newman's quest for origins into one of continued, and possibly continuous, deferral. Similarly, within this later passage the Patristic God either holds himself or is held back from the theophanies of biblical narrative. Instead he hides himself within a human order made numinous by his concealed presence. But as the Apostolic Tradition usurps the reality it witnesses, as the ecclesiastical miracles define the world in which fallen humanity must live, so this belated vision of God comes to assert its authority. It insinuates itself as the only power capable of engaging—not just a post-lapsarian world—but a post-Enlightenment Europe. Within the limited context of these two passages, virtually all the god-terms of Romanticism make an appearance: manifold, inscrutable, uncontrollable; glory, gleams, shadows, traces. But they appear divorced from any natural landscape which they would illumine within the poetry of Wordsworth, Coleridge, or Shelley. Within the broader context of Newman's Sicilian landscapes, however, these invocations succeed, as Newman could not at the time, in baptizing his secular Eden and finding it a home within the Patristic Church. Simultaneously, they succeed in giving his God a new habitation and a new set of names within the modern world.[46]

CHAPTER 11

The Context of Conversion

❁

AS WE SAW in chapter 10, Newman worked to include within his image of God the anomalous forces which encroached upon him during the 1830s and early 1840s. Yet as the God-self dyad grew to encompass the triangle of God, self, and intruder, this reconceptualized God grew just as hard to deal with as the intruders themselves. Although they reach very different conclusions, Rajan and Mellor find similar incursions undermining both the Romantics' claims for imaginative transcendence and Hegel's claims for the progressive appropriations of *Geist*. For Rajan, as we saw, these darker intimations inhabit the subtexts of much Romantic poetry; for Mellor, they transform Schlegel's original affirmations of flux and becoming into a denial of any human subjectivity. Both critics note that for early Nietzsche, this undifferentiated Dionysian reality denies the possibility of individual identity or social coherence.[1] Mellor concludes that "by the time he published his doctoral dissertation, *The Concept of Irony*, Kierkegaard had concluded that the psychology inherent in romantic irony could only produce an individual filled with anxiety, melancholy, boredom, and despair" (181).[2]

For Schopenhauer, Marx, and Nietzsche, the same reality which dooms Romantic claims is equally fatal to claims for a personal God. Though vastly different in their stance and tone, both Kierkegaard and Newman come to see their God as encompassing this invasive reality. Anticipating Kierkegaard's insistence on unconditional choice and on dread, Newman wrestles throughout the 1830s with the threat God poses to his spiritual dialogue, his Church, even his salvation. As he reevaluates his own "Church Catholic" against the Catholic Church he encountered on his tour, his lovingly constructed "paper church" seems increasingly impotent to protect its flock against the spiritual anarchy which surrounds them. As he reevaluates church history, early Christianity comes to anticipate the arbitrary demands made by contemporary Catholicism upon its followers—and by his God upon him. Finally, as he reevaluates his earlier Romantic claims within the metaphorical context of his second conversion, their language and a new language of institutional authority join in unresolved conflict.

Augustinian Parallels

The new conflicts threatening Newman's dialogue with his God are fore-shadowed in Newman's own excerpt from the *Confessions:* "[W]hen I thought of Thee, Thou wast not to me any solid or substantial thing. for Thou wert not Thyself, but a mere phantom, and my error was my God. If I offered to discharge my load thereon, that it might rest, it glided through the void, and came rushing down against me; and I had remained to myself a hapless spot, where I could neither be, nor be from thence. For whither should my heart flee from my heart? whither should I flee from myself?" (quoted in *HS* 2: 146). As we suggested in chapter 8, the same dilemmas which haunt the unconverted Augustine also haunt Newman as he vacillates between one conversion and another. Because none of the nouns in this passage—God, phantom, error, load, self, heart—have clearly defined referents, none of the pronouns have clear antecedents. Though what "glided through the void, and came rushing down against" him should be his load, it displays very animated behavior for an inanimate object. Yet attributing this activity to the phantom or to his error would grant either a reality which the context tries to deny. In thus reanimating that which he sets against God, Augustine brings his conceptually dead Manicheism back to narrative life as he portrays its demise.

In much the same way, Newman must acknowledge his own familiar spirits as familiar even as he distances himself from them. By embodying these spirits within his God, moreover, he bestows on this new entity the power to redefine him or to define him out of existence. As we have amply shown, the earlier vision of God was hardly lenient, but Newman had been anticipating his demands almost from birth. Throughout the 1830s, however, Newman encounters a God who manifests seemingly incompatible qualities: the "gleams, shadows, traces of Almighty Power" within a Romantic nature spirit, "the sport and terrible mischievousness of an insulted [Dionysus]," and the arbitrary righteousness of an Old Testament Jehovah who "overcomes when He is judged."

Divine Condemnation and Balaam

Thus refigured, Newman's God becomes his most dangerous adversary. Sometimes, as we saw, he can himself occupy Sunden's God-role, at least as God's surrogate, but more and more often God's indirection grows personally threatening. Satan's "thousand eyes and his many instruments avail him nothing against the . . . holy imperturbable calm which reigns through the providences of God" (*PS* 4 [17]: 259-60); "when in His providences He seems to hurry, He still keeps time. . . . He can condense into an hour a life of trial. . . . Adam fell in a moment; Abraham was justified upon his seizing the knife; Moses lost Canaan for a word; . . . our Lord baffled Satan in three sentences; He redeemed us in the course of a day" (*PS* 5 [4]: 51-52).

As Newman finds himself haunted by ghosts, spirits of place, revenants, and "nephews of mauvais honte," so even those who deny the power of conscience find themselves obsessed by mere thought of God: "The difficulties of science may be dismissed from the mind. . . . But what at once demands attention, yet refuses to satisfy curiosity, places itself above the human mind, imprints on it the thought of Him who is eternal, and enforces the necessity of obedience for its own sake. And thus it becomes to the proud and irreverent, what the consciousness of guilt is to the sinner; a spectre haunting the field, and disturbing the complacency of their intellectual investigations" (*Ari.* 272). Like Byron, the Tractarian Newman was "not unwilling to play with a man, who asked me impertinent questions" (*Apo.* 51), but his God can be equally baffling: "[T]he All-wise, All-knowing God cannot speak without meaning many things at once. . . . [A]s far as we may reasonably infer them, we must thankfully accept them" (*PS* 1 [21]: 271-72). Like Guido in Dante's *Inferno,* who learns to his sorrow that the devil too is a logician, Newman learns that his God is no mean ironist:

> Religious men cannot but feel, in various ways, that His providence is guiding them . . . ; yet when they attempt to put their finger upon the times and places, the traces of His presence disappear. . . . Who has not had thoughts come upon him with a sort of mysterious force, for his warning or his direction? . . . but [God] seems so frequently to undo what He has done, and to suffer counterfeits of His tokens, that a conviction of His wonder-working presence can but exist in the individual himself. (*PS* 6 [17]: 248-50)

Though convinced that he remains the object of a personal providence, Newman can win no sure insight into its intent towards him: God "can convert us, if He will, through the very obstinacy, or self-will, or superstition, which mixes itself up with our better feelings. . . . The simple question is, *has* He, in this particular case, commanded, has He promised? and how far? If He has, and as far as He has, all is easy; if He has not, all is, we will not say impossible, but what is worse, undutiful or presumptuous" (*Ess.* 2: 342-43). In an 1846 letter to Bowden's widow, he extrapolates from his own recent conversion to those contemplated by friends. By this point, providence has taken on the grotesque, episodic incongruity of a romance narrative: "Sometimes too I have known at the very morning of acting, a letter has come [to the one converting], saying for instance, that the step will be the death of some near relative of his, with strong representations of the recklessness of his conduct, so that he is like some hero in a romance who has to make his way to the object of his search amid magical terrors" (*LD* 11: 141).

It is the *ad hoc,* unrehearsed quality of these confessions which separates them from Kierkegaard's apparently similar claims. According to Mellor, his "sense of self . . . must be founded on a conviction of spiritual inadequacy; 'as against God we are always in the wrong.' For Kierkegaard, the self-restraint of romantic irony must become a specifically religious dread, a deep sense of guilt and personal inadequacy. This is the redemptive fear and trembling before God that Kierkegaard described in his later theological, 'upbuilding treatises.'" (182-83).[3] Kierkegaard, however, is writing as one who has seen the meaninglessness of existence outside Christianity; he is writing for those, either nominal Christians or freethinkers, who can dimly perceive this meaninglessness within their own lives. To quote Hermann Diem, it was "Kierkegaard's opinion that it was no longer possible, within a world turned 'Christian,' to gain any impression of the passion of the Christian faith. . . . He spoke as a 'poet' because he was neither willing nor able to be himself a witness to his faith" (43).[4] Although Newman never stood as far away from his age as he claimed, he never stood with those lost multitudes he describes in the *Apologia,* "having no hope and without God in the world" (217). Because he cannot choose to disbelieve in God, he cannot, like Kierkegaard, choose to dread. He cannot even anticipate this dread; he can only respond to each new instance of the "magical terrors" with which his God may visit him.

In 1836, confessing to Jemima that his prayers may have disrupted their family, he describes their efficacy with the superstitious dread of someone granted wishes in a fairy tale:

> About a year since, when I found myself getting into debt, I began a prayer . . . "that God would either give me the means of doing what I wished to do towards you all, or remove the necessity—." . . . When your engagement was formed, it stuck me strangely—and, when we were overtaken with our affliction last May [their mother's death], it seemed just as if I had been praying for the death of her.

. . . But so I have most remarkably found it, and I suppose others find it too—that my prayers in a variety of cases are most strangely answered—so much so that to pray seems to be using an edged tool. (*LD* 5:322–23)[5]

Thus Newman comes to fear that even his spiritual and imaginative powers may only be bait proffered by an affronted God.[6] Repeating the "pane of glass" metaphor in his own journal, he admits to Henry Wilberforce that all his ability to inspire others may profit him nothing: "I dare say I *am* doing good—but I have no consciousness that I retain any portion of it myself—or that I am more of an instrument of God than Solomon or Jehu might be" (*LD* 6: 57).[7] This fear of becoming an expendable instrument reappears in his obsessive references to yet another Old Testament figure.

That the Mesopotamian diviner Balaam should confuse Newman is understandable if only because of the unreconciled accounts of him within chapters 22–24 and 31 of Numbers. In the last account he is killed, along with most of the Midianites, because he is held responsible for their sexual corruption of Israel at Peor. In the folktale of Balaam's ass (Numbers 22:21–35), the seer undertakes a journey against God's will and has to be reprimanded by his lowly mount before he can see the angel barring his path.[8] In the surrounding text, however, Balaam is celebrated as a pagan witness to Israel's manifest destiny. When he is summoned by the Moabite king Balak to curse the invading Israelites "come out of Egypt," Balaam blesses them instead, rationalizing that he could not "go beyond the word of the Lord, to do either good or bad of my own will; what the Lord speaks, that will I speak" (24:13).

In the essay on Scripture, Newman intimates that in Balaam he is confronting irreconcilable traditions.[9] While he would never admit that this inconsistency was real, others like it he simply notes and then tactfully ignores. Balaam, however, worries him—and so he constantly worries Balaam. In *Arians* he claims that "a heathen is made the oracle of true divine messages about doing justly, and loving mercy, and walking humbly; nay, even among the altars of superstition, the Spirit of God vouchsafes to utter prophecy" (82).[10] And in positing authentic religious origins for the Temple at Segesta, he notes that "Even among the altars of Balak, a prophet of God officiated—even in the corrupt heart of Balaam an uncongenial spirit of truth spoke for the edification of others" (*LD* 3: 291–92). Yet elsewhere, "The old Prophet of Bethel was the involuntary instrument of God's wrath, though he condemned himself the while . . . with a covetous heart and amid heathen enchantments" (*PO* 344).

Among Newman's most visionary sermons—and composed at about the same time[11]—we find one devoted entirely to Balaam: "[A] man divinely favoured, visited, influenced, guided, protected, eminently honoured, illuminated,—a man possessed of an enlightened sense of duty, and of moral and religious acquirements, educated, high-minded, conscientious, honourable, firm; and yet on the side of God's enemies, personally under God's displeasure, and in the end (if we go on to that) the direct instrument of Satan, and having his portion with the unbelievers" (*PS* 4 [2]: 26). Because this figure bears so little resemblance to any of the different Balaams in Numbers, we may suspect that it bears considerable resemblance to Newman himself. If Newman finds his story "fearful," it is not just that Balaam had misapplied his gifts; Newman dismisses many such figures in sermons equally stern but much more self-assured. It is not even that Balaam, "admitted to conscious intercourse with God" (21), wields the same potentially dangerous prophetic powers which Newman has been appropriating for himself. It is rather "that at this very time, *while* [Balaam] so spoke and acted, he seems, as in one sense to be in God's favour, so in another and higher to be under His displeasure" (25). In crossing into Moab, "He had sinned, and nothing happened outwardly, but wrath was abroad and in his path. *This* again is a very serious and awful thought. God's arm is not shortened. What happened to Balaam is as if it took place yesterday. God is what He ever was; we sin as man has ever sinned. We sin without being aware of it. God is our enemy without our being aware of it" (34). Balaam may indeed have sinned "as man has ever sinned," but it is Newman personally who becomes aware that God may be his enemy, that "wrath [is] abroad and in his path." It is Newman who realizes that he has been tempted "to act towards God . . . as towards a mere system . . . , not as against a Person" (31), one "who chooses whom He will choose, and exalts whom He will exalt, without destroying man's secret responsibilities or His own governance" (21). It is Newman who convicts himself of trying to subsume his God into a projection of his own spiritual aspirations.

Thus when he "reads in Scripture what the many cannot see there, the course of [God's] providence," Newman may also see himself standing outside the pale. Later in this same passage, he acknowledges, "Well is it for those who are so gifted, that they do not for certain know their privilege; well is it for them that they . . . contemplate it as external to themselves, lodged in the Church of which they are but members" (*PS* 3 [24]: 363–64). Perhaps because Newman feared that this "privilege" would prove his own damnation, he chose to lodge it, and ultimately his own future, within the safety of an institutional church.

Early Images of Catholicism

Even Newman's choice of this church depended upon its affinity with the God who afflicted Balaam. His later references to Roman Catholicism describe it as a bastion against the inroads of modern skepticism or a safe harbour from the open sea of relativism. During the Oxford Movement, however, Rome conjured up in Newman the same awed fascination that he otherwise reserved for his God. The *Apologia* is right in claiming that his most knowledgeable comments on Catholicism come relatively late, but it understates Rome's influence during his grand tour.[12] Although he began his trip secure in Anglican insularity, he was challenged almost from the start.[13] After several months and many miles, his letter to Christie from Rome explores the moral relativism which this cultural pluralism has awakened. Greek fasts and Roman Masses he now interprets as "an opiate to the conscience. . . . Not that [the natives] are likely to consider their bandit-kind of life as requiring some makeup. . . . [A] bravo adopts a *profession* indeed, and one in which murder *may* be added to plundering, but he is not in any sense more *habitually* disobedient to his conscience, or more pained or sensitive, than a dishonest servant in England—who picks up stray halfpence of his master's or purloins his tea and sugar" (*LD* 3: 239–40).

The actual experience of Rome, because so much more daunting, produces even more conflicting impressions. Each letter may sound characteristically self-assured, but when read in chronological order they suggest that Newman knows not what to make of the Catholic Church—only that he must make something of it. His first letter from Rome itself is a rare example of unreflective, uncritical awe:

And now what [can] I say of Rome, but that it is of all cities the first, and that all I ever saw are but as dust, even dear Oxford inclusive, compared with its majesty and glory. . . . In St Peter's yesterday, and St John Lateran today, I have felt quite abased—chiefly by their enormous size, which . . . makes one seem quite little and contemptible. . . . [T]he sight of the very arena where Ignatius suffered, the columns of heathen pride with the inscriptions still legible, the Jewish candlestick still perfect in every line on the arch of Titus, brand it as the vile tool of God's wrath and again Satan's malice.—Next when you enter the Museum etc, a fresh world is opened to you—that of imagination and taste. (*LD* 3: 230–31)

While Newman affects an Augustan contemplation of discrete objects, the whole passage offers a very Romantic fusion of different Romes and different responses: respect for antiquity in St. John Lateran, submersion in the Counter-Reformation grandeur of St. Peter's, terror inspired by the clash between Roman power and Judeo-Christian zeal. Rome as a whole—pagan and Christian; ancient, Renaissance and modern—becomes simultaneously the instrument of God and of Satan.

In a letter to his mother from the relative safety of Naples, he could still prophesy an inevitable decline from Catholicism into secularism; yet this church retains enough power to involve the rest of Christendom in its ruin: "[H]ere also they have infidelity and profaneness—as if the whole world (Western) were tending towards some dreadful crisis" (*LD* 3: 224). Even in decay, the architecture moves him to that empathy with human transience first called up by the artifacts from Pompeii and the ruins at Segesta: "[T]here are such traces of long sorrow and humiliation, suffering, punishment and decay, that one has a mixture of feelings, partly such as those with which one would approach a corpse, and partly those which would be excited by the sight of the spirit which had left it" (*LD* 3: 234).[14]

While Newman was prepared by his classical reading for the decay of classical Rome, he was surprised and disconcerted to find a vigorous church usurping its place (Brent, "Moral," 82–87). To Pusey, therefore, he invokes more hopeful biblical cataclysms in which the fall of Catholicism will leave Israel's saving remnant or those survivors of the last times within the Synoptics: "How fast events are going. . . . and tho' we shall not live to see it, can we doubt it is intended to effect the purification of that divinely founded body, for its edification in love, and for the re-union to it of those well-meaning but mistaken dissentients who at present cause so great a scandal?—By no means short of some terrible convulsion and thro' much suffering can this Roman Church, surely, be reformed" (*LD* 3: 259). Unable to conceive of Christian Rome as either damned or redeemable, he resurrects those powers he had divined within *Arians*, spirits from some middle realm who shape the destinies of races, sects, and nations. Although Thirlwall compared these spirits to the mock-epic machinery in *The Rape of the Lock*, they cannot be reduced either to machinery or to the confines of a neo-classical poem. Closer to the anarchic powers rampant in the *Arabian Nights*, they are able to hold the largest body in Christendom under their sway:

[I]t has been supposed that the *Christian Church* is that new form of the old evil, whereas it is really a sort of Genius Loci which enthralls the Church which happens to be there. . . . [T]he religion it upholds is still polytheistic, degrading, idolatrous—and so strictly is all this connected with Rome *as a local source*, that its authorities lose their power if they quit Rome. . . . I am a great believer in the existence of Genii Locorum. Rome has had one character for 2500 years—of late centuries the Christian Church has been the instrument by which it has acted—it is its slave. (*LD* 3: 288-89)[15]

Yet because Newman is himself in Rome and under the power of this *genius loci*, he feels himself in danger of becoming its slave as well.[16] After attending a mass celebrated by the Pope, he confesses to his mother that he can neither dismiss contemporary Catholicism nor separate its power from its superstition:

[T]here is much unedifying dumbshow . . . , nor can I endure the Pope's foot being kissed, . . . nor do I even tolerate him being carried in on high. . . . And yet as I looked on, and saw all Christian acts perform[ed,] the Holy Sacrament offered up, and the blessing given, and recollected I was in church, I could only say in very perplexity my own words, "How shall I name thee, Light of the wide west, or heinous error-seat?" and felt the force of the parable of the tares—who can separate the light from the darkness but the Creator Word who prophesied their union? (*LD* 3: 268)[17]

The next letter to his mother still attempts to distinguish ideal from actuality: "As to the Roman C. system, I have ever detested it . . . but to the *Catholic* system I am more attached than ever" (*LD* 3: 273). Yet from Froude we learn that the very next day he and Newman met with Wiseman to explore some future union between their churches (*LD* 3: 276).[18]

As if anticipating Wiseman's rebuff, Newman's letters periodically predict Rome's immanent downfall. The Naples letter goes on to hope "that England is after all to be the 'Land of Saints' in this dark hour, and her Church the salt of the earth" (*LD* 3: 224-25); but while he can gloat that the Roman hierarchy may lose their property, he must admit to Henry Wilberforce that the English clergy are no more secure: "[I]t is useful to dwell upon this [seizure], because it is so likely to be the case with ourselves at home. I think I should feel a great deal at being ejected from St Mary's, and seeing another person appointed to it" (*LD* 3: 247).[19] Tract 20, written six months after his return to England, replaces prediction with militant denunciation: Catholics "cannot repent. Popery must be destroyed; it cannot be reformed." Yet now Rome's error, which had been its fatal weakness, becomes the source of its continuing power: "Human nature cannot remain without visible guides; it chooses them itself if it is not provided for them. If the Aristocracy and the Church fall, Popery steps in" (*Tracts* 1 [20]: 3-4).

Because transcendence, union, and destruction all seem equally unpromising, Newman's unspoken alternative remains some form of appropriation. While he cannot countenance the *fact* of Rome's authority until he rediscovers Augustine's "Securus judicat orbis terrarum," he cannot deny the power of beliefs unquestioningly held and vigorously implemented. His letter to Jenkyns shows a grudging appreciation for the organization and drama in Catholic liturgy (*LD* 3: 279); that to Rickards offers a similar response to its politics: "Its policy is still crafty, relentless, inflexible, and undeviating through a succession of rulers—it still sacrifices the good of its members to the splendour and strength of the republic" (*LD* 3: 288–89).[20] In the *Apologia,* Newman was to describe the Oxford Movement in very different terms: "I had a lounging, free-and-easy way of carrying things on" (63). Yet if we follow the dizzying progression of strategies and counter-strategies through which he hoped to instantiate his Church Catholic, we may suspect that he had learned much from the singleminded dedication he witnessed among the Roman clergy.

By 1838 and the *Prophetical Office,* Newman could acknowledge that Roman Catholicism had surmounted the barrier between scriptural miracle and Patristic legend, but he still feared the power which it vested in its fallen members: "Revelation so melts into Providence that we cannot draw the line between them. Miraculous events shade off into natural coincidences, visions into dreams, types into resemblances. . . . [W]hat an opening is given by a theology of so ambitious a character to pride and self-confidence. It has been said that knowledge is power. . . . Now religion is the great chastiser of human pride; . . . [but] when thus turned into an intellectual science, even polytheism answers such a moral purpose better than it" (*PO* 136). Yet he has already claimed a similar power for the Church Catholic of his via media. The image of Adam naming the animals will come to figure human amazement before the daunting variety of creation; here, however, it figures the power of the Church to encompass the equally daunting variety of religious opinion: "What man is amid the brute creation, such is the Church among the schools of the world; and as Adam gave names to the animals about him, so has the Church from the first looked round upon the earth, noting and visiting the doctrines she found there" (*Ess.* 2: 232). By the late 1830s, Newman's problem is not whether to vest the Church with such power but which church to vest with it: Jesus' "Name is a Name of power; we must seek *where* He has lodged His power, if we would speak with power. He has not left His Name at large in the world, but He has lodged His Name in a secure dwelling-place; and we have that Name engraven on us only when we *are in* that dwelling-place" (*PS* 6 [14]: 200).

Religious Anarchy

In chapter 1 I suggested that Newman would come to substitute the Church's authority for that of his mother. The year after her death, he outlined this metaphorical transference within the *Prophetical Office:* "The Church Catholic is our mother. . . . She does not assume infallibility. . . . Sometimes, perhaps, she mistakes in lesser matters, and is set right by her child; yet this neither diminishes her prerogative of teaching, nor his privilege of receiving dutifully. . . . She makes her way by love, she does not force a way by violence. All she asks is [her children's] *confidence*" (274–75). From this time forward, however, the irrational forces we have been tracing, joined by incursions from liberal secularism, began to fray this fragile parental bond, the authority it granted to the Church, and the confidence it inspired in at least one of her children:

> We see the Kingdom of God to all appearance broken into fragments—authority in abeyance—separate portions in insurrection—brother armed against brother—truth a matter not of faith but of controversy. And looking at our own portion of the heavenly heritage, we see heresies of the most deadly character around us and within us; we see error stalking abroad in the light of day and over the length of the land unrebuked—nay, invading high places; while the maintainers of Christian truth are afraid to speak, lest it should offend those to whom it is a duty to defer. We see discipline utterly thrown down, the sacraments and ordinances of grace open to those who cannot come without profaning them and getting harm from them. Works of penance almost unthought of; the world and the Church mixed together. (*SD* [25]: 382)[21]

In another remarkable sermon passage, this pervasive, progressive dissolution points beyond entropy or even apocalypse; it prefigures a kind of Christian *Götterdämmerung* which will involve both Church and world in the common cataclysm:

> But if [the Church] be an empire, if it be a philosophy, as it had its rise, it will have its fall. This is what unbelievers prophesy. . . . [W]ere not Scripture pledged that it should continue to the end, when Christ shall come, I see nothing to startle us, though it were to fall, and other religions to succeed it. God works by human means. . . . Nay, it *may* actually be destined so to expire; it may be destined to age, to decay, and at length to die;—but we know that when it dies, at least the world will die with it. . . . The world shall

never exult over the Church. If the Church falls sick, the world shall utter a wail for its own sake; for, like Samson, the Church will bury all with it. (*SD* [8]: 100–1)

He claims that this prospect holds "nothing to startle us," but as we saw in chapter 6, his flock and his followers would not let him off so easily. In 1842, he suggests that receiving communion can both reenact and reinterpret the otherwise terrifying intimations of imminent apocalypse: "But while the times wax old, and the colours of earth fade, and the voice of song is brought low, and all kindreds of the earth can but wail and lament, the Sons of God lift up their heads, for their salvation draweth nigh. Nature fails, the sun shines not, and the moon is dim, the stars fall from Heaven, and the foundations of the round world shake; but the Altar's light burns ever brighter; . . . and all above the tumults of earth the command is heard to show forth the Lord's Death, and the promise that the Lord is coming" (*PS* 7 [11]: 158).[22] Other contemporary sermons, however, question "whether our services, our holy seasons, our rites, our Sacraments, our institutions, really have with them the Presence of Him who thus promised? If so, we are part of the Church; if not, then we are but performers in a sort of scene or pageant" (*SD* [23]: 354).

With this passage, Newman's attention shifts from the viability of *the* Church to that of *this*, the Anglican Church. While Wiseman claimed that the Anglicans had never shared this promise, Newman is not yet ready to deny his past religious experience. Projecting his disillusionment, his own fears, his own visions of imminent cataclysm, he suggests that Christ is only in the *process* of abandoning them: "[Y]ou will, perhaps, ask, 'Is there no chance of Christ ever leaving a home where once He was? and if His Presence leaves it, must not we leave it also?' Yes, verily; did He leave His home, we must follow Him; who doubts it? But let me ask, Does He commonly leave without tokens that He is leaving? and if we have tokens that He is still with us, we have sufficient tokens that He has not yet left us" (*SD* [21]: 320–21). To forestall this ominous "yet," the Anglican is sent off on a quest for tokens of Christ's continued presence, a quest uncomfortably similar to those which Newman ridiculed among the Evangelicals:

[I]f you can recollect times when you visited holy places, and certainly gained there a manifestation such as the world could not give; . . . or if strange providences, and almost supernatural coincidences have hung about the Church's ordinances; if mercies or judgments have descended through them upon yourselves, or upon those about you; or if you have experience of death-beds, and know how full of hope the children of our Church can die;—O! pause ere you doubt that we have a Divine Presence among us still, and have not to seek it. (322)

This passage virtually reenacts the dilemma Newman has so pointedly identified within Protestantism and private judgment. When forced to bolster the Anglican Church with such subjective, experiential evidence, he is forced to see it—and to react against it—as a human creation: "Let us enjoy what we still have, though the world deride us;—though our brethren tell us . . . it is all a dream, and rudely bid us seek elsewhere. . . . [W]e humbly trust that Christ is in [the Church]; and while He is in it, we will abide in it. He shall leave before we do. He shall lead, and we will but follow; we will not go before Him" (322-23). As the "evidence" here is transparently his own, so too are the objections foisted off upon "brethren" or "the world." Playing both defense and prosecution, Newman tells his flock first to stay the course, then only to "pause," then to follow Christ, whose lead Newman already knows, whose departure is already a foregone conclusion.

In part, Newman's disillusionment may grow from his suspicion that no one is following *him*. A passage above claims that the Church is in anarchy because "those who discern and mourn over all this [are] looked upon with aversion, because they will not prophesy smooth things and speak peace where there is no peace" (*SD* [25]: 382). In an earlier sermon, however, Newman had explored a role different from that of beleaguered defender of the religious establishment. Identifying Elijah as a type of the departing Christ, he implicitly identifies with this Old Testament renegade: "[W]hen . . . the Prophet had to flee for his life for fear of Jezebel, and in his heart thought that his mission had failed, he sought not the kingdom of David, he honoured not the precept of unity, he had no heart for that outward glory of holier times; he passed by Jerusalem, he passed on, along a forlorn and barren way, into that old desert in which the children of Israel did wander, till he came to Horeb the Mount of God" (*SD* [24]: 376). As he here rejects unity and "holier ties" in favor of individual visionary encounter, Newman may be telling us that he must leave the Anglican Church, not just because it is becoming increasingly Protestant, but because it is causing him to become increasingly Protestant.

Catholicism within the Development

Brent suggests that Newman did not convert until he realized that Roman Catholicism was no longer the imperious institution he had encountered at Rome, that it was now just as beleaguered as Anglicanism ("Moral" 89-93). Yet this image of militant Catholicism is only intensified in "The Church of the First Centuries" from the 1845 *Development*. In any context, this account must remain one of the most remarkable since Eusebius. Newman structures the whole section to climax in its famous page-and-a-half long concluding sentence: "If there is a form of Christianity now in the world which is accused of gross superstition, . . . it is not unlike Christianity as that same world viewed it, when first it came forth from its Divine Author" (*Dev.* 228-29). The above ellipsis conceals over twenty clauses sliding between early Christianity as seen by pagans and modern Catholicism as described by Protestants. As Lash points out, Newman himself acknowledged this strategy to be imperfect: "What I *want* to do and can't . . . is to construct a *positive* argument for Catholicism. The negative is more powerful—'Since there must be one true religion, it can *be none other* than this'" (*LD* 13: 319; in *Development* 18).[23] Even more dangerous, however, this strategy commits him to see the Church, like Gibbon, exclusively through pagan eyes; it even commits him to admit charges which Gibbon could only imply: When the disparaging dismissal of Christianity by cultured pagans "continues from age to age, it is certainly an index of a fact, and corresponds to definite qualities in the object to which it relates" (*Dev.* 207). Where Gibbon was only titillated by his accounts of sex and violence,[24] Newman's darker world-view can comfortably accommodate both within the early Church: "[I]nscriptions found at Cyrene . . . contain the Carpocratian tenet of a community of women. I am unwilling to allude to the Agapae and Communions of certain of these sects, which were not surpassed in profligacy by the Pagan rites of which they were an imitation" (*Dev.* 206).

Elsewhere Newman is more than willing to expand upon pagan hostility; like them he even includes Christianity among the "magic, superstition, barbarism, jugglery," which "in various ways attracted the attention of the luxurious, the political, the ignorant, the restless, and the remorseful" (*Dev.* 202-3). He appeals specifically to Plutarch: "Tacitus, Suetonius, and Pliny, call [Christianity] a 'superstition.' . . . But Plutarch explains for us the word at length: '. . . he who fears the gods fears everything, earth, seas, air, sky, darkness, light, noises, silence, sleep. . . . [H]e sits at home, with sacrifice and slaughter all round him, while the old crones hang on him as on a peg, as Bion says, any charm they fall in with'" (208-10). After seeming to countenance Plutarch's mockery, Newman suddenly equates such superstition with early Christianity: "[I]t was the imagination of the existence of an unseen ever-present Master; . . . horror at guilt, apprehension of punishment, dread, self-abasement, depression, anxiety and endeavour to be at peace with heaven, and error and absurdity in the methods chosen for the purpose" (*Dev.* 211). Here he virtually recapitulates the sermon passage, cited in chapter 4, which advises us "to wait in miserable suspense, naked and shivering, among the trees of the garden, for the hour of [God's] coming, and meanwhile to fancy sounds of woe in every wind stirring the leaves about us" (*US* [6]: 118).

Turning Plutarch's parody into an indictment of his smug classical humanism, Newman implies that if these pagan caricatures of early Christianity match the smug Protestant caricatures of contemporary Catholicism, then the realities of both institutions will match as well. Yet nowhere does he take pains to distinguish caricature from reality; he even seems comfortable with the possibility that pagan critics saw the early Church more accurately than New Testament apologists: "'Read this,' says Paley, after quoting some of the most beautiful and subduing passages of St. Paul, 'read this, and then think of *exitiabilis superstitio,*' and he goes on to express a wish 'in contending with heathen authorities, to produce our books against theirs,' as if it were a matter of books. Public men care very little for books; . . . they look at facts. . . . [W]hat Christians said, what they thought, was little to the purpose. They might exhort to peaceableness . . . ; but what did they *do?*" (*Dev.* 214–15). By contrasting books to "facts," Newman follows Gibbon's implication that whatever the early Christians said, they had from the beginning engaged in arcane practices like those the pagan authors criticized:[25]

Such was Christianity in the eyes of those who witnessed its rise and propagation;—one of a number of wild and barbarous rites which were pouring in upon the Empire from the ancient realms of superstition . . . ; a horrible religion, as inflicting or enjoining cruel sufferings, and monstrous and loathsome in its very indulgence of the passions; a religion leading by reaction to infidelity; a religion of magic . . . ; a secret religion which dared not face the day; an itinerant, busy, proselytizing religion, forming an extended confederacy against the state, resisting its authority and breaking its laws. (*Dev.* 222–23)[26]

Gibbon himself might have received a *frisson* from this passage—but only because of his emotional distance from Christianity. Part of Newman, I think, stands with Gibbon; he knows that the Protestants in his audience, committed to recreating the Apostolic Church, are writhing under the cumulative insinuations of his parallel clauses. Part of him, however, may stand with them, afraid that the caricature may *be* the reality, even more afraid that the psychological excesses discovered in the sect by pagans may match the theological excesses he has discovered in his

God. Ultimately, I think, Newman accepts the excesses inherent within both God and Church because they *do* in fact correspond. It is not just that the Patristic Church mirrors the modern Catholic Church, but that both of them faithfully mirror their God.

Catholicism as Self-Defining

It is no longer even shocking to suggest that the Catholic Church to which Newman converted existed largely within his own mind: "There certainly grew up within the Oxford Movement a new sense of the Catholic Church as the great divine society," Brilioth admits, "but it was often fashioned according to the ideas of individuals" (*Evangelicalism* 40).[27] In his last year as an Anglican, Newman himself admitted to Faber his distaste for Italianate devotion: "I have a great repugnance at mixing religions or worships together, it is like sowing the field with mingled seed. . . . I do not like decanting Rome into England; the bottles may break. Indeed I look with much anxiety . . . to the inculcation of extraordinary degrees of asceticism; extreme strictness about indifferent matters, heights of devotion and meditation, self-forgetfulness and self-abandonment" (*KC* 356-57). The passages cited above from the *Development,* however, suggest that during his conversion, Newman's fantasy Church was less a product of wish-fulfillment than a stay against fear.

The conversion experience itself, enshrined in the *Apologia,* is also hinted at in the sermon on divine calls, referred to obliquely in letters, expanded in the twelfth lecture on *Difficulties of Anglicans,* and qualified in a note appended to "The Catholicity of the Anglican Church" (*Ess.* 2: 74-111). The actual event divides neatly in two: first, Newman's study of fifth-century heresies and his subsequent discovery that he "was a Monophysite"; second, Williams's repetition of Augustine's "Securus judicat orbis terrarum" (from Wiseman's article on the Donatists) and Newman's subsequent replacement of antiquity with Catholic authority.[28] In both of these episodes, the Church of Rome shares characteristics with the early Church of the *Development,* characteristics which he later softened within the *Apologia.*

In the first episode, "The Church then, as now, might be called peremptory and stern, resolute, overbearing, and relentless" (*Apo.* 109). In a note to his note on the Catholicity essay, Newman defends the above phrases, but not because he finds them true now—"when I have been a Catholic for so long." Instead, "this is what I felt, as I then expressly said, *before* 'experience' of her 'rule,' and an impression which did not deter me from becoming a Catholic, or rather helped me to become one"

(*Ess.* 2: 75).[29] Within the second episode, the issue at stake is no longer heresy but schism. Newman is won not by Catholicism's truth, or fidelity, or consistency, but by the bald fact of its authority.[30] As Svaglic points out Newman's 1864 paraphrase ("that the deliberate judgment, in which the whole Church at length rests and acquiesces, is an infallible prescription" etc.) backs away from Augustine's words and Wiseman's translation ("Structure" 543n–44n). So too does the conclusion of his note to the Catholicity essay: "[N]o Catholic would contend that this aphorism precludes or supersedes appeal to Antiquity" (108).[31]

In 1839, however, Newman saw more deeply—or at least differently— into the Patristic Church than he would thirty years later. He saw "miracles, monkery, Popery" rampant; he saw a divine presence which "show[ed] itself as it would, and when it would, and without fixed rules," a presence "manifold, variable, uncertain, inscrutable, uncontrollable, like the natural atmosphere; dispensing gleams, shadows, traces of Almighty Power."[32] When he insists within the *Difficulties* essay that "to imbibe into the intellect of the Ancient Church as a fact, is either to be a Catholic or an infidel" (393), he implies that such incursions of the Romantic sublime leave him only these two alternatives. He could retreat into the scoffing rationalism of Hume and Gibbon, or he could accept the mediation of an institution "resolute" enough to shelter him but "peremptory," "relentless," "awful" enough to embody a portion of the ineffable power it mediated.[33]

Confronted later with the less-than-sublime imperiousness of the Roman hierarchy, he would come to hedge this interpretation of Augustine's "Securus," but in 1839, I think, he read it as Wiseman had written it. Lash laments that even in the 1845 *Development,* Newman rather uncritically "shared . . . a [monolithic] concept of church unity" (*Development* 16).[34] As Inge explains the issue, however, "If we . . . ask on what grounds he chooses to prefer the authority of the Catholic Church to other authorities, . . . we are driven again to lay great stress on the almost political necessity which he felt that such a Divine society should exist" (190–91). Specifically, Newman needed to find vested within the Roman Church a power of almost unlimited self-determination, a power to incorporate otherwise incompatible terms because it controlled the syntax and vocabulary of religious speech. In the *Development,* he illustrates the Church's analogous powers of theological appropriation:

> She alone has succeeded in thus rejecting evil without sacrificing the good, and in holding together in one, things which in all other schools are incompatible. Gnostic or Platonic words are found in the inspired theology of St. John; . . . the prophets of the Montanists

prefigure the Church's Doctors, and their professed inspiration her infallibility, and their revelations her developments, and the heresiarch himself is the unsightly anticipation of St. Francis. . . . The theology of the Church is no random combination of various opinions, but a diligent, patient working out of one doctrine from many materials. (341–42)[35]

The Imagery of Conversion—the Hand

Catholicism's control over religious language manifests itself as power over the numerous figures through which Newman tropes his conversion. Though justly famous, the hand, the call, the ghost, and the mirror do not really cohere within themselves or with one another, as would the images within a Wordsworthian or Joycean epiphany.[36] Instead, they both extend and subvert one further aspect of Romantic irony. In chapter 10 I suggested that as a writer, the Anglican Newman was not ready to "embrace" the universe of directionless process which he was discovering. He was not ready to "permit [his] creative self to hover above its image and representational system and thereby glor[y] in its own self-activity" (13), to borrow Ryals's paraphrase of Friedrich Schlegel's project.[37] In his conversion narrative, however, Newman could authorize a similar figural play while denying that he, as author, was doing the playing. It is rather the context itself, vested with both divine and ecclesiastical power, which engages a host of earlier contexts within Newman. In these earlier contexts hands, calls, ghosts, or mirrors appeared in different and often conflicting senses.[38] As they reappear within his conversion, however, each of these figures is challenged and then recontextualized by this new narrative and the new forces which govern it.

The image of the hand, for example, appears in two separate passages within the narrative. The second, as Newman is reflecting upon the whole experience, echoes most of his earlier contexts in referring to the hand of God, but here the hand is not raised in any gesture of guidance, blessing, or protection: "[S]o far as this was certain,—I had seen the shadow of a hand upon the wall. It was clear that I had a good deal to learn on the question of the Churches" (*Apo.* 111). Here the Hand of God, writing its own secret language upon the wall, retains unfettered powers of judgment; yet whether Newman can learn to read it and what it will avail him to do so remain in doubt; Belshazzar, we remember, pays Daniel to read what turns out to be his death sentence and is slain the same night.

The first passage, following Newman's discovery that he was a Monophysite, describes his own hand. Until now human hands, when implementing God's will, have been granted great power: "[T]he Sacraments are put into the Church's hands to *dispense*—and are dispensed at different times differently according to her discretion" (*LD* 5: 258); "[T]he Church discriminated by imposition of hands, not a tyrant's jurisdiction, I love indeed" (*LD* 5: 301). Even more dramatic, as we have seen, is the power of intercession: "Hands raised in blessing . . . have now become the 'unutterable intercessions' of the Spirit" (*Jfc.* 196). Because of "the influence of the prayer of faith upon the Divine counsels[, the] Intercessor directs or stays the hand of the Unchangeable and Sovereign Governor of the World" (*PS* 2 [18]: 211–12). But Newman has also accorded human hands considerable autonomy: "[W]e are under the eye of One who, for whatever reason, exercises us with the less evidence when He might give us the greater. He has put it into our hands, who loves us" (*US* [11]: 215). Hence, as we saw, the genius of faith "makes progress not unlike a clamberer on a steep cliff, who, by quick eye, prompt hand, and firm foot, ascends how he knows not himself" (*US* [13]: 257).[39]

In his conversion, however, Newman's hand is in danger of being rendered powerless by an angry God: "Be my soul with the Saints! and shall I lift up my hand against them? Sooner may my right hand forget her cunning, and wither outright, as his who once stretched it out against a prophet of God! anathema to a whole tribe of Cranmers, Ridleys, Latimers, and Jewels!" (*Apo.* 109). In both Old Testament references, the maiming or threat of maiming follows an attempt to forestall divine vengeance: Jereboam (1 Kings 13) attempts to thwart a prophecy that his altar will be destroyed; after first offering to forfeit his hand if he forgets Jerusalem, the Psalmist goes on to envision the destruction of all infants in Babylon (137). Among those "Protestant Martyrs" to whose memorial Newman had refused to subscribe, Cranmer had offered to the flames the hand with which he had signed his original recantation. Newman here preserves the strength and cunning of his own hand by reaffirming Queen Mary's original anathema and by symbolically reenacting her sentence.[40]

The Call

The call Newman receives to this new militancy has been as important for his religious experience as for that of an inner-light Evangelical. Before 1839, he tended to see these calls as affirmations of his current course. To Robert Wilberforce he argues that praying for the dead "is so very natural, so soothing, that if there is no command against it, we have (it would seem) a call to do it" (*LD* 5: 260). After 1839, however, the calls become more ambiguous: "I sometimes have uncomfortable feelings as if

I should not like to die in the English Church. It seems to me that, while Providence gives one time, it is even a call upon one to make use of it *in* deliberateness and waiting—but that, did He cut short one's hours of grace, this would be a call to make up one's mind on what seemed most probable" (*KC* 301).

Within this conversion experience, Newman's call participates in a more complex sequence characteristic of his major crises, a sequence of disobedience, reprimand, turn, and reacceptance. During his Sicilian fever, for example, his admission of willfulness won him "a revelation . . . of God's love to His elect," then a call to go out to meet him, and then a Divine response: "[I]t certainly seems like some instinct which He put within me and made me follow" (*LD* 4: 8).[41] Apart from its pattern of call and response, his conversion narrative appears quite different: "For a mere sentence, the words of St. Augustine, struck me with a power which I never had felt from any words before. To take a familiar instance, they were like the 'Turn again Whittington' of the chime; or, to take a more serious one, they were like the 'Tolle, lege,—Tolle, lege,' of the child, which converted St. Augustine himself" (*Apo.* 110).

The contemporary sermon on divine calls, however, suggests several parallels between this encounter and the one in Sicily. First, as we saw in chapter 6, the call is reserved for God's elect. Second, it employs intermediaries and coincidences: "[W]e get acquainted with some one whom God employs to bring before us a number of truths which were closed on us before; and we but half understand them, and but half approve of them; and yet God seems to speak in them, and Scripture to confirm them" (*PS* 8 [2]: 29). Besides referring to Robert Williams's repetition of Wiseman's "Securus judicat," this sermon passage also hints at a third parallel, the initial incomprehensibility of the message: "[A] sudden trial . . . will be the means of advancing [the one called] to a higher state of religious excellence, which at present he as little comprehends as the unspeakable words heard by St. Paul in paradise" (25).[42] In the conversion account, Newman's Sicilian hallucinations are replaced with an encoded language like that written on the wall. Despite these similarities, however, when the "Turn again Whittington" and the "Tolle, Lege," are taken together, they frame this call in a new, more compelling, more troubling context. The fairy-tale Whittington is called back to fame and glory in a gesture of amoral, wish-fulfilling, natural magic. Augustine is called back to a life of repentance, self-denial, and reaffirmation of his mother's religious values. Newman is called in both incompatible directions at once.

To be called with Augustine's words to Augustine's calling, however, reconciles Newman to him. Chadwick remarks: "It is curious and striking how Newman never had any feeling of friendship with the greatest of the

Fathers, St Augustine" ("Bremond" 193). Culminating the Patristic age, Augustine may have seemed too belated, too self-conscious a theologian for the Anglican Newman to feel comfortable with.[43] Even though Newman claims that Augustine's writings were providentially saved from the Vandals' sack of Hippo (*HS* 2: 140–41), he found them already too schematic to reveal the "atmosphere" of primitive doctrine: "Augustine's theology," he argues, "transmi[ts] the primitive stream through an acute, rich, and powerful mind" (*Ess.* 1: 287). Because Newman wanted this stream to reach his own powerful mind untreated, unadulterated, unpurified, he preferred the Alexandrians, who codified the creed but not its philosophical ramifications. As we saw in chapter 8, however, Newman shows many affinities with the proto-Byronic Romanticism of the pre-Christian Augustine. And as we saw at the beginning of this chapter, Augustine's false god prefigured the incursions of the Romantic sublime during Newman's last years as Anglican. Now, by re-enacting Augustine's renunciation of Manicheism, he can simultaneously renounce its Romantic legacy and identify himself with the mature saint. In the now-fused context of their conversions, both he and Augustine escape from belatedness and self-consciousness by testifying to the divine favor and divine guidance bestowed upon them.

The Ghost

Because both these testimonies are mediated, Augustine's by the child's voice and Newman's by this host of figures, their release from spectral incursions must be effected by another spectral incursion. The ghosts in Newman's conversion narrative both climax and complicate the sequence we traced in chapter 10. There the congenial *genius loci* of Cambridge yielded to the Lazaretto ghost, then to the spectral landscape at Alton, then to the grotesques of the "new" Oxford, and finally to the "nephews of mauvais honte" haunting his *Arians* manuscript. Here in 1839, two separate specters appear: The first—personifying the parallels between the fifth, sixteenth, and nineteenth centuries—"was like a spirit rising from the troubled waters of the old world, with the shape and lineaments of the new" (*Apo.* 109). This ghost attacks Newman's most cherished beliefs and undermines his most reliable strategies: he has established Patristic Christianity as an ideal against which the present can be measured and found wanting. Now this idealized past clothes itself with the present and takes its shape. It thus forces upon him the conclusion we suggested in chapter 3; it insinuates that in searching for the Patristic Church, Newman has never actually left home.[44]

The second apparition, arising as Newman reflects on both experiences, may reflect back on the first spirit: "He who has seen a ghost, cannot be as if he had never seen it" (*Apo.* 111). If a reflection, however, it now literalizes the "spirit rising," itself only the vehicle of a simile, the tenor of which was yet another figure, the "shadow" of a century. This tension between instantiation and infinite regression is further intensified within the larger company of Newman's other familiar spirits. Except in dream, Newman has never *seen* a ghost; his closest encounter has been with the bumps in the night at the Lazaretto. The terror inspired by the earlier ghosts remained in inverse proportion to their objective credibility, but this apparition—in the service of a Church which controls its own spiritual language—claims a similar control over its ontological status. It insists that its self-figuration must count for and be accounted as experiential fact; Newman must believe that he has, and act as if he has, seen a "real" ghost.

The Mirror

In this conversion narrative, therefore, the epistemological criteria for the process of seeing and the objects of sight are brokered by an authority beyond the self. By 1839, as we saw, Newman had grown increasingly troubled by historical flux, by a Patristic world which offered increasingly cloudy, increasingly distorted reflections of the Apostolic past which it was supposed to witness. Yet within this spiritual fun house, he suddenly encounters the "mirror," which can subvert change, which can support a Patristic instead of a biblical typology, which can superimpose one historical period upon another, which can reflect the fifth century (in this strange, new, "Catholic" light) as the norm and model for subsequent history: "Here, in the middle of the fifth century, I found, as it seemed to me, Christianity of the sixteenth and nineteenth centuries reflected. I saw my face in that mirror, and I was a Monophysite" (*Apo.* 108).

This mirror has often been linked with the later mirror reference which prefaces Newman's defense of his Catholic beliefs: "If I looked into a mirror, and did not see my face, I should have the sort of feeling which actually comes upon me, when I look into this living busy world, and see no reflexion of its Creator" (216). And in this postmodern climate, critics cannot resist playing on the conflation of reality and reflection in these "mirror images." Michael Ryan pounces upon the implications of Newman's analogy: "[W]e [might just as well] be surprised that Newman is alive, since, from the lack of any image in the mirror, we would expect him to be dead. . . . [T]he metaphor thus implies a relationship of complicity between opposites" (152). Fleishman admits that in this second passage, "There is some reciprocity of the two beings . . . , but the main emphasis falls on belief in oneself" (170). Heather Henderson is even more severe: "Despite the attempt to make 'face to face' serve as a metaphor for his unmediated relation to God, Newman is caught in a self-reflective circle. With what Thomas Vargish calls 'breathtaking egocentricity' Newman reaffirms the primacy of the self, while God drops out of the picture" (61).[45]

As we have seen, however, the relation of self and God reflected in Newman's writings has remained equally problematic throughout the Tractarian period. Just after his return to England, he did quote a relatively unambiguous use of the mirror metaphor in St. Gregory Nazianzen: "[N]othing seemed to me so great, as by closing up the senses, . . . and conversing with one's self and God, to live above things visible, and to bear within one the divine vision always clear, pure from the shifting impressions of earth,—a true mirror unsullied of God and the things of God" (HS 2: 82). But in many other passages, Gregory's "true mirror unsullied of God" has come to include Newman's own image. Recall, for example, "With astonishment and fear, [Disciples] would become aware that [in the Teacher of Truth] Christ's presence was before them"; or "What mortal heart could bear to know that it is brought so near to God Incarnate?"; or "The Almighty Father, looking on us, sees not us, but this Sacred Presence, even His dearly beloved Son." As O'Leary says of the Justification, "each sentence he composed is a mirror reflecting the perfection of his ideal self. . . . [T]he 'continual motion of mind' which animates Newman's style is a rhythm of first striving to fulfil a self-ideal and then cherishing his ideal self in delighted self-recollection" (181).

The mirror within the conversion narrative, however, counters both the solipsism in the later mirror image and the apotheoses in these earlier texts; it redresses the balance of forces within Augustine's "trial of the center"; it demands orthodox self-transcendence instead of Romantic self-replication. As Loesberg puts it: "If in the mirror of the Godless world Newman could not see himself, in the historical mirror [of the Monophysite passage] he saw a self he did not want to see" (159). He sees in "the fifth century . . . Christianity of the sixteenth and nineteenth centuries reflected. I saw my face in that mirror and I was a Monophysite." Within this narrative, the mirror of history reflects his Anglicanism as sixteenth-century Protestantism and hence as fifth-century heresy. In order to see the past superimposed upon the present and reaffirmed within it, Newman must see himself as the transhistorical reality of Catholicism chooses to reflect him.

Heresy as Imagination

Of course *heretic,* as Loesberg notes, is "a label no heretic . . . applies to himself" (159). He takes the term as earnest that Newman is already in the process of abandoning the via media; yet as Newman reinscribes this self-recognition, first in the *Difficulties* essay and then in the *Apologia,* he cannot escape seeing himself as a heretic. He cannot escape the specific heresies of the nineteenth century because his spiritual vision presupposes these very heresies.[46] They remain for him what the "Intimations" remain for Wordsworth—

> Which, be they what they may,
> Are yet the fountain light of all our day,
> Are yet the master light of all our seeing.
> (152–54)

Each of the four figures in these narratives has been created and sustained by imaginative power, a power which may have its origins in Old Testament prophecy and Christian conversion stories, but which constantly acknowledges its own post-Enlightenment subjectivity. When Newman reads the handwriting on the wall, he is at once its prophetic interpreter, its potential victim, and its author. Whether his hand refrains from blocking an Old Testament anathema or reaches out to confirm a sixteenth-century one, he remains the (gentle)man described in the *Apologia:* "[N]ot even when I was fiercest, could I have even cut off a Puritan's ears, and I think the sight of a Spanish *auto-da-fe* would have been the death of me" (53). The war in which he smites or forbears is now fought less over beliefs than over ideologies; and with the mere recognition of this change, the war is transformed into the night battle of his university sermon and Newman is transformed into a combatant for both sides at once.

In much the same way, the call Newman heeds would be inaudible to anyone with pre-Enlightenment hearing. True, it mimics that of Augustine, but in so doing it sets up the spiritual father of Romanticism as its indispensable mediator. Just as no one could write like Newman about angels before Wordsworth, so no one could self-consciously reappropriate the *Confessions* before assimilating the later *Confessions* of Rousseau.[47] The Romantic recapitulation implicit in Newman's call appears as early as the sermon quoted in chapter 5: "He calls you by your roused affections once and again, ere He leave you finally. He brings you back for a time (as it were) to a second youth by the urgent persuasions of excited fear, gratitude, love, and hope. He again places you for an instant in that early, unformed state of nature when habit and character were not" (*PS* 1 [9]: 121–22).

The passage on divine calls which concludes the conversion narrative holds up vision as the goal of both call and conversion: "What gain is it to be applauded, admired, courted, followed,—compared with this one aim, of 'not being disobedient to a heavenly vision'? What can this world offer comparable with that insight into spiritual faith?" (*Apo.* 111). The two ghostly mediators of this vision claim to supersede all Newman's earlier, more obviously Gothic visitations, challenging their authority and undermining their implications. Yet these two also remain nineteenth-century apparitions, invisible to an earlier imagination because inconceivable to an earlier mind. The first spirit embodies, personifies, clothes itself in the very historical relativity which its rising claims to transcend. The second demands, as a condition for its acceptance, an equally sophisticated distinction among levels of theoretical, symbolic, and experiential truth.

Finally, in the context of his Anglican writings, Newman's mirror reflects him less as a fifth-century heretic than as the reluctant representative of "Christianity of the . . . nineteenth centur[y]"; it reflects him as a child of his post-Enlightenment age, by turns Latitudinarian or Liberal or Romantic, but always self-consciously aware of the dangers and the inevitability of spiritual self-creation; to quote Valerie Pitt: "He was *not* a proxy Monophysite but a nineteenth-century scholar" (23). If Newman's mirror reflects this dilemma as simple heresy or his self-creating spirituality as simple blasphemy, it can do so only by denying the truth of its own reflection. In claiming that "I saw my face in that mirror, and I was a Monophysite," Newman has had to affirm and deny his own Romantic heritage in the same breath; he has had to use his imaginative power to win the insight that such power is not only superfluous but false. The whole metaphorical construct thus shows a marked propensity to self-destruct; it offers what it claims to be a real picture of its own impossibility.

Newman wants to figure the moment of his conversion to Catholicism as a decisive turn, but the figures themselves reinscribe this moment as an anomalous standoff. In this standoff, spiritual and institutional forces claim precedence over any subjective autonomy while the subject claims autonomy as a precondition for recognizing any such forces. This anomaly, in turn, offers a better paradigm for Newman's 1839 conversion— and for his Anglican career—than any of the many explanations he offered in the *Apologia,* in his other Catholic works, or in his letters. The *Apologia* may not portray Newman as the "troubled soul in its passage from darkness to darkness," as Oscar Wilde saw him (109), but his Anglican writings trace his equally troubled passage from one Romantic irony to another.

NOTES

INTRODUCTION

1. I am using the adjective "Anglican" here as a shorthand reference to the forty-four years of Newman's life before his conversion to Roman Catholicism in 1845. The term is suspect in that it disguises the important changes in his thought as he passed through his Evangelical, Noetic, and Tractarian periods. It remains accurate, however, to the extent that all of these positions could be maintained, with varying degrees of comfort, within the Church of England during the first half of the nineteenth century.

2. Besides those who are literally writing hagiography in the cause of Newman's canonization, we find a conscientious historian like Meriol Trevor trying to rationalize all of Newman's political and religious feuds, and scores of subtle theologians trying to pin down and categorize his slippery and often inconsistent doctrinal statements. For a curt rejection of this approach, see Levine (166n).

3. For a similar summary of these conflicting interpretations, see Stephen Thomas (255).

4. Brilioth somewhat more tactfully suggests that Abbott's study "has too partisan a stamp owing to the self-satisfied peevishness of the author" (*Anglican* 109n). David Newsome's *The Convert Cardinals* (13-14) describes Abbott's mathematical background and his earlier challenge to Newman's credulity in *Philomythus*. In our penultimate chapter we will consider further this mind-numbing assault on the *Ecclesiastical Miracles* and Newman's later theories of probability. Here we can point out that Abbott himself admits his obsession with Newman. Beginning with a casual comparison between him and Huxley, Abbott finds that "the section grew beyond the limits of a section. . . . Still I read on, and the more I read, the more my article expanded. . . . Newman was a magnet, and I was magnetized. I must go on reading and thinking, and giving up every other occupation till I had come to some solution" (*Philomythus* lxvi–lxvii).

5. Though Newman claimed he could not get past the second chapter because of its inaccuracies, Chadwick speculates that his real annoyance was Mozley's revelation (in chapter 2) that Newman's father had failed even as a brewer (141).

6. Prickett gives even more emphasis to Newman's Catholic thought, particularly the development of doctrine and the psychology of belief (*Romanticism* 173-208).

7. David Nicholls and Fergus Kerr cite the same problematic as evidence for a very different evaluation, arguing that "The Canonization of Newman . . . would be seen as something of a blow . . . to the cause of Christian unity." Presumably within this context, they claim that Newman's metaphors "raise questions about Newman's orthodoxy as well as about his common sense and sanity. Great as

Newman is, do not his writings often invite readings which run against the grain of his rhetoric? The essays in this book [the anthology they have edited] seek to explore, in various ways, some of the crucial ambiguities in Newman's work" (8).

8. In this context, see Stephen Finley's response to Ryan's reading of the *Apologia:* "What Ryan finds in Newman's empty mirror, i.e., death, occurs too often in deconstructive readings for its discovery here to reveal a particularly Newmanian crisis" ("Natural" 172n).

9. While we will explore Newman's complex sexuality more thoroughly in chapters 1 and 6, we must acknowledge here the methodological implications of his aggressively male conception of God, of intellectual culture, and of spiritual holiness. I have worked to keep my own prose inclusive, but to modify or subvert Newman's insistently gender-specific pronouns would do real violence to the specifically anthropomorphic, specifically male images at the center of even his most inclusive ideals.

10. "His rhetoric has a limited appeal—to the waverers in the Anglican fold in a time of re-alignment after the Reform Act. The deployment of 'heresy' precludes the universality to which his rhetoric aspires" (Thomas 167). While it is hard to convict Thomas of any pre-existent bias, his researches seem to have left him appalled at Newman's own bias and, worse, at his slipshod treatment of issues which concerned him so deeply. See, for example, page 57, where Thomas describes Newman's "almost hysterical dramatization of the controversy over Church and State"; page 67, where he wonders whether Newman "was *applying* to the contemporary polemical scene principles discovered during scholarly research, or, conversely, if the immediate background first affected his method of research"; page 88, where he points out that "Newman writes as if there is an obvious connection between the edition of Dionysius . . . and Apollinarianism. In fact there is no historical connection between them"; page 106, where, on Newman's assertion that "all heresies run into one," Thomas counters, "It is hard to avoid the suspicion . . . that the whole argument is circular"; finally page 131, where he concludes, "It therefore seems not inappropriate to apply a 'tu quoque' to Newman, touching his final remarks on Abbott." Thomas's best explanation for Newman's "hysteria" (59–60) is that he, like Keble and Pusey, equated the imminent collapse of the *ancien regime* with an apocalyptic assault upon Christianity; yet, unlike his friends, Newman abandoned Anglicanism both as a faith and as an institution. Thomas's excellent study has thus persuaded me of two points: (1) we need to look more deeply into the psychological roots of Newman's intellectual and scholarly lapses, and (2) to see Newman at his best, we need to search out those areas in which he is least threatened and most comfortable.

11. As we shall discover, Newman himself acknowledged in the *Grammar* (76) that the voice resembled that of a parent.

12. I certainly cannot claim that my own efforts to win a professional-sounding "objectivity" in my treatment of Newman have been easy or consistently successful. My personal discomfort arises, I think, less from the reason DeLaura offers than from one which Stephen Finley once suggested in conversation: "Newman is so smart he sees through everything." No matter what ground I choose in order to gain some perspective on Newman, I keep discovering that he, like some intel-

lectual or spiritual Kilroy, has already been there and has rejected the position as untenable.

13. I see this subjectivity as more layered, more problematic, and less self-transparent than Newman would admit. In Kantian terms, Newman's *cogito* cannot predicate an *ens cogitans* within his spiritual universe; in more Heideggerian terms, the questioning self which prompts the *cogito* cannot find itself in the answer. In tracing Newman's early career with a vocabulary unavailable to him, I am only following what Robert Langbaum describes (*Poetry* 75–108) as Browning's response to a relativistic age, i.e., allowing his subjects to define themselves and their world, but focusing on those parts of their text which define them in ways counter to their own intentions. In keeping with the fundamentally Romantic paradigms of this study, I am not pushing my critique to the skepticism of Lacan's parody of the *cogito:* "It thinks; therefore I seem."

14. As Newman himself will insist, a skepticism like that of Feuerbach is no mere absence of belief but a positive metaphysics. Hence Feuerbach's etiology of religion, like those offered by Marx, or Nietzsche, or Freud, remains an imposition on the unknown, no more self-evident than the orthodox etiology that Newman preached or the Romantic one that he practiced.

15. In confronting the liberal historian Milman, he is actually confronting "those momentous principles, which he has adopted indeed, but which are outside of him, and will not be his slaves" (*Ess.* 2: 229).

16. Newman learns from "Blanco [White]'s analysis of his own conversion to Unitarianism [that] a form of words conceals a shift which has *already* taken place without the subject's conscious knowledge" (Thomas 85). And later, "this external contemplation of Christianity necessarily leads a man to write as a Socinian or Unitarian *would* write, whether he will or not" (*Ess.* 2: 202).

17. "In his treatment of heresy[, Newman] psychologized rhetoric into a form of investigation, and it led him where he did not expect to go" (Thomas 255). "When he came to portray his *own* period of doubt and self-questioning from 1839 to 1843, he presented the analogical and critical structure of his own rhetoric as *turning back upon himself,* as he found his own position the subject of an inner inquest, in the same style of interrogation to which he had subjected his opponents" (203).

18. As a procedure, this is no different than what various editors have been doing for well over a century, making collections of Newman quotations on one topic or another. The occasional nature of his Anglican writing in particular has made this almost the only way to salvage his ideas from the oblivion of long-dead controversies. The difference between their practice and mine lies only in the kinds of passages collected.

19. Despite their different and often hostile conclusions, Pattison and Thomas shed valuable light on the intellectual, historical, and social contexts of his writings.

20. Sayre and Lowy go on to support this claim: "If our hypothesis—that the romantic worldview represents in essence a reaction against the conditions of life in capitalist society—is justified, it would follow that the romantic stance should continue to retain its vitality as long as capitalism exists" (32).

21. Lacoue-Labarthe and Nancy support this claim with a representative list of romantic anticipations of "modern" critical practice: "[I]t is not difficult to arrive at the derivatives of these romantic texts, which still delimit our horizon. From the idea of a possible formalization of literature (or of cultural production in general) to the use of linguistic models . . . ; from this problematic of the (speaking or writing) subject to a general theory of the historical or social subject; from a belief that the work's conditions of production or fabrication are inscribed within it to the thesis of a dissolution of all processes of production in the abyss of the subject. . . . And the massive truth flung back at us is that we have not left the era of the Subject" (16).

CHAPTER 1

1. These would be Maisie Ward's *Young Mr. Newman,* Sean O'Faolain's *Newman's Way,* and Martin Svaglic's "Charles Newman and His Brothers."

2. In a letter of 1840 to Rogers, Newman notes the book with guarded approval: "My sister H. has been writing a juvenile novel, which has come before Mr. Gresley, who is so taken with it that they talk of beginning a new series of tales, &c., with it for the first. It has its faults, of course, as a first publication, but it is certainly very good" (Moz. 2: 287).

3. The moral significance of this dedicated effort comes clear in a passage from his *Arians:* "Moral feelings do not directly contemplate and realize to themselves the objects which excite them. . . . [A] child feels not the less affectionate reverence towards his parents, because he cannot discriminate in words, nay, or in idea, between them and others. As, however, his reason opens, he might ask himself concerning the ground of his own emotions and conduct towards them; and might find that these are the correlatives of their peculiar tenderness towards him, long and intimate knowledge of him, and unhesitating assumption of authority over him" (143-44).

4. Martin Svaglic, for example, after quoting Harriett on John's "great respect . . . for his parents," comments, "Can we be surprised at the veneration he would soon accord, even as an Evangelical, to the Fathers of the Church?" ("Charles" 372n).

5. See also the guilt-ridden journal entry of 21 February 1826: "Why could I not have said how much I owed to him, his kindness in sending me to Oxford &c &c" (*AW* 208).

6. Donald Capps makes much more of both parents' efforts to maintain their influence over him, even after his ordination ("Vocational" 38-39). I see Newman's efforts to pacify them as *pro forma* gestures at filial obedience. Capps also makes an interesting case for the influence of Newman's paternal grandmother as a supporter of his religious commitment, an embodiment of traditional, more settled values, and a source for his later identification of the Catholic Church as a spiritual mother (43-48).

7. According to Ragland-Sullivan's Lacan, "In the neurotic's myth—which avoids the Real in favor of living out fantasies or promoting symptoms—the Real

father was often split. . . . [T]he child was bequeathed the function of living out the (m)Other's Desire, the father's Symbolic function having been somehow weakened (through death, defection, alcoholism, or other cause). Lacan argues that in this type of Desire-and-Law interaction, although the nodal point of neurosis is the mother as Desiring (i.e., unsatisfied), a very special form of narcissistic splitting [occurs] in the psychic conception of the father so that he is idealized and denigrated at the same time, sought and fled simultaneously, and so on" (264). In several ways, Newman actually anticipates Lacan: both have a strong sense of structure, linguistic and institutional, and both think desire is a cheat.

8. Even the relatively cerebral Thomas Scott begins his *Force of Truth*, "[T]ill the sixteenth year of my age, I do not remember that I ever was under any serious conviction of being a sinner, in danger of wrath or in need of mercy. . . . 'Being alienated from God through the ignorance what was in me,' I lived without him in the world; and utterly neglected to pay him any voluntary service, as if I had been an *Atheist* in principle." David Newsome focuses instead on endings: "If Newman had never acknowledged his debt to Scott, a reading of *The Force of Truth* would still have revealed the close parallel between the religious experiences of these two men. . . . [Newman] held in his mind . . . Scott's moving peroration when he came to write the memorable closing words of his last Anglican publication. 'And now, dear Reader, time is short, eternity is long'" ("Evangelical" 19).

9. See also Gilley (20–21) and Sheridan (174). Newsome puts a darker coloring on the same continuity: "His Calvinist conversion did not turn him into an individualist. What it did was to direct the talents of an inflexible and proud young man . . . into the service of the Church" ("Evangelical" 22). As he later restates it, Newman's "Evangelical conversion, in clarifying his vision of 'two and two only supremely and luminously self-evident beings . . . ,' was actually only the confirmation of what he had been groping towards during his childhood" (*Convert* 37).

10. Newman worked tirelessly, however, to ensure that this "weakness" in others could not be found (or found out) within him. According to Henry Staten, he "describes God as a sort of monitor of the unconscious, who 'sees with most appalling distinctness all . . . the windings and recesses of evil within us.' . . . [The Christian's] duty is to bring to consciousness the influences which operate upon his behavior and thought" (71). And as George Levine points out: "Despite Newman's talk about the irrational, he tended to an almost formal equation of consciousness with man's full psychic life. . . . The dark, romantic will of Schopenhauer, Nietzsche, and Lawrence is swept under the carpet, and thus, while we can talk about Newman's extraordinary psychological perceptiveness, we must recognize that his psychology is, finally, only a brilliant extension of the rationalist introspective psychology of the British Empiricist tradition" (216–17).

11. Faber himself suggests that such psychological reduction is not the most fruitful approach to Newman: "There is an initial vigour in men of genius. . . . They do not go to others to be healed, nor do they run away from the conflict between the world and their dreams. In one way or another, at whatever cost of suffering, they work out their own salvation" (24). Anticipating Christopher

Dawson's criticism, he even suggests, like Wordsworth, that such psychological naturalism murders spirituality in the process of dissecting it: "[B]y treating belief as a pathological curiosity, unworthy of influencing [one's] conscious actions, I defeat my own object of making the dead bones live. If I reduce the belief of a Newman or a Froude to a mere morbid symptom, I reduce them to puppets. And what are the *Eminent Victorians* but a diverting puppet-show, designed to tickle the self-conceit of a cynical and beliefless generation?" (196).

12. Faber is right to point out that as the eldest John would be both the most susceptible to her influence and the most vulnerable to any parental anxiety, but he goes on to claim that "A trained psychologist can argue back, with a considerable degree of certainty, from the abnormal characteristics of a grown man to the decisive influences which he encountered in infancy" (10). At this point he is simply arguing in a circle, from the supposed "abnormal characteristics" back to the upbringing and from the upbringing forward to the adult character, with little hard evidence for either. That Mrs. Newman depended on her eldest son in his twenties hardly establishes that she dominated him in his youth. Newsome quotes J. B. Mozley's opinion that for Newman, "the maternal influence has been but slight in forming the man" (*Convert* 27).

13. In attacking Faber, Christopher Dawson claims that "A psychology which ignores religious values must inevitably misinterpret the behavior of men whose whole lives are ruled by religious motives. . . . Such mistakes are the nemesis for a psychology which regards every spiritual or self-transcending tendency as a disguised form of the sexual impulse" (vii–viii). Rebutting Faber's insinuations of homosexuality, Dawson asserts that "The Freudian method is entirely indifferent to moral considerations, but as soon as it is transferred from the consulting room . . . , it becomes contaminated with the moral convictions and prejudices of the lay critic" (ix). Dawson's own case is theologically if not psychologically suspect. As he moves closer to the 1840s, he unobtrusively shifts his focus from Newman to Keble and Pusey so that he may contrast the dogmatic Tractarians with the later Modernists, who claimed Newman's *Development* essay as their bible.

14. As a pattern for such loss, he offers St. John, dying, like Tennyson's Bedivere, "last of the Apostles": "He had to experience the dreariness of being solitary, when those whom he loved had been summoned away. He had to live in his own thoughts, without familiar friend, with those only about him who belonged to a younger generation. Of him were demanded by his gracious Lord, as pledges of his faith, all his eye loved and his heart held converse with. . . . He sent forward his friends on their journey, while he stayed himself behind" (*PS* 4 [20]: 305).

15. Where we might read this response as evidence of depression, Newman would probably claim it as insight into the human condition. During Lent he pleads, "Earth must fade away from our eyes, and we must anticipate that great and solemn truth, which we shall not fully understand until we stand before God in judgment, that to us there are but two beings in the whole world, God and ourselves. The sympathy of others, the pleasant voice, the glad eye, the smiling countenance, the thrilling heart, which at present are our very life, all will be

away from us, when Christ comes in judgment. Every one will have to think of himself" (*SD* [3]: 38).

16. Newsome comments: "This must stand as perhaps the saddest self-revelation that Newman ever vouchsafed; and it is all of a piece with a propensity to express his deepest emotions for people by the medium of letters, while reserving any physical expression purely to inanimate objects" (*Convert* 124).

17. An early sermon, anticipating this famous quotation from the *Apologia*, views all material creation as illusory and hence dangerous: "To understand that we have souls, is to feel our separation from things visible, our independence of them, our distinct existence in ourselves, our individuality. . . . The unprofitableness and feebleness of the things of this world are forced upon our minds; they promise but cannot perform. . . . And then its changes are so many, so sudden, so silent, so continual. . . . We feel that, while it changes, we are one and the same; and thus, under God's blessing, we come to have some glimpse of the meaning of our independence of things temporal, and our immortality . . . and we begin, by degrees, to perceive that there are but two beings in the whole universe, our own soul, and the God who made it" (*PS* 1 [2]: 19–20).

18. Thomas Gornall, "The Newman Problem," *The Clergy Review* 62 (1977), 138; cited in Jay Newman 19.

19. It is the Spirit "by whom also you were made the instrument of good to me, and by whom my heart was softened to receive your instructions, [that] he steer me safe through the dangers, to which I may be exposed at College" (*LD* 1: 31).

20. Although the *Memoir* claims that Newman's parish responsibilities caused him to drop out after a year, Thomas Sheridan cites evidence (86–87) that he continued intermittently for at least an additional year.

21. Sheridan concludes (87), "[I]t is difficult to disagree with Middleton's statement (*Newman at Oxford* 48) that 'the Professor's wide learning, his historical, biblical, and liturgical knowledge, together with his Catholic outlook, must have greatly helped in [Newman's] mental and spiritual development.'" I would suggest only that "helped" may be too bland a verb.

22. Capps points out ("Vocational" 39–41) that the condemnation of his early sermons by Mayers and Hawkins for diametrically opposite reasons brought Newman to the point of leaving the Church if he could not resolve the issue of baptismal regeneration (see *AW* 202, and 77–78).

23. And two days later, "I cannot alter my views. . . . I earnestly trust that, if you leave me Tutor in the way you propose, it is not under the idea of my probably changing my mind in the course of time" (*LD* 2: 242).

24. The *Memoir*, as we have come to expect, celebrates this intellectual fearlessness: "Sad to say, it is our ordinary experience in life that men are cowards to those who make fight and bullies to those who yield. So was it not with a man, who, whatever were his faults, was in generosity, in boldness of speech, and in independence of mind, a prince. . . . [H]e could not convert men by logic, he would not subdue them by authority; what he could do . . . was to break to pieces the idols which blocked out the light. . . . It was his to preach . . . that religion need not be afraid of argument, that faith can fearlessly appeal to right

reason" (*AW* 84-85). By the 1870s, however, Newman had recuperated enough of Whately's values that the *Grammar* has often been seen as a Noetic document.

25. Chadwick contextualizes this apparent discourtesy: "The early Victorian age, and even later, had a feeling that to be seen to be friendly with a person of the wrong principles was to compromise the right principles. . . . Newman and Keble and Pusey all shared this view" ("Bremond" 180).

26. "I have had great alternations and changes of feeling, . . . according as the affectionate remembrances which I had of you rose against my utter aversion of the secular and unbelieving policy [of] the Irish Church. . . . [These] are but the legitimate offspring of those principles . . . with which your reputation is especially associated . . . which seem to my present judgment to be based in the pride of reason and to tend toward infidelity."

27. Throughout Tract 73, however, Newman will claim that he has escaped from the horns of this dilemma, will claim that he is denying the appeal to reason only on theological issues where it cannot apply.

28. The intersection of these two patterns produces the possibility of adopting the "God role" itself (Capps, "Sunden," 58-62). We will explore later Newman's covert assumption of this role. Edwin Abbott, as we would expect, gives a more cynical slant to the same strategy: "If he deceives others, it is never without first deceiving himself. . . . [A]lthough he is always thinking about himself while preaching, yet it is without the slightest trace of . . . conceit. . . . If his friend lies dying, he comforts himself with the thought of the mission of the dead to the living; if his own life seems a tissue of disappointments, he exhorts himself with a sermon on Jeremiah" (*Anglican* 2: 32, 34).

29. As early as the fifteenth of the *Tracts for the Times,* he insists that in Antiquity, "if a Bishop taught and upheld what was contrary to the orthodox faith, the clergy and people were not bound to submit" (1: 11).

30. See particularly the same letter in which he pledges to oversee Frank's education after his father's bankruptcy: "*Every thing* then as far as relates to Francis and myself is to be cut off from your anxiety. . . . I can only protest, that however other places may *agree* with me, I am not in my own proper element when I am away from you and my sisters. Land animals may plunge into the water and swim about in it, but they cannot live in it" (*LD* 1: 155).

31. Compare this passage from the letters: "Home has the memory of too many trying events to inspire a merely earthly pleasure. What confidence can I have, or you, or any of us, that we shall continue blest in each other's love, except as we are members of Him whose life and rule belong to another world?" (*LD* 2: 108).

32. If the submission to providence here sounds more self-righteous than resigned, in some of the sermons it sounds even more uncomfortably eager: "[H]e who has friends or kindred, and acquiesces with an entire heart in their removal while it is yet doubtful, who can say, 'Take them away, if it be Thy will, to Thee I give them up, to Thee I commit them,' who is willing to be taken at his word; he too risks somewhat, and is accepted" (*PS* 4 [20]: 303-4). O'Faolain warns us that his "gift of analysis has to be constantly and carefully guarded against. . . . All Newman's biographers have taken him too admiringly at his word in these post-

mortems, failing to realize that in analyzing his own inward crises he always transformed emotion into intellect, and that once the experience passed into the refinery of his mind it was, in a sense, falsified" (37). It is nevertheless astonishing how much of life he "passed through the refinery of his mind" before it ever became experience.

33. Surrounding passages from this letter reveal how clearly Newman had come to understand and analyze the grieving process: "At home I feel more the reality of things, a greater but a more tangible pain;—I can grapple with it more.—Do not ask me—suffer me. I know you will press me;—but to be among new scenes, it turns away my heart from the fact not from the pain; it makes me confused and puzzles me—I must look my affliction in the face, if I would get a calm mind. . . . Had I been at home all this time, my distress would have been vastly more poignant, but by this time I would have been softened and subdued" (*LD* 2: 82).

34. Note Thomas Mozley's demurral: "Newman seemed to have had hope of everybody. Whoever was not against him might be for him" (1: 315).

35. Newman's intuition of the nature and role of women anticipates that analyzed in Ragland-Sullivan's study of Lacan: "Insofar as the primary unconscious Desire is the (m)Other's, the daughter is closer to the personal and the narcissistic (the *moi*), while the son is urged by the oedipal structure and by language to 'transcend' the Other's influence to 'find' himself within the social (public) group" (296). But when Newman displaces his own desire into the spiritual realm and sets Mary over it, Ragland-Sullivan would claim that he is internalizing her: "Woman is alien and dangerous, then, not because a patriarch wills it so, but because she reminds all of us of our own psychic Otherness" (289). For her, man "puts [woman] in the place of the dark face of his own unconscious being. And he identifies her with the unconscious, the unknown, and truth—what Lacan tellingly terms the face of God" (292).

36. For the further adventures of Klepper, see T. Mozley 1: 203.

37. The allusion here to Sophocles' *Electra* conveniently transforms their dead father from failure to victim.

38. Quoting a passage from Harriett in which the John character rebukes the Charles character for refusing to wear gloves, Svaglic comments: "Charles would take only so much of this elder-brotherism, and eventually he rebelled" ("Charles" 372).

39. That Newman himself became painfully aware of this dilemma is clear from "Mr. Kingsley's Method of Disputation" in the *Apologia:* "There is a story of a sane person being by mistake shut up in the wards of a Lunatic Asylum, and that, when he pleaded his cause to some strangers visiting the establishment, the only remark he elicited in answer was, 'how naturally he talks! you would think he was in his senses'" (396).

40. Frank actually articulates this causal claim: Charles's "moral ruin was from Robert Owen's *Socialism and Atheistic Philosophy*," and he goes on to articulate the same domestic determinism which so incensed John about *his* siblings: Charles "had *all the same dear sweet influences of home* as all of us; yet how unamiable and useless has he become!" (quoted in M. Ward 170-71; italics Frank's).

41. In 1830, for example, he writes Jemima that the exercise of copying over one of Charles's letters has "put me in so much clearer possession of his position and mine in contrast than any reading could do" (*LD* 2: 285).

42. He even makes careful room in his theology for such relationships: "[I]t might be supposed that the Son of God Most High . . . would not have had only one friend, but, as being All-holy, He would have loved all men more or less, in proportion to their holiness. Yet we find our Saviour had a private friend; and this shows us . . . that there is nothing contrary to the spirit of the Gospel . . . in having our affections directed . . . towards those whom the circumstances of our past life, or some peculiarities of character, have endeared to us" (*PS* 2 [5]: 52).

43. Even these friendships may thus follow a pattern well-established in childhood, one which Harriett captures in her portrait of "George" "quizzing" his playmates and which Frank belabors so spitefully: At Ealing "the boys . . . told me that he *quizzed* everybody. Gradually it leaked out that he had initiated a number of the boys into a special Order, . . . marked by ribbons of different colours, with J. H. N. as Grand Master" (4). As Robbins puts it: "[F]riendship with Newman usually involved a complete surrender to his personality and exalted ideals" (84). To be fair to him and to Newman, we need to add his subsequent qualification: "[I]t is true too that he missed and longed to renew relations with some men of independent mind who held their own course."

44. For those with different values, he kept his distance as much as possible. The anguished letters to Mr. Mayers about college temptations and the tragicomic episode in the *Memoir* (*AW* 32, 156–57) in which some fun-loving undergraduates fail to get him drunk, both suggest that he held equally aloof from most fellow students at Oxford. As he boasted: "I was never taken in by an equal, continually by a superior" (*LD* 5: 304). Having first tried to assume the mantle of his parents, now he tries on that of his teachers: in his first year he proudly writes his mother: "In discipline [Trinity] has become the strictest of Colleges. There are lamentations in every corner of the increasing rigour; it is laughable, but it is delightful, to hear the groans of the oppressed" (*LD* 1: 48). Ten years later, as a fellow of Oriel, his self-parody is surer but his attitude is little changed: "Our undergraduates are getting great—and like German students, affect to give an opinion upon what their Superiors do. The debating Society, as it is called, is the organ and the index of this flippancy. . . . Is not all this German American and odious?—I am pretty well determined to use all my influence . . . to put down that spouting club, or at least to modify it greatly. See what a bigot I am getting" (*LD* 2: 133). As we will see in chapter 10, this "bigotry" reappears five years later still when a nightmare at Naples reveals his fear that by losing his position as tutor he has abandoned Oriel to the Stanley Kowalskis of this world. For Frederic Rogers, "As the Movement gathered power in his hands he became somewhat more disinclined to men who affected an independent position, and was quick in detecting a growing divergence" (quoted in M. Ward 248). We need to contrast this cliquishness, however, with Thomas Mozley's opinion that in potential disciples, "He expected rivers out of the dry ground. . . . Wise and experienced Ox-

ford observers smiled at the confidence he reposed in men who were at best broken reeds and bulrushes, if not stocks and stones" (1: 313).

45. Faber interprets this letter as lover's pique, a rejection of Froude because Newman had to share him with the Archdeacon (286–87). For Faber's case for a homosexual attraction between Newman and Froude see also 215–32. His evidence is less than conclusive.

46. While Bremond's aggressively psychological approach to Newman has often been criticized by other biographers, it is defended in a balanced evaluation by Roger Haight (350–79). Haight claims that while Newman cannot be identified as the father of Modernism, the similarity of his theological method to that of the Modernist faction cannot be denied.

47. Goodwin, following Shairp, suggests an interesting contrast between Newman, who remained perpetually dissatisfied with father surrogates, and Keble: "J. C. Shairp notes that Keble, even after his marriage, lived with his father, who did not die until age ninety. Keble 'never outgrew the period of absolute filial reverence, never questioned a single opinion or prepossession which he had imbibed from his father'" (Shairp 259; quoted in Goodwin 480). But John Griffin ("Keble" 167–73) counters this prevailing view with evidence that Keble, from 1827 to 1834, was quite radical, at least in the sense of being anti-erastian.

48. This same realm also enables Newman to avoid another problem within his image of God. Without it, his positing of the ultimate reality as negation would place him within an Eastern religious tradition, not within an incarnational religion like Christianity.

CHAPTER 2

1. See Harrold: "The increasing tendency of the day was to turn away from the supernatural . . . and to assume that man could save himself unaided. . . . Newman is thus an un-Romantic insofar as he fought the implicit or explicit Pelagianism of his day" (Newman 253). Newsome further suggests that in his effort to move behind the Romantics to the Fathers, he was really affirming a Platonism common to both: "He stepped at once into the world of the Neoplatonists, and found himself—perhaps without knowing it—translating into theological language the esoteric teaching of dedicated Platonists like Thomas Taylor and William Blake" (Two Classes 70). But as we will see in the next chapter, Dean Inge disputes Newman's Platonism.

2. On Newman's use of the Patristic Church to type or "encode" the present, see Thomas: "Encodement brings the ancient uncomfortably close; aspects of Fathers and heresiarchs live again in contemporary figures and situations. Conversely, the uncomfortable present is glorified" (166).

3. The delicate balance of Aristotelian and Platonic elements in this concept is well analyzed in Robert Pattison's "Arian" (143–47), where he details Newman's effort to maneuver around the theological dilemmas implicit within this heresy.

4. Robert Pattison offers an unexpected parallel to Newman's Patristic model: "'One must be accustomed to living on mountains,' Nietzsche said. His mountain was located in a future beyond liberalism, while Newman's was situated in the past before liberalism" (*Dissent* 211).

5. That Newman's own words troubled his conscience we can see in the qualification he feels obliged to insert into his defense of the Tracts: "I challenge the production of any thing in the Tracts of an unkind, satirical, or abusive character; any thing personal. One tract only concerns individuals at all, No. 73; and that treats of them in a way which no one, I think, will find to be an exception to the remark" (*Tracts* 4 [82]: viii). In actuality he feared that Abbott in particular might take exception; he not only offered him an apology but published it in the *English Churchman:* "I stated to him that if in my remarks in the 'Tracts for the Times,' upon one of his publications, I was betrayed into any expressions which might be considered personal, instead of confining myself to the work itself which I was criticizing, I am sorry for them and wish them unsaid. I saw him but for half an hour . . . [but] he has my good wishes and my kind remembrances" (Moz. 2: 373).

6. The complete passage is even more remarkable, positing for Adam an extended celibate existence.

7. Cunningham remarks, "Newman's constant practice is to put words into people's mouths" (236).

8. Thomas traces Newman's evident attraction for Apollinarianism, the denial of a human mind in Christ, in his response to the heretic himself within an unpublished draft: "The defection of Apollinaris from the Catholic Faith excites feelings of especial pain and [regret] . . . from his high character and former services to the Church" (Thomas 90).

9. In his *Newman and the Gospel of Christ* Strange argues at considerable length for the orthodoxy of Newman's Christology (47–86). For Prickett, "The tendency to hypostatise the 'idea,' to treat it as if it were a person, which we find in some passages, [Nicholas Lash] suggests, is partly due to the fact that one of the themes of the fugue is an explicit identification of the 'idea' with the person of the living Christ striding, as it were, through history" (*Romanticism* 164).

10. It is the related distinction (within the "Literature" essay appended to the *Idea*) between the objective truth of science and the personal expression of literary creation which T. R. Wright pronounces as an untenable denial of the metaphorical basis of all revelation (185–96). As Robert Pattison shows, however, the price of agreeing with Hampden's incipient relativism was high indeed (*Dissent* 79–85). Graham Shute (233) actually finds in Newman a fluid conception of language prefiguring Wittgenstein, whom Pattison cites as Hampden's logical successor. And Cunningham notes that a similar nominalism is put in the mouth of the hero of *Loss and Gain:* "'What are words but artificial signs of ideas?' said Charles; 'they are more musical but as arbitrary'" (250).

11. Pattison quotes Hampden's conclusion that "whatever is recorded in those books is indisputably true; and that nothing independent of these books, or not taken from them, can possess the same authority,—not to say in *degree* only,—but

even in *kind*. For this is *divine* truth; whatever is distinct from it, is *human*" (quoted in *Dissent* 89). Despite his personal distaste for Hampden, Newman acknowledged the force of his argument: "[H]ow can human words, how can earthly images, convey to the mind an idea of the Invisible? They cannot rise above themselves. . . . The metaphors by which [doctrines] are signified are not mere symbols of ideas which exist independently of them, but their meaning is coincident and identical with the ideas" (*PO* 338). Thomas presents Hampden as considerably less radical and less relativistic: "Moral conclusions [for Hampden] *are* allowed because incitement to duty is the very purpose of revelation. . . . Man can make moral inferences from Scripture because there is an analogy between his natural moral knowledge, and the enlarged and elevated form of revealed morality" (74).

12. Pattison argues that "The spirit of Hampden lives on in the theories of modern criticism, and fashionable theories of deconstruction have their origin in the detritus of nineteenth-century theology" (*Dissent* 90). A much more direct link could, I think, be drawn to Kantian critique. Pattison does acknowledge that "nineteenth-century Anglicanism independently asked and answered the same questions the German philosophy had confronted half a century earlier. What issue was raised by Kant that was not addressed in Hampden's own critique of pure reason, the Bampton lectures of 1832?" (169). Yet given Pusey's learning, his book on German thought, and his presence on the Oxford scene, Pattison may be claiming too much for Hampden's originality.

13. The published title is "Holy Scripture in Its Relation to the Catholic Creed." Interestingly, Newman had recently edited Froude's *Remains,* within which its editors felt obliged to temporize in a footnote because their friend's journal had expressed a view of scriptural inspiration so critical and delimited: e.g., "We cannot be certain that the inspiration which dictated the Sacred Writings differed at all in kind, or very materially in degree, from that which suggested such a work as Bishop Butler's Analogy" (1: 124).

14. A few years later, in the *Development,* Newman openly admits that the positions of these massed opponents had grown far more promising than his own: "For three hundred years the documents and the facts of Christianity have been exposed to a jealous scrutiny; works have been judged spurious which once were received without a question; facts have been discarded or modified which were once first principles in argument. . . . [I]nfidelity itself is in a different,—I am obliged to say in a more hopeful position,—as regards Christianity. The facts of Revealed Religion, though in their substance unaltered, present a less compact and orderly front to the attacks of its enemies. . . . The assailants of dogmatic truth have got the start of its adherents of whatever Creed; philosophy is completing what criticism has begun" (29). One could plausibly argue that by the time of this quotation, however, Newman had already abandoned Scripture as the bastion of revealed truth in favor of an established church. It is tempting to conjecture that Matthew Arnold had Newman's mournful cadences in his ear when he opened his "Study of Poetry" with this self-quotation: "There is not a creed which is not shaken, not an accredited dogma which is not shown to be question-

able, not a received tradition which does not threaten to dissolve. Our religion has materialized itself in the fact, in the supposed fact; . . . and now the fact is failing it (161)."

15. An 1840 letter to Jemima singles out liberal Protestantism as leading an almost Apocalyptic assault on scriptural authority: "I expect a great attack upon the Bible. . . . Those wretched Socialists on the one hand—then Carlisle [sic] on the other. . . . Then again you have Arnold's school, such as it is (I do hope he will be frightened back) giving up the inspiration of the Old Testament or of all Scripture (I do not say Arnold himself does). Then you have Milman clenching his History of the Jews by a history of Christianity which they say is worse; and just in the same line. Then you have all your political Economists who *cannot* accept (it is impossible) the Scripture rule about almsgiving, renunciation of wealth, and self denial etc. And then your geologists giving up part of the O. T. All these and many more spirits seem writing and forming into something shocking" (*PL* 45).

16. The essay abounds in lists of apparent inconsistencies: "[A]ccording to Matt. xxviii., it might seem that Christ did not appear to His disciples, till He met them on the mountain in Galilee; but in St. Luke and St. John His first appearance was on the evening of the day of Resurrection. Again: in . . . St. Mark and St. Luke, the Ascension seems to follow immediately on the Resurrection; but in the Acts our Lord is declared to have shown Himself to His disciples for forty days" (*DA* 168). Ostensibly Newman is worrying about the inferences of his audience: "I conceive the impression left on an ordinary mind [by the Synoptics] would be, that our Saviour was a superhuman being, intimately possessed of God's confidence, but still a creature" (*DA* 184). But the fact that so many of these examples support the dreaded specter of Socinianism suggests that he is citing those which have long troubled him personally.

17. Culler quotes, already at second hand, a characterization of Milman as "a kind of Christian Gibbon, without the indecency and without the fun" (*Victorian* 101).

18. This assertion is echoed in the *Development:* "No one has power over the issues of his principles; we cannot manage our argument, and have as much of it as we please and no more" (30). Just how far Newman's theory (really his methodology) is taking him is evident even in his 1825 letters to Charles. There he admits that "There is nothing, for example, to prevent my considering the Canticles erroneously inserted in the Jewish Canon, and yet the Jewish religion true, and the books in substance authentic. There is every difference between thinking the *books not inspired* or corrupted and interpolated, and the *religion false.* Michaelis and Less, two of our standard writers on the Canon of the New Testament, *reject the Apocalypse,* yet they do not dream that *in consequence* they must reject the other books" (*LD* 1: 254; italics Newman's). As G. R. Evans's evidence suggests, John may be arguing so aggressively with his brother because he is actually arguing against himself. Evans points out that the letters to Charles contain a long list of Scriptural problems suggested primarily by Newman's own thinking and reading (96–97). This supports my contention that Charles is being used throughout as his brother's stalking horse.

19. In the *Prophetical Office* similar reservations are foisted off upon the Roman Catholics, but without even a gesture at rebuttal: Catholics observe that the New Testament "is but an incomplete document on the very face of it. There is no harmony or consistency in its parts. There is no code of commandments, no list of fundamentals. It comprises four lives of Christ, written for different portions of the Church, and not tending to make up one whole. Then follow epistles written to particular Churches on particular occasions, and preserved, (as far as there can be accident in the world,) accidentally. Some books, as the Epistle to the Laodiceans, are altogether lost; . . . some delivered down with barely sufficient evidence for their genuineness, as the Second Epistle of St. Peter" (*PO* 294–95).

20. In the *Prophetical Office* Newman's insight into the *ad hoc* nature of revelation suggests the need for a flexible response: "[A]ny one book of Scripture would be sufficient, provided none other were given us; . . . the whole Volume, as we have received it, is enough, because we have no more. There is no abstract measure of what is sufficient. Faith cannot believe more than it is told. It is saving, if it believes as much as that, be it little or great" (299).

21. In his last university sermon, during his last years as an Anglican, Newman does at least peer over the brink: "[I]t is a question whether that strange and painful feeling of unreality, which religious men experience from time to time, when nothing seems true, or good, or right, or profitable, when Faith seems a name, and duty a mockery, and all endeavors to do right, absurd and hopeless, and all things forlorn and dreary, as if religion were wiped out from the world, may not be the direct effect of the temporary obstruction of some master vision, which unconsciously supplies the mind with spiritual life and peace" (*US* [15]: 322).

22. He develops this claim in his *Arians:* "Surely the Sacred Volume was never intended, and is not adapted, to teach us our creed. . . . [F]rom the first, it has been the error of heretics . . . to attempt of themselves . . . the eliciting a systematic doctrine from the scattered notices of the truth which Scripture contains. . . . The insufficiency of the mere private study of Holy Scripture for arriving at the exact and entire truth which Scripture really contains, is shown . . . by the discordance of opinions which exists wherever [creeds and teachers] are thrown aside" (50–51). Later in the book, he hedges still further: "[T]he text of Scripture [is] addressed principally to the affections, and of a religious, not a philosophical character" (146).

23. In a similar passage, here equating Jesus' authority with that of the "Sacramental system," Newman's hunger for Augustan propriety even drives him to acknowledge his usually covert fascination with Gibbon by privileging the skeptic's testimony as unbiased: "[S]ome have considered the doctrine of our Lord's Divinity to be an addition upon the 'simplicity' of the Gospels. . . . [T]his has been the belief . . . of infidels, such as the historian Gibbon, who looked at things with less of prejudice than heretics, as having no point to maintain. I think it will be found quite as easy to maintain that the Divinity of Christ was an afterthought, brought in by the Greek Platonists . . . , upon the simple and primitive creed of the Galilean fisherman . . . as that the Sacramental system came in from the same source" (*DA* 187).

24. His reliance, not just on tradition, but on an institutional locus for it, underlies the even harsher judgments on Scriptural reliability in the essay on ecclesiastical miracles: "[T]he earliest of the Evangelists wrote some years after the events recorded, while the latest did not write for sixty years. . . . [T]he greater part of the Miracles of Revelation are as little evidence for Revelation at this day, as the Miracles of the Church are now evidence for the Church" (*Mir.* 233-34). Dean Inge complains that "We can imagine nothing more calculated to drive a young and ingenuous mind into flippant scepticism than a course of Newman's sermons. The *reductio ad absurdum* of his arguments is not left to the reader to make; it is innocently provided by the preacher" (188). And Holmes argues that the then-Tractarian James Anthony Froude did indeed lose his faith as a result of this equation of Scriptural and Patristic evidence ("Froude" 29-34).

25. In the *Apologia,* Newman insists that he took the criticism in stride: "When I was Editor [of *The British Critic*], in my very first number I suffered to appear a critique unfavorable to my work on Justification, which had been published a few months before, for a feeling of propriety" (63-64). In a contemporary letter on the critique, Newman actually grumbled that Le Bas, the reviewer, was "so directly against me that I am hindered from defending my own views" (*LD* 2: 263). Mysticism is likewise Bremond's stock explanation for Newman's beliefs, and even for O'Faolain, "reality . . . was something about which he had had the gravest doubts since childhood. It was, in a sense, the core of his philosophy" (238). Thomas suggests that Newman's distaste for Milman's *History of Christianity* may stem in part from the latter's effort to historicize and debunk the rise of mystery (161-62).

26. See Chadwick (*Bossuet* 119). See also his broader discussion of the influences on Newman (96-138).

27. Collected as "Primitive Christianity" and "The Church of the Fathers" in *HS,* 1: 333-446 and 2: ix-210, respectively. For Newman's portrait gallery within *Arians,* see Thomas (43-45).

28. In a remarkably candid letter to Jemima, Newman asserts that acknowledging moral and spiritual intimations renders philosophical knowledge superfluous: "As to Berkeley, I do not know enough to talk—but it seems to me, while a man holds the moral governance *of God as existing in and thro' his conscience,* it matters not whether he believes his senses or not. For at least he will hold the external world to be a *divine* intimation, a scene of trial, (whether a reality or not) just as a child's game may be a trial. I have tried to say this in the Arians" (*LD* 4: 253).

29. As early as the 1826 *Essay on Miracles,* the plausibility of miracles is made to rest on the perception of a moral order paralleling the natural one: "The Miracles of Scripture, for instance, are irregularities in the economy of nature, but with a moral end. . . . Thus, while they are exceptions to the laws of one system, they may coincide with those of another. . . . To consider them as mere exceptions to physical order, is to take a very incomplete view of them" (*Mir.* 4-5).

30. Even in 1825 he was haranguing Charles about similar psychological failings: "And now you are in an unquiet state of mind altogether at variance with that calm, equable, candid, philosophical temper which is necessary for balancing such nice matters. . . . You are apt *in every thing* . . . to be self-willed[,] to de-

cide precipitately, to run away with a part for the whole, to form conclusions from very partial inductions, to suffer your feelings to be soon excited: you are slow in observing character; you have very little judgment" (*LD* 1: 213).

31. Newman is always convincing in his portrayals of an afterlife; one from the fourth volume of *Parochial Sermons* anticipates the *Dream of Gerontius:* "When we have wound up our minds for any point of time, any great event, . . . when it comes, and is gone, we have a strange reverse of feeling from our changed circumstances. Such . . . may be the happy contemplation of the disembodied spirit; as if it said to itself, 'So all is now over; . . . against which I have prepared, fasted, prayed, and wrought righteousness. Death is come and gone,—it is over. Ah! is it possible? What an easy trial, what a cheap price for eternal glory! . . . We should consider ourselves to be in this world in no fuller sense than players in any game are in the game; and life to be a sort of dream, as detached and as different from our real eternal existence, as a dream differs from waking; . . . in itself a kind of shadow, without substance" (*PS* 4 [14]: 220–22).

32. Well before this, however, Newman uses the same conjecture to come to terms with the imminent loss of Bowden's wife: "[R]eally we cannot afford that those should be cut off, who by their prayers are doubtless doing more for the cause of Truth than all the exertions of those who are called to labor—but God knows best.—One is irresistibly led on to hope that their intercessions will not stop, though they be removed from us into the invisible world" (*LD* 4: 336).

33. Thomas Mozley reports that if someone suddenly died, for Newman he "had done all the good work he could do or was likely to do. He was withdrawn because he would do no more, or could do no more" (1: 209).

34. By 1841 Newman can challenge Robert Peel to find any means of transferring secular values from one generation and age to another as powerful as the spiritual transmission of Christianity: "Each one of us has lit his lamp from his neighbour, or received it from his fathers, and the lights thus transmitted are at this time as strong and as clear as if 1800 years had not passed since the kindling of the sacred flame. What has glory or knowledge been able to do like this? Can it raise the dead?" (*DA* 271).

35. Newman addresses the intermediate state between death and the Last Judgment much more tentatively within Tract 79, a thoughtful but largely hostile analysis of the Roman Catholic doctrine of Purgatory. While he finally rejects it as "but a violent hypothesis to give meaning to a usage for which other hypotheses . . . equally conjectural with it, may be assigned" (4: 20), he does agree with an unnamed source that it answers the perceived dilemma that "Most men, to our apprehension, are too unformed in religious habits either for heaven or for hell, yet there is no middle state when Christ comes in judgment." Even in the writings of the Fathers, Purgatory thus grows out of "the musings of serious minds feeling a mystery, and attempting to solve it, at least by conjecture" (4: 23). For an account of this issue in the context of nineteenth-century sectarian disputes, see Rowell (100).

36. The above-mentioned four sermons were preached in 1832, 1834, 1835, and 1837, respectively.

37. The metaphor of suffering as dance prefigures Callista's dream just before

her martyrdom, in which, encouraged by the heavenly court, "she began a solemn measure, unlike all the dances of earth, with hands and feet, serenely moving on towards what she heard some of them call a great action and a glorious consummation" (*Callista* 355). In a roughly contemporary sermon, the gap between the cosmic harmony which suffering should achieve and the imperfect human means of achieving it occasions the replacement of an aesthetic discipline by an ascetic one: "[T]o practice a heavenly life on earth, certainly, is a thing above earth. It is like trying to execute some high and refined harmony on an insignificant instrument. In attempting it, that instrument would be taxed beyond its powers, and would be sacrificed to great ideas beyond itself. And so, in a certain sense, this life, and our present nature, is sacrificed for heaven and the new creature; that while our outward man perishes, our inward man may be renewed day by day" (*SD* [7]: 87). For another example from the *Plain Sermons* (*PS* 7 [10]: 134), see Brilioth (*Anglican* 235). His chapter on "Forms of Tractarian Piety" (211-59) includes an excellent discussion of the spiritual realm in Newman's sermons.

38. See also *Tracts* 3 (73): 11, and *PS* 3 (17): 237.

39. See also both an earlier and a still later sermon: "Who can say that all of us, or at least all who are living in the faith of Christ, have not some strange but unconscious life in God's presence all the while we are here, seeing what we do not know we see, impressed yet without power of reflection" (*PS* 3 [12]: 168). And later, "Who shall limit the power of the gracious Spirit of God? . . . As the earth goes round the sun, yet the sun is said to move, so our souls, in fact, may be taken up to Christ, when He is said to come to us. . . . May [the Spirit] not in less than a moment bring our souls into God's presence, while our bodies are on earth?" (*PS* 6 [10]: 127-28).

40. See, for example, the complex reworking of John's spiritual and military imagery in this passage from the sixth volume of the sermons: "[T]he Saints are ever taking possession of the kingdom, and with the weapons of the Saints. The invisible powers of the heavens, truth, meekness, and righteousness, are ever coming in upon earth, ever pouring in, gathering, thronging, warring, triumphing, under the guidance of Him who 'is alive and was dead, and is alive for evermore.' The beloved disciple saw Him mounted on a white horse, and going forth 'conquering and to conquer.' 'And the armies which were in heaven followed Him upon white horses, clothed in fine linen, white and clean'" (*PS* [22]: 316).

41. In the *Prophetical Office,* he speculates on why this spiritual power is not more manifest: "If the Christian Church was intended to come on earth in the power and spirit of Christ Himself, . . . if she was destined to compel the nations with an irresistible sway, smiting and withering them if rebellious, though not with earthly weapons, and shedding upon the obedient overflowing peace, and the holiest and purest blessings, . . . that these prospects have been disappointed, may be owing, as in the case of the Jews, to the misconduct of her members" (225).

42. Later in this passage, the same island metaphor which Matthew Arnold uses to enforce his own isolation in "To Marguerite, Continued" here explains the apparent diffusion of Christian churches as the result of a Flood brought

upon an otherwise sinful world: "[T]hough the visible Churches of the Saints in this world seem rare, and scattered to and fro, like islands in the sea, they are in truth but the tops of the everlasting hills, high and vast and deeply rooted, which a deluge covers" (*PS* 4 [11]: 178). Indeed Bremond describes companionship as his principle motive in seeking out this age: "When he is free to follow nothing but his own inclination, it is the man, it is the saint, whom he looks for above all in each of the Fathers. Before taking them for masters, he wishes to have them as friends" (77). With their friendship, Newman wins sanction, pattern, and company for his solitary devotions.

43. While this passage may seem to approach a crude Manicheism, a contemporary sermon portrays Satan and God as operating on vastly different levels: "[H]is thousand eyes and his many instruments avail him nothing against the majestic serene silence, the holy imperturbable calm which reigns through the providences of God. . . . [H]e appears like a child or a fool, like one made sport of. . . . He makes a guess here, or does a bold act there, but all in the dark. . . . [H]ow can we hope to see [this providence] except by that way which the devils cannot take, by a loving faith?" (*PS* 4 [17]: 259-60).

44. In Newman's defense of Pusey's baptism tract, he takes on again the claim that Voltaire, as baptized, was better than Adam. Newman replies that Voltaire was moved into a new, higher mode of being, but not one which would assure him of salvation (*VM* 2: 163).

45. In the *Development*, Newman quotes St. Justin defending devotion to Angels: "Him, (God) . . . and the host of the other good Angels who follow and resemble Him, and the prophetic Spirit, we worship and adore, paying them a reasonable and true honour" (384).

46. The dangers latent in both may have occasioned this monitory appeal to economy within his essay on ecclesiastical miracles: "When the [Jewish] people had lately come out of Egypt, with all the forms of idolatry . . . impressed upon their hearts, . . . to have disclosed to them truths concerning angelic natures . . . might have been the occasion of the withdrawing their heart from Him who claimed it whole and undivided" (*Mir.* 359).

CHAPTER 3

1. Duncan Nimmo argues (160-62) that Newman's theory of development was anticipated by Mark Pattison as early as his response to Hampden's Bampton Lectures of 1832, but as Williams here suggests, the idea seems already implicit within Newman's conception of Patristic hermeneutics in *Arians* (265-66). This context makes doubly ironic Thomas's discovery (76) that the same argument appears in Hampden as well. See also Weatherby (214-15).

2. "To read allegorically is to acknowledge that God's revelation itself employs the same pedagogy as the skilled catechist. . . . [I]ts importance abides as a means of uniting the language of theology with the essentially *progressive* nature of Christian discipleship—faith as a paideia [Gr], a process of being shaped by the truth over time" (268).

3. Note the similarity of this account to a roughly contemporary one of the Movement itself: "[I]t is a spirit afloat, neither 'in the secret chambers' nor 'in the desert,' but everywhere. It is within us, rising up in the heart where it was least expected. . . . It is an adversary in the air, a something one and entire, a whole wherever it is, unapproachable and incapable of being grasped" (*Ess.* 1: 272).

4. Thomas Hummel points out that Newman here distinguishes this, the Prophetical Tradition, from an unchanging Episcopal Tradition (267–69), but Nicholas Lash counters that Newman is remiss in not acknowledging that "the content of the 'Episcopal Tradition' is itself subject to significant historical change and variation" (*Change* 99). Besides, Newman claims that the Prophetical Tradition is "in its first origin . . . equally Apostolical, and viewed as a whole, equally claims our zealous maintenance" (*PO* 268).

5. See Cameron: "Newman began to see that the problem of development is more pervasive, raising questions about the relation of the earliest Fathers to the New Testament" ("Tractarian" 96). See also Hummel: "When Newman found he could no longer maintain that the doctrines expressed in the Creeds and tradition were consciously taught by the apostolic church everywhere, by everyone, and always (the Vincentian Canon), he turned to a theory of development for the answer" (265). Williams posits much the same difficulty: "Newman is still reluctant to commit himself to the idea that the ante-Nicene divines might not have recognized Nicene doctrine at once as identical with their own teaching; but this presentation moves discernibly in this direction. . . . [A] crack has opened in the confident assertion that doctrine does not change, even if only in the recognition that its idiom changes" (271).

6. Brent has Newman's approach cutting several different ways at once, both Aristotelian and Platonic, and Platonic in both an essentialist and developmental sense ("Conversion" 265–78). He claims that Newman was moved both by Aristotelian reasoning and Platonic dialectic in his conversion, that the former produced his early interest in Bull as defending the solidity of dogma against Petavius (265) and also the syllogistic effort to show such dogma fixed within the Thirty-Nine Articles within Tract 90 (275–78). But the Platonic dialectic was an essentialistic claim for unchanging form underneath shifting matter.

7. Thomas Arnold's "Malignants" article describes church history as a perpetual, implicitly Hegelian, development: such history "shows that the world has on the whole advanced;—that the heresy of one period becomes the orthodox faith of another;—and that that which great and good men taught at the price of their blood, obtains in the end so sure a triumph, that even the low and the wicked are obliged to . . . make use of its name to exclude that further developement of truth which is indeed its own genuine child" (234).

8. This process is taken to its ultimate, if not necessarily its logical, conclusion by Edward Said: "Publication of a text, or at least the appearance of the text as an object to be diffused, is a ceremonious repetition of the parricidal deed by virtue of which copies proceed to supplant . . . an inaccessible source. . . . [The] Gospel[s'] physical existence commemorates a communal guilt and redemption. If Jesus is the father of the Christian community, every instance of writing signifies

his death. . . . [H]is presence is transmuted into or sacrificed for words, just as, conversely, he was the Word made flesh" (210-11).

9. In a note within *Arians,* he even attacks Milton's effort to return to an un-mediated biblical literalism: "[T]he theological language of the Paradise Lost [*sic*] . . . becomes offensive as being dwelt upon as if it were literal, not figurative. It is scriptural to say that the Son went forth from the Father to create the worlds; but when this is made the basis of a scene or pageant, it borders on Arianism. Milton has made Allegory, or the Economy, *real*" (93n).

10. In the *Church of the Fathers* Newman quotes a letter of Basil to Gregory recommending ritual as the figure of life: "Pious exercises nourish the soul with divine thoughts. What state can be more blessed than to imitate on earth the chor-uses of Angels?—to begin the day with prayer, and honour our Maker with hymns and songs?—as the day brightens, to betake ourselves, with prayer attend-ing on it throughout, to our labours, and to sweeten our work with hymns, as if with salt?" (*HS* 2: 64). As translated for his flock, however, this labor is neither sweet nor light: "Is it an easy thing to pray? It *is* easy to wait for a rush of feel-ings, and then to let our petitions be borne upon them; and never to attempt the duty till then; but it is not at all easy to be in the habit day after day and hour after hour, in all frames of mind, and under all outward circumstances, to bring before God a calm, collected, awakened soul" (*PS* 4 [5]: 75).

11. To Jemima he claims that the ancient "worshipper did not think of himself—he came *to* God—God's House and Altar were the Sermon which addressed him and roused him. His Sacraments were the *objects* of regard. Words were unneces-sary" (*LD* 6: 79), and in much the same way Newman's followers, as we saw in chapter 2, are inspired by "The very disposition of the building, the subdued light, the aisles, the Altar, with its pious adornments" (*PS* 3 [17]: 251).

12. Newsome puts this strategy more positively: "[H]e had an uncanny knack . . . of catching the spirit of a tradition, absorbing its ethos, and then . . . of imposing upon the teaching received his own distinctive interpretation, his own idiosyncratic twist." Newsome goes on to anticipate Harold Bloom's paradigm: Newman's practice reveals "the stamp of the true philosopher who, while he learns from all who can teach him, is never content with an interpretation which is not his own" ("Newman" 74).

13. It is on this charge that the anonymous *Edinburgh* reviewer is most relent-less: "Mr Newman in all this matter is a partisan, and not an historian" ("New-man's *History of the Arians*" 55); "the literary theology of the age, explains the rise, or rather the existence, of the Arian and other heresies. They are the genuine offspring of the peculiar form of mental developement at that day" (58); and analogously, "The theological system, then, of the Alexandrian Church is . . . exactly the form of teaching which men educated in the prevailing philosophy . . . would be likely to adopt" (61). The reviewer can be so skeptical about his-torical claims because of his assumption, far more naive than Newman's, that he does not need them: "[T]he views entertained by men placed under various cir-cumstances of Christian doctrine, are a most valuable record . . . ; but they have only an historical, and not an authoritative value" (65).

14. Inge equates Newman's anti-intellectualism with the "Personalism" of Julius Hare: here "the intellect, in forming concepts, has to be content with an approximate resemblance to concrete reality. . . . [P]ersonalism is beyond question a self-sufficient, independent, individualistic doctrine. When it is combined with a nominalist theory of knowledge, it naturally suggests that every man may and should live by the creed which naturally suits his idiosyncrasies" (190).

15. With a cultural distance approaching Foucault's, he will come to perceive in even the "most direct and severe" arguments an unacknowledged reservoir of unacknowledged bias, "subtle assumptions . . . traceable to the sentiments of the age, country, religion, social habits and ideas, of the particular inquirers or disputants, and passing current without detection, because admitted equally on all hands!" (*GA* 176).

16. Arnold would hardly have included Newman with the rest of his world as "Light half-believers of our casual creeds" (172). See also Thomas's later comment: "Newman was the child of British empiricism, hypersensitive to epistemological issues, concerned with the psychology of impressions and ideas, agnostic about their object" (182).

17. See also the 1819 letter of Shelley to Charles and James Ollier: "A certain similarity all the best writers of any particular age inevitably are marked with, from the spirit of that age acting on all" (10: 96). This phrase and concept, of course, are signatures of Hazlitt.

18. Since Schiller's paradigm itself secularizes a *Verfallstheorie* on the loss of biblical inspiration, historians of religion have not been slow to explore and adapt its hermeneutic consequences. Gerhard Ebeling describes the sacramental element in Roman Catholicism, which Newman was trying to incorporate into the via media, as the "realistic," "metaphysical" strategy of realizing the past in the present (33–34). While the Reformation initiated an attack on this mode of recuperation (45–49), the Enlightenment was needed to complete its work by developing the critical-historical method.

19. Maurice "is of the Cambridge School—and from the little I have seen of those men, they seem to me never satisfied to take things as they find them, but to be always meddling and (as they think) improving truths which have been from the beginning—and to believe sacred doctrines, not because they have received them, but because they can prove them from philosophy" (*LD* 5: 180).

20. Tennyson points out that "Keble's primary-secondary division roughly parallels Coleridge's distinction between the Imagination and the fancy" (*Victorian* 64–65). As with Schiller, the distinction is not purely chronological. Both see Shakespeare as a primary/naive poet, but in this, as Goodwin implies below, Keble ducks the question of whether fervent religious emotion is achievable outside a naive, mythic mindset.

21. Keble's illustration of this distinction in the person of Virgil is documented by Goodwin: "As long as he [Virgil] kept to epic conventions in the *Aeneid,* 'working evidently by rule and against the grain,' he produced secondary poetry. Virgil wrote primary poetry when he departed from the convention and allowed for the 'development of his true self'—the expression of his melancholia channeled and veiled by reference to 'country sights and sounds'" (478).

22. Robert Pattison quotes Bagehot's sexist quip that the "*Christian Year* is Wordsworth translated for women" (*Dissent* 43).

23. Even Satan's instrument remains vulnerable, however, and twelve years later in the *Development*, Newman is able to trace it, not to the broad classical foundations of the still formidable Gibbon, but to the jejune, cerebral Manicheism which "seduced" the young Augustine: "[N]othing else was the cause of my falling into their hands, than their professing to put away Authority which was so terrible, and by absolute and simple Reason to lead their hearers to God's presence, and to rid them of all error. For what was there else that forced me, for nearly nine years, to slight the religion which was sown in me . . . but their assertion that I was terrified by superstition. . . . Who would not be seduced by these promises, and especially a youth . . . with a contempt of old-wives' tales" (*De Utilitate Credendi;* cited in *Dev.* 308).

24. I suspect that this last image owes its intensity to some cruel and painful prank once played on the young Newman by a classmate.

25. Rajan argues further that this strategy "unsettles any vision of art as progressing toward the historical recovery of naivete, because it tacitly concedes that this naivete has never existed" (34).

CHAPTER 4

1. For Bernard Reardon, the Tractarian Movement "appears as an aspect of the general cultural renaissance denoted by the word romanticism. . . . [A]lways freedom and spontaneity were deemed the vital conditions of [the] pursuit" of its ideals (*Coleridge* 92). O'Faolain claims that all the Tractarians were "more indebted to the romantic poetry of the century than they knew. Nobody would have dared talk [as Newman did of angels] before 1789" (157). For a description of Newman's use of "imagination" as an amalgam of Addison and Johnson, see Merritt Lawlis (73–80). Henry Staten attempts to identify Newman with the Romantics in their common effort to reconcile inner and outer (69–75). See also Basil Willey's elegant formulation of this relation (90–93).

2. Coulson's "differences" involve both Newman's solitary presence as the most innovative thinker among the Tractarians and his subsequent rejection of what Coulson sees as the movement's most significant value—an imaginative, Coleridgean reappropriation of seventeenth-century sacramental language.

3. James's conclusion to this chapter clarifies this assertion: When Coleridge celebrates the Incarnation as the source and basis for all human symbolism, then "in this, in acceptance of the mythology which is divinely given as history, the long and difficult history of Romanticism in England comes to its end. After the labour of mighty imaginations in the creation of myth and allegory, we return to the mythology enacted in time and through the free act of God" (209). It is just this return which Newman, I would claim, tries and fails to make. Despite this, and despite his strategy of making Newman the serene Catholic counterpart of Coleridge's Protestant speculation, James's early-written and under-read analysis

anticipates many of the conclusions reached by Gore, Prickett, Reardon, Goodwin, et al.

4. Pattison goes on to debunk any attempt to link Newman with even an attenuated Romanticism (*Dissent* 40-45).

5. T. R. Wright also argues, against Newman's patent intention, that Newman did not succeed "in escaping the Romantic predicament" (182), but Wright focuses on Newman's grudging acknowledgment of the inevitable metaphoricity of language. Pitt classes him as a high Romantic, but only by condescending to the whole group; Newman shares their retreat "from the treacherousness of Enlightenment rationality to something like the condition of faith, or at least to that feel for the reality of things which grows in the interaction of the mind and its world" (23-24). Brilioth, through equally unhappy for theological reasons, admits that "self-mirroring . . . may be observed in the leaders of the Oxford Movement, and in its measure contributes to heighten their purely personal interest" (*Anglican* 57).

6. This use of pantheism as a catch-all term is also evident in Pusey's analysis of the German pre-Romantic Lessing: "A too prominent indulgence of the taste for elegant literature and the arts, in which he was so great a master, seem[s] to have enervated in him the moral earnestness, and precluded him from the self-knowledge, necessary for a thorough and satisfactory examination; and though he perhaps rightly preferred Pantheism to the then existing systems, he had neither the boldness to take the 'saltum mortalem,' by which Jacobi escaped it, nor a philosophy sufficiently deep to see the deficiencies of Pantheism itself" (1: 156).

7. See also Chadwick's broader discussion of the influences on Newman (*Bossuet* 96-138). Mark Pattison is quoted as claiming that they were at least in the air of the Oriel Common Room: "I could not have handled the Oriel philosophy paper [for a fellowship in 1837] in a way to meet the views of the examiners, but for this strong infusion of Coleridgean metaphysics" (Prickett, *Romanticism*, 190).

8. Alexander Whyte praises Pusey's book as a "long denied and forgotten essay": "[I]t will yet be pronounced to be the best book that its learned author ever wrote. At any rate, there is a strength in it, and a sanity, and a true catholicity, that are not always exhibited in Pusey's later writings" (29-30). Brilioth, however, wonders whether Pusey's "philological training was the best equipment for a champion of a movement that was in its essence historical" (*Evangelicalism* 56). C. G. Brown points out the hostility with which German thought was met in England by noting that William Palmer attacked Newman's *Development* as influenced by German rationalism (14).

9. Newman's own ongoing failure to understand Kant is well summarized in Johannes Artz's article. While mentioning Pusey, Artz concentrates on Newman's use of an 1854 English translation of H. M. Chalybaus's *Speculative Philosophy from Kant to Hegel*. Against A. M. Fairbairn's 1885 charge that both Kant and Newman deified morality, Artz argues that Kant's moral goal is freedom while Newman's is relationship and that Kant's base is epistemological while Newman's is psychological (531-35). This conclusion seems more viable to me than Robert Pattison's, i.e., that "Newman's reply to Kant was his habitual scholastic reply to

Socinianism" (*Dissent* 171). Culler notes that in Newman's library at the Oratory, "his copy of Kant was opened only to page 184, his copy of Auguste Comte only to page 40, his Fichte only to page 16. We know what he read, and we know what he apparently did not read as well" ("Remembrance" 61).

10. Harriett had written, "'Maria' [Pusey's wife] is a person we should like;—perhaps as much as you do Pusey. Only I am afraid she is beyond me a very great way. I should fear besides she has not escaped his radicalism; what a desperate radical he is!" (*LD* 2: 62). While Pusey's style, compared to Newman's, is prolix and tangled, friends' stories of its incoherence and incomprehensibility probably owed more to the novelty of the ideas he was presenting.

11. Pusey's "view of inspiration I think you will be much pleased with. It is one which has by fits and starts occurred to me, he has put it into system, and I do believe it is the old orthodox doctrine.—He holds the inspiration of the Church, and all good men (e.g. Socrates)" (*LD* 2: 164). In assessing Pusey's influence, John Griffin distinguishes him from other Tractarians in his lack of interest in the Apostolic succession, his praise for the Reformation, and his acceptance of the Anglican Church as Protestant ("Pusey" 139-43).

12. See, for example, *LD* 4: 303 and 320. Before the publication of his university sermons in 1843, he claimed to Jemima that the consistency of his theory constituted his only incentive to publish, "considering its unpopularity and my own ignorance of metaphysical writers" (Moz. 2: 363).

13. See Faber's account of Pusey's traumatic and compulsive studies in Germany (134-37).

14. In volume 2 Pusey defends this praise of Schleiermacher against Hugh J. Rose's charges of speculative heresy, but he adds almost nothing of substance to his original, rather vague comments (89-96).

15. Nos. 18 and 19 (April and July 1835) of an American journal, *The Biblical Repository*.

16. Thomas also quotes an unpublished early memorandum: "I do not even like the words Trinity, Person, Procession, etc etc—indeed any systematic exposition of the doctrine but what is *relative to us and practical*" (18). Such passages also complicate Robert Pattison's claim that Newman's "*Odium Theologicum*" for Hampden grew from the relativism inherent in his neo-Arianism: "The fact of the Trinity is real and imperishable, but the God whom we perceive in our own linguistic formulations is 'a relative Deity'—relative to our own fallible interpretations" (*Dissent* 80).

17. For earlier studies of this influence, see the rather anecdotal one by Castle, and the gruffer but more thorough one by Davis.

18. Robert Pattison takes both Prickett and Coulson to task for reading Romanticism into Newman's terminology while ignoring his explicit conclusions (*Dissent* 157n). Newman's 1829 "Essay on Poetry," to be sure, specifically claims that "Revealed Religion should be especially poetical—and it is so in fact. While its disclosures have an originality in them to engage the intellect, they have a beauty to satisfy the moral nature. . . . With Christians a poetical view of things is a duty,—we are bid to colour all things with hues of faith, to see a Divine meaning in every event, and a superhuman tendency. . . . [T]he virtues pecu-

liarly Christian are especially poetical—meekness, gentleness, compassion, contentment, modesty, not to mention the devotional virtues" (*Ess.* 1: 23). This effort to enlist Christianity in the service of eighteenth-century sensibility, however, is neither the deepest nor, fortunately, the most characteristic strain in Newman's mature thought.

19. Engell continues, "This is the promise of the imagination in Blake's prophetic books, and it is an idea later stressed by Arnold" (364).

20. Prickett continues "that the 'poetic' use of language, *by its very nature,* raises questions that are inescapably 'religious,' and that for Coleridge, poetry, like all art, is essentially incomplete in that it points beyond itself to areas of experience not open to literary or aesthetic criticism" (*Romanticism* 11). McFarland, although he wants to clear the mature Coleridge of pantheism, must acknowledge that pantheism shares three "analogies of structure" with poetry: "First of all, both . . . tend to make particular awarenesses involve, or symbolically imply, more extended awarenesses. . . . [secondly] both tend to allow a scrambling, as it were, of ordinary reference. . . . [T]hirdly, both . . . tend to obliterate the boundaries between the realm of thing and the realm of mind: for poetry, objects are invested with meaning, spiritual states are correlated with states of nature . . . , while for pantheism either matter is conceived as an appearance of spirit, or spirit as an extension of matter" (274-75).

21. "'It would be hard to believe,' declares Keble, that poetry and theology 'would have proved such true allies unless there was a hidden tie of kinship between them.' If the images of poetry point towards another world of greater reality, it is also true that the hidden tie of kinship binds religion to poetry in the very structure of the language by which those images are created. If religion is the 'tenor,' then poetry is the 'vehicle'" (Prickett, *Romanticism,* 114). Prickett continues, "The poet, in creating a poem, allows the translucence of the eternal in and through the temporal; his work is a part of the whole which it describes. Similarly, the Christian's experience of God is essentially 'poetic,' revealing to us the poetic nature of the whole universe—in which he shares. Poetry makes us aware of the sacramental nature of all human experience" (116). For an interesting comparison of this program with the more secular one of Matthew Arnold, see Alvan Ryan (121-30).

22. Pusey's use of a similarly sacramental language is documented from previously unpublished lectures by A. M. Allchin (56-73).

23. John Coulson appeals to Coleridge to heal a very similar split, though he describes it in terms more reminiscent of T. S. Eliot: "Between ourselves and the Elizabethan and Caroline poets and theologians exists a change in consciousness, describe it how we will—as a dissociation of sensibility, the rise of scientific rationalism, or the birth of the machines. Is the divide unique, or can we remain in continuity? Have we now to say that all metaphors are but projections which require correction, or—if we follow Marx—reduction to the contradiction they reveal in their secular basis? If so, then the first [Elizabethan] use of metaphor has been superseded" (33). Newman saw, I think, that the effort of the later Coleridge to baptize the imagination seduced him and his followers into a kind of nostalgic idolatry. Coulson lets a similar fascination with the primitive, earthy,

culturally-bound use of metaphor seduce him into lumping the nihilistic metaphors of Shakespeare's tragic vision with the assurances of the Caroline divines (18–27).

24. Newman's comments during this year and the next plough the same ground: "I could not in my first talk make out to my satisfaction that he [Stephen] was not too much of a philosopher—looking (in Coleridge's way) at the Church, Sacraments, doctrines etc rather as symbols of a philosophy than as *truths,* as the mere accidental signs of principles, But when I dined with him (tête a tête) I find he was far from this" (*LD* 5: 225). He abruptly dismisses the new book of Pusey's friend: "I had seen it for weeks in the Papers and said to myself with some contempt—'Cambridge all over.'—viz. 'History of the formation of my opinions—' or 'history of my opinions—' 'by a fellow of a College'" (*LD* 6: 99). To Charles Cornish he complains, "These fellows [at Cambridge] take up every thing as a matter of literature—and their opinions come and go like Spring fashions. . . . They are all for what is Catholic, and their definition of Catholicism in any subject matter is an abstraction taking in the widest extent of opinion" (*LD* 6: 363). Finally, he reports to Rogers that Faber "says that two parties are formed [at Cambridge], Hookites, which *in fact* includes us, and a sort of Latitudinarians, who *consider* they maintain 'Oxford views.' . . . An external *bond* is what they want, and what they shrink from. Are they not like Greeks, and we like Romans? 'Graiis ingenium,' etc. 'Tu, Romane, memento . . . parcere subjectis et debellare superbos'" (*LD* 6: 365).

25. The third and fourth volumes of *Parochial Sermons* are good illustrations of this pattern.

26. As we will see below, in practice Keble did not approve of modern attempts to explore his sacramental universe, but he saw less clearly than either Coleridge or Newman the subjective premises underlying his project. Drawing from Coleridge's more inclusive version of economy, Prickett makes a similar distinction between power and truth: "For Coleridge the bi-focal symbolizing power of the imagination had always seemed to carry with it some kind of self-authenticating guarantee of truth. For Newman, this was plainly not so in all cases. The problem of the truth or falsity of the imagination was one that became very important to him" (*Romanticism* 195).

27. It is my focus upon these privileged moments which, I would argue, allows me to circumvent Prickett's cogent argument that Newman's psychology of belief "stems directly from a bold inversion of Locke and seems to owe almost nothing to Kant or his repudiated followers such as Fichte or Jacobi. Whereas the Kantian 'reason' applies only to a limited range of innate ideas, the whole point of Newman's account of what he calls the 'illative sense' is that it applies equally to the entire range of mundane sense-experience" ("Physiognomy" 274). This shift from privileged to mundane in Newman's criteria for evidence may epitomize a larger shift from his Anglican practice to his Catholic theorizing.

28. Stephen Maxwell Parrish argues that this quotation from the 1829 "Essay on Poetry," omitted from the 1871 revision, was actually Blanco White's editorial addition.

29. This is certainly the conclusion of D. G. James's extended parallel between

the speculating, assertive Coleridge, simultaneously Gothic and Protestant, and the acquiescent, self-delimited, Romanesque Newman (243-61). Here, James implies that Protestant Justification inevitably betrays Catholic self-transcendence by anticipating Romantic self-exaltation.

30. For Newsome, "almost every page of Newman's sermons testifies to his own awareness of that privileged, yet awesome, relationship [with God]. . . . Newman spoke of the haven for which the soul craves as if he had already found it himself" (*Convert* 104-5). As Chadwick describes the sermons: "The more overwhelming the reality, the more th[is] preacher's personality started to hide. Popular preachers create their effect by making their personality large. Newman created his effect by disappearing in the reality of which he spoke, as though he must get out of its way. . . . Yet the kind of man preaching comes through" (*Newman* 21, 24). Eric Griffiths offers further evidence of this self-effacement (66-67).

31. Chadwick suggests that Tyrrell's effort to balance Newman's "negative qualities as well as his virtues" made Bremond's decision to let him write the Introduction "an error of judgment. . . . Occasionally someone would quote one of the more extreme utterances of Tyrrell in it as though its author were Bremond" ("Bremond" 174).

32. A late sermon explores some of the reasons for this reticence: "[I]t is very difficult to draw out our reasons for our religious convictions, and that on many accounts. It is very painful to a man of devout mind to do so; for it implies, or even involves a steadfast and almost curious gaze at God's wonder-working presence within and over him, from which he shrinks, as savouring of a high-minded and critical temper. And much more is it painful, not to say impossible, to put these reasons forth in explicit statements, because they are so very personal and private" (*SD* [23]: 348).

33. Taylor, of course, has dramatized the Enlightenment dilemma of subject and object in order to highlight the brilliance of Hegel's solution (44-49). Thomas compares the process of doctrinal development in Newman to Hegelian dialectic, but he feels that Newman has succeeded in protecting revelation "from the 'vicissitude and change' to which doctrine is open" (242).

34. Jost, while he rejects comparisons with Hegel, acknowledges "Newman's move . . . toward an ontology and epistemology grounded in contingency" (62) and develops what he calls "Newman's Principle of Antagonism" (158-61).

35. Livingston expands on this contrast: "For Hegel man was conceived as God in his self-alienation; for Feuerbach the exact opposite is the truth, i.e., *God is man in his self-alienation*" (*Modern* 181).

36. For similar attacks made by Coleridge on Kant's effort to derive God from morality, see Wellek (89-92).

37. For background on this interchange with Stephen and an extensive discussion of Newman's homiletic harshness, see Newsome's *Convert Cardinals* (106-15). To earlier criticisms, Newman himself replied, "Comfort is a cordial, but no one drinks cordials from morning to night" (*LD* 1: 191).

38. In his second university sermon he admits that, "Natural Religion . . . gives little or no information respecting what may be called [God's] *Personality*.

. . . The philosopher aspires towards a divine *principle;* the Christian, towards a Divine *Agent.* . . . [T]he doctrine of original sin is centred in the person of Adam. . . . The Evil Principle is revealed to us in the person of its author, Satan" (*US* [2]: 22, 28–30).

39. Paradoxically, this antidote to rational disinterestedness effects a balance among our human faculties, but where we might expect the balance of awe and terror within a Burkean Sublime, the imagery of this early sermon returns to an Augustan aesthetics of taste. Because "in this world, *fear and love must go together,*" this apparently superstitious mix holds "untold and surpassing pleasure to those who partake it. The bitter and the sweet, strangely tempered, thus leave upon the mind the lasting taste of Divine truth, and satisfy it; not so harsh as to be loathed; nor of that insipid sweetness which attend enthusiastic feelings, and is wearisome when it becomes familiar" (*PS* 1 [23]: 303–5). Without this divinely induced and directed fear, the faculties war against one another and foster a truly degrading form of superstition. Were we "like the Angels," we could see within the incorrigible "the anguish of pride and impatience, where there is no sorrow,— the stings of remorse, where yet there is no repentance,—the wearing, never-ceasing struggle between conscience and sin,—the misery of indecision,—the harassing, haunting fears of death, and a judgment to come,—and the superstitions which these engender" (*US* [6]: 115).

40. Marshall remarks that Wordsworth's "principle of generosity or dialectic of love mediates the relation of man to nature but without ever condensing into a fixed or traditional symbol or series of symbols, located in an unspecifiable interaction or process of exchange often stated in a language of nearly maddening abstraction" (83).

41. As Langbaum quotes him, Hume "wrote: We 'are nothing but a bundle or collection of different perceptions, which succeed each other with an inconceivable rapidity, and are in a perpetual flux and movement.' We arrive at the sense of self through error, through the process of association; and in order to justify this absurdity, says Hume, . . . we imagine 'something unknown and mysterious, connecting the parts'" (*Word* 22).

42. Alan Crowley explores Newman's relation to Ricoeur's hermeneutics of suspicion and of belief, suggesting that both authors "pursu[e] a balance between icon building and icon breaking in their understanding that discursive acts exist in a mutual relation of will and structure" (85).

43. My title, "Romanticism and the Anglican Newman," suggests two options for proceeding: (1) we can work through the various schools of Romantic criticism now current and speculate on the perspective that each offers on Newman's project, or (2) we can work through the various aspects of that project and speculate on the perspectives which each offers on Romanticism. Of these, I have opted for the second. The first virtually demands, if not some master discourse to order all the competing theories, at least a plan for moving among them. Newman's project, as peripheral to either English Romantic poetry or German Romantic philosophy, can only frustrate the search for such a center. By focusing on Newman, I maintain a better hope for coherence, and even if authorial coherence remains a logocentric or psychological illusion, an author who spent his life con-

structing his persona deserves to have its integrity—if not respected—at least closely examined.

CHAPTER 5

1. For Cameron, "the *Apologia,* an autopsychography rather than an autobiography, is in some ways very like *The Prelude* of Wordsworth" ("Tractarian" 92).

2. Our best recourse, therefore, is to follow the lead of Newman's first biographer, Anne Mozley. According to Louis Bouyer, she not only "went gleaning among his sermons" for hints about his childhood, but did so "in all probability . . . not without guidance from Newman himself" (15).

3. See Newman's gloomy reflections on the children under his pastoral care: "Consider their amusements, . . . and what they dream about themselves in time future, when they grow up; and say what place religion holds in their hearts. Watch the reluctance with which they turn to religious duties, to saying their prayers, or reading the Bible; and then judge. Observe, as they get older, the influence which the fear of the ridicule of their companions has in deterring them even from speaking of religion, or seeming to be religious" (*PS* 7 [2]: 15). These youths, dragged all unwilling through their religious training, look even worse when compared with others, "alas not a few, who look upon acquaintance with evil as if a part of their education. . . . [T]hey throw themselves into the manners and opinions of all in turn. . . . [T]hey see persons of opposite creeds and principles, and whatever they fall in with they take . . . merely as facts of human nature, not as things right or wrong" (*PS* 8 [18]: 261–62).

4. Thomas notes that in Tract 73, "the Gospel should not be used to effect conversion, for this is the job of natural theology. . . . '[A] man who does not obey God under natural religion, will not under the Law, nor under the gospel.' Newman's emphasis upon natural religion seems to leave little for revelation to do" (112).

5. Newman's deep anxiety about God's action in and on childhood helps account for his otherwise incongruous struggle with the issue of baptismal regeneration. Analyzed thoroughly by Sheridan, this struggle pits God's power against various manifestations of contingency and contextualization (31–167).

6. In an earlier sermon, Newman even brackets doctrinal issues in favor of what he posits as irrefutable empirical evidence that a child remains a being not of this world: "Who can tell how God makes the soul, or how He new-makes it? We know not. . . . Whether it is created in Heaven or hell, how Adam's sin is breathed into it, together with the breath of life, and how the Spirit dwells in it, who shall inform us? But this we know full well,—we know it from our own recollection of ourselves, and our experience of children,—that there is in the infant soul, in the first years of its regenerate state, a discernment of the unseen world in the things that are seen, a realization of what is Sovereign and Adorable, and an incredulity and ignorance about what is transient and changeable, which mark it as the fit emblem of the matured Christian" (*PS* 2 [6]: 64). Here only the word "regenerate" makes any gesture towards baptism.

7. A later sermon offers the same religious rationale but distances the premise itself: "[S]ome have thought that the minds of children have on them traces of something more than earthly, which fade away as life goes on, but are the promise of what is intended for them hereafter" (*PS* 7 [6]: 81). Brilioth's *Anglican Revival* (209 and note) offers further examples. Wilfrid Ward's biography gives a recollection of Father Ryder: "never shall I forget—I was a boy at the time, just recovering from an illness—his coming and reading to me the famous Ode 'On the Intimations of Immortality.' There was a passion and a pathos in his voice that made me feel that it was altogether the most beautiful thing I had ever heard" (2: 354).

8. In one of his few emotional overtures to Charles, John appeals to a less focused restiveness: "In every one of us there is naturally a void, a restlessness, a hunger of the soul, a craving after some unknown and vague happiness, which we suppose seated in wealth, fame, knowledge, in fact any worldly good which we are not ourselves possessed of" (*LD* 1: 170).

9. Butler continues by showing that Southey wrote the poem as a deliberate revision of the *Ancient Mariner* on Enlightenment terms ("Repossessing" 73-81). The Romantics subsequently pillaged *Thalaba* for plot devices, while Shelley and Byron rewrote its Enlightenment politics, but they all remained more stylistically conservative than the "vulgar," lower-class, eclectic Southey. She finds that the youthful Southey's literary and prophetic models "range from Isaiah and Jeremiah to the Rousseau who wrote *On the Origins and Foundations of Inequality among Men*. Models for a text which is the symbolic history of the life of a nation through its cultural stages to its fall include the Bible, . . . Homer, . . . and Gibbon" ("Plotting" 143).

10. Culler sees Newman's goal as Proustian; the papers are his "effort to recapture the past and to keep himself in communion with it" ("Remembrance" 66).

11.

> my boat
> went heaving through the water like a swan;
> When, from behind that craggy steep till then
> The horizon's bound, a huge peak, black and huge,
> As if with voluntary power instinct,
> Upreared its head. I struck and struck again,
> And growing still in stature the grim shape
> Towered up between me and the stars, and still
>
> . . . .
> Strode after me.
>
> (*Prelude* 1.375-82, 385)

12. The passage goes on to qualify this intuition: "[W]hile discovering He loves them individually, [men] do not advance one step, on that account, to the general truth, that He loves other men individually also" (118).

13. Compare Prickett: "Nothing happened in Newman's world that did not have an immediate and personal meaning for him; nothing held a meaning for

him that did not also have a direct bearing on the rest of creation" (*Romanticism* 176).

14. During the cholera attack of 1832, it is true, to Henry Wilberforce he shaped this Providence into an heroic defiance of consequences: "One may be as tough a fatalist as a Turk here. If it were not for this, I should think myself likely to be taken by it" (*LD* 3: 68). To Rogers he was more candid about both his bravery and his belief: "[W]hether imagination would get the better did I actually *see* a case, I cannot tell—but at present I am unable to realize the danger. Surely one's time is come or it is not—the event is out of our power. . . . [T]here is on one's own mind the strong impression, (I know it is not a good argument, but fear is but an impression, and this works by a counter imagination) that one is destined for some work" (*LD* 3: 72). Later, however, these echoes of Shakespearean stoicism give way to an active search for tokens of divine guidance.

15. "In his excellent book *Epiphany in the Modern Novel,* Morris Beja distinguishes modern epiphany from traditional vision by two criteria: the criterion of Incongruity (the epiphany is irrelevant to the object or incident that triggers it) and the criterion of Insignificance (the epiphany is triggered by a trivial object of incident). . . . I would add four more criteria . . . Psychological association: . . . arising from real sensuous experience. . . . Momentousness: the epiphany lasts only a moment, but leaves an enduring effect. . . . Suddenness: a sudden change in external conditions causes a shift in sensuous perception that sensitizes the observer for epiphany. Fragmentation or the Epiphanic Leap: the text never quite equals the epiphany" (Langbaum, *Word,* 40).

16. Culler is kinder; while he does compare Newman to a pair of hoarding recluses, he concludes that "he has been called the prisoner of his own journals and memoirs, but if so, it was a prison he delighted to inhabit" ("Remembrance" 63).

17. This tendency is pointedly illustrated in the memorandum noting March 1836 as "a cardinal point of time" because of the deaths of Froude and his mother, the editorship of the *British Critic,* and his sister's marriage, among other things (*LD* 5: 246-47). Edwin Abbott also scoffs at Newman's intimation that waiting seven years before converting would somehow enhance the validity of this step (*Anglican* 2: 360-65).

18. "He has now no longer need to consult the omens continually. The sacraments of the Church preserve him from this feverish and disquieting expectation, which formerly paralyzed him" (Bremond 324).

19. Weiskel points specifically to Blake as heir to the "radical, visionary tradition [of] Milton and Spenser" (7).

20. We could play out for Newman Weiskel's psychological reduction of the sublime to a sublimated recuperation of Oedipal conflict. In the process, however, we should not forget (1) that Newman insists his transcendent order is always already dominated by God the Father and (2) that Newman seems to have marginalized his own father from a relatively early age.

21. To Harriett he implies that modern morals, English and Italian, have not improved since classical times: "At the Sciarra Palace we have seen Guido's picture of the Cenci, which I admired extremely till I heard her story which is so shocking that I only hope it is not she (which by the bye is like[ly so])—It is

worthily the subject of a tragedy by Shelley, and I did not know this, tho' every one I met did. I wonder at the perversion of people's minds—to read such authors, such works, and speak coolly of such persons" (*LD* 3: 275). To W. J. Trower he is after Shelley again for being both a Romantic and an immoral Romantic: "Now really do believe me to despise sentimentality. I am up in arms against the Shelleyism of the day, which resolves religion into feeling, and makes it possible for bad men to have holy thoughts" (*LD* 3: 291). As O'Faolain sardonically comments, "Newman on the arts is almost always deplorable" (156n). His more typical response, however, is the *nil admirari* pose he adopted in the Naples museum. He uses the phrase himself: "All this [experience] is gain, and I suppose is part of that nil admirari which one gets by travelling" (*LD* 3: 241). Rather like the adolescent Prince Olavsky in *Fledermaus,* who longs to be young again, to Rogers he tries to sound at least twice his actual age: "Pleasures I have had in abundance, and most rapturous; yet somehow (as was natural) *aliquid desideravere oculi mei.* It might have been different were I younger; but when one's mode of life is formed, one is often more pained than interested by what is novel" (*LD* 3: 233).

22. Characteristically, Newman needs a theory to explain why he feels such sympathy, not why the sympathy appears to him so dangerously secular.

23. A contemporary poem with this epigraph (*VV* 129) explores, rather more pretentiously, the same dilemma.

24. It is not until some five years later, in the letter to Wood quoted in chapter 2, that he acknowledges such beings may be guiding his own movement: "That *we* are under the superintendence of some supernatural power, I cannot doubt for an instant—we have a game to play, a course to run. But then comes the question, is it not something short of God?" (*LD* 6: 113).

25. Faber is convinced that in reconstructing the ruins, Newman and Froude "misinterpreted all they saw; missed the chief secret of the civilization whose poets they had got by heart; reading into its ruins the fugitivism of Wordsworth and Coleridge and Southey" (293). Newman may see the temple's present through Wordsworth, but he sees its past through a thoroughly classical mythos.

26. "Toward the ruinous parts of the present world [Thomas] Burnet [*The Sacred Theory of the Earth*] exhibits the complex attitudes which helped form the new aesthetics of the following century. For he finds positive values in those aspects of the landscape which are vast, misproportioned, terrifying, and by traditional aesthetic standards, ugly; but these values are both aesthetic and quasi-theological, for in them the speaking face of earth declares the infinity, the power, and the wrath of a just deity. . . . Even in later naturalistic treatments of these categories, . . . the vast and disordered in nature express his infinity, power, and wrath, and so evoke a paradoxical union of delight and terror, pleasure and awe" (Abrams, *Natural,* 100-2).

27. Subsequent accounts to college friends grow bolder in their narrative sweep. For Ryder, Sicily becomes "an emblem of its own past history, i.e. the history of heathen countries, being a most noble record stone over the grave of high hopes and aims, pride, sin, and disappointment" (*LD* 3: 248). For Trower, he reads there "the history of all that is great and romantic in human nature, and the man

in all his strength and weakness, with high aims and manifold talents corrupted by sin and humbled by continual failure" (*LD* 3: 291).

28. D. G. James offers a sacred parallel to this secular golden age in the Catholic Newman's celebration of the simple Benedictine life as "a return to the 'primitive age of the world, of which poets have so often sung, the simple life of arcadia or the reign of Saturn, when fraud and violence were unknown' [*HS* 2: 385]" (259).

29. For background on these real-life models for Eliot's Casaubon, who saw all myths as corruptions of Old Testament history, see Edward Hungerford (3-34).

30. A 1 July 1833 continuation of an earlier letter to Jemima does state that "God is giving me a severe lesson of patience, and I trust I am not altogether wasting the discipline" (*LD* 3: 310). But here his thwarted desire is not to go to Sicily but to return home quickly.

31. Faber argues on somewhat different grounds that Newman's interpretation of his sickness as a divine mandate cannot be sustained. He had announced his mission for England to Wiseman before leaving Rome, and Keble's Assize Sermon would have been preached without him: "The contrast between the illness and the sudden fierce outburst of energy on his return to Oxford was exciting, in his own mind; but there was no causal relation" (302).

32. Brilioth (*Anglican* 215-16) offers further examples. For a more vital conception of Newman's nature imagery, see John Holloway (183-88).

33. The poem "Taormini" (*VV* 135), composed at this time, contains another reference to Jacob and the angels.

CHAPTER 6

1. In this he is anticipating Feuerbach's critique of religion as projection.

2. Most fittingly, one of the impressive essays which won him the Oriel fellowship analyzed the debilitating effects of this fear: Diffidence arises "from the excessive fear of shame—a shuddering at repulse, defeat, or even criticism. . . . Thus an indolence is brought on, torpidity of the faculties, and rigidity of the *joints* of the mind (if I may be allowed the expression) which is [a sad] contrast to that elasticity under any failure" (*LD* 1: 148). Although not citing Newman's essay, Geoffrey Faber accounts for Newman's collapse during the Schools in similar terms: "You cannot renounce your belief in the desirability of a double first in the middle of your examination. All you can do is to save your face by a breakdown. Which was what Newman did" (59). For a good discussion of the importance of the Schools in Newman's life and that of Oxford, see Svaglic ("Oriel" 1016-18).

3. Two years later he has learned to avoid a like assault; he writes his mother: "They wish me to go into the Schools again. I have refused it point blank and unconditionally" (*LD* 2: 136).

4. "He was two men at once, the master and the servant, the one ambitiously determined to leave his mark upon the world, the other going in perpetual fear of

consequences, the one always successful, the other always turning success into failure" (Faber 178).

5. Maisie Ward observes the same psychological rhythm, but for her, "this is often the result of precocity. There has to be a long pause, a falling-back to take breath, a fresh start, for young minds which have begun too early" (97).

6. Brilioth sees throughout his career a "dualism which can never entirely be overcome" between the "true" Church as "the body of the elect" and the Church as "constructed on a purely historical foundation" (*Anglican* 261).

7. O'Faolain, I think, blurs election and sainthood in his claim that the fifteen-year-old Newman's confession of sinfulness "is to be accepted as a picture of reality only as one accepts the words of all men who strive after sainthood" (43).

8. This hostility extended even to his own family: "Many thanks for your congratulations about my Sister. I never can approve of a fellow like Mozley marrying—but if it must be, it is great happiness to find him brought nearer to me by his offence against monastic rule" (*LD* 5: 345). In a more private context he begrudged even this "happiness": "[B]e sure of this, that every one when he marries is a lost man—a clean good for nothing—I should not be surprised to be told that Mozley would not write another letter all his life" (*LD* 6: 18).

9. Blanco White, by contrast, saw Hurrell Froude's celibacy as a threat to himself and the Movement: "There are dark points in our University, there are men who strongly remind me of monks and inquisitors. . . . I am sorry that [Froude?] has become a practical Malthusian. I believe it would be good for him to add two or three individuals to the population of these kingdoms. He would have some one to drill in succession for a number of years, which, by giving vent to his hegemonic powers and tendencies, would keep down the bile, and make him happy till old age shall subdue him. . . . [A]s long as he remains fellow of Oriel, he will keep you all in hot water" (*LD* 3: 85).

10. The latest in a long line of critics to exploit this passage are Nicholls and Kerr in the Introduction to their anthology (6-7).

11. Bremond, in fact, attributes this need for distance to the intensity of Newman's visions: "[W]hen, in other respects, [people] have been familiarized with the fairest prospects of faith, they find it harder to resign themselves to this mediocrity. It is hard not to enter into a promised land when one has had full liberty to view that country on one of those clear days which reveal all the wonders of the scene" (268-69).

12. This stance moves dangerously close to the self-conscious posturing which we saw Newman attacking among the Evangelicals and trying to avoid in his own behavior.

13. It is this difference, I believe, which renders Kingsley the more conventionally and more dangerously sexist of the two.

14. Robbins offers a convenient summary: "'His friends,' said Wilfrid Ward, loved his very faults as one may love those of a fascinating woman.' His early dedication to celibacy and the ideal of virginity, and his annoyance at the marriage of disciples, together with the anguish in passages of the *Journals* and in Froude's *Remains* over unnamed sins, are used by Geoffrey Faber in *The Oxford Apostles* to suggest a homosexual strain in Tractarian friendships" (83). Faber himself,

more melodramatically, claims that Newman embraced virginity because "His sexual appetites must be somehow appeased. A negative abstinence was not enough. Only a positive ideal could subdue the beast within him" (222).

15. For an engaging summary of these, see Culler ("Introduction" viii–xii).

16. See too the divine compensation Newman offers those suffering from alienation and misunderstanding. Unlike men, God "knows what is in thee, all thy own peculiar feelings and thoughts, thy dispositions, and likings, thy strength and thy weakness. He views thee in thy day of rejoicing and thy day of sorrow. He sympathizes in thy hopes and thy temptations. He interests Himself in all the anxieties and remembrances, all the risings and fallings of thy spirit" (*PS* 3 [9]: 125).

17. Such efforts to generalize from his own experience do qualify Newman's frequent litanies of personal and ecclesiastical betrayals: To Froude in 1834, "Keble and Pusey (and Williams) take my part—else I am solus. Abused beyond measure by high and low—threatened with a pelting, and a prosecution—having anonymous letters—discountenanced by high Church and low Church. It should be you" (*LD* 4: 279). To Froude in 1836, "I suspect the Dissenters here are hating me with a perfect hatred—as the Psalmist says—and I know there are a large party of people who abominate me. . . . I have been told I am 'a marked man—there is no question of it.' I am getting callous, I believe—all this would have made me quite sick at one time—but somehow I wag on sluggishly" (*LD* 5: 190). To Pusey in 1838, "[W]hat warrant have I for putting myself so forward against the world? . . . I have nothing to appeal to in justification, but my feeling that I am in the main right in my opinions. . . . My sole comfort has been that my Bishop has not spoken against me. . . . Yet, I say it sorrowfully, though you are the only person I say it to, he has never been my *friend*—he has never supported me. . . . His kindness to me, which has always been great, is from the kindness of his nature" (*LD* 6: 307).

18. The autobiographical associations of this passage are also explored by Sr. Julia of the Trinity (55–60).

19. See Harrold: "Like Newman and Hurrell Froude, these two [saints] were great in friendship, and at one in having a 'profound sense of the world's nothingness'" (*Newman* 229).

20. That this was a long cherished idea of Newman's is evident from the 1826 essay on miracles: "The power of displaying them is, according to the Scripture narrative, intrusted to certain individuals, who stand forward as their interpreters, giving them a voice and language, and a dignity demanding our regard; who set them forth as evidences of the greatest moral ends, a Revelation from God" (*Mir.* 18). Newman's high standards provoke a grudging admiration even from Geoffrey Faber. Accounting for Newman's limited sense of humor, he asks, "What is humour, after all, but a means of coming to terms with our own imperfections and with the imperfections of others? Newman's whole strength lay in his refusal to come to terms with imperfection" (381).

21. The passage continues with an unflattering comparison to the secular replacement being offered: "This Christian idea Lord Brougham has borrowed for his new Pantheon, which is equally various in all attributes and appendages of mind, with this one characteristic in all its specimens,—the pursuit of Knowl-

edge. . . . Nothing comes amiss to this author; saints and sinners, the precious and the vile, are torn from their proper homes and recklessly thrown together under this category of Knowledge. . . . Milton could have helped him to some angelic personages, as patrons and guardians of his intellectual temple, who of old time, before faith had birth, 'Apart sat on a hill retired / In thoughts more elevate, and reasoned high / Of providence, foreknowledge, will, and fate'" (*DA* 288, 290). I will argue later that Newman's spiritual hierarchy may have more parallels with Milton's diabolical one than he cares to admit.

22. Buried within that self-acknowledged manifesto of the via media, the *Prophetical Office,* several passages celebrate an individual faith approaching inner-light Protestantism, a faith which defines the church more than it is defined by it: "Without some portion of that Divine Philosophy which bids us consider 'the kingdom of God' to be 'within us,' and which . . . assimilates to itself all that is around us, . . . the Church Catholic anywhere, or at any time, Primitive, Roman, or Reformed, is but a name" (*PO* 338).

23. Edwin Abbott offers a perceptive, though (as always) prejudiced, analysis of Newman's intense idealization of his dying friend (*Anglican* 1: 170-77). But Gavin White notes that both Newman and Froude were toying with India at the time as a possible refuge for the Movement (268-69).

24. The same idea is echoed in the *Development:* "Saints are often characterized by acts which are no pattern for others; and the most gifted men are, by reason of their very gifts, sometimes led into fatal inadvertences" (175).

25. When combined with his vision of parallel realms, the mountain offers the elect a foretaste of heaven on earth: "[H]oly souls . . . have risen with Christ, and they are like persons who have climbed a mountain and are reposing at the top. All is noise and tumult, mist and darkness at its foot; but on the mountain's top it is so very still, so very calm and serene, so pure, so clear, so bright, so heavenly, that to their sensations it is as if the din of earth did not sound below, and shadows and gloom were no where to be found" (*PS* 6 [15]: 209).

26. In chapter 5 we visited "the everlasting mountains, grow[ing] as we recede from them." In chapter 7 we will explore "the mountains of truth" scaled only by genius.

27. The passage continues, "University men attend—I cannot say I am sorry—but I would do any thing I could to keep them from being excited" (*LD* 6: 275). According to Thomas Mozley: "[H]e repeatedly maintained that for a parish priest to publish his addresses to his flock was as shocking as it would be for a man to publish his conversations with his wife and children" (1: 136-37). As Chadwick describes the scene, "The church had few parishioners in Oxford, and they not likely to understand what he said. . . . [S]ome fell asleep. But slowly the special gifts came clear to a growing group of sensitive Oxford minds. . . . As he grew famous, Oxford tutors started . . . discouraging young men from going to hear, and so encouraged them to go" (*Newman* 18).

28. Note that in his early ministrations to the dying girl, Newman had compared himself to Paul in Galatians.

29. John's "hard-hearted" response testifies that his own consternation has rendered him incapable of counseling or consoling others: "Your letter and

_____'s to you, would have brought me to many tears unless I had so hard a heart. You must take what I do in faith at least; if not, I fear I cannot find a better way of consoling you. . . . If others, whom I am pierced to think about, because I cannot help them, suffer, shall not I suffer in my own way?" (Moz. 2: 377). The whole episode offers an ironic parallel to that described in his lecture on university preaching within the *Idea*. There, at the conclusion of the service, the preacher "resumes himself, and comes to us in the gifts and associations which attach to his person. He knows his sheep, and they know him; and it is this direct bearing of the teacher on the taught . . . which is his strength and influence when he addresses them" (344).

30. Earlier, O'Leary claims that Newman's insistence on ontology blinds him to the young Luther's realization that "such an anthropology of substance, habits and qualities has no validity for our existence before God" (155).

31. See Brilioth's analysis of these same passages (*Anglican* 286-89). Sheridan quotes an unpublished college paper claiming that justification "is irresistible . . . because it is *interior* to the will itself: . . . 'when God imparts *a will*, . . . it is not a *wish* merely that He imparts,—not a wishing mind, but a willing soul'" (47-48). Sheridan also quotes Newman's later translation from Athanasius: Christ "was not first man and then became God, but He was God and then became man, and that in order to make us gods" (225). Chadwick notes that "Pusey almost *feels* the individual's incorporation in the Body [of Christ]. His language is more mystical . . . than the language of any other Tractarian" (*Mind* 48). Pusey's sermons, however, always achieve the self-transcendence enjoined by Augustine.

CHAPTER 7

1. Bremond continues that it is only "by an irresistible association he immediately regards each of these commands or prohibitions as the infallible expression of the will of God in Three Persons, of the Incarnate Word" (334).

2. These conjectures recapitulate those from an earlier university sermon already cited in chapter 2: "[L]ove of the great Object of Faith, . . . fear of the risk of slighting or missing what may really come from Him; . . . these are the feelings which make us think evidence sufficient, which falls short of a proof in itself" (*US* [10]: 193).

3. These critics fragment even Feuerbach's core of Romantic subjectivity. For Faber, "psychology lies between us and [the Victorians]. We cannot help looking for those animal roots. And though we may declare to ourselves that the origin of a sentiment has nothing to do with its value, the very terminology in which we are obliged to speak of it seems often to imply a sneer at its pretensions. Let us try to keep our language clear of these question-begging pretensions" (218). As his other quotations have already made clear, Faber kept his own advice very imperfectly. Robert Pattison remarks: "It would be easy to find psychological explanations for the apparently self-destructive way in which Newman ruthlessly extracted defeat from every occasion for victory. But psychology is only another manifestation of the liberal spirit against which Newman battled all his life, and it seems

only fair to his memory to explain his failure on his own terms, as a failure of his own intellectual and moral choosing" (*Dissent* 52–53). Since I have been arguing that Newman remains complicit with the thought of his age, I consider myself under no such restraint. I might suggest that Pattison's last sentence brings in psychology through the back door—as does his later summary from the same source: "Everything Newman held true depends on the unprovable assumption that subjective human instincts have objective metaphysical correlatives. Is there a God? Yes, because he complements the lonely soul" (166). If this, as Pattison claims, constitutes Scholasticism, then it would be hard to deny the same label to Schleiermacher's feeling of total dependency. Drew Morgan suggests that the "Seven Notes" of Newman's *Development* constitute their own hermeneutics of suspicion (241).

4. Robbins quotes a passage from his late *Letter to the Duke of Norfolk* in which he acknowledges that for moderns conscience is "a twist in the mind of primitive man, a guilt notion, and imagination, an irresponsible element in a network of cause and effect" (132).

5. Any refusal to privilege Newman's claims should not, I admit, automatically privilege those of his skeptical successors. The claim, to take an analogous example, that Augustine's intensely overdetermined relations with his mother complicate his account of his conversion seems to me irrefutable. The stronger claim that these relations explain away his conversion seems a leap of faith less warranted than Augustine's own. In the same way, we cannot stand in a position to know either the source of Newman's conscience or the provenance of his visions of that source.

6. Margaret Grennan derives a similar conclusion from the heroine's arguments in *Callista:* "You may tell me that this dictate [of conscience] is a mere law of my nature, as to joy or to grieve. I cannot understand this. No, it is the echo of a person speaking to me" (quoted in Grennan 101). Reardon argues that the thrust of Newman's argument from conscience is less ontological than phenomenological: "His claim is that the nature and implications of the moral consciousness itself are at once and essentially religious" ("Psychology" 321). This claim is further worked out by Graham Shute, and by Harry Klocker (150–51). Reardon's reading of Newman, however, brings him dangerously close to the Kantian postulate that religion is at once and essentially moral.

7. As Coulson puts it, "certitude is, for him, the reward, not the pre-condition of faith. . . . [H]e held that an assent to religious objects, as if they were objects of sight was not directly available for the asking, so to speak, but was the privilege of a devout nation only" (40).

8. This appeal to mystery leaves itself vulnerable to René Wellek's criticism of Coleridge for letting religion in through the back door: Kant's "doctrines on the limits of our knowing power become a sort of back-door through which the whole of traditional theology is admitted. . . . At length, [Coleridge] seduced the struggling spirit to acquiesce in immediate knowledge and faith, he lured it to enjoy a mere feeling of mystery and to give up the labor of thinking penetration into problems. . . . He made a philosophy out of this incapacity" (115, 134). More pragmatically, however, I am only following Stanley Fish's premise in *Do-*

ing What Comes Naturally, that anyone claiming to escape from ideology into truth (even with a small "t") is only replacing one ideology with another (14–25).

9. To his mother, Newman does acknowledge a secondary role for reason, but only a restorative one: "Listen to my theory. As each individual has certain instincts of right and wrong, antecedently to reasoning, on which he acts and rightly so, which perverse reasoning may supplant, which then can hardly be regained, but, if regained, will be regained from a different source, from reasoning, not from nature" (*LD* 2: 130). He goes on to extrapolate from a personal to a collective conscience. God's revelations "are transmitted as 'the wisdom of our ancestors.' . . . [M]any of the generations, through which they are transmitted, are unable to prove them, but hold them either from pious and honest feeling (it may be) or from bigotry or from prejudice. . . . Keble's book is full of such truths; which any Cambridge man might refute with the greatest ease" (130–31). This conjecture softens Newman's allegations in this same letter that the Anglican Church depended on such bigotry and prejudice.

10. For Coleridge, God's moral claims arise here as a Kantian extrapolation from the parity necessary for interpersonal relations. Though Newman saw this attempt to "derive" God's voice as more evidence of Coleridge's wanton speculation, Reardon offers a more balanced summary of the interplay of reason and responsibility in Coleridge's thought: "Coleridge is a religious man in the process of thinking out his faith, and although the relationship between faith and speculative thought may defy precise formulation, in the full context of a living experience the problem assumes a different aspect. Coleridge's religious philosophy is in this sense a practical one" (*Coleridge* 72). Several decades earlier, D. G. James wrote that in "the 'reason' as Coleridge upheld it, . . . the truths it discovers are not the discovery, if that were possible, of a curious intellect, but of a life which is being lived and which is seeking increasing fulfillment" (201).

11. Contemporary letters constantly translate this belief into personal advice: to Henry Wilberforce: "[W]ith what comfort, or rather how without apprehension, can you resign yourself night after night to the unconscious and helpless state of sleep, without being able to show good works, done in the course of the day, as an evidence to yourself of your heart being right with God?" (*LD* 3:14); to Ryder: "I certainly think you too young to marry. . . . [Y]ou have been just swayed by two pathe [Gr.] to and fro, indolence and love,—you yourself, the proper *you,* having no power or will of your own.—Do you know yourself enough?" (*LD* 3: 70); to Henry Wilberforce again: "Aut Caesar aut nullus is a bad maxim; and be sure of this, that inactivity is the very reason of temptation; fill your mind with manly objects, and all evil spirits will leave it. . . . [I]t seems a sensible thing for a conscience-stricken sinner to inflict some penance on himself as a continual humiliation" (*LD* 3: 106); to Ryder: "I considered you under (what may be called) a ceremonial uncleanness, in not having presented yourself fully for examination—and therefore (if it could be avoided) ought not for the look of the thing travel" (*LD* 3: 124); and yet again to Henry Wilberforce: "You must have more work, responsibility and anxiety, if you are to be worth any thing. And next I fear the ladies of the house will make you idle. You will be lounging and idling with them all day" (*LD* 3: 247).

12. Hill (189) quotes a passage from the 1837 essay "The Fall of De la Mennais," which puts into his mouth an extreme form of Newman's eventual theory: "They who look at Antiquity as supplying the rule of faith, do not believe in the possibility of any substantial increase in religious knowledge; but the Romanist believes in a standing organ of Revelation, like the series of Jewish prophets, unfolding from time to time fresh and fresh truths from the abyss of the divine counsels" (*Ess.* 1: 159).

13. It is in this context that Newman makes the unusually Protestant gesture, analyzed in chapter 6 (note 22), of entrusting the life and fortunes of the Church to this inner direction: "Without some portion of that Divine Philosophy which bids us consider 'the kingdom of God' to be 'within us,' . . . the Church Catholic anywhere, or at any time, Primitive, Roman, or Reformed, is but a name" (*PO* 338). While carefully specifying the correct attitude and spiritual discipline, Newman does not specify where this spiritual guidance will lead either Church or individual.

14. In an even later sermon, the cyclical "holy seasons" of Patristic life contribute to a more individual development, a Romantic, almost Blakean, vortex which subsumes repetition within organic growth: "I do not say [a religious man] need recollect any definite season when he turned to God and gave up the service of sin and Satan; but in one sense every season, every year is such a time of turning. I mean, he ever has experience, just as if he had hitherto been living to the world, of a continual conversion; he is ever taking advantage of holy seasons and new providences, and beginning again. . . . [I]n the course of years a religious person finds that a mysterious unseen influence has been upon him and has changed him" (*SD* [23]: 349-50). Coming from his last days in the Anglican Church, this assurance of a development both organic and teleological is itself both impressive and essential. For Blake's vortices, see Abrams (*Natural* 259-61).

15. For Prickett, "The idea that living within a particular set of conditions in some way cramps our style and limits us is a fundamental philosophic error, Newman argues. It perpetuates the Lockean fallacy of supposing a 'sensorium,' or, crudely, a 'watcher' inside the head who is somehow separate from the sense which feeds him with partial and imperfect data. This simply puts off the problem of consciousness within the machine in a kind of infinite regress" (*Romanticism* 180).

16. D. G. James takes much of this imagery as signalling a quintessentially Catholic acceptance of divine inscrutability: "It is not for us to try, even if we could hope to be successful, to wrest light from a world from which we are shut out. . . . This world is indeed dark; but so much light has the Divine wisdom seen right to allow to enter into it" (223). Newman's own confrontation with this darkness seems to me far more anguished than James implies here.

17. After a subtle exploration of this waffling as reflexive and self-critical, Jost must admit: "Love, it is fair to say, does not get clearly defined in this passage" (60-61). Livingston is blunter: "Many of Newman's contemporaries found this aspect of his argument as unconvincing as we do today" (*Modern* 141n).

18. Newman's passage, probably also drawing on Thucydides, precedes Matthew Arnold by over ten years. This dating assumes, on internal evidence, that

Arnold wrote the poem on his honeymoon. In a footnote, Robert Pattison also traces this image back to Gibbon and to the Patristic Church historian Socrates Scholasticus (*Dissent* 116n). Culler finds further references in Thomas Arnold, Clough, and Carlyle (*Victorian* 3).

19. David Shaw summarizes the dilemma: "If faith is a presumptive judgment and if its propositions are performative, how can faith be grounded in a truth that is antecedent to a believer's affirmation of it?" (240).

20. See, for example, Carlyle's demurral at including Jesus among his cadre of heroes: "[A] noblest godlike Form of Man,—is not that the germ of Christianity itself? The greatest of all Heroes is One—whom we do not name here! Let sacred silence meditate that sacred matter" (Lecture 1 of *Heroes, Hero-Worship, and the Heroic in History*).

21. The same invidious comparison appears in a poem, entitled "The Apostolic Fathers," sent to his mother from the Hermes in December 1832:

> Sequel of holy Paul! more favoured ye
> Than the world-harassed Saint, from earliest youth
> Blest in the arms and by the voice of Truth.
>
> (*LD* 3: 161)

Evident here is another implied parallel with Newman's scripting of his own childhood. Elsewhere he works to salvage Paul by suggesting that his former life undermined evangelical claims that conversions must entail a total transformation: "Here is no ease, no self-indulgent habits, no wilful sin against the light" (*PS* 2 [9]: 104). Thus Paul's former life can win the same saving reprimand that Newman's "willfulness" won him in Sicily.

22. He also invokes Paul to Rickards in the course of making a less-than-convincing rationale for Tractarian militancy: "We have nothing to do with politics, i.e. with party politics—for I suppose in one sense St Paul was political" (*LD* 4: 59).

23. In still another sermon this pollution even denies them access to the "Temple" of full spirituality: "Men of energetic minds and talents for action are called to a life of trouble; they are the compensations and antagonists of the world's evils; still let them never forget their place; they are men of war, and we war that we may obtain peace. They are but . . . soldiers in the open field, not builders of the Temple" (*PS* 2 [28]: 351-52).

24. One sermon does acknowledge a need for some criteria to distinguish self-actualization from apostasy: "Christian Zeal . . . renounces all hope of hastening [Christ's] coming, all desire of intruding upon His work. . . . It plans no intrigues; it recognizes no parties; it relies on no arm of flesh. . . . It acts according to God's will, this time or that, as it comes, boldly and promptly; yet letting each act stand by itself. . . . In a word, Christian Zeal is not political" (*PS* 2 [31]: 389). Newman's earliest expressions of such zeal, while not overtly political, are engagingly ambitious. To Rickards in 1826, he exults, "my spirits most happily rise at the prospect of danger, trial, or any call upon me for unusual exertion—and as I came outside the Southampton coach to Oxford, I felt as if I could have

rooted up St Mary's spire and kicked down the Radcliffe" (*LD* 1: 304). And in 1830 he was already justifying to Jemima his effort to pack the Evangelical Church Missionary Society with high-churchmen: "Now, if it be a silly thing, why, I am exposing myself, and doing what is unsafe—But one must run risks to do good, and fortune favors the bold—so I must hug myself, if no one else will hug me" (*LD* 2: 193).

25. Edwin Abbott likens Newman's new militancy to the unpremeditated violence of Coleridge's Hamlet: "[B]oth saw so many aspects of a question . . . that they could never take any important action except with the eyes of the reason momentarily closed. Then, when they opened them again, . . . [they] felt a passionate necessity . . . to discern a special Providence in [the event.] . . . [H]aving so far done violence to his nature as to plunge into the conflict, such a one will often be more logically austere, more consistently unkind, sometimes even more insolently aggressive, than a . . . professional controversialist" (*Anglican* 1: 300, 311). Newsome cites in H. Scott Holland's 1914 *Bundle of Memories* an even earlier description of the same dilemma: a "spiritual fastidiousness, that makes him conscious always of the personal element itself, to a degree that weakens action" ("Evangelical" 21). To me, the situation itself released Newman's otherwise conflicted urge to act.

26. The care with which he separated his sermons from his controversial works is evident in his fretful letter to Jemima on the publication of the sixth volume: "I am anxious about it; it will be the most doctrinal set [of sermons] I have published, and that on the subject of the Eucharist. I should be sorry to get my sermons into the disfavour which attends some of my writings; but I must take my chance" (Moz. 2: 315).

27. For such revisionist readings, see in particular the books by David Riede (passim) and Janice Carlisle (43–79).

28. Some of these strategies, I would suggest, address the problem Jost raises concerning Newman's rhetoric, i.e., "that his elevation of the importance of 'antecedent probabilities and considerations' in informal inference is intrinsically conservative and even reactionary" (106). Yet Basil Willey claims that in him, "some of the deepened insights of the age found utterance: insights none the less 'advanced' because of their 'reactionary' colouring" (74). Thomas also makes extensive reference to Newman's rhetoric, but for him the term seems to encompass almost any instance of logical fallacy, emotional appeal, contemporary application, or self-reference.

29. On Newman's use of the "view," see Culler (*Imperial* 196–97). Jost (116–21) reinterprets views as rhetorical *topoi,* and Katherine Tillman (605–7) also treats his educational program for formulating and breaking down preliminary hypotheses.

30. The passage continues, "[Yet never] could I have even cut off a Puritan's ears, and I think the sight of a Spanish *auto-da-fé* would have been the death of me." These last two humorous disclaimers fail to mitigate either the ferocious antagonism of his earlier examples or the present relish with which he cites them. At best they throw up the same rhetorical smoke-screen as this already-quoted

protestation: "[I]n spite of what you say . . . I am especially moderate in Church matters. . . . [I]f there is one merit I have, it is extreme moderation" (*LD* 4: 232).

31. Such advice sounds disconcertingly like that given fifty years later by Ko-Ko, the newly appointed Lord High Executioner in *The Mikado*. After entering with his own "list / Of society offenders who might well be underground," he concludes his patter song: "But it really doesn't matter whom you put upon the list, / For they'd none of 'em be missed—they'd none of 'em be missed!"

32. He finds a similar value even in the works of opponents. He writes to Bowden: "I have heard from Manning, who fears Mr. Osburn [author of *Doctrinal errors of the apostolical and early Fathers*. London, 1835] and the Record are doing harm. Yet I hardly can think so—so that they rouse people to think, it is every thing" (*LD* 5: 345). Edwin Abbott condescendingly describes the strategy as one "known in commerce as 'haggling'—of asking more than one hopes to get in order to get more than one's commercial adversary expects to give" (1: 295).

33. If not kind, the conduct is certainly *in* kind. In private, at least, Newman admits that taking it is a lot harder than dishing it out: "I suspect that the Dissenters here are hating me with a perfect hatred—as the Psalmist says. . . . Indeed I have been told I am 'a marked man—there is no question of it'" (*LD* 5: 190).

34. Newman thus attributes his self-pity to a difficulty with self-definition: "[W]hen others resist . . . I feel a sort of bad conscience and disgust with what I have done" (*LD* 6: 353).

35. D. G. James (216) cites a passage from Newman's 1859 essay on St. Chrysostom justifying his own practice: The "Ancient Saints . . . do not write a *summa theologiae*, or draw out a *catena*, or pursue a single thesis through the stages of a scholastic disputation. They wrote for the occasion, and seldom on a carefully-digested plan" (*HS* 2: 223).

36. This passage anticipates one in the *Idea*, but the differences between them are more significant than the similarities: "[T]he multiplicity of external objects, which [sailors] have encountered, forms no symmetrical and consistent picture upon their imagination; they see the tapestry of human life, as it were on the wrong side, and it tells no story. . . . [T]hey gaze on Pompey's Pillar, or on the Andes; and nothing which meets them . . . has a history or a promise. Every thing . . . comes and goes in its turn, like the shifting scenes of a show, which leave the spectator where he was. . . . Such is mere acquisition . . . no one would dream of calling it philosophy" (122). Both of Newman's sailors merely acquire experience; both fail to appreciate it; but they lack different things. The one in the *Idea*, lacking a disciplined intellect, cannot correlate this present experience with either past or future. The sailor of the earlier letter lacks an actual controversy for which he can gather up his experiences like weapons, lacks an occasion which compels him to use them. See also Walter Jost's analysis (1-2) of a similar passage in the 1839 "Theology of St. Ignatius."

37. Mitchell invokes both aesthetic and philosophical parallels to pin down (and tone down) Newman's claims for this faculty: "There is, after all, nothing

controversial in the claim that innate sensitivity and rigorous training are required for the discovery and recognition of certain truths. . . . It may call for a certain 'temper of mind' which not everyone has" (245). Such qualification, however, seems to slight the insistence of Newman's imagery on the ineffable, unrepeatable, almost unrecognizable nature of religious evidence; as Walter Jost defines it, "Implicit reason is thus often hidden, subtle, complex, personal" (39). Newman's passage echoes the portrait of the Apostolic Tradition in the *Prophetical Office,* but where that tradition rekindled fading vestiges of a numinous past, the course of this visionary explorer is not just uncharted but unknowable both in its paths and in its ultimate destination.

38. The *Prophetical Office* includes such genius with other forms of intuitive knowledge. In this context, the mountainous terrain of the quest appears more daunting: "Truth is struck out in the course of life. Common sense, chance, moral perception, genius, the great instruments in the discovery of principles, do not reason. The discoverers have no arguments, no grounds; they see the Truth, but they do not know how they see it; and if at any time they attempt to prove it, it is as much a matter of experiment with them, as if they had to find a road to a distant mountain which they see with the eye, and they get entangled, embarrassed, and perhaps overthrown in the superfluous endeavour" (296). See also D. G. James (189).

39. Christ's tender regard for such individuality Newman prizes over all other blessings: "[T]he most winning property of our Saviour's mercy . . . is its dependence on time and place, person and circumstance; in other words, its tender discrimination. It regards and consults for each individual as he comes before it" (*PS* 3 [9]: 120).

40. The sentence ends with the portentous addition, "—till, that is, the event confirms it." Exactly what kind of confirmation would convince the multitude or what kind of event would suffice is left carefully undefined. We must remember, however, that Newman's quester sees himself as discovering realities, even if he may seem to be creating them as he goes along. In any case, he knows himself justified by God's affirmation of his quest, though it often remains an affirmation which he alone can perceive. Apart from the Augustan balance of his cadences, Newman's analogy between aesthetic and spiritual inspiration and his insistence on their common indeterminacy could both find a home in Schelling: "Each artist is accordingly able to produce only so much as the perpetual conception of his own being is bound up in God. Now the more he already perceives the universe in this manner, the more organically he proceeds" (cited in Engell 320). Newman's analogy remains, if anything, too radical for the later Coleridge, with his firsthand experience of human frailty.

41. Like Newman's other exemplars, Patristic and modern, the Teacher has so far internalized the visionary universe he inhabits that he cannot articulate or defend it: "[T]he gifted individual whom we have imagined, will of all men be least able (as such) to defend his own views, inasmuch as he takes no external survey of himself. . . . The longer any one has persevered in the practice of virtue, the less likely is he to recollect how he began it. . . . He holds the whole assemblage of

moral notions almost as so many collateral and self-evident facts. Hence it is that some of the most deeply-exercised and variously gifted Christians, when they proceed to write or speak upon Religion, either fail altogether, or cannot be understood except on an attentive study" (*US* [5]: 83–84). Unlike Newman's more passive visionaries, however, the Teacher possesses a more active genius, one which Newman is again not afraid to compare with its aesthetic counterpart: "[I]t is considered the highest of gifts to possess an intuitive knowledge of the beautiful in art, or the effective in action, without reasoning or investigating; that this, in fact, is *genius;* and that they who have a corresponding insight into moral truth . . . have reached that especial perfection in the spiritual part of their nature, which is so rarely found and so greatly prized among the intellectual endowments of the soul" (84). A sermon entitled "The Self-Wise Enquirer" describes the drift toward heresy of one differently "circumstanced" than the Teacher, one "in whom intellectual power is fearfully unfolded amid the neglect of moral truth" (*PS* 1 [17]: 222).

42. The Teacher's militancy arises partly from within, partly from his hostile audience, partly from the goal Newman has set for him, and partly from the empathy invoked in us, the congregation. The eclectic sources of his power thus deflect any suspicions that he is using it solely to imprint himself upon his followers: "[W]e must invest our Teacher with a certain gift of power, that he may be feared. But even then . . . he is, from the nature of the case, thrown upon his personal resources . . . ; for it is plain that he cannot commit his charge to others as his representatives, and be translated (as it were), and circulated through the world, till he has made others like himself" (*US* [5]: 86–87). The danger of self-idolatry is further rendered moot because the Teacher can only reenact the parable of the Sower: "Some hearers of it had their conscience stirred for a while, and many were affected by the awful simplicity of the Great Teacher; but the proud and sensual were irritated into opposition; the philosophic considered His doctrines strange and chimerical; the multitude followed for a time in senseless wonder, and then suddenly abandoned an apparently falling cause. For in truth what was the task of an Apostle, but to raise the dead?" (87).

43. Newman goes on to admit his own involvement with this issue: "How grand all this is and how con[ducive] to indolence and self-indulgence.—I shall turn philosopher—rail at the world at large and be content with a few friends who know me" (*LD* 2: 255). But his hunger for some recognition from posterity, while it can be indefinitely deferred, cannot be completely stifled: "Say that [a member of the elect] is alone, his faith counted a dream, and his efforts to do good a folly, what then? He knows . . . present opinions are the accident of the day, and that they will fall as they have risen. . . . He can bear in faith to wait five hundred years, to wait for an era long, long after he has mouldered into dust" (*PS* 3 [17]: 249–50).

44. As the passage continues, figures of past saints and prophets intervene within Newman's characteristic dyad of self and Christ: "A few highly-endowed men will rescue the world for centuries to come. Before now even one man [Athanasius (Newman's note)] has impressed an image on the Church, which,

through God's mercy, shall not be effaced while time lasts. Such men, like the Prophet, are placed upon their watch-tower, and light their beacons on the heights. Each receives and transmits the sacred flame, trimming it in rivalry of his predecessor, and fully purposed to send it on as bright as it has reached him" (*US* [5]: 97). The introduction of Athanasius, Newman's spiritual mentor, and the frank admission of a "rivalry" both point toward a spiritual anxiety of influence. Certainly the whole sermon, far more daring in its claims than anything in Athanasius, establishes Newman as a "strong" prophet, usurping his predecessor's place in the very act of imitation.

45. How difficult such change would be he acknowledges in a critique of Froude's writings: "You send home flaming papers . . . but after all I fall back to what I said last year. . . . Not that it is not right (very right) to accustom men's imagination to the prospect of changes, but they cannot *realize the arguments*— they are quite beyond them" (*LD* 4: 274).

46. In his "Oxford Malignants" essay, Thomas Arnold dismisses Tractarianism in similar terms as "the fanaticism of mere foolery. A dress, a ritual, a name, a ceremony;—a technical phraseology;—the superstition of a priesthood without its power;—the form of Episcopal government, without the substance" (235). Brilioth suggests that "To Newman, the *via media* was his controversial stronghold in the discussion with Romanism, a stronghold which he used his singular powers to fortify. To Keble, Isaac Williams, and others, the *via media* was an obvious reality" (*Evangelicalism* 58).

47. Though I know from personal correspondence that David DeLaura remains dubious about the weight I give these metaphors, DeLaura posits similar powers of self-instantiation for one of Newman's books: "[T]he *Apologia* . . . does make its way, as any prophetic book must in the modern world, on its own and literarily; it *creates* its own authority and authenticity" (496).

48. These claims are echoed in the passage already quoted from Cunningham (243): "metaphor is reality, becomes reality," but Newman is addressing Scripture, the only text from which, according to Newman, "we can argue freely" (*PO* 291). See also similar parallels supporting a slightly different point in D. G. James (192–93), and Wright's comment that Newman brings "Romantic criteria of originality and unity" to bear on Scripture: "It is this same Romantic tradition, of course, which lies behind Heidegger, the New Hermeneutic, and later postliberal arguments that particular uses of language reconstitute the world" (185).

49. The first sentence and the title of this sermon, "Intercession," both suggest that the influence Newman enjoins on us comes through prayer and not some more active intervention.

50. Such visions are surprisingly frequent even in the early sermons: "We are the elect of God, and have entrance 'though the gates into the' heavenly 'City,' while we 'do His commandments.' . . . His confidential servants . . . are the real agents in the various providences which occur in the history of nations, though overlooked by their annalists and sages. They bring before him the temporal wants of men, witnessing His marvelous doings with the barley loaves and fishes. . . . And, when He brings trouble and distress upon a sinful people, they

have truest knowledge of His will, . . . and while others praise the goodly stones and buildings of the external Temple, [they] have heard from Him in secret how the end shall be" (*PS* 2 [1]: 11-12).

CHAPTER 8

1. As late as the *Difficulties Felt by Anglicans* of 1850, according to Prickett, Newman's metaphor of the Church as a "sentient human being" continued to lure him into a similarly "Romantic shift of perspective. Just as Wordsworth . . . had answered his own question 'What is a Poem?' by defining the nature of a poet, so Newman answers his own question 'What is the Church?' by . . . shifting to the mind of the individual who is doing the imagining" ("Physiognomy" 271-72).

2. For McGann's complex categorization of "primary" and "secondary" works, see particularly his chapter, "Phases of English Romanticism," in *The Romantic Ideology* (107-18).

3. Rajan, for example, sets up the Romantics' supposedly novel claims for immanence as holdovers from the Enlightenment through which they tried intermittently to shield themselves from the modern realization that such claims were actually imposed upon an unreceptive universe—were constructs and not discoveries (13-16). See also Hamilton's attack on another critic's effort to undermine Romantic claims: "Siskin still replicates the literary, generic character of the writing he historicizes, and so still models a Romantic aesthetic redeploying itself through self-difference. There seems to be no escape from the Romantic circle embracing the critical idea" (17). Much less globally, Don Bialostosky praises Jonathan Arac's *critical genealogies,* working out of Wordsworth's Supplementary Essay to the 1815 Preface, as "showing how the disciplined study of poetry can set itself up as an iconoclastic center of power to oppose the power which Foucault sees in all civilized institutions" (412-19). Even more down to earth, L. J. Swingle suggests that "Perhaps the Romantics are confronted, not with a void to be filled, but rather with some sort of burden of presences—structures or pressures that loom over them, hindering free movement and hedging them in. . . . Romanticism has more to do with the state of mind that drives the romantic writer from one momentary infatuation toward another and that prevents him from committing himself completely to some particular ideology" (20, 34).

4. Clifford Siskin, for example, exposes Romantic "development [as] an all-encompassing formal strategy underpinning middle-class culture itself. . . . Thus a self-made mind, full of newly constructed depths, is an object of the new knowledge of those depths. . . . [B]y requiring and expecting unlimited development, it always opens deeper depths to surveillance" (12-13). See also McGann's reading of the *Rime of the Ancient Mariner:* "[T]he purpose of the poem is to 'lift [its more literal belief systems] to a higher point of view' whence they will be open to a critical, self-conscious, but sympathetic valuation. This 'higher point of view,' . . . is Coleridge's own system. . . . *What* that whole truth constitutes is (a) that

there is a whole truth which justifies and is the ground of all the fragments of the truth; and (b) that this whole truth is in a perpetual process of becoming" ("Meaning" 222).

5. Paul Privateer attempts to split the difference here by splitting Romanticism itself: "The first kind of romanticism can be characterized as a response consistent with bourgeois power; an ideology that inscribes the individual in terms of an absolute and autonomous self; a self that pursues its annihilation in terms of a higher, transcendental version of itself; a transcendental ego primarily homocentric, linear, and concentrist in its orientation. . . . [T]he second kind of romanticism also relies on the imagination and the instability of language and figuration but does so to undermine bourgeois control over what constitutes legitimate forms of the self" (225).

6. See for example Paul Hamilton: "Literature becomes in this way an ironic history of itself, inviting the corollary that the critic's literary history must be another version of the same. By unmasking the distinctive features of a literature, criticism participates in the same function by which literature propagates itself" (22). Lacoue-Labarthe and Nancy offer an intriguing vision of the Romantic project, not as surpassing or replacing older forms but as interpreting, reconstructing, complementing, supplementing them (110-13).

7. In this essay, to be sure, Culler distinguished this "Christian-humanist" tradition from both Romanticism and Utilitarianism, but, as Svaglic pointed out in a reply two issues later, these categories seemed rather too rigid even then, and with the renaissance in Romantic studies of the 1960s, they have come to seem even more so.

8. This may only state positively what McGann, speaking of Blake, puts negatively: Blake "was first and last a Christian, and his own work remained open—as it still remains open—to those clerical interpretations which survive in the valley of their saying, which make nothing happen beyond what has been established as possible or acceptable" ("Third" 98). I would hope to have shown that Newman's claims remain slightly less predictable.

9. In another sermon, he asks us to "Consider how such [holy] men show forth their light in a wicked world, yet unconsciously. Moses came down from the mount, and 'wist not that the skin of his face shown' as one who had held intercourse with God" (*PS* 1 [12]: 155–56). Alan Hill, however, quotes an 1838 article from *The British Critic* (24: 61–82) in which Newman accepts enough of the psychological premises in Keble's *Lectures on Poetry* to relax his normal strictures against reading fiction: "The human intellect needs some play, as it may be called, and Providence has mercifully consulted this peculiarity. . . . [T]he consequence of forbidding what God has not forbidden will be like stopping a safety-valve. . . . The irritation of the reason being denied its natural course, will strike inwards and fall upon vital parts" (23–24).

10. According to Culler, this precocious passage cultivates "that strange feeling which psychologists call *deja vu,* the feeling that we have been here before, that, although time has flowed under our feet and all is changed, yet also it is mysteriously the same" ("Remembrance" 67).

11. Realizing his hypocrisy, however, did not automatically cure it. The following year, as he contemplated standing for the Oriel Fellowship, he boasts to his aunt: "[M]y heart beats high at the thought that God is cutting away all ties which might bind me to the world and preparing me of that Kingdom of which perfect holiness is the characteristic glory" (*LD* 1: 116). By 1837 this reflexivity is more apologetic but no less intense. He concludes a long letter to Rogers, "What an egotistical letter this is!—as all mine are" (*LD* 6: 9). And again in 1844: "[N]ow what a deal I have said about myself! I wonder how many I's are in this letter" (Moz. 2: 399).

12. Advising his assistant, R. F. Wilson, Newman laments, "I am continually very cold and unimpressed, and very painful it is; but what can be done?" (*LD* 4: 281).

13. O'Faolain continues: "The next world revolved around him; but that it was the next and not this was his salvation, since his doubts about his soul's future induced humility in his body's present, a check which he fully needed, since he had an abundance of self-conceit" (77). Bremond describes much the same trait as portrayed by Newman himself in *Callista* (121-22): "This Agellius who dreams of a second baptism, equally efficacious, equally miraculous as the first, this delicate conscience which needs to be reassured even respecting its devotional impulses, this uneasiness which sees the shadow of a fault in the simple remembrance of past sins, and, on the other hand, that assured confidence—'I have never believed that Hell was reserved for me'—all this, I can say it with absolute conviction, draws to the life the sentiments of the author himself" (214).

14. For a good summary of his religious pilgrimage, see Thomas (80-87).

15. See this passage among others: "[A]n intellectual question may strike two minds very differently, may awaken in them distinct associations, may be invested by them in contrary characteristics, and lead them to opposite conclusions" (*GA* 196). On the issue of religious assent, which remains the book's focus, Newman's insistence on individual experience leads him to claim that only an early formation of the conscience can foster a "religious imagination" (*GA* 80).

16. To Pusey he offers examples of this psychological isolation: "Ask a dozen educated persons their respective reasons for the belief in a God?—or again their mode of reconciling St James and St Paul?—or again to analyze the peculiar beauty of a certain passage in Shakespeare or to criticize the character of Hamlet,—how triumphantly one might show . . . that St Paul was diametrically opposed to St James, that Hamlet's character was a mere extravagance!" (*LD* 5: 70).

17. The poem quoted is "Man's responsibility," later entitled "Substance and Shadow." Newman's isolation is made slightly less confining by the intensity of his own internal dialogues. In chapter 7 we examined his description of writing as conversation, but he uses similar terms to describe the spiritual life in general: "All the necessary exactness of our obedience, the anxiety about failing, the pain of self-denial, the watchfulness, the zeal, the self-chastisements which are required of us, as little interfere with this vision of faith, as if they were practiced by another, not by ourselves. We are two or three selves at once, in the wonderful structure of our minds, and can weep while we smile, and labour while we meditate" (*PS* 4 [9]: 147).

18. Elsewhere this depth is not just available to God but a measure of Jesus' omniscience: "[E]ven human philosophers or poets are obscure from the depth of their conceptions. What then must be the marvellous abyss of love and understanding in Him who, though partaker of our nature, is the Son of God?" (*PS* 3 [10]: 128).

19. Reardon specifically critiques the late-written *Grammar* for "maintaining that the illative sense . . . supplies 'no common measure between mind and mind.' . . . [W]hat Newman overlooks are the logical connections between individual reasoning . . . and the general reasoning of the race" (*Coleridge* 143). Curiously enough, Prickett reads the *Grammar* as acknowledging this very cultural dependence: "We can describe our 'form of life' as resting upon a network of interlocking certitudes which are analogous to our perceptions in that we reason with them rather than about them: they are, as it were, the groundwork on which our consciousness itself is based" (*Romanticism* 196).

20. Livingston notes that Huxley "held Newman to be 'the slipperiest sophist I have ever met with,' and thought Kingsley 'was entirely right about him'" (*Ethics* 3).

21. See J. M. Cameron ("Night" 101-2); and also Thomas Mozley: "[H]is carefulness to master the other side of the great question[s?] has suggested to some critics that his faith and his scepticism contended for the ascendancy on such equal conditions as to leave the issue sometimes doubtful" (1: 40).

22. See, however, the contrary premise within the last university sermon: "As God is one, so the impression which He gives us of Himself is one; it is not a thing of parts. . . . When we pray, we pray, not to an assemblage of notions, or to a creed, but to One Individual Being" (*US* [15]: 330).

23. In Discourse VI of the *Idea,* Newman implicitly includes himself among those susceptible to such temptations: "[T]he first time the mind comes across the arguments and speculations of unbelievers, . . . and, as if waking from a dream, begins to realize to its imagination that there is now no such thing as law and the transgression of law, that sin is a phantom, and punishment a bugbear, . . . who will deny that the fruit of the tree of knowledge . . . has made it one of the gods, with a sense of expansion and elevation,—an intoxication in reality, still, so far as the subjective state of the mind goes, an illumination?" (119).

24. By 1835 he could claim astonishment at the enthusiasm with which Blanco White converted to Unitarianism: "Socinianism is no *new* thing to him, and to be in raptures about what he has known these 17 years, seems like insanity" (*LD* 5: 123). In 1825, however, he could still understand the fascination of doctrinal novelty.

25. Writing to Wood, he seems to find the fascination with new secular studies more deceptive but less dangerous: "What a strange feeling it is to have begun a new pursuit. . . . A new field is opened, and one has a variety of thoughts and views one never had before—and first is eager, and then checks the intention, to tell others all our new notions, about which they of course have no interest, if they can understand them. I do not wonder the acquisition of knowledge leads in so many instances to self confidence and arrogance—nor again to the utter depreciation of all pursuits and objects compared with that which has fascinated and

engrosses us,—which I suppose is the essence of narrow-mindedness and pedantry" (*LD* 3: 89).

26. Newman here clothes Milton with the mantle of his own Satan; for Newman, as for Blake, he "was of the Devil's party without knowing it."

27. Newman recalled the phrase when readying himself for battle on his return from Sicily; see the *Apologia* (44-43). For the structural and psychological implications of this allusion, see also Svaglic ("Structure" 448) and Colby (454).

28. Such inferences may seem only to establish the tenuousness of metaphorical extrapolation. The *Decline and Fall* is indeed most scathing in its attacks on the Patristic Church and the specifically Catholic institution which grows out of it. The book, however, contains another Rome—one of humane, rational stoicism—which Gibbon celebrates in its unequal struggle against what he called "barbarism and religion" (7: 321).

29. Cameron continues with a quotation from a then-unpublished letter of 1887 at the Oratory: "It will not be surprising if the sensitive or the melancholy should find that the argument has cast them 'into a wild deserted hopeless region'" ("Night" 106).

30. Riede is here following Frederick Garber. As we shall see, Valerie Pitt attributes this attraction to Newman's "habit of making a drama out of a spiritual crisis" (18). Father Ryder suggests that "he could have admired Byron heartily if his moral disapprobation had allowed him" (quoted in W. Ward 2: 354).

31. Newman notes that Augustine, moved by the preaching of St. Ambrose during a particularly anguished stage in his conversion, "began to eye and muse upon the great bishop of Milan more and more, and tried in vain to penetrate his secret heart, and to ascertain the thoughts and feelings which swayed him. He felt he did not understand him" (*HS* 2: 148). In the postscript to a letter of 19 May 1838 to Henry Wilberforce, Newman adds, "Rogers well suggests that St Aug's account of St Ambrose's conduct to him, (sitting still and reading a book) is a remarkable and happy specimen . . . of the Catholic mode of effecting conversions" (*LD* 6: 246).

32.

> His heart was form'd for softness—warp'd to wrong;
> Betray'd too early, and beguiled too long;
> Each feeling pure—as falls the dropping dew
> Within the grot—like that had harden'd too.
> (3.662)

33.

> My sole resources in the path I trod
> Were these—my bark, my sword, my love, my God!
> The last I left in youth!—he leaves me now—
> And Man but works his will to lay me low.
> (2.475)

34. This insistence on imaginative identification underlies Newman's claim

faith, an obeying prior to reason, and *proving* its reasonableness by making experiment of it—a casting of heart and mind into the system, and investigating the truths by practice" (*LD* 5: 196).

35. Four months later, nursing his former college roommate Bowden through the terminal stages of tuberculosis, he draws a parallel between physical and psychological sickness: "To show that [my religious doubts] may possibly be otherwise explained, as you kindly do, is to *my feelings* like the conduct of a patient in a consumption and of his friends, who satisfactorily show that not one of his symptoms but may be referred to some cause short of the fatal malady, not one which involves the necessity of death. Yet a bystander or physician has a view, though he cannot out-argue; and the event justifies it" (*KC* 329). Here self-judgment, challenged by the judgment of friends, is reinforced by that of a disinterested third party.

36. While he was still secure within the via media, his indignant response to R. F. Wilson's accusations of bigotry can be archly tongue-in-cheek: "What do you mean by thinking me violent, and talking of my stern orthodoxy? . . . I am especially moderate in Church matters— . . . if there is one merit I have, it is extreme moderation" (*LD* 4: 232).

37. Tillman uses this passage to illustrate the flexible, self-correcting methodology built into Newman's educational ideal (606-8).

38. During his Tractarian period, responding to this challenge often seemed demeaning: to Samuel Rickards he "observe[s] it is *inconsistent* in her [Lady Winchelsea], calling me a Pelagian and yet spiritually-minded. Let her be quite sure that when I think a person a heretic, *I* shall never call him religious. A spiritually minded heretic may exist in the 'Protestant' world, but not in the Church" (*LD* 4: 315).

39. Even the year before his grand tour, Newman shows considerable sophistication in cautioning Keble against importing the figurative intensity of Hebrew psalms into the Anglican service: "That different places have different manners is proved by the (to us unaccountable) custom of many parts of the Primitive Eastern and African Churches, of violently applauding with hands and feet preachers that pleased them—yet I would not dare say that this was more than a custom, a peculiarity, which is strange to Northern sluggishness, but suitable to fervid minds. I think several of the Fathers notice it as a thing of course" (*LD* 2: 355).

40. Newman himself celebrates his absorption in his message: "[I]f what we preach is truth, it must be natural, it must be seasonable, it must be popular, it will make itself popular. . . . [T]hose who thought its voice strange and harsh at first, will wonder how they could ever so have deemed of sounds so musical and thrilling" (*PO* 70).

41. At one point, when he appropriates John 4 and the Samaritan woman's description of Jesus as "a man who told me all that I ever did," his self-conscious assumption of power even threatens to lapse into self-worship.

42. Even Culler's language here echoes the *locus classicus* of this phenomenon in *The Prelude:*

The days gone by
Return upon me almost from the dawn
Of life: the hiding places of man's power
Open; I would approach them, but they close.
I see by glimpses now; when age comes on,
May scarcely see at all.
          (12.277–82)

CHAPTER 9

1. O'Faolain goes on to quote an 1831 letter from Froude to Keble: "Things are still in a bad way down here [in Devon]. The labouring population, as well as the farmers, seem thoroughly indifferent to the welfare of the parsons and the squires" (177). On Newman's fearful and unsympathetic portrayal of the mob in *Callista,* see Levine (186–93).

2. The last ellipsis hides a particularly bald expression of Newman's intellectual contempt for women: "[N]ay and [my preaching] is attractive to those whom it would seem least likely to attract, I mean, women, (who do not reason, and only feel)" (*LD* 5: 32).

3. This passage conflates the letter in *LD* 5: 45 and a draft of it reprinted in David Newsome's "Justification" (49). Newsome's account of the fascinating three-way correspondence of Newman, Stephen, and Samuel Wilberforce (37–53) is fuller and more sympathetic to the low-church position than that in *Letters and Diaries.* Newsome's transcript reveals that the debate turns largely upon social class. Stephen argues that even at Athens, Paul set the pattern for evangelical preaching by appealing to the poor. Newman counters that in the gospels, even "publicans and harlots" display tasteful reverence toward Jesus.

4. Newman's objection to the Evangelicals is the same one he leveled at secularism: "I have spoken strongly . . . that that spirit tends to liberalism and Socinianism, I ever must. This is the reason for my strong language, my fear of a system of doctrine which eats out the heart of godliness" (*LD* 5: 32).

5. Despite Frank's allegations that John tried to rewrite the annual report of the Church Missionary Society and pack its rolls with high-church sympathizers, Stunt argues that Newman's hostility was primarily directed toward the radical wing of an already factionalized movement (65–74). Thomas adds that even "His strictures . . . would have been acceptable to moderate evangelicals within the Church of England, such as the Clapham sect, who were also appalled by the pentecostal excesses of such as Edward Irving" (20).

6. For a good discussion of the whole issue see David Newsome ("Evangelical" 11–30). Newsome agrees that "Evangelical scripturalism caused him more and more offense," but he offers a very different reason—"it betrayed an incipient rationalism" (21). He seems, however, to be referring here to the effort to educe doctrine from Scripture.

7. Chadwick points out that "the Evangelicals contributed perhaps more than

any other group to transforming the high and dry men into the new high church-men of the nineteenth century. There is a certain continuity of piety between the Evangelical movement and the Oxford Movement" (*Mind* 27).

8. While he goes on to construct a defense of traditionally received moral in-tuition, it hardly offsets his portrait of the Church party.

9. After exhaustive study, Thomas is forced to conclude that liberalism "be-came a catch-all for everything [Newman] saw as bad in the application of intel-lect to religion" (43).

10. For another perspective on the Hampden controversy, see R. W. Grieves (212-15).

11. Perhaps still smarting from this incident, Arnold attacks the "Oxford Ma-lignants" in similar terms for their treatment of Hampden: "[I]n such a proceed-ing we see nothing of Christian zeal, but much of the mingled fraud, and baseness, and cruelty, of fanatical persecution" (239).

12. Arnold's sudden death in 1842 left Newman still discomforted about the man and about his conduct toward him. Though eventually dissuaded, he consid-ered contributing to the Arnold Memorial: "I think there would be nothing in-consistent or hypocritical, . . . because I am conscious of having always done jus-tice to his great merits at Rugby—nay, having always defended him . . . as being more real and earnest than his friends; as having done a work when they are merely talkers. I think I never spoke harshly of him except on the occasion [at Rome] which gave me the opportunity [on his taxing me with it sharply] of do-ing so, and which I really cannot reproach myself with" (Moz. 2: 359-60). For Newsome's balanced account of the whole exchange, see his *Convert Cardinals* (79-80).

13. For a full treatment of Newman's analogical strategy of finding modern parallels within the Ancients, see Thomas (passim). He quotes J. D. Walsh, for example, to show that Newman's introduction to the Fathers in Milner, though thoroughly Evangelical, employed these same techniques: "The moderns comi-cally deluded themselves on the modernity of their views: it was not new philoso-phy they propagated but ancient heresy" (48).

14. In Thomas Mozley's summary of Newman's ideas on "the moral probation and proper excellence respectively of the rich and the poor," the same hierarchy is rationalized with much less tact and sympathy: "The former have more to do; the latter more to bear. The former have greater powers and opportunities . . . ; they have also greater temptations. . . . The latter have to endure hunger, thirst, cold, heat, sickness, weariness, and dulness. The higher class borders dangerously on the angelic state; the lower on the brutish. . . . [E]ach class has to consider its own mission and end" (1: 404-5).

15. As Robert Pattison puts it: "[I]t was a basic point of Newman's philosophy that the world cannot renounce its obligation to judge" (*Dissent* 8), and he con-tinues by reminding us of Newman's fascination with the "Securus judicat" of Augustine. While Pattison offers an impressively detailed account of Newman's indictment of his age, he sees Newman as standing within a dogmatic Scholasti-cism outside the confines of post-Enlightenment thought. As the passages below

should illustrate, however, Newman attacks his age from anywhere and nowhere, and this maddening opportunism suggests to me that his ultimate appeal is not to dogma or Scholasticism but to an image of God as Himself opportunistic.

16. In particular, within what to my knowledge remains his only piece of feminist criticism, Newman can expose the implicit paternalism delimiting the apparent inclusiveness of Peel's invitation to the life of the mind. Peel claims that "'great injustice would be done to the *well-educated and virtuous* women of the town and neighbourhood' had they been excluded. A very emphatic silence is maintained about women not virtuous. What does this mean? Does it mean to exclude them while bad men are admitted? . . . What has virtue to do with a Reading Room? It is to *make* its members virtuous; . . . and who else would prove a fitter experiment, and a more glorious triumph, of scientific influences? And yet he shuts out all but the well-educated and virtuous. Alas that bigotry should have left the mark of its hoof on the great 'fundamental principle of the Tamworth Institution'! . . . *Cannot* we prevail on him to modify his principle, and admit into his library none but 'well-educated and virtuous' *men?*" (281–82).

17. Robert Sayre and Michael Lowy specifically reject such attempts to drive a wedge between Marxist and Romantic critique: "This reduction of romanticism to a bourgeois ideology . . . is in fact the dogmatic commonplace of those who violently deny the affinities between the Marxist and romantic worldviews. The error of this position is to ignore the *essence* of the romantic phenomenon. For in spite of the fact that a part of its authors and public belong to the bourgeoisie, romanticism represents a deep-seated revolt against this class and the society that it rules. . . . The traditional intelligentsia . . . inhabits a mental universe governed by *qualitative* values. . . . But the central characteristic of capitalism is that its functioning is entirely determined by *quantitative* values. . . . There is a fundamental opposition, then, between these two worlds" (61–63).

18. Marjorie Levinson maintains the continued power of Marxist critique "to sidestep historicism's Hobson's choice of contemplation or empathy: in the Romantic idiom, knowledge or power. . . . [B]y rewriting 'knowledge' as possession *of* the object, and 'power' as possession *by* the object, we begin to appreciate both high ambitions as reflections of the commodity form" (Introduction 2). Even she, however, must acknowledge the contingency of what Marx saw as Other and the potential naivete of his utopian hope, must acknowledge that he invokes "a matter which is always already transformed—a Nature which is always already culture," and that he "permits no victimization which will not be, in the fullness of time but not by any divinity (including Chronos) surpassed" ("New" 32, 34). Admittedly, these phrases cannot do justice either to the sophistication or to the fundamental defensiveness of her argument. In a talk at the 1993 MLA convention in Toronto, "'Little I against the Whole Alphabet': Coleridge, Imagination, and the Cost of the Social," Steven Cole suggested that Levinson inadvertently reduces her own utopian hopes to quietism by insisting that an age's ideological boundaries can only be seen in hindsight.

19. Again, Ferber agrees: "In seeking pockets of resistance against capitalism, where else can we look but at survivals of older traditions, religious, ethnic, aesthetic, or whatever? A postcapitalist society exists only in our imaginations, and

we must draw from precapitalist societies . . . for evidence that it is possible" (82–83).

20. After detailing Newman's persistent refusal to observe historical objectivity, Thomas concedes that "it was not entirely out of ignorance: an instinct, a scepticism, held him back—and it is this which brings him remarkably close to what may be termed a 'postmodern' perspective" (256).

21. Newman had encountered this doctrinaire refusal to consider such evidence twenty years before in the letters of Charles. One of these, attacking the probability of Revelation, he answers by invoking the probable basis of all such knowledge: "[W]e know historical facts only from moral (i.e. *probable* [Newman's addition]) evidence: we are informed of the presence of material objects only through our senses etc etc" (*LD* 1: 240).

22. Just as shoddy for Newman was the rationalist's sophistic itch to exploit all such evidence as material for disputation. While he attacked Constantine for dismissing doctrinal distinctions as trivial or unknowable, he claimed, "far greater was the evil, when men destitute of religious seriousness and earnestness engaged in the like theological discussion, not with any definite ecclesiastical object, but as a mere trial of skill, or as a literary recreation" (*Ari.* 32). In Tract 45, he argues that such disputations came to "make light of mere probabilities. . . . In the course of time all the delicate shades of truth and falsehood, the unobtrusive indications of God's will, the low tones of the 'still small voice,' in which Scripture abounds, were rudely rejected" (1: 2).

23. Newman's earliest intuitions of such contingency, however, appear bundled up with very different emotions. Vexed by Charles's provocative assertion that "Mr [Robert] Owen for practical motives to action . . . beats St Paul hollow" (*LD* 1: 212), John claims that his brother cannot stand in a position to weigh the two men or the two systems: "[I]t is but proper you should defend your line of argument before you enter upon it. Admitting even you have the most subtle and plausible proofs, you must first convince the judges of the court, *that you are entitled to a hearing*. . . . [T]ill you do, you have no right to pen another line about Mr Owen's system: a system, which it would not be difficult but irrelevant to answer" (*LD* 1: 224–26). Here, to be sure, the effort to contextualize Charles within nineteenth-century English Christianity grows entangled with sibling rivalry. It remains unclear whether the "Judges of the court" are pronouncing the verdict of history, or of God, or of an autocratic elder brother.

24. In a passage already cited, the self-idolatry implicit within scientific investigation frequently leads to self-worship. Sir Robert Peel "considers that greater insight into Nature will lead a man to say, 'How great and wise is the Creator, who has done this!' True: but it is possible that his thoughts may take the form of 'How clever is the creature who has discovered it!' and self-conceit may stand proxy for adoration. . . . So, this is the religion we are to gain from the study of Nature; how miserable! The god we attain is our own mind; our veneration is even professedly the worship of self" (*DA* 301).

25. "The natural man," Newman continues in a university sermon, "dissects [the Gospel's] evidence without reverence, without hope, without suspense, without misgivings; and while he . . . sums up its result with the precision and pro-

priety of a legal tribunal, he rests in it as an end, and neither attains the farther truths at which it points, nor inhales the spirit which it breathes" (*US* [10]: 193-94). Newman is on safer ground, or at least on ground closer to home, when he attacks this same affectation of moral and intellectual disinterestedness on the part of modern Christian apologists: "[H]ad they been the Samaritans to whom St. Philip came, or the Ephesians who were addressed by St. Paul, they would have thought it their duty to have felt neither 'much joy' with the one, nor 'fear' with the other; . . . if Samaritans and Ephesians had acted on the modern view of what is rational and what is evidence, what sound judgment and what credulity, Christianity would not have made way and prospered, but we all should have been heathen at this day" (*Mir.* 201).

26. Within an 1834 sermon, disinterested patience can offer neither insight nor surety because it cannot make good on its claim to transcend the human condition: Rationalists "can bear the first news of God's having spoken to man, without being startled. They can patiently wait till the body of evidence is brought out before them, and then receive or reject as reason may determine for them" (*PS* 2 [2]: 20-21). Newman admits that these preconceptions may sound plausible: "If religion be not a practical matter, it is right and philosophical in us to be sceptics. Assuredly higher and fuller evidence of its truth might be given us" (21). In a university sermon, however, he grants only that unbelief "employs itself in doing what a believer could do, if he chose, quite as well, . . . in showing that the evidence might be more complete and unexceptionable than it is" (*US* [12]: 230).

27. Any secular reduction of the moral to the rational is itself reduced to an old sinner's itch to avoid God's demands by subsuming his role: "[H]e who sets about to seek God, though in old age, must . . . begin again with the very beginning as if he were a boy. . . . Now it is plain how humbling this is to his pride: he wishes to be saved; but he cannot stoop to be a penitent all his days; to beg he is ashamed. Therefore he looks about for other means of finding a safe hope. And one way among others by which he deceives himself, is this same idea that he may gain religious knowledge merely by his reason. Thus it happens, that [such] men . . . settle down into *heresies* in their latter years. . . . [T]hey *think* themselves judges" (*PS* 1 [17]: 226-27).

28. Eldon Eisenach points out that the central chapters in Mill's *Autobiography* and his *Utilitarianism* both turn on his discovery that Bentham's mechanistic psychology cannot ground either his ethics or his politics (165).

29. At this same period, to be sure, he worries even more about schemes for secular morality which threaten to succeed; seconding Pusey, he sees the Victorian self-help movements in particular as mere vehicles for promoting self-satisfaction: "Certainly our worldly morality is already bearing its fruits in making us very proud of ourselves. This is P[usey]'s notion of the evil of the Temp[erance]. Soc[iety]., viz that persons, puffed up by the sense of their superior decency, illumination etc etc., will get more harm than good from their temperance" (*LD* 3: 55). By the time of the *Idea*, Newman will be more willing to acknowledge, albeit grudgingly, an internal coherence in the ethical system of a Gibbon or a Shaftesbury. In 1832, however, such gestures of individual or communal hubris seem to

invite not just psychological demons but real ones: "And with Saul's sin, Saul's portion awaits his followers,—distraction, aberration; the hiding of God's countenance; imbecility, rashness, and changeableness in their counsels; judicial blindness, fear of the multitude; alienation from good men and faithful friends; subserviency to their worst foes, the kings of Amalek and the wizards of Endor" (*US* [9]: 175).

30. Note how Raymond Williams's Marxist critique of high culture replicates Newman's theological vocabulary here: "The religious emphasis weakened, and was replaced by what was in effect a metaphysics of subjectivity and the imaginative process. . . . 'Culture' was then at once the secularization and the liberalization of earlier metaphysical forms. . . . [Q]uasi-metaphysical forms—'the imagination,' 'creativity,' 'inspiration,' 'the aesthetic,' and the new positive sense of 'myth'—were in effect composed into a new pantheon" (15).

31. Such a pursuit "is not meritorious of heavenly aid or reward; but it does a work. . . . It expels the excitements of sense by the introduction of those of the intellect. . . . [I]s it nothing to substitute what is in itself harmless for what is, to say the least, inexpressibly dangerous?" (*Idea* 161).

32. Here Newman dismisses secular morality as psychologically ineffectual; several pages later, he sees any reduction of ethics to aesthetics, culture, or knowledge as equally unfair to all parties: "If we attempt to effect a moral improvement by means of poetry, we shall but mature into a mawkish, frivolous, and fastidious sentimentalism;—if by means of argument, into a dry, unamiable long-headedness;—if by good society, into a polished outside, with hollowness within, in which vice has lost its grossness, and perhaps increased its malignity;—if by experimental science, into an uppish, supercilious temper, much inclined to scepticism. . . . But reverse the order of things: put Faith first and Knowledge second; . . . and then classical poetry becomes the type of Gospel truth, and physical science a comment on Genesis or Job, and Aristotle changes into Butler, and Arcesilas into Berkeley" (*DA* 275). By the time of the *Idea*, Newman is much more dubious about the wisdom of letting theology intrude so boldly into the territory of the other disciplines. With this slighting allusion to Burke's defense of Marie Antoinette, compare his later, more explicit reference in the *Idea* (173).

33. Four years later Newman is brooding over Blanco White's defection to the Unitarians and the theological sterility he sees in their doctrines: "[W]hat a view does it give one of the Unitarians and id genus omne? They really do think it is no harm whatever being an Atheist, so that you are sincerely so, and do not cut people's throats and pick their pockets" (quoted in W. Ward 1: 80).

34. M. H. Abrams, for example, finds some Marxist criticism dreary and predictable: "[S]uch a reading is in effect self-confirming because empirically incorrigible; it is the product of a discovery procedure that presupposes the political meanings it triumphantly finds. . . . For a rigorously political reading is not only a closed, monothematic reading; it is also joyless, casting a critical twilight in which all poems are gray" (325–26). See also Charles Altieri: "Poetry must be allowed its sense of excess if we are not to castrate it. To impose Freud's concept of the subject in the self-righteous moralizing mode of critical historicism allows ourselves no intruding sky, no pressures defining our own limitations" (402).

35. This vision, appropriately enough, has itself been conscripted for ideological service. Terry Eagleton argues that "The thrust of Arnold's social criticism is to convert a visionless, sectarian bourgeoisie, pragmatically sunk in its own material interests, into a truly hegemonic class—a class with cultural resources adequate to the predominance it has come to hold in history" (104).

CHAPTER 10

1. "This," Pitt continues, "is how the Almighty manages events; how, like an experienced stage producer he conjures the high spectacle of this salvation" (19). While her satire is well directed, it assumes that she has some privileged access to this divine script, the same access she denies to her subject.

2. These specters personify what D. G. James reads as Romanticism's inevitable, self-defeating conclusion: "For to Coleridge no less than to Newman, 'clear and distinct ideas' about God and the end of the moral life cannot be forthcoming. . . . Yet the sense of this darkness is also necessary to the health of the soul which can be sustained only through acknowledgement of an enveloping unknown. Thus, at his last stage in the growth of Romanticism, does the 'mystery' of all true religion, which Blake had so passionately (and so perversely) opposed, find a frank and eager acceptance" (212). Michael Bright also links Romanticism and Tractarianism as turns toward the supernatural in reaction to empiricism, but he fails to consider, I think, how many of Newman's specters come unbidden. I would even suggest that these specters inform, if not the content, at least the imagery in which Newman cloaks the secular forces ranged against Christendom in the last chapter of the *Apologia:* "[T]he fierce energy of passion and the all-corroding, all-dissolving scepticism of the intellect in religious inquiries" (218).

3. Again, Cameron offers a valuable caveat to my description of these scenes as Romantic. For him, empiricism "offers a wild poetry which creates in us a strange view of the commonplace, much as an unusual light will give a familiar scene a look of enchantment" ("Empiricist" 94–95). Such claims, however, have been made about Wordsworth as well.

4. Harrold cites notes from a Newman lecture in which he remarks on the Ancient Mariner's being saved "by suddenly admiring the beauty of nature" (*Newman* 250).

5. When we move from sermons on heaven to letters about his own experiences, however, we find this mystery compromised by the personal need it must fill. As we saw in chapter 2, Newman darkens the physical circumstances of his own losses to obscure the finality of death and thus highlight his faith in an afterlife. We have already examined the progression through which he first projects Mary's spirit into the landscape ("Dear Mary seems embodied in every tree and hid behind every hill" [*LD* 2: 69]) and then points both her and the now-darkened landscape toward their spiritual counterparts ("Her form is almost nightly before me, when I have put out the light and lain down" [*LD* 2: 108]). When he loses Walter Mayers, he completes this transference of matter into spirit: "[T]his world is but a shadow and a dream—we think we see things and we see them not—they

do not exist, they die on all sides, things dearest and pleasantest and most beloved. But in heaven we shall all meet and it will be *no* dream" (*LD* 2: 58).

6. As in his other efforts to baptize Romanticism, however, Newman immediately extrapolates from psyche to spirit: "[N]ay, in heaven itself, such may be the high existence of some exalted orders of blessed spirits, as the Seraphim, who are said to be, not Knowledge, but all Love" (*US* [15]: 323).

7. Once again, however, the favor bestowed compromises the witness. The same encounter prized for its evidence of spiritual presences outside the self is valorized by the conformity of these presences to the self.

8. But Sheridan indirectly suggests that Newman had not come on this interpretation unassisted. He quotes Newman's early mentor, Walter Mayers, writing that conversions come "oftentimes from causes which appear at the time fortuitous, but which the mind when enlightened will discern to have been directed by God. Under some visitation of Providence either of sickness or adversity a person may have been awakened to a sense of religion" (40).

9. Froude's letter of 1835 agrees that "doubtless bodily pain is the sublimest of all disciplines to those who are up to making use of it" (*LD* 5: 68).

10. Earlier he had queried the indolent Henry Wilberforce "whether you might not (could your health stand it) enter upon some rigid course—supposing you determined to fast at certain times etc etc" (*LD* 3: 46). Geoffrey Faber notes that Froude's diary draws a similar link between spirituality and the disorientation caused by fasting: "The vacancy left in my mind by abstinence, fits it for spiritual ideas" (214).

11. A letter of 1835 to Pusey does explore another cause of Newman's asceticism, the physical and (probably) psychological impediments to his enjoyment of food: "If I were to talk much when I eat, the chance is (not always) I have a fit of indigestion—sometimes am kept awake all night etc. In like manner, if I eat but one mouthful after I take disgust at anything, if in any sense I eat as a duty (so to say) I am *sure* to suffer" (*LD* 5: 92).

12. Two years later in the *Development,* Scripture is again imaged as a landscape, not identifiably Eden, but Edenic in its very wildness: "[I]t must be an unexplored and unsubdued land, with heights and valleys, forests and streams, on the right and left of our path and close about us, full of concealed wonders and choice treasures" (*Dev.* 65-66). The caution with which Newman greeted spring in the sermon analyzed in chapter 5 vanishes two pages later. He first appeals to Mark: "'So is the kingdom of God, as if a man should cast seed into the ground, and should sleep, and rise night and day, and the seed should spring and grow up, he knoweth not how; for the earth bringeth forth fruit of herself.'" But this natural growth is then made to figure forth the growth of doctrinal truth: "Here an internal element of life, whether principle or doctrine, is spoken of . . . [and] the spontaneous, as well as the gradual, character of the growth is intimated. . . . [It] comes of its own innate power of expansion within the mind in its season" (*Dev.* 67-68).

13. Goodwin claims that the imagery here is Dantean, that this poet is being tempted to remain in the dark woods and reject the invitation to paradise; yet Dante goes first to Hell and, I will argue, Newman's own journey to the Catholic

Church has its own infernal implications. Wright finds Newman's claims for the Catholic Church as a safe haven from hermeneutical problems equally suspect (183–84).

14. Prickett sees Newman here as reverting to his empiricist past by mounting a Humean attack on the perceptions (*Romanticism* 179). In "Physiognomy," Prickett develops the imaginative reality of Catholicism, before which Anglicanism is only a "similacrum," by invoking a metaphor from Keats's letters: "[T]he Imagination may be compared to Adam's dream—he awoke and found it truth" (272–73). Finley, citing the prophet's scroll passage from the *Apologia* in the context of Ryan's deconstructive reading, questions even the image of Rome as the safe harbor after his perilous voyage from Anglicanism: since the outer world belies God's presence, then "the 'voice of conscience,' dependent as it is upon the way 'God lies,' must be not only 'an echo, but the echo of a lie'" (163). Continuing with Newman's admission that the formal proofs of God's existence cannot "make the buds unfold and the leaves grow within me" (*Apo.* 217), Finley argues that Newman has adopted the figure only "to enforce the lifelessness, or suspended animation, of his moral being in crisis" (164).

15. Cameron is one of the few who quote this passage, citing it as one "of the characteristic statements of his mature position . . . continuous with [his] accounts of 'childish imaginations'" ("Night" 108–9).

16. By Discourse VI of the *Idea*, Newman is working hard to assimilate such threats into a program for intellectual growth: "[L]et a person, whose experience has hitherto been confined to . . . these islands, . . . go for the first time into parts where physical nature puts on her wilder and more awful forms, . . . [he will] find for a time that he has lost his bearings. He has made a certain progress, and he has a consciousness of mental enlargement. . . . And so again, the sight of beasts of prey and other foreign animals . . . throw[s] us out of ourselves into another creation, and as if under another Creator, if I may so express the temptation which may come into the mind. We seem to have new faculties" (118). In a long note to this page Svaglic qualifies Culler's claim that even here Newman is rejecting the Enlightenment recipe for mental enlargement (606–7).

17. Weiskel (35–36) cites Schiller's "On the Sublime," where he posits a similar lack of teleology in Nature as producing the sense of alienation requisite for the sublime moment.

18. Much of this evident distaste, in Newman at least, arises from his still very limited, very English version of "the Ineffable." Despite his efforts to champion the Asiatic style of Scriptural and Patristic writers, he shows little appreciation for the kind of delight which Job's God showed in Behemoth or Leviathan. In 1831, as we saw, he warns Keble that his attempt to capture Hebrew poetry in a new translation of the Psalter would remain "strange to Northern sluggishness" (*LD* 2: 355).

19. The same assurance is included in a letter to Pusey: "St Antony is bright and cheerful, . . . and he looks on evil spirits as utterly contemptible and weak to the *believer in Christ*—as powerful only towards the timid, and cowards towards the bold" (*LD* 5: 198–99).

20. See Finley's interpretation of this passage (155–56). Newman's discomfort

with any demiurge appears as early as the 1826 essay on miracles, where it is only "on the authority of Scripture, [that] we admit the occasional interference of agents short of divine with the course of nature" (*Mir.* 46). Subsequently he employs Occam's razor against any efforts to rationalize miracle as spiritual intervention: "Nature attests, indeed, the being of a God, but not of a race of intelligent creatures between Him and Man. In assigning a Miracle, therefore, to the influence of Spirits, an hypothetical cause is introduced merely to remove a difficulty" (50).

21. This same structural dilemma pervades the *Apologia* as a whole, where Newman is tracing his development toward a position which must remain always already present. Jonathan Loesberg, in particular, explores Newman's effort to portray his conversion as the inevitable progression of a stable consciousness: "Newman's progress involves more a decoding of what he has always been and what has always been there, a decoding of the true content of his beliefs" (146–47). Yet this same progression has been simultaneously reducing Newman's consciousness to a series of mutually incompatible textual moments, held together only by the literal reflections and metaphorical reflexiveness of his self-questioning rhetoric.

22. Thomas Mozley claims that even before the trip, "as he said long after, a 'ghost' was pursuing him" (1: 292).

23. In an 1832 poem entitled "The Sign of the Cross" Newman wonders whether, when he crosses himself, "hateful spirits around, / For their brief hour unbound, / Shudder to see, and wail their overthrow?" (*VV* 69).

24. Discourse VI of the *Idea* attributes this force to the "youthful community" of students: "It will give birth to a living teaching, which in course of time will take the shape of a self-perpetuating tradition, or a *genius loci*, . . . which haunts the home where it has been born, and which imbues and forms . . . every individual who is successively brought under its shadow" (130).

25. Given that Alton was the scene of his father's precipitous decline and that Newman has just been indulging in guilty recollections of him (*LD* 4: 331), his spirit may be the one called forth.

26. The dream itself may be a distortion of another nighttime incident from his undergraduate years when he and a friend climbed an Oxford tower to observe the stars: "[W]hile his friend was busily engaged with the pointers, he, earthly-minded youth, had been looking down into the deep, gas-lit, dark-shadowed quadrangles, and wondering if he should ever be Fellow of this or that College" (*AW* 50).

27. Culler notes: "All his life the shrubbery at Ham was an image of security to him, as the snapdragon on the walls of Trinity was a symbol of his cloistered life" ("Remembrance" 65). Faber's detailed Freudian analysis of the first nightmare is often convincing (310-15). He argues that its opening, before the excerpt quoted here, transfers Newman's contest with Hawkins for control of Oriel to the unlikely figure of Jenkyns, who as one of Hawkins's henchmen had objected to Newman's assumption of the deanship in 1832 (*LD* 3: 58-64). Faber goes on, rather less persuasively, to interpret the end of the nightmare as a displacement of homosexual desires. The father and son who visit his rooms are Hurrell and the

Archdeacon, and the lady under the arm of his travelling companion is "none other than Newman himself" (315). In the slightly later, fever-induced nightmare quoted in chapter 1, childhood is no longer even a failed refuge but instead the occasion of some preternatural fear: "I had some miserable nights—the dreamy confusion of delirium—sitting on a staircase, wanting something, or with some difficulty—very wretched—& something about my Mother & Sisters" (*AW* 131).

28. C. W. Le Bas, "Newman and Faber on Justification," *British Critic* 24 (July 1838). Conversely, Walter Houghton notes that the review of Le Bas' *Life of Archbishop Laud* in volume 19 of the *British Critic* (April 1836) was by Newman ("New" 241). For the contents of both these issues, see Esther Houghton (125, 128).

29. Even here, however, he must acknowledge the dangerous circularity of this argument: "Others . . . have exposed themselves to the plausible charge of adducing, first, the Miracle to attest the divinity of the doctrine, and then, the doctrine to prove the divinity of the Miracle" (*Mir.* 51).

30. Thomas analyzes this incident as well (251), but he focuses on Newman's wrestling with Victorian decorum over how explicitly to describe Arius' gastric distress.

31. Newman even finds himself in bed with the infamous liberal historian Milman. On his supercilious account of Samson, Newman comments: "[W]hat else has the writer done towards the inspired narrative, but invest it in those showy human colours which legendary writers from infirmity, and enemies from malice, have thrown over the miracles of the Church? There is certainly an aspect of romance in which Samson may be viewed . . . ; and so again there may have been a divinity in the acts and fortunes, and a spiritual perfection in the lives, of the ancient Catholic hermits and missionaries" (*Mir.* 169).

32. Chadwick's emendation of this passage is to the point: "Newman never thought of the sacrifice of the intellect . . . in Evangelical language. He thought always of the inadequacy of the intellect to probe the mysteries of God; which is a different idea" ("Bremond" 193).

33. In his essay on Newman and Bremond, however, Chadwick extends to the essay every benefit of the doubt: "[H]e struggles, and twists, and turns, and does his best, and comes out not quite with a certainty but with a sort of hope that everything will be all right. . . . [A]nd as we ought to share [the Fathers'] outlook in all we can, so we ought to share their outlook in this openness of mind to the direct intervention of God in our lives. . . . His mind needed to be persuaded; but his faith did not rest there" (192).

34. The most exhaustive (and exhausting) indictment of Newman's credulity is Edwin Abbott's *Philomythus*. Abbott, however, attributes it to a pervasive fideism. Similar passages appear, as Holmes has shown ("History" 254-57), in Newman's contributions to *The Lives of the English Saints,* and the *Ecclesiastical Miracles* uses the same dubious slippery-slope arguments we have encountered in the essay on Scripture: "[T]he narrative of the combats of St. Antony with evil spirits is a development rather than a contradiction of Revelation; viz, as illustrating such texts as speak of Satan being cast out by prayer and fasting" (*Mir.* 158). Even more insidiously, the argument can be run backwards: "Those [miracles] of Elisha

in particular are related . . . with a profusion and variety very like the luxuriance which offends us in the miraculous narratives of the ecclesiastical authors" (*Mir.* 167). Culler notes that in his introduction to the "Legend of St. Gundleus," Newman abandons any claims for historical accuracy and treats the narrative as a moral exemplum (*Victorian* 116–17).

35. From praising miracles the critic moves to doubting them, to circumscribing God, to dispensing with the need for revelation. The passage thus dramatizes the insidious, gradual, dissolving power Newman will come to find in rationalism, the power that will make "Christianity . . . melt away in our hands like snow; we shall be unbelievers before we at all suspect we are" (*Ess.* 2: 241–42). As he puts it in a sermon, Doctrines "will fade away insensibly like hues at sunset, and we shall be left in darkness" (*PS* 6 [23]: 340).

36. Transfixed by a natural variety which engulfs any tidy classification, Newman even flirts with a normally suspect analogy between creation and creator: "As in the natural world the animal and vegetable kingdoms imperceptibly melt into each other, so are there mutual affinities and correspondences between the two families of miracles as found in inspired and uninspired history, which show that, whatever may be their separate characteristics, they admit of being parts of one system" (*Mir.* 162).

37. Though now alienated from the Anglican Church, he describes himself in his 1843 essay on ecclesiastical miracles as part of a growing movement which sees *some* church as the locus of an ongoing miraculous dispensation: "[I]f we believe that Christians are under an extraordinary Dispensation, such as Judaism was, and that the Church is a supernatural ordinance, we shall in mere consistency be disposed to treat even the report of miraculous occurrences with seriousness" (*Mir.* 185).

38. Ryals's book is suggestive in its extension of Romantic irony to include many of the seemingly more stolid Victorian authors. Even Ryals, however, shies away from including Newman.

39. In Mellor's formulation, "the romantic ironist . . . must acknowledge the inevitable limitations of his own finite consciousness and of all man-made structures or myths. But even as he . . . consciously deconstructs his mystifications of the self and the world, he must affirm and celebrate the process of life by creating new images and ideas. Thus the romantic ironist sustains his participation in a creative process that extends beyond the limits of his own mind" (5).

40. David Simpson finds a similar double movement in Keats, citing the ironic function of the chameleon poet (183–85) but also pointing out a Keats letter where he admits to having "in my own breast so great a resource" (191). While Simpson rejects any neo-classical irony that relies on a concealed norm (xii, 22), his distinctively English version of Romantic irony sets up an epistemological indecidability, not the Schlegelian sense of play with and against a fertile flux: it "consists in the studied avoidance on the artists' part of determinate meanings, even at such times as he might wish to encourage his reader to *produce* such meanings for himself; it involves the refusal of closure, the incorporation of any potentially available 'metacomment' within the primary language of the text, the provision of a linguistic sign which moves towards or verges upon a 'free' status,

and the consequent raising to self-consciousness of the authoritarian element of discourse, as it effects both the author-reader relation and the intentional manipulation, from both sides, of the material through which they communicate" (190).

41. Newman may have been attracted to Byron because of his deeply Calvinistic insistence on God's vengeance as the condition of his own defiance.

42. In a still later sermon, the literal account in Joshua prompts a grotesque anticipation of Patton's "Kill 'em all and let God sort 'em out": "All those Canaanites, whom the children of Israel slew, every one of them is somewhere in the universe, now at this moment, where God has assigned him a place. We read, 'They utterly destroyed all that was in' Jericho, 'young and old.' . . . Every one of those souls still lives. They had their separate thoughts and feelings when on earth, they have them now" (*PS* 4 [6]: 83). In such rationalizations, we may be hearing Newman's inner debate with the ghost of Gibbon, who mocked the Gnostics' asceticism but applauded their outraged repudiation of Old Testament morality: "As those heretics were, for the most part, averse to the pleasures of sense, they morosely arraigned the polygamy of the patriarchs, the gallantries of David, and the seraglio of Solomon. The conquest of the land of Canaan, and the extirpation of the unsuspecting natives, they were at a loss how to reconcile with the common notions of humanity and justice" (Gibbon 2: 13).

43. Boehme was an important source for Coleridge's religious thought, a fact which would not have endeared Coleridge to Newman, had he known it. According to Abrams's summary of Boehme's theology: "The coincidence of opposites in the one God manifests itself in the opposition of positive and negative forces that constitute all of nature. For 'there is a single God; He is himself all existence, He is evil and good, heaven and hell, light and darkness, eternity and time, beginning and end; where His love is hidden in a being, just there is His anger apparent'" (*Natural* 161). While Newman's emerging universe seems too anarchic to dramatize those proto-Hegelian imaginative efforts at divine synthesis and self-realization which so fascinated Coleridge, yet it does dramatize what Abrams calls Boehme's "compelling vision of a fallen universe which is constituted throughout by an opposition of quasi-sexual contraries, at once mutually attractive and repulsive, whose momentary conciliations give way to renewed attempts at mastery by opponent powers, in a tragic conflict which is at the same time the very essence of life and creativity" (162).

44. Newman's only other theologically viable option is the Manichean one we examined in chapter 8.

45. Rajan points out (45) that by positing Dionysus before Apollo, Nietzsche reverses Schiller's Golden Age myth, showing form as a modern construct upon the unconscious abyss. And DeLaura notes that Pater's "view of Greece is considerably more complex than Arnold's" because he added "the Dionysian tradition to the Apollonian" (*Hebrew* 177). Well before either of these revisionists, however, Newman intimates that he and Pentheus are dealing with some aboriginal reality.

46. In the essay "Literature" appended to the *Idea,* Newman himself quotes Theseus' lines to illustrate the powers of instantiation vested in literary language (238).

CHAPTER 11

1. For Rajan, "Schopenhauer defines reality in terms of two categories, will and representation, which Nietzsche was to rename Dionysos and Apollo, respectively" (35).

2. Mellor continues: "In *Either/Or* (1843), Kierkegaard portrays the romantic ironist as A, the aesthete whose life is arbitrary and thus without purpose or historical actuality. . . . [A]s Kierkegaard insisted, 'Irony is free, to be sure, free from all the cares of actuality, but free from its joys as well, free from its blessings. For if it has nothing higher than itself, it may receive no blessings, for it is ever the lesser that is blessed of a greater.'"

3. See in particular the 1844 "Edifying Discourse" on Paul, "The Thorn in the Flesh": "To have stood personally in God's presence, and now forsaken by God. . . . [T]o discover that in God, too, there is change, alternation of light and darkness, that there is an angel of Satan who has power to banish a man from bliss!" (quoted in Diem 48).

4. "My only analogy is Socrates. . . . I do not call myself a Christian (keeping the ideal free), but I can reveal the fact that others are still less entitled to the name than I am" (Kierkegaard quoted in Thomte 15).

5. Brilioth acknowledges that "The invisible world to Tractarian piety is above all *mysterious* and *awful*. . . . To the Oxford men . . . the realities of religion form a *mysterium tremendum*. How could they do anything but tremble?" (*Anglican* 216). For him, however, "The Tractarian feeling of *awfulness* is not a consequence of dread of judgment, but of a lively sense of the nearness and majesty of God" (217).

6. In one sermon he justifies his refusal to play the odds with the assurance that the worldly goals being sacrificed aren't worth much in the first place: "This, then, is what is meant by faith going against reason, that it cares not for the measure of probabilities; it does not ask whether a thing is more or less likely; but if there is a fair and clear likelihood what God's will is, it acts upon it. [If there were nine chances against the truth of Scripture, and but one for it, yet the greatness of the prize and of the punishment weighs far more than nine times the consequences of the word of Scripture failing.] If Scripture were not true, we should be left where we were; we should, in the event, be no worse off than before; but if it be true, then we shall be infinitely worse off for not believing it than if we had believed it" (*PS* 6 [18]: 259; the bracketed passage, later deleted, appears in the 1840 Rivington edition, 281). The odds quoted are less good than those reported by Chadwick: "Newman admitted, in a phrase which struck into W. G. Ward's mind, that the chances on a revelation were possibly three to two in favour" (*Bossuet* 128). Such reasoning echoes Pascal's Wager or Cicero's assurance that we should believe in an afterlife because we will never have occasion to be proved wrong. In all these cases, the wagerers are betting with play money. On Newman's brief flirtation with religion as self-interest, see Cameron ("Empiricist" 89).

7. The corresponding passage from "My Illness in Sicily" reads: "Indeed this is how I look on myself; very much (as the illustration goes) as a pane of glass, which transmit[s] heat being cold itself. . . . I have a vivid perception of the

consequences of certain admitted principles . . . and, having no great (i.e. no vivid) love of this world, whether riches, honors, or anything else, . . . take the profession of them upon me, as I might sing a tune which I like . . . for I believe myself at heart to be nearly hollow" (*AW* 125). Elsewhere he argues that "the election of St. Matthias" (who replaced Judas) proves "how easily God may effect His purposes without us. . . . It often happens that those who have long been in His favour grow secure and presuming" (*PS* 2 [11]: 118).

8. Balaam is also accused of these failings in Revelation 2:14, and of greed in Jude 1:11 and 2 Peter 2:15-16. In Micah 6:5, however, he is mentioned as a prophet. Geoffrey Faber recounts that Pusey heard, but was not amused by, the annual spectacle of the learned Eichhorn parodying the episode of Balaam's ass (134).

9. "[I]n the history of Balaam we read, 'God came unto Balaam at night, and said unto him, If the men come to call thee, rise up and go *with them;* but yet the word which I shall say unto thee, that shalt thou speak.' Presently we read, 'And God's anger was kindled, *because* he went; and the Angel of the Lord stood in the way for an adversary against him.' Now supposing the . . . permission given him to go . . . was only the received belief of the Church, would it not be at once rejected by most men as inconsistent with Scripture?" (*DA* 157-58).

10. In the essay against Milman he sees the antecedents of revelation so scattered throughout the ancient world that he "could readily grant . . . that Balaam was an Eastern sage, or a Sibyl was inspired" (*Ess.* 2: 233). As early as the first volume of the Sermons, Newman portrayed Balaam as unwillingly *possessed* by evil: "Alas! there are men who walk the road to hell, always the while looking back at heaven, and trembling. . . . They hasten on as under a spell. . . . Such was Balaam. . . . How did he revere God in speech! How piously express a desire to die the death of the righteous! Yet he died in battle among God's *enemies*" (*PS* 1 [13]: 168-69).

11. Newman's diary records his preaching the Balaam sermon on 2 April 1837, only ten days before he confessed to Henry Wilberforce his fear of being cast aside by God in spite of the good he was doing others (*LD* 6: 51).

12. "We kept clear of Catholics throughout our tour. . . . I do not recollect being in a room with any other ecclesiastics [besides Wiseman], except a Priest at Castro-Giovanni in Sicily, who called on me when I was ill, and with whom I wished to hold a controversy" (*Apo.* 41).

13. Upon his first encounter with Greek churches, he buttresses his chauvinism with a characteristic appeal to morality: "I fear outward ceremonies are the substitute for holiness, as among the Jews. The Greeks are very rigid in their fasts . . . and the pirates etc are as rigid in keeping them as others" (*LD* 3: 181). Yet even here he is surprised not to find murder and mayhem condoned in the liturgy: "I turned over leaves of one or two devotional books in the country church. One was a collection of prayers by John of Damascus. There was little objectionable (that I saw) in either, and much that was very good" (181). To his mother three weeks later, he admits that he is strangely drawn to the church services themselves: "[I]t is fearful to have before one's eyes the perversion of all the best, the holiest, the most exalted feelings of human nature. Every thing in St John's Church is admir-

able, if it did not go quite so far—it is a beautiful flower run to seed" (*LD* 3: 204). The outdoor processions, on the other hand, he is happy to fob off on the Evangelicals: "[S]tatues of Madonnas and Saints in the Streets, etc etc [are a] more poetical but not less jading stimulant than the pouring-forth in a Baptist Chapel" (206).

14. To Ryder his moral indignation reasserts itself and he invokes the curses of Revelation against pagan Rome: "Here we see the only remnant of the 4 great Enemies of God—Babylon, Persia, and Macedon have left scarce a trace behind them—the last and most terrible beast lies before us as a subject for our contemplation, in all the visibleness of its plagues. . . . I confess I am not of those who can mourn over the ruins of the Coliseum, or censure the early Christians for destroying the monuments of heathen greatness. I wish them to be as they are— just so much remaining as to show how powerful was the enemy which the Gospel overthrew" (*LD* 3: 248-49). Even here, however, he argues solicitously that his favorite authors shielded themselves from the general ruin: "[T]o what Roman writer can one turn with any real satisfaction, except so far as they withdrew themselves from the system in which they lived, and (like Virgil and in part Cicero) bewailed amid the thick shades of the garden the toils and vexations of human life?" (*LD* 3: 249). The last image anticipates by a month Newman's nightmare and his effort to escape the decline which Hawkins was bringing upon Oriel by retreating to the shrubberies at Ham.

15. Faber perceptively connects this spirit of place to the one evoked by Cambridge (304). See also Paul Misner (387). Misner is at pains to point out (386–94) that Newman's position towards Rome softened much more quickly than the *Apologia* implies. Even within the *Prophetical Office,* where he has worked to marginalize Catholicism by subsuming its power and authority within the via media, vestigial connections between it and such ambiguous forces persist. The powers which characterize Catholicism, however, he also begins to find rampant both within the Patristic church and within his own religious imagination.

16. To Christie he appeals to antiquity to sort out his conflicting responses: "[W]hat mingled feelings come upon one. You are in the place of martyrdom and burial of Apostles and Saints—you have about you the buildings and sights they saw—and you are in the city to which England owes the blessing of the gospel— But then on the other hand the superstitions;—or rather, what is far worse, the solemn reception of them as an essential part of Christianity" (*LD* 3: 240-41).

17. To his mother he admits a rather patronizing respect for the simple piety of those not yet corrupted by hierarchy or power: "I feel much for and quite love the little monks [seminarists?] of Rome—they look so innocent and bright, poor boys" (*LD* 3: 273). But to Christie he acknowledges something approaching the refined simplicity of his own Oxford in other, higher-ranking ecclesiastics: "There is so much amiableness and gentleness, so much Oxonianism, (so to say) such an amusing and interesting demureness, and such simplicity of look and speech, that I feel for those indeed who are bound with an iron chain" (*LD* 3: 277). Yet as the letter continues, we find that his judgmental attitude is itself a defense against his having already been judged: "What a strange situation it is, to be with those who think one in a state of perdition, who speak calmly with one, while they have aw-

ful thoughts! what a mixture of grief and indignation, what a perplexity between frankness and reserve comes over one!"

18. Abbott also quotes this letter in detail (*Anglican* 1: 272-73). Since he claims that Newman was, unbeknownst even to himself, an implicit Catholic a full decade before his formal conversion, Abbott gives his initial response to Rome a full and quite perceptive analysis (1: 266-78).

19. A letter to Jenkyns predicts a similar end to the Donation of Constantine: "I suppose in some way the Roman system will be broken up, yet without destroying the essentials of the Church system. . . . Foreigners here seem to think this state of affairs cannot last, and that the Papal power is falling. Would the fall of the system follow?" But again he pulls himself up short, recollecting that a former fellow of Oriel has been busy redefining the national church to include virtually all of Protestantism: "[W]e must not anticipate the downfall of others; when we have so much cause to look with anxiety at our own home. So, that precious Dr Arnold is for making us pig three in a bed with the Baptists and Socinians!" (*LD* 3: 280-81).

20. Tract 71 spells out this sacrifice for the individual believer: "[C]onsider the number of points of faith which the Church of Rome has set up. You must believe every one of them; if you have allowed yourself to doubt any one of them, you must repent of it, and confess it to a priest" (3: 11).

21. In a contemporary letter to Lyall, he draws an even bleaker parallel between the Church and the collapse of an institution not secular but pagan: "[T]he present state of the Church is like that of an empire breaking or broken up. At least I know of no better illustration. Where is the Turkish Empire at this day? . . . For the most part, a Turk speaking of precepts, prerogatives, powers, speaks but of former times. . . . Our Lord founded a kingdom: it spread over the earth and then broke up. Our difficulties in faith and obedience are just those which a subject in a decaying empire has in matters of allegiance. . . . [W]hen we are asked, 'Where is the Church?' I can but answer, 'Where it *was*'—the Church only *is* while it is one" (Moz. 2: 357).

22. In the penultimate of his university sermons, he simply casts their common plight onto God. Those acting on faith "profess a sincere belief that certain views which engage their minds come from God; that they know well that they are beyond them; . . . that a divine blessing alone can carry them forward; that they look for that blessing; that they feel that God will maintain His own cause; that *that* belongs to Him, not to them; that if their cause is God's cause, it will be blessed, in His time and way; that if it be not, it will come to nought; that they securely wait the issue" (*US* [14]: 301).

23. Nicholls, following early Anglican critics of the *Development*, argues that the work "was a historical explanation of how the church of Rome came to be as it was, and not a general theory of development of which the Roman church *happens to be* the only valid instance to be found" ("Anglican" 394). Dean Inge is more cynical: "Newman shows with great force and ingenuity that all the developments in the Roman system which Protestantism rejects as later accretions were natural and necessary. But this only means that the Catholic Church, in

order to live, was compelled to adapt itself to the prevailing conditions of human culture in the countries where it desired to be supreme" (196).

24. As G. M. Young observes: "[W]henever women or religion are the theme[, h]e cannot let them alone: like an ill-bred talker, he is constantly forcing the unwanted note" (126–27).

25. "Their gloomy and austere aspect, the abhorrence of the common business and pleasures of life, and their frequent predictions of impending calamities, inspired the Pagans with the apprehension of some danger which would arise from the new sect" (Gibbon 2: 78). See also E. J. Oliver's comment: "[Because] the average Roman official had as little regard for Christianity [as he], Gibbon has given a valid account of Christian development from that point of view" (126). Peter Toon (50–51) states that George Stanley Faber's otherwise obtuse review of Newman's essay notes that he had made all the unbelievers' points for them.

26. In his essay on the *Development,* John Ford is equally nonplussed by this strategy: "[I]t is at best ambivalent, particularly insofar as 'there is a certain general correspondence between magic and miracle. . . .' One is left wondering what criteriological grounds there are for distinguishing between genuine developments and counterfeit similes" (25–26). Later in the *Development,* Newman will present the opposite caricature: "[W]hile the world's first reproach in heathen times had been that Christianity was a dark malevolent magic, its second has been that it is a joyous carnal paganism;—according to that saying, 'We have piped unto you, and ye have not danced; we have mourned unto you, and ye have not lamented'" (*Dev.* 394).

27. A note in Brilioth's *Anglican Revival* comments: "When Newman, in *Apologia,* says: 'From the time I became a Catholic, of course I have no further history of my religious opinions to narrate . . . ,' it is difficult not to see in this a species of self-deception" (107n). Lynn Feider summarizes: "[W]hile Newman never surrendered his Catholic ideal nor his conviction that it could only be found in the Roman Church, the 'reality therapy' of years of actually living in the actual Roman Catholic Church tempered somewhat his views on how well that ideal was truly realized in that body" (178).

28. Thomas rightly questions the accuracy of these late-written accounts, especially since contemporary drafts on the Monophysites reveal nothing like the anxiety which Newman will so graphically describe. Thomas argues persuasively that Newman's discovery of his own heresy was itself a back-formation from his encounter with Wiseman's claims for Catholic authority: "The idea of the Monophysite 'face in the mirror' arose out of the turmoil provoked by Wiseman's adept public challenge, rather than the scholarly researches of his closet some weeks before" (219).

29. Within this first episode it is the heretics who were "shifting, changeable, reserved, and deceitful" (*Apo.* 109), traits more like those he would ascribe to the early Church in the *Development:* "a secret religion which dared not face the day; an itinerant, busy, proselytizing religion" (223).

30. Thomas quotes from Wiseman's article: "[B]y the Fathers . . . the question was essentially considered one of fact rather than of right" (220).

31. As William Seth Adams points out (82–85), the quasi-Tractarian William Palmer also denounced both of Wiseman's articles on Anglican claims because they posited the Roman Church as the source and arbiter of change. In published letters to Wiseman, he rejected the "fact" of Papal supremacy because he denied the validity of development (Adams 85–87). In 1843, Palmer's *Narrative of Events,* what Adams (92–98) calls the first history of the Oxford Movement, claims that the first generation of Tractarians, including Newman, sought only to return the Anglican Church to its Patristic roots, but that the movement was being corrupted by a new generation of Romanizers.

32. As was suggested in chapter 10, the Church's aggressive mediation was called forth by a power far more cosmic than what Newman described in the *Apologia* as "the immense energy of the aggressive, capricious, untrustworthy intellect" (220).

33. This analysis complicates but in the main supports Josef Altholz's paradigm: "Newman thus used history to release theology from mere reason, conscience to release it from mere history, and Authority to release it from private judgment" ("History" 294). While I would also qualify the direct connection Nicholls finds between Newman's need for this authority and his insistence upon human individuality, Nicholls does posit an interesting source for such a connection: The source "is of course Thomas Hobbes, who combined a profound scepticism and a pervasive individualism with an uncompromising authoritarianism in religion and politics" ("Individualism" 208). Without such a Church, in other words, even our spiritual life would be "nasty, brutish, and short."

34. Inge is again much blunter: "His 'orbis terrarum' was the Latin empire. . . . He first says 'The judgment of the great world is final'; and then 'If the world decides against Rome, so much the worse for the world'" (195).

35. John Holloway compares the seamless web of lived Catholicism to the figurative interaction within Newman's description of it (179–81). Robert Pattison notes that the Arian heresy's acceptance by virtually everyone including the then Pope raised a special problem for Augustine's "Securus judicat orbis terrarum" ("Arian" 152–53). He suggests that development for Newman is not an historical process at all but the unfolding of a hidden spiritual idea. From the recognizability of the Catholic Church in different ages, Prickett concludes that Newman's unwritten criterion for development is actually an increase in organic complexity, by analogy with the growth of an individual human being in body, mind, and spirit ("Physiognomy" 270–73).

36. Walter Houghton offers a formalist analysis of the passages, but the connections he draws seem more emotive and figurative (*Art* 56).

37. In Furst's paraphrase of this same strategy: "Irony . . . stems from the artist's critical self-detachment and unremitting self-consciousness; it denotes his complete freedom, his superiority over the work-in-progress; and it becomes manifest in the liberty with which he creates, de-creates, and re-creates" (28).

38. In chapter 4 I demurred at Prickett's suggestion that Newman's prose possesses the imaginative richness of a Shakespeare play. I suggested that instead of thinking through images, Newman delimited their implications within parallel clauses and rhetorical situations. In its figurative anarchy, his conversion narrative

hardly lends itself to rigorous metaphorical analysis; yet in their *repetition* within a series of very different contexts, these images can become unexpected indices of his mind and spirit.

39. While not physically violent, Newman's hand could be deadly indeed when it seized a pen. As he wrote his mother: "My head, hand, and heart are all knocked up with the long composition I have sent Charles" (*LD* 2: 284).

40. As early as 1833 he confessed to his sisters: "I will tell you, what I cannot tell to the world. I *do not* like Cranmer's character—his death must ever make him an object of reverence—but his conduct! his marriage! his taking part against Catherine! I cannot bear it" (*LD* 3: 270).

41. The corresponding passage in "My Illness in Sicily" begins, "I had a strange feeling on my mind that God meets those who go on in *His* way, who remember Him in His way, in the paths of the Lord, that I must put myself in His path" (*AW* 127).

42. This state bears an uncanny resemblance to the "other world" revealed by the spiritual visitant within the dream recorded in Newman's 1821 journal, the world in which "every thing . . . was so *very, very plain*" (*AW* 166).

43. However, see Cameron: "The essential note of his character is reflexivity, as it was for Augustine and Pascal and Kierkegaard" ("Tractarian" 90).

44. Shaw describes this ghost more as a function of Newman's epistemological waffling: "Is the ghost a mere specter, to be exorcised with more learning and erudition? Is it a mere demon or obsession? . . . Had he had a glimpse into heaven or merely been enchanted? Newman wants to pause. . . . [H]e is genuinely uncertain of the ghost's status, like Hamlet, unwilling to take a leap of faith until he sees better where he is likely to land" (247).

45. Thomas concludes his book with yet another postmodern "reflection" on, and of, Newman's mirror: "The texts beckon, but in the end render up above all the reflected image of the investigator, who is startled to behold there the inescapable outline of his own obsessions" (256).

46. His letters of 1843 and 1844 to Mrs. Froude offer preliminary accounts of this same experience. But as their editor, Gordon Harper, notes, "whereas in the *Apologia* . . . he elaborated even the smallest points in his effort to show a sincerity of purpose[, h]is private letters proceeded along more strictly intellectual lines" (60).

47. Deen argues that "the *Apologia* does not entirely escape the influence of Rousseau, [in] whose *Confessions* . . . the personality and sufferings of the writer are even more central" (228). See also Peterson: "With the *Apologia*, the autobiography becomes self-conscious as a genre: it realizes its hermeneutic intention" (119).

WORKS CITED

Abbott, Edwin A. *The Anglican Career of Cardinal Newman.* 2 vols. London: Macmillan, 1892.

———. *Philomythus: An Antidote against Credulity.* 2nd ed. London: Macmillan, 1891.

Abrams, M. H. *The Mirror and the Lamp: Romantic Theory and the Critical Tradition.* New York: Oxford UP, 1953.

———. *Natural Supernaturalism: Tradition and Revolution in Romantic Literature.* New York: Norton, 1971.

———. "On Political Readings of *Lyrical Ballads.*" In *Romantic Revolutions: Criticism and Theory,* ed. Kenneth R. Johnston et al. Bloomington: Indiana UP, 1990: 320–49.

Adams, William Seth. "William Palmer's *Narrative of Events:* The First History of the 'Tracts for the Times.'" In *The Divine Drama in History and Liturgy,* ed. John E. Booty. Allison Park, PA: Pickwick, 1984: 81–106.

Allchin, A. M. "The Theological Vision of the Oxford Movement." In *The Rediscovery of Newman: An Oxford Symposium,* ed. John Coulson and A. M. Allchin. London: Sheed and Ward, 1967: 50–75.

Altholz, Josef L. "Newman and History." *Victorian Studies* 7 (1964): 285–94.

———. "Some Observations on Victorian Religious Biography: Newman and Manning." *Worship* 43 (1969): 407–15.

Altieri, Charles. "Wordsworth's Poetics of Eloquence: A Challenge to Contemporary Theory." In *Romantic Revolutions: Criticism and Theory,* ed. Kenneth R. Johnston et al. Bloomington: Indiana UP, 1990: 371–407.

Arnold, Matthew. *English Literature and Irish Politics.* In *The Complete Prose Works.* Vol. 9, ed. R. H. Super. Ann Arbor: U of Michigan P, 1973.

———. *Poems,* ed. Kenneth and Miriam Allott. 2nd ed. London: Longman, 1979.

Arnold, Thomas. "The Oxford Malignants and Dr. Hampden." *Edinburgh Review* 63 (1836): 225–39.

Artz, Johannes. "Newman in Contact with Kant's Thought." *Journal of Theological Studies* 31 n.s. (1980): 517–35.

Beer, John. "Newman and the Romantic Sensibility." *The English Mind: Studies in the English Moralists Presented to Basil Willey.* Cambridge: Cambridge UP, 1964: 193–218.

Bialostosky, Don H. "Wordsworth, New Literary Histories, and the Constitution of Literature." In *Romantic Revolutions: Criticism and Theory,* ed. Kenneth R. Johnston et al. Bloomington: Indiana UP, 1990: 408–22.

Bouyer, Louis. *Newman: His Life and Spirituality.* Trans. J. Lewis May. London: Burns and Oates, 1958.

Bremond, Henri. *The Mystery of Newman*. Trans. H. C. Corrance. Intro. George Tyrrell. London: Williams and Norgate, 1907.

Brent, Allen. "Newman's Conversion, the *Via Media*, and the Myth of the Romeward Movement." *Downside Review* 101 (1983): 261-80.

———. "Newman's Moral Conversion." *Downside Review* 104 (1986): 79-94.

Bright, Michael H. "English Literary Romanticism and the Oxford Movement." *Journal of the History of Ideas* 40 (1979): 385-404.

Brilioth, Yngve. *The Anglican Revival: Studies in the Oxford Movement*. London: Longmans, Green, 1933.

———. *Three Lectures on Evangelicalism and the Oxford Movement*. London: Oxford UP, 1934.

Brown, C. G. "Newman's Minor Critics." *Downside Review* 89 (1971): 13-21.

Butler, Marilyn. "Plotting the Revolution: The Political Narratives of Romantic Poetry and Criticism." In *Romantic Revolutions: Criticism and Theory,* ed. Kenneth R. Johnston et al. Bloomington: Indiana UP, 1990: 133-57.

———. "Repossessing the Past: The Case for an Open Literary History." In *Rethinking Historicism: Critical Readings in Romantic History,* ed. Marjorie Levinson et al. Oxford: Basil Blackwell, 1989: 64-84.

Byron, George Gordon, Lord. *Complete Poetical Works,* ed. Jerome J. McGann. Oxford: Oxford UP, 1980 ff.

Cameron, J. M. "John Henry Newman and the Tractarian Movement." In *Nineteenth Century Religious Thought in the West,* ed. Ninian Smart et al. Vol. 2. Cambridge: Cambridge UP, 1985: 69-109.

———. "Newman and the Empiricist Tradition." *The Rediscovery of Newman: An Oxford Symposium*. London: Sheed and Ward, 1967: 76-99.

———. "The Night Battle: Newman and Empiricism." *Victorian Studies* 4 (1960): 99-117.

Capps, Donald. "John Henry Newman: A Study of Vocational Identity." *Journal for the Scientific Study of Religion* 9 (1970): 33-51.

———. "Sunden's Role-Taking Theory: The Case of John Henry Newman and His Mentors." *Journal for the Scientific Study of Religion* 21 (1982): 58-70.

Carlisle, Janice. *John Stuart Mill and the Writing of Character*. Athens, GA: U of Georgia P, 1991.

Carlyle, Thomas. *On Heroes, Hero-Worship, and the Heroic in History*. In his *Works,* ed. H. D. Trail. Vol. 5. London: Chapman and Hall, 1898-1901.

———. *Sartor Resartus*. In his *Works,* ed. H. D. Trail. Vol. 1. London: Chapman and Hall, 1898-1901.

Cascardi, Anthony J. *The Subject of Modernity*. Cambridge: Cambridge UP, 1992.

Castle, W. R., Jr. "Newman and Coleridge." *Sewanee Review* 17 (1909): 138-52.

Chadwick, Owen. *From Bossuet to Newman: The Idea of Doctrinal Development*. Cambridge: Cambridge UP, 1957.

———. "Henri Bremond and Newman." In *The Spirit of the Oxford Movement: Tractarian Essays*. Cambridge: Cambridge UP, 1990: 167-97.

———. *The Mind of the Oxford Movement*. Stanford: Stanford UP, 1960.

———. *Newman*. Oxford: Oxford UP, 1983.

————. "The Oxford Movement and Its Reminiscencers." In his *The Spirit of the Oxford Movement*. Cambridge: Cambridge UP, 1990: 135–53.

Colby, Robert A. "The Poetical Structure of Newman's *Apologia Pro Vita Sua*." In *Apologia Pro Vita Sua*, by John Henry Newman, ed. David J. DeLaura. New York: Norton, 1969: 452–65.

Coleridge, Samuel Taylor. *Table Talk*, ed. Carl Woodring, 1990. In his *Collected Works*. Vols. 14–15. Princeton, NJ: Princeton UP, 1969 ff.

Coulson, John. *Religion and Imagination*. Oxford: Clarendon, 1981.

Crowley, Alan J. "Theory of Discourse: Newman and Ricoeur." In *Discourse and Context: An Interdisciplinary Study of John Henry Newman*, ed. Gerard Magill. Carbondale: Southern Illinois UP, 1993: 81–92.

Culler, A. Dwight. *The Imperial Intellect: A Study of Newman's Educational Ideal*. New Haven: Yale UP, 1955.

————. Introduction to *Apologia Pro Vita Sua*, by John Henry Newman, ed. A. Dwight Culler. Boston: Houghton Mifflin, 1956: vii–xix.

————. "Method in the Study of Victorian Prose." *Victorian Newsletter* 9 (spring 1956): 1–4.

————. "The Remembrance of Things Past." In *A Newman Symposium*, ed. Victor R. Yanitelli. New York: Fordham UP, 1952: 59–70.

————. *The Victorian Mirror of History*. New Haven, CT: Yale UP, 1985.

Cunningham, Valentine. "Dangerous Conceits or Confirmations Strong?" In *John Henry Newman: Reason, Rhetoric and Romanticism*, ed. David Nicholls and Fergus Kerr. Bristol, U.K.: Bristol Press, 1991: 233–52.

Darwin, Charles. *The Origin of Species*. London: Dent, 1975.

Davis, H. Francis. "Was Newman a Disciple of Coleridge?" *Dublin Review* 217 (1945): 165–73.

Dawson, Christopher. *The Spirit of the Oxford Movement*. London: Sheed & Ward, 1933.

Deen, Leonard W. "The Rhetoric of Newman's *Apologia*." *ELH* 29 (1962): 224–38.

DeLaura, David J. *Hebrew and Hellene in Victorian England: Newman, Arnold, and Pater*. Austin: U of Texas P, 1969.

————. "Newman's *Apologia* as Prophecy." In *Apologia Pro Vita Sua*, by John Henry Newman, ed. David J. DeLaura. New York: Norton, 1969: 492–503.

Diem, Hermann. *Kierkegaard: An Introduction*. Trans. David Green. Richmond, VA: John Knox, 1966.

Eagleton, Terrence. *Criticism and Ideology: A Study in Marxist Literary Theory*. Atlantic Highlands, NJ: Humanities Press, 1976.

Ebeling, Gerhard. *Word and Faith*. Trans. James W. Leitch. Philadelphia: Fortress, 1963.

Eisenach, Eldon J. *Two Worlds of Liberalism: Religion and Politics in Hobbes, Locke, and Mill*. Chicago: U of Chicago P, 1981.

Engell, James. *The Creative Imagination: Enlightenment to Romanticism*. Cambridge: Harvard UP, 1981.

Evans, G. R. "Newman's Letters to Charles." *Downside Review* 100 (1982): 92–100.

Faber, Geoffrey. *Oxford Apostles: A Character Study of the Oxford Movement.* London: Faber and Faber, 1933.

Falck, Colin. *Myth, Truth, and Literature: Towards a True Post-Modernism.* Cambridge: Cambridge UP, 1989.

Feider, Lynn A. "John Henry Newman: His Via Media." *Proceedings of the American Theological Library Association* 44 (1990): 177–90.

Ferber, Michael. "Romantic Anticapitalism: A Response to Sayre and Lowy." In *Spirits of Fire: English Romantic Writers and Contemporary Historical Methods,* ed. G. A. Rosso and Daniel Watkins. Rutherford, NJ: Fairleigh Dickinson UP, 1990: 69–84.

Finlay, John. "The Dark Rooms of the Enlightenment." *Southern Review* 23 (1987): 309–31.

Finley, C. Stephen. "Newman, the Snapdragon, and Natural Theology." *ELH* 57 (1990): 151–73.

Fish, Stanley. *Doing What Comes Naturally.* Durham, NC: Duke UP, 1989.

Fleishman, Avrom. *Figures of Autobiography: The Language of Self-Writing in Victorian and Modern England.* Berkeley: U of California P, 1983.

Ford, John T. "Faithfulness to Type in Newman's *Essay on Development.*" In *Newman Today,* ed. Stanley L. Jaki. San Fransisco: Ignatius, 1989: 17–48.

Froude, Richard Hurrell. *Remains.* 4 vols. London: Rivington, 1838.

Furst, Lilian R. *Fictions of Romantic Irony.* Cambridge, MA: Harvard UP, 1984.

Gibbon, Edward. *The History of the Decline and Fall of the Roman Empire.* Ed. J. B. Bury. 7 vols. London: Methuen, 1901.

Gilley, Sheridan. *Newman and His Age.* London: Darton, Longman and Todd, 1990.

Goodwin, Gregory H. "Keble and Newman: Tractarian Aesthetics and the Romantic Tradition." *Victorian Studies* 30 (1987): 475–94.

Grennan, Margaret R. "Newman the Novelist." In *A Newman Symposium,* ed. Victor R. Yanitelli. New York: Fordham UP, 1952: 97–107.

Grieves, R. W. "Golightly and Newman, 1824–1845." *Journal of Ecclesiastical History* 9 (1958): 209–28.

Griffin, John R. "Dr. Pusey and the Oxford Movement." *Historical Magazine of the Protestant Episcopal Church* 42 (1973): 137–53.

––––––. "John Keble: Radical." *Anglican Theological Review* 53 (1971): 167–73.

Griffiths, Eric. "Newman: The Foolishness of Preaching." In *Newman after a Hundred Years,* ed. Ian Ker and Alan G. Hill. Oxford: Clarendon, 1990: 63–91.

Gunton, Colin. "Newman's Dialectic: Dogma and Reason in the Seventy-Third *Tract for the Times.*" In *Newman after a Hundred Years,* ed. Ian Ker and Alan G. Hill. Oxford: Clarendon, 1990: 309–22.

Haight, Roger. "Bremond's Newman." *Journal of Theological Studies* 36 n.s. (1985): 350–79.

Hamilton, Paul. "'A Shadow of a Magnitude': The Dialectic of Romantic Aesthetics." In *Beyond Romanticism: New Approaches to Texts and Contexts, 1780–1832,* ed. Stephen Copley and John Whale. London: Routledge, 1992: 11–31.

Harper, Gordon Huntington. *Cardinal Newman and William Froude, F.R.S.: A Correspondence.* Baltimore: Johns Hopkins UP, 1933.

Harrold, Charles Frederick. *John Henry Newman: An Expository and Critical Study of His Mind, Thought, and Art.* London: Longmans, Green, 1945.

———. "Newman and the Alexandrian Platonists." *Modern Philology* 37 (1940): 279-91.

Hartman, Geoffrey. "'Was it for this . . . ?': Wordsworth and the Birth of the Gods." In *Romantic Revolutions: Criticism and Theory,* ed. Kenneth R. Johnston, et al. Bloomington: Indiana UP, 1990: 8-25.

Henderson, Heather. *The Victorian Self: Autobiography and Biblical Narrative.* Ithaca, NY: Cornell UP, 1989.

Hill, Alan G. "Originality and Realism in Newman's Novels." In *Newman after a Hundred Years,* ed. Ian Ker and Alan G. Hill. Oxford: Clarendon, 1990: 21-42.

Holloway, John. *The Victorian Sage: Studies in Argument.* London: Macmillan, 1953.

Holmes, J. Derek. "John Henry Newman's Attitude towards History and Hagiography." *Downside Review* 92 (1974): 248-64.

———. "Newman, Froude and Pattison: Some Aspects of Their Relations." *Journal of Religious History* 4 (1966): 28-38.

———. "Newman's Attitude towards Historical Criticism and Biblical Inspiration." *Downside Review* 89 (1971): 22-37.

Houghton, Esther Rhoads. "*The British Critic* and the Oxford Movement." *Studies in Bibliography* 16 (1963): 119-37.

Houghton, Walter E. *The Art of Newman's Apologia.* New Haven: Yale UP, 1945.

———. "'New' Articles by Cardinal Newman." *TLS* 3033 (15 April 1960): 241.

Hume, David. *Dialogues Concerning Natural Religion.* Ed. Henry D. Aiken. New York, Hafner, 1957.

Hummel, Thomas C. "John Henry Newman: A Search for Development with Continuity." *The Saint Luke's Journal of Theology* 20 (1977): 265-81.

Hungerford, Edward B. *Shores of Darkness.* New York: Columbia UP, 1941.

Inge, William Ralph (Dean). "Cardinal Newman." In his *Outspoken Essays.* London: Longmans, Green, 1919: 172-204.

James, D. G. *The Romantic Comedy.* London: Oxford UP, 1948.

Jost, Walter. *Rhetorical Thought in John Henry Newman.* Columbia: U of South Carolina P, 1989.

Julia of the Trinity. "Self Revelation in Newman's Sermons." *Catholic World* 162 (1945): 55-60.

Kamenka, Eugene. *The Philosophy of Ludwig Feuerbach.* New York: Praeger, 1969.

Keats, John. *Letters,* ed. Hyder Edward Rollins. 2 vols. Cambridge: Harvard UP, 1958.

———. *Poems,* ed. Miriam Allott. London: Longman, 1970.

Ker, Ian. *John Henry Newman: A Biography.* Oxford: Clarendon, 1988.

Klocker, Harry R. "The Personal God of John Henry Newman." *The Personalist* 57 (1976): 145-61.

Lacoue-Labarthe, Philippe, and Jean-Luc Nancy. *The Literary Absolute: The Theory of Literature in German Romanticism*. Trans. Philip Barnard and Cheryl Lester. Albany: State U of New York P, 1988.

Langbaum, Robert. *The Poetry of Experience: The Dramatic Monologue in Modern Literary Tradition*. New York: Norton, 1957.

_____. *The Word from Below: Essays on Modern Literature and Culture*. Madison: U of Wisconsin P, 1987.

Lash, Nicholas. *Change in Focus: A Study of Doctrinal Change and Continuity*. London: Sheed and Ward, 1973.

_____. *Newman on Development: The Search for an Explanation in History*. Shepherdstown, WV: Patmos, 1975.

Lawlis, Merritt E. "Newman on the Imagination." *Modern Language Notes* 68 (1953): 73-80.

Le Bas, C. W. "Newman and Faber on Justification." *British Critic* 24 (July 1838): 61-82.

Levine, George. *The Boundaries of Fiction: Carlyle, Macaulay, Newman*. Princeton, NJ: Princeton UP, 1968.

Levinson, Marjorie. Introduction to *Rethinking Historicism: Critical Readings in Romantic History*, ed. Marjorie Levinson, et al. Oxford: Basil Blackwell, 1989: 1-17.

_____. "The New Historicism: Back to the Future." In *Rethinking Historicism: Critical Readings in Romantic History*, ed. Marjorie Levinson, et al. Oxford: Basil Blackwell, 1989: 18-63.

Livingston, James C. *The Ethics of Belief: An Essay on the Victorian Religious Conscience*. Tallahassee, FL: American Academy of Religion, 1974.

_____. *Matthew Arnold and Christianity: His Religious Prose Writings*. Columbia: U of South Carolina P, 1986.

_____. *Modern Christian Thought: From the Enlightenment to Vatican II*. New York: Macmillan, 1971.

Loesberg, Jonathan. *Fictions of Consciousness*. New Brunswick, NJ: Rutgers, 1986.

Macheray, Pierre. *A Theory of Literary Production*. Trans. Geoffrey Wall. London: Routledge and Kegan Paul, 1978.

Marshall, Donald G. "Secondary Literature: Geoffrey Hartman, Wordsworth, and the Interpretation of Modernity." In *Romantic Revolutions: Criticism and Theory*, ed. Kenneth R. Johnston, et al. Bloomington: Indiana UP, 1990: 78-97.

McFarland, Thomas. *Coleridge and the Pantheist Tradition*. Oxford: Clarendon, 1969.

McGann, Jerome J. "The Meaning of the Ancient Mariner." In *Spirits of Fire: English Romantic Writers and Contemporary Historical Methods*, ed. G. A. Rosso and Daniel Watkins. Rutherford, NJ: Fairleigh Dickinson UP, 1990: 208-39.

_____. *The Romantic Ideology: A Critical Investigation*. Chicago: U of Chicago P, 1983.

———. "The Third World of Criticism." In *Rethinking Historicism: Critical Readings in Romantic History,* ed. Marjorie Levinson, et al. Oxford: Basil Blackwell, 1989: 85–107.

McGrath, Alister. "John Henry Newman's 'Lectures on Justification': The High Church Misrepresentation of Luther." *Churchman* 97 (1983): 112–22.

Mellor, Anne K. *English Romantic Irony.* Cambridge, MA: Harvard UP, 1980.

Merrigan, Terrence. "Newman's Progress towards Rome: A Psychological Consideration of His Conversion to Catholicism." *Downside Review* 104 (1986): 95–112.

Mill, John Stuart. *Autobiography and Literary Essays,* ed. John M. Robson and Jack Stillinger. Toronto: U of Toronto P, 1981.

Misner, Paul. "Newman and the Tradition Concerning the Papal Antichrist." *Church History* 42 (1973): 377–95.

Mitchell, Basil. "Newman as a Philosopher." In *Newman after a Hundred Years,* ed. Ian Ker and Alan G. Hill. Oxford: Clarendon, 1990: 223–46.

Morgan, Drew Phillip. "Hermeneutical Aspects of John Henry Newman's *Essay on the Development of Christian Doctrine.*" *Horizons* 16 (1989): 223–42.

Mozley, Dorothea, ed. *Newman Family Letters.* London: S.P.C.K., 1962.

Mozley, Thomas. *Reminiscences: Chiefly of Oriel College and the Oxford Movement.* 2 vols. London: Longmans, Green, 1882.

Newman, F. W. *Contributions, Chiefly to the Early History of Cardinal Newman.* London: Kegan Paul, 1891.

Newman, Jay. *The Mental Philosophy of John Henry Newman.* Waterloo, Ontario: Wilfred Laurier UP, 1986.

Newman, John Henry. *Apologia Pro Vita Sua.* Ed. Martin J. Svaglic. Oxford: Clarendon, 1967.

———. *The Argument from Conscience to the Existence of God.* Ed. Arian J. Boekraad and Henry Tristram. Louvain: Editions Nauwelaerts, 1961.

———. *The Arians of the Fourth Century.* London: Longmans, Green, 1908.

———. *Autobiographical Writings.* Ed. Henry Tristram. New York: Sheed and Ward, 1957.

———. *Callista: A Tale of the Third Century.* London: Longmans, Green, 1901.

———. *Certain Difficulties Felt by Anglicans in Catholic Teaching.* London: Longmans, Green, 1908.

———. *Correspondence of John Henry Newman with John Keble and Others.* London: Longmans, Green, 1917.

———. *Discussions and Arguments on Various Subjects.* London: Longmans, Green, 1899.

———. *An Essay in Aid of a Grammar of Assent.* Ed. I. T. Ker. Oxford: Clarendon, 1985.

———. *An Essay on the Development of Christian Doctrine.* Ed. C. F. Harrold. New York: Longmans, Green, 1949.

———. *Essays Critical and Historical.* 2 vols. London: Longmans, Green, 1903.

———. *Fifteen Sermons Preached before the University of Oxford.* London: Longmans, Green, 1901.

———. *Historical Sketches.* 3 vols. London: Longmans, Green, 1901.

———. *The Idea of a University Defined and Illustrated.* Ed. I. T. Ker. Oxford: Clarendon, 1976.

———. *Lectures on the Doctrine of Justification.* London: Longmans, Green, 1900.

———. *Lectures on the Prophetical Office of the Church: The* Via Media *of the Anglican Church.* Ed. H. D. Weidner. Oxford: Clarendon, 1990: 58–358.

———. *Letters and Correspondence of John Henry Newman.* 2 vols. Ed. Anne Mozley. London: Longmans, Green, 1903.

———. *The Letters and Diaries of John Henry Newman.* Ed. Charles Stephen Dessain et al. Vols. 1–6 (Oxford: Oxford UP, 1978-84), 11–22 (London: Thomas Nelson, 1961-72), 23–31 (Oxford: Oxford UP, 1973-77).

———. *Loss and Gain: The Story of a Convert.* London: Longmans, Green, 1910.

———. *A Packet of Letters: A Selection from the Correspondence of John Henry Newman.* Ed. Joyce Sugg. Oxford: Clarendon, 1983.

———. *Parochial and Plain Sermons.* 8 vols. London: Longmans, Green, 1901.

———. *Sermons Bearing on Subjects of the Day.* London: Longmans, Green, 1902.

———. *Tracts for the Times: By Members of the University of Oxford.* 5 vols. London: Rivington, 1840; individual tracts are paginated separately.

———. *Two Essays on Biblical and on Ecclesiastical Miracles.* London: Longmans, Green, 1907.

———. *Verses on Various Occasions.* London: Longmans, Green, 1903.

———. *The Via Media.* 2 vols. London: Longmans, Green, 1908.

"Newman's *History of the Arians.*" *Edinburgh Review* 63 (1836): 44–72.

Newsome, David. *The Convert Cardinals: John Henry Newman and Henry Edward Manning.* London: John Murray, 1993.

———. "The Evangelical Sources of Newman's Power." In *The Rediscovery of Newman: An Oxford Symposium,* ed. John Coulson and A. M. Allchin. London: Sheed and Ward, 1967: 11–30.

———. "Justification and Sanctification: Newman and the Evangelicals." *Journal of Theological Studies* 15 n.s. (1964): 32–53.

———. "Newman and the Oxford Movement." In *The Victorian Crisis of Faith,* ed. Anthony Symondson. London: S.P.C.K., 1970: 71–89.

———. "'Newmania.'" *Journal of Theological Studies* 14 n.s. (1963): 420–27.

———. *Two Classes of Men: Platonism and English Romantic Thought.* London: John Murray, 1974.

Nicholls, David. "Individualism and the Appeal to Authority." In *John Henry Newman: Reason, Rhetoric and Romanticism,* ed. David Nicholls and Fergus Kerr. Bristol, U.K.: Bristol Press, 1991: 194–213.

———. "Newman's Anglican Critics." *Anglican Theological Review* 47 (1965): 377–95.

Nicholls, David, and Fergus Kerr. Introduction to *John Henry Newman: Reason, Rhetoric and Romanticism.* Bristol, U.K.: Bristol Press, 1991: 1–12.

Nichols, Ashton. *The Poetics of Epiphany: Nineteenth-Century Origins of the Modern Literary Moment.* Tuscaloosa: U of Alabama P, 1987.

Nimmo, Duncan. "Towards and Away from Newman's Theory of Doctrinal Development: Pointers from Mark Pattison in 1838 and 1846." *Journal of Theological Studies* 29 n.s. (1978): 160-62.

O'Faolain, Sean. *Newman's Way.* London: Longmans, Green, 1952.

O'Leary, Joseph S. "Impeded Witness: Newman against Luther on Justification." In *John Henry Newman: Reason, Rhetoric and Romanticism,* ed. David Nicholls and Fergus Kerr. Bristol, U.K.: Bristol Press, 1991: 153-93.

Oliver, E. J. *Gibbon and Rome.* London: Sheed and Ward, 1958.

Parrish, Stephen Maxwell. "Newman on Rousseau: Revisions in the Essay on Poetry." *Notes and Queries* 199 (1954): 217-19.

Pattison, Mark. *Memoirs.* London: Macmillan, 1885.

Pattison, Robert. *The Great Dissent: John Henry Newman and the Liberal Heresy.* New York: Oxford UP, 1991.

——. "John Henry Newman and the Arian Heresy." *Mosaic* 11, no. 4 (summer 1978): 139-53.

Peterson, Linda. *Victorian Autobiography: The Tradition of Self-Interpretation.* New Haven, CT: Yale UP, 1986.

Pitt, Valerie. "Demythologizing Newman." In *John Henry Newman: Reason, Rhetoric and Romanticism,* ed. David Nicholls and Fergus Kerr. Bristol, U.K.: Bristol Press, 1991: 13-27.

Prickett, Stephen. "Newman: The Physiognomy of Development." *Christianity and Literature* 40 (1991): 267-76.

——. *Romanticism and Religion: The Tradition of Coleridge and Wordsworth in the Victorian Church.* Cambridge: Cambridge UP, 1976.

Privateer, Paul Michael. *Romantic Voices: Identity and Ideology in British Poetry, 1789-1850.* Athens: U of Georgia P, 1991.

Pusey, E. B. *An Historical Enquiry into the Probable Causes of the Rationalist Character Lately Predominant in the Theology of Germany.* 2 vols. London: Rivington, 1828, 1830.

Ragland-Sullivan, Ellie. *Jacques Lacan and the Philosophy of Psychoanalysis.* Urbana: U of Illinois P, 1986.

Rajan, Tilottama. *Dark Interpreter: The Discourse of Romanticism.* Ithaca, NY: Cornell UP, 1980.

Reardon, Bernard M. G. *From Coleridge to Gore: A Century of Religious Thought in Britain.* London: Longman, 1971.

——. "Newman and the Psychology of Belief." *The Church Quarterly Review* 158 (1957): 315-32.

Riede, David G. *Oracles and Hierophants: Constructions of Romantic Authority.* Ithaca, NY: Cornell UP, 1991.

Robbins, William. *The Newman Brothers: An Essay in Comparative Intellectual Biography,* Cambridge: Harvard UP, 1966.

Rowell, Geoffrey. *Hell and the Victorians.* Oxford: Clarendon, 1974.

Rupp, Gordon. "Newman through Nonconformist Eyes." *The Rediscovery of Newman: An Oxford Symposium.* London: Sheed and Ward, 1967: 195-215.

Ryals, Clyde de L. *A World of Possibilities: Romantic Irony in Victorian Literature.* Columbus: Ohio State UP, 1990.

Ryan, Alvan. S. "Newman and T. S. Eliot on Religion and Literature." In *A Newman Symposium,* ed. Victor R. Yanitelli. New York: Fordham UP, 1952: 119-34.

Ryan, Michael. "A Grammatology of Assent: Cardinal Newman's *Apologia Pro Vita Sua.*" In *Approaches to Victorian Autobiography,* ed. George P. Landow. Athens: Ohio UP, 1979: 128-57.

Said, Edward W. *Beginnings: Intention and Method.* Baltimore: Johns Hopkins UP, 1975.

Sayre, Robert, and Michael Lowy. "Figures of Romantic Anticapitalism." In *Spirits of Fire: English Romantic Writers and Contemporary Historical Methods,* ed. G. A. Rosso and Daniel Watkins. Rutherford, NJ: Fairleigh Dickinson UP, 1990: 23-68.

Schiller, Friedrich. "On Simple and Sentimental Poetry." In his *Essays Aesthetical and Philosophical.* London: George Bell and Sons, 1910: 262-332.

Schlegel, Friedrich. "Talk on Mythology." In his *Dialogue on Poetry and Literary Aphorisms.* Trans. Ernst Behler and Roman Struc. University Park: Pennsylvania State UP, 1968: 81-93.

Scott, Thomas. *The Force of Truth: An Authentic Narrative.* New York: Williams and Whiting, 1810.

Shairp, J. C. *Studies in Poetry and Philosophy.* Edinburgh: David Douglas, 1886.

Shaw, W. David. *Victorians and Mystery: Crises of Representation.* Ithaca, NY: Cornell UP, 1990.

Shelley, Percy Bysshe. *Complete Works,* ed. Roger Ingpen and Walter E. Peck. 10 vols. London: Benn, 1965.

Sheridan, Thomas L. *Newman on Justification.* Staten Island, NY: Alba House, 1967.

Shute, Graham J. "Newman's 'Logic of the Heart.'" *The Expository Times* 78 (1967): 232-35.

Simpson, David. *Irony and Authority in Romantic Poetry.* London: Macmillan, 1979.

Siskin, Clifford. *The Historicity of Romantic Discourse.* New York: Oxford UP, 1988.

Staten, Henry. "Newman on Self and Society." *Studies in Romanticism* 18 (1979): 69-79.

Stephen, Leslie. "Newman's Theory of Belief." In his *An Agnostic's Apology and Other Essays.* London: Smith, Elder, 1893: 168-241.

Strange, Roderick. *Newman and the Gospel of Christ.* Oxford: Oxford UP, 1981.
———. "Newman and the Mystery of Christ." In *Newman after a Hundred Years,* ed. Ian Ker and Alan G. Hill. Oxford: Clarendon, 1990: 323-36.

Stunt, T. C. F. "John Henry Newman and the Evangelicals." *Journal of Ecclesiastical History* 21 (1970): 65-75.

Svaglic, Martin J. "Charles Newman and his Brothers." *PMLA* 71 (1956): 370–85.

———. "Newman and the Oriel Fellowship." *PMLA* 70 (1955): 1014–32.

———. "The Structure of Newman's *Apologia*." In *Apologia Pro Vita Sua*, by John Henry Newsman, ed. David J. DeLaura. New York: Norton, 1969: 441–52.

Swingle, L. J. *The Obstinate Questionings of English Romanticism*. Baton Rouge: LSU Press, 1987.

Taylor, Charles. *Hegel*. Cambridge: Cambridge UP, 1975.

Tennyson, Alfred, Lord. *Poems,* ed. Christopher Ricks. 2nd ed. 3 vols. Berkeley: U of California P, 1987.

Tennyson, G. B. "Removing the Veil: Newman as a Literary Artist." In *Critical Essays on John Henry Newman,* ed. Ed Block, Jr. Victoria, B.C.: U of Victoria P, 1992: 7–21.

———. *Victorian Devotional Poetry: The Tractarian Mode*. Cambridge, MA: Harvard UP, 1981.

Thirlwall, Connop. *Letters Literary and Theological*. Ed. J. J. Stewart Perowne. London: R. Bentley & Son, 1881.

Thomas, Stephen. *Newman and Heresy: The Anglican Years*. Cambridge: Cambridge UP, 1991.

Thomte, Reider. *Kierkegaard's Philosophy of Religion*. Princeton, NJ: Princeton UP, 1948.

Tillman, M. Katherine. "Cardinal Newman on Imagination as the Medium of Intellectual Education." *Religious Education* 83 (1988): 601–10.

Tillotson, Kathleen. "Harriett Mozley's Tales for the Young." *The Listener* 48 (31 July 1952): 187–89.

Toon, Peter. "Newman's Essay on Development Revisited." *Churchman* 89 (1975): 47–57.

Trevor, Meriol. *Newman: Light in Winter*. London: Macmillan, 1962.

Ward, Maisie. *Young Mr. Newman*. New York: Sheed & Ward, 1948.

Ward, Wilfrid. *The Life of John Henry Cardinal Newman*. 2 vols. New York: Longmans, Green, 1912.

Weatherby, Harold L. *Cardinal Newman in His Age*. Nashville, TN: Vanderbilt UP, 1973.

Weiskel, Thomas. *The Romantic Sublime: Studies in the Structure and Psychology of Transcendence*. Baltimore: Johns Hopkins UP, 1976.

Wellek, René. *Immanuel Kant in England*. Princeton, NJ: Princeton UP, 1931.

White, Gavin. "Newman's Missionary Dream." *The Modern Churchman* 14 n.s. (1971): 267–72.

Whyte, Alexander. *Newman: An Appreciation in Two Lectures*. New York: Longmans, Green, 1902.

Wilde, Oscar. "The Critic as Artist: Part I." In *The Writings of Oscar Wilde*. Vol. 6. London: Keller-Farmer, 1907: 107–65.

Willey, Basil. *Nineteenth Century Studies: Coleridge to Matthew Arnold*. London: Chatto & Windus, 1949.

Willliams, Raymond. *Marxism and Literature*. Oxford: Oxford UP, 1977.

Williams, Rowan. "Newman's *Arians* and the Question of Method in Doctrinal History." In *Newman after a Hundred Years,* ed. Ian Ker and Alan G. Hill. Oxford: Clarendon, 1990: 263–85.

Wordsworth, William. *Poetical Works,* ed. E. de Selincourt and Helen Darbishire. 5 vols. Oxford: Oxford UP, 1940–49.

Wright, T. R. "Newman on Literature: 'Thinking out into Language.'" *Literature and Theology* 5 (1991): 181–97.

Young, G. M. *Gibbon*. New York: Appleton, 1933.

INDEX

Abbott, Edwin, 5, 30, 105, 106, 131, 132, 151, 156, 169, 180, 220, 228, 237

Abbott, Jacob, 7, 43–45, 191, 227

Abrams, M. H., 74, 87, 90, 91, 108, 112, 146, 206, 226

Action: as Newman's guide for life, 143; Carlyle's reliance on, 149; self-authenticating, 147

Adam, 44, 59, 77, 96, 101, 133, 136, 211, 212, 226, 231, 238

Adams, William Seth, 245

Adolescence, Newman's as romantic, 101, 102

Aestheticism, 205; as a threat to Newman's spiritual life, 87; as possible response to Newman, 15; Romantic escape into, 167

Aesthetics, 11, 15, 54, 55, 69, 76, 85–89, 96, 112, 142, 152, 158–60, 167, 186, 200, 205; Keble's deriving from Coleridge, 87; Keble's influence, 76; of Coleridge's theology, 86; self-justifying, 152

Alexandrian Church, 9, 41–43, 50, 60, 63, 64, 72, 78, 114

Allchin, A. M., 87

Altholz, Josef, 245

Ambrose, 51, 178

Angels. *See under* Patristic Christianity

Antichrist, the, 43

Antony, 49, 51, 58, 61, 134, 214, 220

Apollinarianism, 7, 13, 44

Arabian Nights, the, 213, 215, 236

Arius, 43, 70, 151, 154, 199, 219

Arnold, Matthew, 48, 58, 67, 73, 86, 87, 114, 149, 177, 206

Arnold, Thomas, 48, 68, 91, 141, 149, 162, 191, 192, 194, 237; demand for an apology, 192; Newman's insult of, 192; Newman's second thoughts on, 193; opposition to the Tractarian agenda, 192; views on church governance, 192

Artz, Johannes, 83

Asceticism: as a criterion for doctrine, 51; as evidence of conviction, 151; no viable model for young Newman, 25

Asceticism, Newman's: his fear of Catholic extremes in, 244; his pride in, 211; self-righteous, 141

Athanasius, 58, 61, 69, 137, 162, 199

Augustine, 26, 51, 64, 71, 78, 81, 90, 91, 94, 99, 123, 137, 141, 165, 173, 177, 178, 190, 196, 230, 238, 244–52; as source of the spiritual autobiography, 90; contrasted with Byron, 177; in Newman's Patristic canon, 51; Manicheism in, 173, 177; Newman's new identification with, 249; restlessness apart from God, 102; "Securus judicat," 196, 238, 244–48; self-divided, 177; "Tolle, lege," 248; too self-conscious for Newman, 249; trial of the center, 81, 91, 94, 99, 123, 137, 165, 251; writings of, 71

Authority: Newman's respect for, 31; Newman's search for, 23, 31

Autobiography: as denial of change, 215; modeled on Augustine, 90; Protestant conversion narratives, 91, 177

Autobiography, Newman's: *Apologia* slighting his personal influence, 238; constructed after the fact, 115; Newman's covert use of, 99; downplaying his early contact with Catholicism, 235; manipulation of, 60; providential in retrospect, 103; revising his conversion experience, 244; self-conscious, 168, 252; shift away from subjectivity, 177

Bagot, Richard, 31, 128, 189

Balaam, 230, 233–35

Barth, Karl, 221

Basil, 51, 58, 60, 64, 71, 129, 177

Beer, John, 81, 85, 205

Bentham, Jeremy, 196, 203–5

A Note about the Author

DAVID GOSLEE IS Professor of English at the University of Tennessee, Knoxville, where he teaches courses in Victorian prose and poetry, rhetoric, and advanced composition. His previous publications include *Tennyson's Characters: "Strange Faces, Other Minds,"* as well as numerous articles on Tennyson, Browning, Newman, and Arnold. Having focused on secular subtexts within Newman in this book, he is currently exploring religious subtexts within ostensibly secular Victorian writers—among them Matthew Arnold, George Eliot, John Stuart Mill, and Thomas Huxley.